Going Home

The adventure of a lifetime

How a sixty-year-old woman dared to drive 20,000km
by herself from Europe
overland through West and Central Africa
in her epic quest to return home to Zimbabwe

Dot Bekker

To find more details, blogs and Africa information related to this journey:

www.goinghometoafrica.com

Follow the continued journey:
Facebook: @GoingHomeToAfrica
Instagram: @GoingHomeToAfrica

ISBN : 978-1-77925-994-3

Editor: Andrea Murphy – www.theperfectwordsmith.com
Proofreaders: Ben Randell, Elitsa Simova
Cover image: Iris Ritchie – Facebook irisritchiephotography
Cover image location: Silwani Reserve www.silwani.co.zw
Rear cover images: Iris Ritchie, Ursula van Eck
Rear map: Google Maps

This book is dedicated to the believers, the supporters and the helpers. It took a 'small village' to get me through this journey. From initial concept to the return home, each one of you helped me to make it, and so a part of my success is yours. I could not have done it without you.

Dot Bekker, November 2020

It always seems impossible, until it is done
~ Nelson Mandela

A percentage from the sale of this book supports Kusasa, a non-profit for the education of high-achieving, vulnerable and disadvantaged girls in Zimbabwe. Our focus is on ensuring that these girls have the opportunity to attend high school rather than face a future as child brides, pregnant, prostituted, trafficked or simply condemned to a life of poverty. To find out more visit www.kusasa.africa.

Table of Contents

Acknowledgements

This journey could not have been possible without the support of a great number of people. I do not have enough space to name each of you: my apologies. "Thank you" seems such a tiny phrase for such a great gift, but they are the only words I have. Please know that I hold you all in gratitude, always.

There are, however, a few people who were vital in their generous moral and financial support and I must thank them first, as without them I would not even have been able to start. Mentioned in order of how long I have known them, they are George and Mehtap Tasiopoulos, Trudy and David Denby, and Andrea Murphy: you were each a key that unlocked so many doors and opened a new future for me. I am indebted to you beyond words.

To Andrea I owe a further enormous debt of thanks for undertaking the mammoth task of editing this book, for tolerating the challenge of bringing semblance to my thinking and for masterfully crafting my words into something readable. Additionally to proofreaders Ben Randell and Elitsa Simova, who improved the formatting and ensured that it all made sense.

My Favourite Niece, Ursula van Eck, who worried about me, kept tabs on where I was and how I was doing and joined me for two weeks on the toughest part of the journey. My Favourite Nephew, Gary Rosema, who provided me with support and advice to convert BlueBelle and is my 'go-to-guy' for technical stuff. And my lovely goddaughter, Megan Halliday, who was my number one fan and buoyed me with wise words of encouragement and so much more. You guys rock and I love you!

A swathe of thanks must go to my family and friends around the world who stood by and cheered me on in numerous ways; the total strangers who became friends through my journey or via social media; the followers, whose comments, observations, and kindness so often humbled me, as did the generosity of a number who supported me with financial contributions when I thought I would surely never make it (see the website for a list of contributors). I must also mention the fellow overlanders I met along the way, with whom I swapped stories of places been and seen and routes yet untouched: I learnt much from you. Special thanks to Laurie and Bruce Heimbigner, who were great travel companions for a brief time and whose encouragement and help was unparalleled; and to Chloe Grant of West Africa Travellers, who was incredibly supportive, chose to become my friend and does more for the overlanding community going through West Africa than can be imagined.

To the people of Africa, who demonstrated over and over again their kindness, warmth, hospitality, grace and humour, and who made my return home such a great adventure: you reawakened my heart and I bless you.

And last, but by absolutely no means least, my BlueBelle, without whom I could not have made this incredible journey: her steadfastness, courage and determination matched my own and I regret that she has not been recognised by her makers as the most extraordinary Transit van *EVER*.

My acknowledgements, however, would not be complete without mentioning the cynics and naysayers, the pessimists and worrywarts, the people who were rude and tried to dissuade me, who mocked me and made fun of me: I am sorry that your balls are smaller than my chesticles!

Foreword

by GRAEME BELL

When was the last time you were alone, completely alone? Imagine, for a moment, being alone, completely alone in a foreign country, a country wracked with civil war or extreme poverty and on the developed world's travel advisory 'do not go to' lists. Imagine sleeping in a van in the darkest of nights, very far from home, or civilization, or any semblance of civilization. Would you dare? Do you have the courage?

At the end of her marriage, Dot Bekker set out from a relatively comfortable home in Europe on a journey of daring, a journey of self-discovery and, with very little experience, took on the last great overland route from Europe to Southern Africa via West Africa. This is a journey fraught with danger, adventure, bureaucracy, discovery and the most challenging roads on the planet's surface. It is a journey which few dare to attempt, few begin and end and even fewer attempt alone. Dot Bekker took on West Africa, alone. Even when she was in convoy with another vehicle, she was alone, responsible for herself and her vehicle and the logistical nightmare which this journey presents. Had she been more timid, less resolute and entirely sane, she would most likely not have succeeded (few of us who have completed this journey are completely sane). But Dot persevered. She took each day as it came to her, accepted eventually that which she could not change and made the most of what she had, challenging preconceived notions of what a sixty-year-old woman can or cannot do, should and should not be, refusing to be anyone but Dot. Alone. With no backup, no daily help, no financial assistance, no regular encouragement, no one to hold when the nights were long and dark and menacing, Dot proved that she did not need anyone but Dot when it really came down to it; when harsh reality replaced courageous dreams.

I was fortunate to meet Dot twice, once at the very beginning of her odyssey on a cool Moroccan beach, and again near the end of her journey, in the dusty suburbs of Windhoek, Namibia. The truth is that the Dot I met in the shadow of Europe was much the same Dot I met again near her home, Zimbabwe; but there was a new streak of confidence born of achievement, a calm after the storm. Dot's physical, mental and emotional journey proves to the world not only that a strong, independent woman can achieve what many consider to be impossible, but also that Africa is not the heart of darkness. Her journey proves to those who are not aware that infamous West Africa has a gentle side – respectful, generous, caring and kind. When BlueBelle's wheels dug deep into the sand or mud, it was the locals who appeared and helped push the big blue van back on to solid ground. When the road was tough and the days hotter than hell, it was the waves of the children, the smiles of the vendors, the welcome of each tiny village which gave her the strength to continue. There were three women I know of traversing Africa solo in 2019: none suffered assault or abuse, and they were safer on the road there than they would be in most industrialised cities. Thank you, Africa, for welcoming these brave women and rewarding their courage and tenacity!

Dot Bekker's journey was exactly what she needed: to return to the land of her birth when many are running the other way; to prove to herself and the world that she can do what she sets her mind to – and that you can too: you just have to want it badly enough, with every fibre of your being; and you have to have belief in yourself when the world says, 'No, you can't.'

Graeme Bell is an author and a member of The Explorers Club. He writes regularly for the *Overland Journal* and *Expedition Portal* and his books tell the story of the Bell family's overlanding adventures across five continents. Follow Graeme or buy his books at **www.a2aexpedition.com**

Introduction

I want this book to demonstrate what you can do with an idea, a dream or a thought. My *absolute certainty* that somehow I could do this, despite not having the knowledge, money or wherewithal to achieve it, should prove that if an ordinary sixty-year-old woman could make something extraordinary happen, then so can you.

I hope that you, and women especially, will see that the limitations placed on us by family, friends and strangers are not our own limitations; that it is entirely possible to do what you choose to do, what your heart wants, what your soul yearns for. That said, it isn't easy to break free from the walls that have been built around us; to break old habits and to dare to do something just for you and no one else. It takes a desire for your life to be better, more meaningful; to be fulfilled in ways that you may not even now be certain of; perhaps you may simply have a desire that things should be different.

I also want this book to demonstrate that Africa is full of good people, kind people, people who have so little and yet are so rich, as opposed to the many people in the world who are so poor because all they have is money. Going into the 'dark continent' with a smile, a handshake and a sense of humour can achieve more than you ever imagined.

I am often asked what set me out on this journey, so I will briefly outline it here to give context.

After twenty-two years in an increasingly hopeless and dysfunctional relationship, I decided that I just didn't want to be living this unhappiness for another five, ten, twenty years; and if that was the case, I had to do something different, because everything I had tried until then hadn't changed or improved a thing.

In a world where a woman approaching sixty becomes increasingly invisible, we lose our looks and our energy, our bodies change (mostly gravity takes over) and we finally realise we're just *never* going to fit into that outfit we looked so great in twenty-five years ago. We are in unhappy relationships with men who haven't understood us or 'seen' us for years; and we are virtually unemployable. So what are our options as 'old women'? We settle for less, we believe we don't deserve more than we have and we should 'be more careful'. Our lives get smaller and we get unhappier.

I had strolled myself into a zombie-like existence. I wasn't in a happy relationship, I hated my life and I hated the way I was forty kilograms more than I had been twenty years before. I felt I had no choices. I put up with verbal abuse daily and I also gave my share of it. I had nothing and no one to live for and I had been debilitated for six months with the excruciating pain of sciatica. I was fifty-eight years old and I just wanted to give up. I had lost Me in the struggle and I couldn't find a way back.

Many who know me will be surprised by that admission, but that's because depression doesn't show itself in ways we recognise. The demons in my head were taking over the show.

I agreed to do a workshop on *Women's Confidence*, co-presenting with a client and friend. It was this workshop that changed my life, because so often we teach what we need to learn. In preparing my talk and organising my thoughts, little did I know that a few weeks later I would realise that I had been speaking to myself too. My talk was on the topic of women's power: how we, as women, avoid it, are uncomfortable with the image and sense of power in women; how we need to own our power, walk in it not just for our own sake but also to inspire other women. Power is a complicated issue for women: often we think we don't need it, or we have it, and suddenly believe that we don't, or we have been brought up to think that power is a 'man thing' and not a desirable attribute for a woman.

It was after another pointless argument with my then-husband that I walked off into my home office and it hit me like a ton of bricks: I had no power here. I was in this yoyo relationship that mostly didn't work, but I was still hanging in there because 'I should'; 'I was married and had made a vow'; 'I loved this man' (but did I love this relationship?) Basically, I was afraid: afraid to walk into the world as myself, fully, totally me... alone; to be reliant only on me and to decide for myself; to make my own mistakes and never hold it against myself; to be my own shoulder to lean on. I had done it before, so what was the issue? After twenty-two years of marriage I was complacently sleepwalking my life, blocking off parts of me that created conflict and attracted insults. I was not owning my power: how could I tell other women to do it? I hate hypocrisy and yet here I was!

So I walked back to the other room and declared, "I'm leaving and I'll be out of this apartment in three months. I need time to pack up my things and decide on a plan."

He said the total sum of, "Fine." I had probably said this same thing before. I know I had thought it a hundred times, so I don't think he believed me – gosh, I didn't really believe myself!

I have a long rope in many instances, but when I get to the end of it I'm done. And I was done! I was going to take back my power, and my life, no matter how hard it would be. I didn't have a plan, I had a decision, and that was enough to start with; I could work out the rest. I hadn't given myself much choice and in that, it was my making.

I then asked myself that popular Life Coaching question I had always considered pointless: What would you do if money was no object? I consider it a pointless question, because all too often we have money as a point of reference for everything and it is really hard to think of a world without it. However, in my marriage we were barely scraping through: my business had taken a knock as I had been incapacitated by sciatica for a full six months and he was out of work. If I left, there was no money to leave with. The answer, then, was that money really *was* no object to my future plans, as, well, there wasn't any.

Scary? Yes. Liberating? Surprisingly so!

I started to think about my life in Europe: how I hated being cold and in a consumerist-centred society, where things have become so much more important than life. I missed the hot sun of Africa, the sultry nights, the warmth of the people and their bright smiles. I should go home. Yes, I should go home to Zimbabwe: a country I had left thirty-six years earlier and not visited for twenty-six; a country deeply troubled and in crisis. Surely I could do something there? With my skills and experience over the past years in five different countries on two continents, I *must* have picked up something I could share to benefit the people. Good idea, go home.

The logistics of returning, the potential cost and where to stay then struck me… but I had an idea. I had motor-homed in Portugal a few years before, travelling, living and working in an old RV. I could do that again: I could get a small van. It would give me independence, freedom, a degree of security, the facility to travel and a place to live. I had driven through North America and all around Europe, so why not Africa? Driving would be exciting. It would take me through countries I had never been to and I would experience parts of Africa that I had never previously considered.

What if I *drove* home?

It took me two and a half years to work it all out. I packed thirty-five plastic crates of my belongings, sold some stuff, left the rest with my ex, and took the crates and €450 into the future with me. I stayed with friends and family for most of that time, and I often lived on €20 a week in food – some weeks even less. I tried not to burden my generous hosts with too many of my needs; it was enough that I had a roof over my head. I survived, and each day I grew stronger in myself, learnt to love myself, to let go of relationships, family and friendships that were not healthy for me; to become more *Me* than I had ever been.

This journey would be more than a drive-through Africa. I hoped it would be a journey back to *ME*.

I have never authored a book, yet so many people wanted to know my story. What I have sought to do here is to take you with me on my journey and share my experiences along the way. This book is a journal of my travels through Africa from 24 November 2018 to 8 August 2019 and a summary of the events leading up to their start. The people and places are all described from my experience and memories of them. Mostly I have used real names, but occasionally I have used a nom de guerre so as not to incriminate myself.

Part I: The Preparation

Nothing worthwhile happens without a good deal of preparation.
~ Dot Bekker

Chapter One: Homeless

I don't believe that anyone deliberately sets out to be homeless. I never had to live on the streets, but only because people were generous and cared enough to help me. I shudder to think where I might have found myself without them – or eventually without BlueBelle.

When I set out, I did not believe that it would be possible to earn enough money to make the journey and support myself. But I'd read about people who walked out on their lives penniless and yet did extraordinary things. So I said to the Universe, "OK, this is where I hand over to you: sort out the details and I'll put my life in your hands and accept what happens." I'd had one instance in my life when I had left an impossible situation in the hands of the Universe, and after many months of stress and distress, suddenly things resolved. It had worked before and, as my options now were few, I just 'let go and let god', as some say.

My first stop was a house-sit for a friend in Portugal, followed by a few weeks in the Netherlands to visit family. I then had to return to our marital home as our dog was seventeen and it was time to see her to rest. It was mercifully brief, and I knew that I was not going back.

My next stop was my friend Trudy in beautiful West Yorkshire in the UK, with her husband David, their daughter and their grandson. I had met Trudy in Portugal and she had been an angel to me some years before. When she knew I needed help, she quickly reached out to offer me a room in her attic, which became my home for six months. During that time I spent nearly every free moment working with my few clients (business coaching or building websites), saving every cent I could for my journey.

The months of sciatica the previous year, followed not long after by my decision to change my life, had impacted my business, and without a fixed address I knew that it would be challenging to keep the clients I had and still earn money. Additionally, those who thought that my idea of driving through Africa would probably end badly bailed on me when I needed them most; nevertheless, there were those who gave me enough to move forward.

I started, with every free moment, to think: to eat, sleep and walk my dream. But it got serious when I started to tell people. At first I didn't want to. They say don't share your dream with people you don't trust because they will destroy it – and it's true: it had happened to me before. But this time I started to feel a sense of certainty deep within myself that was becoming unshakable. I felt that this was not only what I *wanted* to do, but I also *needed* to do it; and I didn't feel like any other doors were open, so I was all in – which in a way made me even more nervous to tell anyone.

My Malawian friend Irene was one of the first I tentatively told. I felt that, being African, she would understand. If you've never been to the continent, you may not fully appreciate the allure that the wildness, grandeur, chaos and uncertainty of Africa hold for some of us. Irene was surprised but excited and inspired: she encouraged me wholeheartedly and helped me to see that this was more than merely a journey, and I was intrigued by her enthusiasm. I then, still hesitantly, told a few more people, and it was interesting that the women used words like 'amazing', 'inspirational', 'awesome', 'wow', while the men mostly used words like 'dangerous', 'unusual', 'insane', 'really?!'

From that point, my uncertainty became certainty, my confidence grew and I started telling more and more people. I was committing – fully – and I realised that if I didn't follow through on this, I would not only disappoint myself but I would also let others down, and I would just be another blow-hard – all talk and no action. The integrity of my word has become a cornerstone of my life and I was putting my life where my words were.

When I left my marriage of twenty-two years I was broken: unhappy and poor; I was without purpose or desire; and mostly I had lost my joy of life. Suddenly, however, a new life was appearing before me: one filled with questions, yes, but my slowly-returning intuition was shouting that this was right.

I was effectively homeless for the next two years.

Chapter Two: Searching for a unicorn

After a few months of housesitting, staying with people in various European countries, talking to everyone who would listen about vehicles and reading everything I could about driving overland, several things were on my must-have list:-

- A 4x4 vehicle.
- Something suitable for me to live in while on the road, so that I didn't have to search for a place to sleep, or tolerate dubious mattresses, or camp (*not* doing those with my back problems), or spend precious funds on accommodation.
- Security was a necessary consideration: being able to just jump into the front of the vehicle and drive off if I ever felt I was under any threat was a non-negotiable aspect. Thankfully this eliminated the idea of rooftop tents: I couldn't see myself climbing on top of, or down from, a vehicle.
- Preferably something I could stand up in or with a lift top: again, the back issues meant that bending over constantly in a low top would add unnecessary strain.
- A mechanical engine: it needed to be a vehicle that could easily be repaired in the middle of nowhere since it was unlikely that there would be diagnostic equipment in many of the areas I was passing through.
- Good wheel clearance: height off the road was important for rough terrain.
- Diesel would be preferable as availability of fuel in Africa is known to be inconsistent, and a diesel engine is more forgiving than a petrol one.
- Right-hand drive, because I could import the vehicle into Zimbabwe and continue to live in it (I would likely not have the money for rent in the immediate future).
- Something that I could afford.

I was looking for a unicorn!

I went to the UK for the specific purpose of finding such a beast and spent every spare moment searching for information and vehicles that would match my requirements. As a 'girl', I knew very little about cars: all I've ever cared about is that they can get me from A to B with the least amount of hassle and cost. So here I was, learning about all things automotive, and I can't say that it was easy; but luckily I'm endowed with good logic and I'm fairly practical, so this helped me a lot.

It quickly became evident that a 4x4 that *didn't* have many hundreds of thousands of miles on the clock (higher risk factor) was going to be out of my price range. I've had men tell me that I could buy an old one at a good price and fix it up, but since I couldn't do the majority of repairs myself, that just sounded more expensive than buying the right vehicle in the first place. Once you take things apart (and I had no clue what I'd be looking at), things are usually worse than you first thought – especially what the mechanics will tell an ignorant woman! I needed something that wasn't yet worn out.

I spoke to several mechanics about one particular vehicle that I had identified. I had read about a van that attracted words like 'smiley', 'indestructible', 'reliable', 'mechanical', and I started to pay attention. The Ford Transit from 1994 – 2000 is also known as the 'Ford Smiley' or the 'Ford with a banana engine'. (The front radiator grille is in the shape of a smile and the manifold looks like a bunch of bananas.) There were few with 4x4 capability – these were again out of my price range and rarer than hen's teeth – but the mechanics all agreed wholeheartedly that this model was a great vehicle. However, they also doubted that I could find one in good enough condition to drive through Africa because at that age they would be well rusted from all the salt thrown on the roads in winter. Somehow their doubt made me even more determined to find that one in a million. The challenge was on!

After an extensive search I listed the vehicles I wanted to see, hired a car and picked up my goddaughter Megan for a girl's weekend to go and check them out. I had seen a few, but as expected they were in pretty bad shape, and some sellers were asking ridiculous prices for high mileage and rust that would see the body and wheels separate at the first pothole.

The first van on the list was not to be found and the second had been sold – not a good start. Next was a 1998 Transit that had been a community bus-cum-ambulance. The farm where she was parked in south-east England looked decidedly dubious, with higher than normal security at the gate and a motley assortment of buildings. I drove to the end of the track, as directed by the intercom, and spotted a variety of vehicles scattered around a 'field'. I met the contact and he took me to see this Blue Ford Transit. As I've mentioned, she had been a community bus and as such had windows down the side and a huge Ratcliff wheelchair lift at the rear. The interior was covered in hard grey carpet (something most vans have in the UK): this tough material helps to insulate the van, protects the metal sides and reduces condensation. However, I didn't want to keep the heat in and I was concerned that the material would accumulate dust. Still, this was not a deal-breaker.

She looked promising. There were a couple of rust bubbles but little evidence of corrosion underneath, and when I looked at the odometer I gasped: nearly fifty-four thousand miles on the clock – not even 'run in' for a diesel engine! I took her for a spin around the grounds and she drove well – as well as I would imagine a van should drive, never having driven one before. I liked her and tried to negotiate the price, but the guy was firm: he wanted £1,700 and not a penny less.

I still had another vehicle to view, so I told him I would get back to him later in the day. We left to visit the last van on the list, which ended up being not at all what I was looking for (and besides, I had been given incorrect details). It seemed as though the Universe was set to seal our fates as there was only one vehicle that was anywhere near appropriate. I called the owner of the blue ambulance and arranged to collect her the next day.

As I took possession of my new home-to-be-on-wheels, I named her BlueBelle... and it stuck.[1] She wasn't a 4x4 and she didn't have all the attributes that I had laid out, but she did tick most of the boxes: she could be converted into a home and was

---

[1] She is a wonderful gentian blue colour and now she even has her own fans!

right-hand drive; she had better wheel clearance than most, easy access from the rear to the driver's seat, a high top so I could stand up inside, and a mechanical diesel engine with not too many miles on the clock – so not quite a unicorn, but not a total donkey!

BLUEBELLE'S SPECIFICATIONS:

Make	Ford
Model	Transit Mini Bus
Engine	2.5 litre
Fuel	Diesel
Transmission	Manual
Length/width/height	5.25m/1.85m/2.6m
Steering	Right
Drivetrain	Rear-wheel drive
Tyres	Front inherited with van; rear all-weather Firestones

Chapter Three: Life is on the other side of fear

Within a week of buying BlueBelle, I began preparing her. One of the first things was to put five per cent window tint film on the side and rear windows. There were two reasons for doing this: firstly, to prevent potential burglars and vandals seeing everything that was inside, and secondly, to reduce the sun and heat. The brilliance of being in the UK was that I could shop for anything online and it would be delivered to my door in a day or two. I ordered what I hoped would be a suitable amount. Installation was a new challenge: I had never attempted such a thing before, but once I did two windows it got a lot easier. The overall result wasn't perfect, however the effect was exactly what I needed. I was satisfied.

She positively reeked of fuel. I was initially worried that there was a leak in the tank but discovered that the seller must have wiped everything with fuel to give it a good shine. After three 'elbow-grease' washes of the entire interior, I was finally pleased with the result and the smell.

To prepare the back of the van for the interior build, I needed to take out the row of three passenger seats in the rear and also the huge wheelchair lift. It took several scrap yards until I found one where they were willing to remove it, but three men and a forklift later, the back door was finally clear. As I drove off, I could feel the significant weight relief as BlueBelle hurtled joyously down the road.

I had decided to cover the floor with vinyl. It would be light, temperature-neutral and easy to clean, but before I could lay the roll I needed to fill the metal lift runners which ran almost halfway along the floor in four rows. I used expanding filler and when it was dry cut it level with the floor. Next, I had to lay strips of thin foam to help keep the vinyl in better shape. I had chosen a neutral charcoal grey with a stone-looking finish, which I hoped would show less dirt and be easy to clean. I had thought it would be a simple thing – after all, a van must be relatively uniform. I can confirm with confidence, however, that a van is *not* evenly shaped and it was the devil of a job to do on my own. Once done, it looked OK although didn't bear up too well under close inspection.

Getting these basic things done meant that I now had a clear area to plan the interior, and I could use the space to get my few possessions from Luxembourg to Barcelona, where I would be building my home-on-wheels.

Alongside the preparation, planning and working, I had begun buying things I considered I would or might need. I had to eke out my limited budget as far as possible, so I spent hours every night before sleeping seeking out items, comparing product specifications, prices and reviews. I accumulated quite a lot of knowledge and a pile of equipment: solar panel, deep-cycle battery, engine oil, cooler box (that would work on 12V or 220V), twenty-three litre fresh and grey water bottles with handles so that I could lift them, portable toilet (a most valuable buy!), dual-fan for my dashboard to act as my air-conditioning, and a few bargain bedding sets, some of which would become curtains.

I am keen on recycling and the UK is a good place to pick up a deal, so I found a variety of useful things at very affordable prices. I acquired a small wooden chest of drawers I thought would come in handy, wire basket shelving that would be ideal to organise clothes, caravan cushions for a potential sofa, and a two-plate camping stove complete with a three-quarters full gas canister with connector and hose. My friend Trudy picked up an assortment of covered cushions for free and found me a great deal on a 220V camping cable and attachments.

There was one thing I knew I could not compromise on and that was seating. At the front BlueBelle had a single dilapidated driver's seat with foam bursting from the side and a two-seater for passengers. These were worn out, uncomfortable and simply had to go, so after much research I set my mind on swivel captain's chairs. Having back issues and knowing that I would spend many days behind the wheel, I needed a really good driver's seat, so it would be not just a luxury but a necessity. I spent weeks searching and finally found what I thought I needed at a price that I felt was reasonable – although they were easily the most expensive item I bought for the van. I was assured that they would fit on to the existing bases and they were in excellent condition.

I attempted to remove the old seats on my own but eventually succumbed to getting expert assistance, especially after discovering that the new chairs would not just 'slip into place'. I had to purchase an additional base for the passenger seat and after several stops I was eventually referred to Preacher Joe. Down the industrial backstreets of Bradford, I found him and his right-hand man. They were a great discovery as they dropped everything else and worked more hours than they expected to remove the old seating and replace with the new. Holes were drilled, bolts and nuts fitted and chairs positioned and affixed. After watching them work, I knew that the notion that I might have been able to do it myself was a fantasy. The result was perfect: the seats not only made BlueBelle look smarter, but they were also much more comfortable and lent a new dimension to her.

When the time came to take on the next stage and leave Yorkshire, it was a motley mix of things which were piled into the van. It was June yet still chilly, and I needed to consider that I was planning to sleep in BlueBelle for two to three nights on my way across the UK, through France and Belgium and back to Luxembourg. I was ill-prepared. Although I had a makeshift bed with the cushions I had purchased, all my bedding was in Luxembourg; however, as usual, Trudy came to the rescue by giving me a sleeping-bag before I left – for which I was extremely grateful on the cold mornings. Trudy's husband, David, fitted a basic temporary kitchen cabinet into the back so that I could carry the gas and cooker that enabled me to make a meal or a hot drink, and this proved to be very handy indeed.

I waved farewell to my dear friends Trudy, David, Leanne and Zach, and hit the road. BlueBelle and I were on the first phase of our adventure across the Channel to mainland Europe.

I hadn't driven very far when it hit me like a sledgehammer: FEAR!

Let me put this into context. I had driven around Southern Africa, up the west coast of the USA into Canada through the snowy Rocky Mountains, and zig-zagged across large swathes of Europe. I had done parts alone but mostly I was with someone; there was someone to talk ideas through, a backup... there was just 'someone'. Now, I was alone. Completely and utterly alone.

BlueBelle had thus far been solid (although driving a transit van took some adaptation), but now I was driving away from a known base and into the void. What would happen if something went wrong? I didn't have much money and if I broke down, what would I be able to do? All the irrational thoughts came flooding in, the things that could go wrong, that might happen, and the worst-case scenarios: leave it up to the imagination to dream up the totally ridiculous.

I'm not a big fan of fear; I don't often go to that place. Since my first exams in high school when I was so terrified I thought I would die, I've learnt to put anything that elicits fear in me into a box and shove it to one side, and I've taught myself to focus on what needs to be done next to get me through.

In this instance, I knew the journey had to start somewhere and I knew I would be alone. I was as prepared as I could be (for the time being), but it was time to take the next step: the box was open and I had to deal with what I had shoved inside. Perhaps I had merely done a better job of locking the box than ever before, but when it opened every crazy and outrageous thought came tumbling out. Getting stuck on the highway in London-bound traffic merely increased my anxiety, so I found a spot to stop, prepare lunch and reassess. My mind was going in loops and it was time to de-loop.

My mother used to do puzzles with me and play card games, to which I attribute my ability to sit with pieces, options and ideas, and mix them around to find the right way to fit them together to present an acceptable framing of the situation – and one that I can live with. Time to put my rational brain to work and employ on myself some of the exercises I practised as a coach. The one that seemed most apt is what I call 'eating the elephant'. I would never eat an elephant, lovely creatures that they are, but they are big; and when you look at something really big your brain often seizes and becomes overwhelmed. Think of being served up an elephant: your first thought would be, Wow, I'm never going to be able to eat all of that! So how do you eat an elephant? The answer is in bite-sized chunks. Anything big and overwhelming becomes doable when you break it down into smaller, eatable/doable pieces. I had to start with one piece at a time.

I needed to get from the UK to mainland Europe. If I didn't make this part of the journey, there just wouldn't be a next step. All my planning and actions thus far would have been wasted as there was no other way to get from where I was to Africa. I listed the first bites of the elephant: getting to the port, on to the ferry, off the ferry, then driving to Luxembourg. These helped me focus and kept my mind off the whole enormous elephant.

My most important realisation, which carried me through so many things, was that *Life is on the other side of fear*. If I let fear hold me in its thrall, I would not be going anywhere. I would be stuck where I was, and I was certain that this wasn't what I wanted. The pain of staying would be greater than facing my irrational fears, so I needed to stop prevaricating and JFDI.[2]

After arriving in Luxembourg (irrational fear be damned!) I spent a few weeks reorganising my boxes and fine-tuning my possessions. I had just thirty-five plastic packing crates, and for the second time I had to make a decision about each item. Did it deserve a space or was it time to let it go? It was exhausting, but eventually twenty-two crates made it into BlueBelle, along with one cane peacock chair, a mid-sized Turkish carpet, a small metal mosaic-topped table (a gift from my cousin) and the few things I had brought with me from the UK. BlueBelle was filled and there wasn't even space for me to sleep in the back, despite planning one. I spent three nights sleeping in the driver's seat on my journey through France to Barcelona, Spain.

---

[2] Just ffffing do it

Chapter Four: Building BlueBelle

I arrived in Barcelona at the end of July 2017 and that meant long, stifling hot days, sweltering summer nights and the beginning of the hectic tourist season. The city seemed to be constantly under siege. I was there to spend time with My Favourite Nephew,[3] Gary, who had been living in Barcelona for several years and had a fully equipped workshop… with POWER TOOLS – exactly what I needed to build BlueBelle.

Gary is a marvel with his hands. He can design, build, create and fix just about anything, and the plan was that he would help me over the summer holidays when his work usually slowed down. At the time, he was living in a section of his workshop that he had adapted as a home, and he offered me this. I chose, however, to sleep in the workshop office as it made more sense to be closer to my van and all the stuff that I would be sorting. It also meant that I was out of the way of Gary's busy social life. The cluttered, modified office would house my computer on a corner desk, my clothes on adapted hangers on an old filing cabinet, and a bed, which was a plank of wood over some cupboards with a mattress on top. I added my cooler box and travel kettle to these basic surroundings, where I lived for the better part of nine months.

August is peak holiday time and I had not taken into account that most businesses were closed for the summer break, so I was not able to purchase boarding and wood. To add to this, Gary scored a big job that was keeping him busy. So far, none of this part of my plan was working out. 'If you can't do one job, start on another' is my approach, so I set to drawing layouts, sorting through my boxes and putting aside things I planned to include in my interior.

I had decided on a fixed bunk. I didn't want to be 'making and breaking' a bed every day and I worked out that it would take up less space if I built it across the width of the van, where I would just be able to fit in. For stability and to optimise storage, I had decided to build the bed on top of that neat second-hand chest of drawers I had bought in the UK and find a similar one to install

---

[3] A bit of family fun: I only have one niece and nephew but I am their favourite aunt!

back-to-back so that I could have one chest of drawers inside and one that I could access by opening the rear door. I placed the bed on a wooden frame atop the two chests and there was still more storage space either side of them that I could also access from the rear.

I wanted a seating area where I could relax, have a meal and even host a visitor with a modicum of comfort. I also hoped there would be places along my journey where I could park up, sit on my comfortable sofa and look out through my sliding door at a stunning view. The seating facilities were also a prerequisite to enable me to change the status of my van from a light commercial vehicle to a camper, and that would mean cheaper insurance.

A kitchen area was of course necessary, as was a clothes closet. I would be crossing through different climates over several months and would need more than just a travel bag. There had to be a place to store the portable toilet and I really wanted to include a shower too, but hadn't yet figured out how. The drawings progressed, measuring and re-measuring and measuring again, trying to find a way to fit everything into the tiny space. The section to be converted was from immediately behind the front seats to the back doors, which measured three metres long and 1.8 metres wide at floor level (but slightly wider in the middle). This would be my future living area: my home.

When September arrived, boards were ordered and BlueBelle was parked outside the doors of the workshop where I would be building on the street. My nephew was still busy at all hours so I proceeded with the simple things, giving everything an essential few coats of varnish to keep the wood dry. You will recall that the interior of the van was covered in grey carpet, which I had feared would get clogged with African dust. Ripping it out would have been a complex, nasty job as it was glued tight to the board that covered the inside walls. I planned to cover as much of the carpet as practicable with a layer of board and retain the rest to reduce internal condensation. I cut the boards to size, painted them white and solicited the help of Leon, a friend of Gary's, to help me rivet them to the roof and sides above and below the windows.

I had unpacked BlueBelle on my arrival but had not removed my father's beloved old munitions box from WWII because it was filled with crockery and very heavy. I had been meaning to take it out but it provided the convenience of a good seat in the back while I was working, and so it remained.

A few weeks into the construction project, I woke to find my right rear window smashed and, from inside the box, a selection of my beautiful Moroccan patterned crockery and some of my few precious personal possessions were gone. In addition, the thieves had taken the dual dashboard fan, tyre pressure gauge, electric cable connectors, compass, some tools and several other items purchased specifically for the journey. It was a dreadful blow: I had saved so hard for these things and I would struggle to replace them. I felt angry, despondent and assaulted. However, after a few days, I blessed the thieves: the Universe had obviously decided that the perpetrators needed those items more than I did, so I said goodbye to them and set about ordering new security measures, which included window alarms, a big lock for the rear doors and an extra latch for the side door. The final addition to my security arsenal was a big, solid, badass clutch lock. My greatest loss would be losing BlueBelle altogether.

At this time I still believed that I needed my nephew to work on the van with me, but his job kept expanding and he was working from early morning to late at night. He did though generously spend whatever free time he had to talk through my plans with me and give me invaluable advice. On the horizon there was also a trip to South Africa to visit family that he had booked some months before. This put more pressure on him and my window of opportunity seemed to be slipping.

I awoke one morning to the realisation that if I didn't knuckle down and get on with the build, it wasn't going to get done. I considered my options: continue living in the workshop office or get on with building my van and moving my plans forward. That moment was a breaking point for me. I had been enormously stressed and worried about my lack of progress, and yet here I was: *I* could do this – or at least I could give it my best shot!

Gary had pulled out a variety of things from his treasure trove of job leftovers for me to use, including an assortment of floorboards, odd pieces of wood, latches and other bits of ironmongery. It had become evident that my lovely vinyl floor was just too soft and had already started to pit, and this would only get worse. I needed to consider another option. Looking through the treasure trove, I found and managed to match enough beautiful oak-on-pine floorboards, and with the right cuts and placement I was able to cover most of the floor.

To make the sleeping area more secluded at the rear of the van, I wanted to secure two vertical panels to the edge of the bed frame with a gap in between where I would be able both to climb into bed and to access the chest of drawers underneath. The panels had to be cut to the shape of the interior walls of the van if they were to act as screens for the bed area, but the sides of the van were anything but regular and it took me weeks to get those panels right! I carried them between the workshop and the van more times than I can count, cutting a little more here, shaving a sliver off there to get a better result; then, finding that I'd cut too much and something wasn't straight, I had to re-shape and glue extra pieces back on! Finally, one side was done. The second panel went better but it was still not perfect.

There were days when I wondered what on earth I was trying to do. I couldn't do this; I had no skill as a carpenter. I hated it. I cried, I kicked things, I swore, I cried some more... But I continued, realising that no one else would do it for me. I kept telling myself that if I wanted a home and I wanted to *drive* home, I simply *had* to do this.

The challenges continued on all fronts. I awoke one Saturday morning and, as was my habit, went straight to the window to check on BlueBelle. I was on the first floor and as I looked down it immediately struck me that something was different. I couldn't place it for a few minutes, but then I realised she looked wrong at the front. I dashed down the metal stairs, unlocked the door and went to investigate. Sure enough, someone had stolen her Smiley radiator grille. And there, just like me, she had lost her smile.

I wept again. There were so few vans like mine, why would someone steal this?! Another unplanned expense – and I had no idea where I would find a replacement. I had to cover the radiator; I could not leave it exposed during the long journey. My search revealed that the only one available was online and it would be grey plastic. Not ideal but better than nothing. My dear friends George and Mehtap came to my rescue and paid for it, providing untold relief.

After a few more weeks of hard work, BlueBelle's interior was complete.[4] It was April 2018, and I decided to make a trial run into the mountains and back down to the beaches south of Barcelona to see if my ideas had translated into a comfortable reality. I spent two weeks in the middle of nowhere, which allowed me to see how much water I would use, how to deal with washing clothes, what sort of food I needed, and so on. All in all it was a big success and I learnt a great deal about life in a van.

The bonus was that, after such a long time living in other people's houses, I was relishing my freedom and independence. At last, I had my own little home, my own space. It was *all mine*, bought and paid for without an ounce of debt, and I was so grateful for this and for everyone who had helped me get to that point. It was again summer, so I decided that I would leave in the autumn to minimise the effects of the extreme heat when passing the Sahara.

This was the end of the beginning.

---

[4] The build and all accessories cost less than €2000.

Chapter Five: Choosing the route

Navigating a desert in my 2WD vehicle was, frankly, not going to be practical. I don't like sand at the best of times, so a Sahara crossing was out. It made the most sense to stick to the coastal route. I considered that this should keep me away from the more radical central African zones where instability, Boko Haram, Isis, kidnapping and such were actual threats. I wasn't too worried: I figured if someone did kidnap me, they would probably be begging someone else to take me off their hands within a few days; and they had zero chance of a ransom. However, although I understood the risk of what I was doing, I wasn't stupid enough to set out looking for trouble.

My anticipated route would take me through Morocco, Mauritania, Senegal, The Gambia, Guinea-Bissau, Guinea (Conakry), Sierra Leone, Liberia, Côte d'Ivoire, Ghana, Togo, Benin, Nigeria, Cameroon, Gabon, Republic of the Congo, Cabinda (Angola), Democratic Republic of Congo, Angola and Namibia. I had not at that point decided whether I would cut through the Caprivi Strip into Zambia or Botswana and then into Zimbabwe, or if I would continue to South Africa and then up to Zimbabwe, but there was plenty of time to finalise that part.

I put the proposed route through Google Maps and it told me it would be about 16,000 kilometres and would take a mere 228 hours, or nine-and-a-half days; but I knew it would take at least that long just to get through all the border posts! I was quite certain that this estimate would not even remotely resemble reality.

It was only when I was driving through the vast continent that I realised how unreliable maps of Africa still are to this day. You can compare a paper map, Google, Maps.me, Tracks4Africa and several other online options and still come up with different variables. I found the most reliable sources to be Facebook groups such as *West Africa Travellers,*[5] *Overlanding West Africa* and *Overlanding Africa* to find current information and ask questions about routes. These communities are incredibly supportive and a great source of information on the ground. It was important to

---

[5] www.facebook.com/groups/WATravellers

learn that opinions about routes a year ago were often irrelevant at the current time due to changing political situations or security issues. Furthermore, the condition of roads in the rainy season often varied vastly from that in the dry.

The secret, I came to discover, was to prepare well but remain flexible enough to face something entirely different and be ready to adapt quickly. I again learnt to eat the elephant, working on one bite at a time and moving forward while planning and preparing for the next bite.

Chapter Six: The side gig

Alongside building the van and doing web design work, I decided to start a fund for girls' education. Having participated in numerous women's organisations over the years, many of them focused on advancing the equality of women, my research had shown that a vast number of projects needed support and attention in Africa. While I'm personally passionate about Africa and its nature, wildlife and people, which project would *really* make a real long-term difference that I could highlight on my journey?

What stood out most in my research was one fact: the education of girls would result in the solution for many of Africa's woes – and this was the deciding factor. My focus would be on the education of girls, and specifically on getting them into high school where the numbers who attended fell away sharply.

I failed to find an organisation where more money went to the grassroots needs than the expensive offices and cars, or met the values and focus that I was interested in. Consequently, I set up a fully registered non-profit whilst I was still resident in Luxembourg.

I named my non-profit Kusasa,[6] which in Ndebele – the language of the area in Zimbabwe where I grew up – means 'Tomorrow'. Kusasa raises scholarship funds for high-achieving and high-performing girls to progress from junior school into high school or vocational training, because the number of girls entering high school falls off significantly in Africa due to cultural prejudices and poverty. After the economic crash of 2008 in Zimbabwe, a full two-thirds of girls failed to enter high school. Now the economic decline in 2019/2020, added to the impact of COVID-19, will most likely put them in the back seat once again.

Before I left I secured scholarship commitments for three girls. Kusasa had taken off.

---

[6] You can find out more about my research and why highlighting this cause was my final choice on www.kusasa.africa where I provide facts and details to support my decision.

Chapter Seven: Departing the known

It was time to set off on my adventure.

Winter was coming, and this meant that driving past the Sahara Desert should not be too taxing; and besides, it was getting too cold to sleep in my van in northern Spain. I had decided that I wanted to be in Africa to celebrate my sixtieth birthday, and that was fast approaching. Time to get off the fence and shift into doing, rather than just talking about it.

The first step was to book a ferry from Barcelona to Tangier Med in Morocco. Although this would mean twenty-four hours of sailing, it would take less time and money overall compared with the shorter ferry journey from the port of Tarifa, which would cost me precious days of driving, fuel and tolls to reach.

I searched online for the best deal. Timing was important as I wanted to be sure I could clear customs and still reach my first camp stop before nightfall. I selected the appropriate option, added my credit card information and then, before continuing, I had what I fondly call an 'Oh shit' moment. I stared at the computer screen for some time while a myriad thoughts came spinning through my mind. Did I want to do this, was I fooling myself, could I do this, *should* I do this, *why* was I doing this?! Doubt had entered with a vengeance and it was hurting my brain. I had managed to ignore the voices and only focus on what needed to be done, but now they were at full volume. I did the most logical thing that anyone should do at a time like this: I went to make coffee.

The voices subsided somewhat and I went back to the screen. When I finally committed to hitting the Enter key, I found that the whole process had timed out and I had to set it up again. The voices returned: was this a sign? Logic finally prevailed with a louder voice: No, silly, you just took too darn long! Rational thought was returning, the voices died, and there were no more reasons or excuses as to why I could/should/would not go… but there was still something very final about that Enter key.

Indecision bores me, so I hit Enter and that was it – done! Two weeks to go, and I would be in Africa by the end of

November: I would be in Africa for my sixtieth birthday. I was both elated and terrified.

Part of my indecision stemmed from the fact that I had only managed to squirrel away about half of the money I believed I would need to make the journey. If I had to save further, working for at least another year, that would mean I would not meet my goal of being in Africa on my sixtieth; and this had become a landmark event for me. However, I had a deep-seated belief that I was meant to do this and faith that all would be fine. Many people have said, "Yes but it might not have worked out so well", and my response is that my expectation was that all *would* be well. I committed myself with *Absolute Certainty*, with faith… and that faith was proven to be justified. In the words of Henry Ford: "Whether you believe you can do a thing or not, you are right."

Two days before my ferry departure I said a sad goodbye to Solsona in Catalonia where I had spent six months, and to all the lovely people I had met in that charming little town. Even though I spoke little to no Spanish – let alone Catalan – they had welcomed me into their community, helped me raise funds for the girls and made me part of their family. I would miss my new friends and their warmth, generosity and kindness.

Barcelona would be an opportunity to make some last-minute purchases and say some more final goodbyes to new friends I had made there. Amongst my acquisitions was a mattress. For some months I had been sleeping on those bargain second-hand caravan cushions, and while they sufficed, they were heavily contoured and contributing to my back issues. Considering that I would be sleeping *in* my van for months on end, I needed to improve what I was sleeping *on*, and thankfully I found a good mattress. It was more money than I wanted to spend, but at the local Scandinavian shop it was cheaper than the alternatives and proved to be a thoroughly worthwhile investment.

Producing some business cards was also a last-minute idea. I found a great place that printed a double-sided card with links to my journey (website/Facebook/Instagram pages) on one side and details of Kusasa on the other. I also wanted to have a small give-away card, and as it was coming up to the new year I designed one with a 2019 calendar on one side, and on the reverse the map of Africa with flag images in each country and the words 'Keep

Calm... This is Africa'. Unlike so many other overlanders, I didn't want stickers with my details; I wanted something useful. And if I wanted someone to have my private details, I would give them a business card. Being a woman on my own, I was cautious about giving away too much personal information.

TIME TO GO

A couple of people turned up to say goodbye and have a drink with me before I spent my last night in Europe. I was wild camping[7] close to the dock so that I could get there early without the stress of morning traffic. An accident almost six weeks earlier, when I'd torn the tendons in my right ankle for a second time, had been exacerbated by another fall off a step two days before leaving; so with my back and shoulder already bad bedfellows, sleeping was an uncomfortable affair. It was a restless night, the type when you keep waking to look at the clock despite having set the alarm. Pain woke me early at 4.00. I brushed my teeth, wiped my face and applied deodorant, which would have to see me through the day. Instructions were to be at the dock by 6.00.

Stress makes me stupid sometimes and despite all my planning I managed to get lost and drive to the wrong dock, but thankfully I was early enough. I found another dock and knew that I was in the right place because the vehicles already waiting there were piled high with goods strapped to roof-racks and packed to the brim with every kind of chattel imaginable. I parked up behind a row of similar travellers and made coffee (the benefits of having your kitchen with you at all times!) It was a little past 5.00.

As time ticked by and more vehicles arrived, squeezing into every gap, I started to worry as it was now 6.30 and nothing was happening. I went for a walk to find out more and rather noticeably, I was the only woman around. I found someone who spoke a little English and learnt that the ticket office only opened at 8.00

By that time the area was bumper to bumper with fully-loaded vehicles. I had taken up position by the door and was fifth in line. I was still limping heavily from my fall, but when the door

---

[7] Wild camping means setting up camp outside dedicated campsites or caravan parks.

opened this did not deter the many men who pushed past me to get to the ticket office. As I looked around, I realised that I was still the only woman to be seen. Where were all the women..?

I progressed through what I can only describe as the most chaotic ferry loading process I had ever encountered. I received a piece of paper at the ticket office and was told to return to my van, which was now holding up the other traffic (remember all those men who pushed past me?!) I was receiving angry glares and the occasional hooting, and vehicles were making nineteen-point turns to get past me. I drove fifty metres to get a stamp on my piece of paper, then was directed to park and return to the ticket office to get a boarding pass! Another long wait and eventually, with boarding pass in hand, I returned to the van feeling decidedly relieved. Nevertheless I was wondering if I had indeed completed all the requirements when I noticed an official-looking man zig-zagging haphazardly through the parked lanes. People were pushing pieces of paper in front of him which he was signing and handing back, so I decided I should investigate.

He was Italian (as was the ferry company). I asked what he needed, to which he responded in Italian something along the lines of, "Where is your vehicle?" I pointed to BlueBelle and he jutted out his chin: "Go back to your vehicle." Some minutes later he reappeared and I handed him all the papers. He was grumpy; he probably dealt with this chaos daily. After a brief interchange that went something like, "Yes, this is my vehicle, it is from the UK and I am the driver," I received a stamp and a signature, and my papers were thrust back at me as he turned to deal with the next person, who looked equally confused.

During the seemingly incessant waiting I had started chatting to some of the people around me, when suddenly, without announcement or indication, the traffic started moving. There was no orderly queuing, just a mass pushing and shoving. Many cars had been left unattended, their drivers in the main building likely getting refreshment, so this added to the mayhem. The driver I had been so pleasantly chatting to just moments before cut me off as I was turning and sped off to the spot a few metres in front of me. People were running everywhere and drivers dodging both the vehicles and the runners, all in a frantic quest to get on to the ship.

As the queue inched along I eventually came to a halt with a small porta-cabin ahead to the right and the ship to my left. A woman, who I assumed was part of the immigration department, was collecting passports, so I handed her mine and watched her walk off with the stack to the porta-cabin. On her return several minutes later she handed the passports back to their owners, and I was so relieved to find that I had got my own back that I didn't bother to check the exit stamp. After what seemed like an eternity inching towards the ship BlueBelle and I were finally on board, where someone in a traffic vest indicated (at the last minute) that I should not follow the vehicle in front of me but park to one side behind a large truck. As I pulled on the handbrake I breathed a sigh of relief. That had to be the most insane ferry boarding process I'd ever been through, and never again will I complain about any others! I switched on the van window alarms and affixed the clutch lock – although in hindsight she wasn't going anywhere in that sardine-packed boat.

I had beforehand stuffed a small holdall with what I considered essential: my laptop and tablet, my pillow, toiletries and a change of clothes for the next day. By the time I got out of BlueBelle there was barely space to walk between the parked vehicles to get to the stairs leading to the decks. When I came to the lifts they were crowded, but at last, there were women and children. How well they had been hidden until now!

I spent the next hour walking around, trying to figure out where I should position myself. To save money I had not booked a cabin, so I found a couple of rooms with free coach seats. They were already mostly taken up with luggage, blankets and bags, but I found one that didn't appear to be too crowded. However, the TV was on full blast – in French. I don't do TV in any language; it had been ten years since I'd last had access to one and I didn't miss it. Even with earplugs in, that was going to get on my nerves.

Off I trundled again to look for a quieter space. Along the corridors and stairs, every corner was piled high with blankets, bags and bodies. It seemed that those on board were frequent ferry-goers and this was where they would be sleeping. I arrived at a front lounge area, relatively deserted with comfortable side benches and good lighting, so I decided this would suffice and settled down. However, soon after we set sail a crowd started to appear in the middle seating area which faced a small stage. An officious little man arrived with a briefcase, from which he took a stamp, a stamp pad, a pen and a pile of forms, and started berating some of the people before him (at least that's how it sounded to me as I couldn't understand what he was saying).

Up till then I had been reading, but I put my book down and began watching the scene unfold in front of me. People were filling in forms, getting passports and forms stamped. At times there was an altercation in Arabic or French (one never really knows in a language one doesn't understand, but there was sufficient volume and gesticulation to indicate that it wasn't polite), and then the crowd would continue to snake forward and fill again from the rear. The officious official certainly was in a bad mood – or perhaps he just didn't like his job. I assumed that he was clearing passengers before they disembarked.

This set me to wondering if I too should have been in the queue. A man seated next to me had greeted me in English earlier so I asked him, but he assured me that it was only for Moroccans. This seemed erroneous when I started to spot obvious Europeans in the crowd; but perhaps they were resident in Morocco, I told myself. By the time the official was finished and packing up, I gathered the courage to approach him. I wanted to be sure I didn't need to fill in the form or get a stamp, so I showed him my passport and asked if I needed to do anything. He looked at me fiercely and I repeated my request, but it became obvious that Mr Grumpy did not understand me, so I pointed to the form and the stamp and then to myself. He responded roughly in Arabic, shook his head and waved me away, so I took that as a No.

I returned to my seat and continued reading. A Moroccan man approached and sat not far from me and when I looked up he greeted me, to which I politely responded. Not long after that, he struck up a conversation. He was in his early forties and seemed pleasant enough. He informed me, without having been asked, that he had been visiting his brother in France and was now returning home to Rabat. During the conversation I revealed that I was driving on my own through Africa and I think that was when he decided that this crazy old woman, on her own on a boat filled mainly with men, needed looking after. He told me he had a shared cabin and was disturbed to hear that I would be sleeping 'rough' on the ship, fearing I would be robbed. I assured him that I would be fine, at the same time becoming wary that perhaps I was giving this strange man too much detail.

The dinner bell finally went, so I wished the man well and set off with my suitcase and bag in tow. No cabin meant I had nowhere to leave them. I had been sensible enough to purchase food vouchers with my ferry ticket and the cost-saving was exceptional since everything on board was over-priced. The queue in the canteen consisted mostly of men (the women were still in hiding then) and with my meal, I decided to splash out and buy a small bottle of wine: I felt I deserved to celebrate having achieved this first major step of my journey. I found a seat and made myself comfortable.

No sooner had I started eating and drunk my first glass of wine than my new Moroccan friend – I shall call him Mr Rabat – asked if he could join me. I was cautious but, as courteously as I could, I said yes. He noticed my wine and asked if I wanted some more. I felt that two small glasses were sufficient and I should keep some wits about me, so I declined the first and the second time he offered; but then he said he felt like some too and went off to buy a small bottle himself. I was surprised because he struck me as a devout Muslim. When he returned with the wine, he proffered it to me and this time my response was firm: "I will not have any more and I will not change my mind about it." His motives were starting to seem suspect.

The entire ship was full, mostly of Moroccans but with a handful from European origin (primarily French and older than me); however, in the dining-room, at the table next to ours, my attention was drawn to a large, very dark-skinned man. I was intrigued about his roots and also needed to break the intensity of my impromptu dinner guest, so as this man and his guest were passing to leave, I greeted him and asked where he was from. He responded in French that he was from Senegal, which accounted for his handsome darkness. He in turn asked me where I came from, to which of course I said Zimbabwe, which elicited the usual surprised response and some hearty laughter, after which we bade each other good night.

I finished my meal, conducted enough conversation with Mr Rabat to appear polite (I now believe that to be my error), and then excused myself. On heading back to the front lounge, where I had set my mind on spending the night, I became aware that there was a musical performance going on and the room was filled with drunken men – not somewhere I felt comfortable. I would have to wait until the performance was over, so I retreated to the smaller bar and asked for a black coffee. As I was waiting I heard from behind me, "Madame Zimbabwe!" and turned around to find the Senegalese man from dinner. What ensued was a conversation in English and Portuguese by me and French and Spanish by him. It was fun and passed the time nicely.

An hour later the performance in the bar had ended and there were only a few groups of men remaining, so I headed to a quiet corner at the far end. On the opposite side of where I was sitting there was a group of about eight young men waving a bottle of whisky around – probably from the fully-loaded duty-free shop. It was clear this was not their first bottle. They were being baited by a smaller but older group of men seated at the entrance bar, which was now closed. These men were Moroccan, sober and obviously disapproving of the young men's loud and drunken performance. I sat and watched, wondering if this was going to escalate and if I needed to get out of there really fast and make alternative arrangements.

While I was watching, Mr Rabat – who was now starting to feel like a stalker – appeared at my table. He took a seat and complained that his cabin with five other men was hot and crowded and a couple of the men who were already asleep were snoring like generators. As he became aware of the young men in the lounge, he disapprovingly informed me that this was what alcohol could do and why it was evil… seemingly forgetting that not long ago he was drinking it himself and quite happy to ply me with some!

After twenty minutes of escalating exchanges, a member of the crew and a security guard arrived to remove the young men and a modicum of silence returned. It was now 10.00pm and I was tired: it had been a very long day. Mr Rabat repeated his concern that I would be sleeping there on my own and suggested he should sleep close by to protect me; however, I was starting to feel that the only person I needed protection from was him! After firmly reassuring him that I was fine and did *not* need his protection, I was finally relieved to watch him return to his cabin.

I ensconced myself in a corner sofa, took out my pillow and a small blanket, put the suitcase next to me on the floor and barricaded myself in with two of the tables an some chairs closely pushed in behind them. Anyone wanting to come near me or steal my belongings would have to get past my barrier first without making a sound. I wasn't too concerned about the very few other men who had similarly chosen to sleep in the lounge and there was also some low lighting. I had settled in and was reading my book when Mr Rabat returned… and by now I was *definitely* feeling that stalker vibe. This time he arrived with his holdall and claimed that he was not going to be able to sleep in his cabin. He appeared surprised that I was quite so well organised and secure but made himself comfortable on the opposite bench seat, looking a bit put out. I decided now to be offhand and ignore him and a while later he got the message, disappeared to the back of the stage and, to my great relief, stayed there. I checked my things and my position, as well as the few other men who had the same idea, before falling asleep.

I woke early the next morning, packed up quickly, found a shower, and then went to see the view from the deck. Gibraltar and mainland Europe lay on one side with a bank of dark clouds hanging overhead and Africa rose in the distance on the other side with clear blue skies. My emotions were running high. I had worked so hard to do this and I was almost there, but it wasn't without a twinge of regret for all the lovely people I was leaving behind. But the allure of Africa was strong and I could smell the earthy, fresh scent that is home.

I was going home to Africa!

PART II: The Journey

Life is on the other side of fear.
~ Dot Bekker

Definition of Overlanding: self-reliant long-distance travel to remote destinations where the journey is the main goal.

Chapter One – Morocco

24 November 2018

After docking at Tangier Med, it took some time before we were permitted to return to the car decks. I couldn't find BlueBelle as I thought she was one level down, but in fact my wanderings the day before had taken me to park another level up. By the time I found her there was a mad mass exodus of foot passengers with their bundles, and vehicles were already pouring off the ferry. Parked in the second to last row, BlueBelle was once again blocking the vehicles in the last row and people were getting touchy. I shoved in my bags, telling one muttering man who was pacing up and down to calm down; I'd be out when I was out and his protestations were not going to make it happen any sooner.

I had driven on to the ferry in Barcelona and parked facing the front, but instead of disembarking forwards, as is common on most ferries, it was now necessary for me to turn around and drive off in the direction I had come on. I was glad I had missed the departure of the rows next to me because it must have been chaos! Getting out took some manoeuvring and the man trying to direct me was an annoying distraction, so I just did it my way and ignored him. Based on how they had done things thus far, I didn't think I could do any worse.

I made it off the ferry and on to beloved African soil… but immediately found myself in a long queue of vehicles. My initial excitement was overridden by the need to ascertain what came next. The queue dissolved into four lanes and they were moving steadily, which was good news. I took the right-hand lane and when I arrived at the front I showed my passport. The official paged through it, then looked up at me… and announced that there was no Spanish exit stamp.

You might recall that when I took my passport from the woman at the ferry terminal in Barcelona, I had only checked to make sure that it was *my* passport, not whether it had an exit stamp. But *why* hadn't it been stamped? My horror was very real, but I was certain that whatever happened next, I was not going back! I was told to pull over to the left. All four lanes of traffic were stopped and I drove across, feeling somewhat embarrassed. No one knew why I was being pulled aside and I noted all the male eyes watching me. I got out of my van with my papers and was directed to some porta-cabins about fifty metres behind me.

I approached a man – as usual there were only men – and explained my situation. I'm not sure he understood me, but he walked off and another man came to see me. I again started describing my predicament, when who should pass by but Mr Grumpy, the official from the ferry. His humour had not improved! He handed me a form and indicated that I should complete it (could I not have done this on the ferry?), so as I was not permitted to enter his office, I sat on the step of the concrete block outside the porta-cabins and filled it in.

When I was done, I returned to the cabin where Mr Grumpy was now seated at one of the two desks that had been crammed inside. My passport and the form were taken and I stood just inside the doorway, waiting. Mr Grumpy gave me a scathing look and waved me away, indicating that I should remove myself from his presence. I smiled sweetly (my way of highlighting his boorish behaviour) and stepped outside into the increasing heat as the door was shut firmly behind me. I have no earthly idea how it could possibly take that long to stamp a passport, but after ten agonising minutes I was gruffly called in, my passport was thrust back at me and the cabin door swiftly shut again in my face. I walked back to BlueBelle and showed my passport to the officer at the now-dwindling queue of vehicles. He nodded and I was finally permitted to leave.

Still there was no chance to enjoy the moment because within a hundred metres I found myself in another queue, where I inched along to another checkpoint with a man handing out forms. I took mine and followed the traffic, uncertain where I needed to go next but heading towards what looked like a customs check where I noticed several vehicles parked to one side. When I reached the front of the queue, I was asked if I was carrying guns. "No!" was my confident response, nonetheless I was directed to park up with the ten or so other sundry vehicles. I would be lying if I said that there was some order to the entire two-hour process, but it was evident that the system was another of total chaos.

Welcome to Africa!

Happily, I had my home with me, so after thirty minutes of absolutely nothing happening, I made coffee, had a biscuit, took out my book, opened the side door and sat on my step reading. I wasn't bothered by what anyone thought. Everyone around me was speaking either Arabic or French and again I saw only men; if there were any women they didn't leave their vehicles, so I was mostly invisible anyway.

In time, a customs officer drifted over in my direction and gesticulated that I must open the back door and again I was asked if I had guns. I was surprised by the repeated question and my blank look drew a sharp tone: "Guns, do you have guns?" It evidently looked like I would have not just one but probably a whole arsenal! "No!" came my firm reply. I went to open the rear doors (which could only be opened from the inside as I had broken the external handle mechanism some time before), but by the time I emerged again mere seconds later, he was gone.

When it was clear that he was not immediately returning, I shut the doors again. I was taking no chances: being on my own, I understood that I was vulnerable by leaving any part of the vehicle open when I was not present, so my strict rule was to lock everything, even if it was just for a few minutes.

Over an hour later, one young man could no longer take the waiting in the sun and started a heated exchange with one of the customs officers. Before long all the officers had left what they were doing and were weighing in on the argument, which was then joined by other people in the queue. It was a mass of men all shouting and gesticulating at the same time. Oh, this was going to be bad. The longer this went on, the longer we would all be waiting since none of the officers were actually 'working'! Fortunately, after ten minutes they started to drift off, but the young man took a forward offensive position and I could sense he had more coming in the way of argument.

Having lived with men long enough, I recognised the effects of a 'hangry'[8] man. It had been many hours since breakfast and was now well past lunchtime and hunger inevitably escalates anger, especially in men. I picked up my packet of biscuits and a

---

[8] Hungry and angry

'Keep Calm TIA' card and confidently approached the young man and offered him a one. (I have no idea what possessed me to do this, but I am sometimes compelled to do strange things.) He looked at me as if I had come from Mars. I just smiled and said, "I know it is frustrating and has been a long time since breakfast, so please have a biscuit – it will make you feel better." It certainly broke the focus on his exasperation, although I don't believe he understood me fully as the look on his face was one of utter confusion. He carefully took the proffered biscuit and when I asked him if he would like another, he bemusedly shook his head, so I gave him the card with a smile and turned around to head back to BlueBelle.

I hadn't thought this through. As I turned I realised that there were now a dozen men, standing leaning against various cars around BlueBelle, so I took my packet of biscuits and walked down the line offering one to each – after all, it would have been rude not to do so. Some declined and some accepted, but the looks on their faces made me smile: it was a mixture of surprise and concern. What they must have thought I have no idea, but assuredly they now had something else to discuss. As I reached BlueBelle and took up my seat again, the first young man turned to me as I looked in his direction, smiled and said, "Merci," probably realising that in his shock he had forgotten to thank me. I smiled and nodded acceptance as I returned to reading my book. There were no further outbursts so my objective had been achieved!

Earlier I had seen an officer with a sniffer dog walking nonchalantly between the vehicles. He must have noticed my actions and now walked over to investigate what mischief I was up to. I love dogs and since I wasn't carrying weapons, drugs or illegal people, I considered myself safe. He asked me in French where I was from and we had a short cross-cultural exchange. I asked if I could say hello to his dog, and although most working handlers will not allow you near their animal, he agreed. I moved closer to allow the dog to sniff my hand and then stroked him gently on the face. The dog's response was to lean against my leg in a most affectionate way, at which the handler shot me a look of utter surprise. I smiled and stroked the dog some more... and the officer again asked if I had a gun. Extraordinary!

Nothing much happened for a while. Some cars that had arrived after me were inspected and released, while others and I were still waiting. The dog handler returned to me and asked me to give him my passport. I had heard of passports being held ransom so I was at first reluctant, however I felt I could trust him (although I did watch his every move!) He approached one of the customs officers and there was some gesticulating in my direction. He returned with the officer, and *again* I was asked if I had weapons. "No," I sighed, my patience starting to wear thin. What was this obsession with weapons? Were all the white women who arrived in Morocco gun-runners?!

Eventually I was told that my passport would go to be stamped along with my form and then I could leave, and no further inspection of BlueBelle took place. Progress, I thought as I watched my passport disappear into a small office. However after waiting patiently for another fifteen minutes, I decided that it was now time to act and walked over to the office. There was some shuffling around of papers until I indicated which one was mine, and it was then stamped and handed back to me… but where was the vehicle form? More shouting ensued before I was directed to another office where finally my form appeared, signed, sealed and delivered. *Merci!*

I was off! Outside the barrier there were more porta-cabins and some shops, where I needed to stop. I had to buy my vehicle insurance before I continued so I waited in a queue of – yes, you guessed it: only men. I had decided not to purchase a SIM card for my mobile phone from the port. While there was no shortage of people selling them, there had been reports of cards that were invalid or only worked for one day, so I determined to use my international roaming until I could find a proper shop.

Next I had to change some cash. I had a few dirham (the Moroccan currency) with me, but the insurance had taken a good portion and I thought I might need more. I had installed an exchange rate app on my phone so that I could compare euro, US dollar,[9] dirham and various other currencies all at the same time, therefore I knew the general rate I would be looking at, more or less. But the *bureau de change* quoted me an I'm-going-to-con-this-woman rate, so I laughed ironically, replied, "I'm not stupid, thank you so much!" and walked resolutely away. Behind me I heard, "Come back, we can talk about it!" but I did not turn around.

THE FIRST NIGHT IN AFRICA

It was getting late. I had identified a wild camping place not too far from the port with a guard, where I would be able to park in return for tipping him. It was also nicely situated next to the ocean. I put the destination into my phone, which would serve as my GPS throughout the entire journey. I had been wired all day not knowing what to expect, and so far I'd done ok. I gave myself a good pat on the back, smiled and reminded myself that *I was in Africa*! The first bite of the elephant was done.

I entered the bare parking area and sited myself on a reasonably level spot with my side door facing the small bay. A few metres away was an overlanding vehicle, and working on it was a large, well-built man with grey-white hair and a beard. I greeted him and when he replied I faltered. "Where are you from?" I asked him, knowing already. "South Africa," he answered. Of all the places in the world to meet a neighbour..!

Graeme and Luisa Bell and their two teenage children, Keelan and Jessica, had been driving overland continuously for seven years, covering East Africa, the Americas, Europe and some of Asia. Now they were on their way down West and Central Africa to return to their home in Cape Town, to stay for a few months before resuming their journey to as yet unknown destinations. Graeme has written several overlanding books (some of which Luisa has co-written) and I am most grateful to him for writing the foreword to my book.

With a few hours of daylight still remaining, I decided that my priority was to make space inside BlueBelle. The last round of shopping had meant that the floor was full as I'd not had time to put it all away. The main task was to change the mattress, and the old cushions had to go. Working in a confined space with such big bulky items proved to be a challenge, especially as there was a mattress topper and a zipped cover that needed to be taken off the cushions and put on to the new mattress. With my aching shoulder, it was frustrating and taxing and took longer than I expected, and the van was blue inside and out by the time I was done. I considered keeping the old cushions, but I had to be practical as there was simply nowhere to keep them. The good thing about tiny living is that you have to let stuff go: being a hoarder just isn't possible unless you're prepared to sacrifice comfort.

When I was travelling in Portugal in my previous RV, some years before, I had met a lovely Scottish couple, Carol and Roy. Carol had schooled me on travelling in confined spaces with weight limitations. "When you look at buying something," she'd said to me, "ask yourself, 'Do I want it, or do I need it?' If you decide to buy it, then the next question is, 'If this goes in, then what comes out?'" She was entirely right: this is the quintessential way to approach life in a van.

I decided to give the guard the cushions. He was delighted, and when I looked around at my new mattress and bed I was pretty pleased with myself too. My reward was the bottle of wine I had been saving for my first evening.

The Bells and I had earlier agreed to get together later to drink the traditional African *sundowner*, which translates to 'drinking anything alcoholic as the sun sets'. It was a glorious African sunset too: I was welcomed home with a vast golden sky filled with pink streaks that wove their way through the clouds. I took a deep breath, smiled with pleasure and finally toasted my return to my home continent.

We spent a convivial evening together and I learnt a lot from these seasoned overlanders who, over the duration of my journey, became my friends. In conversation I had mentioned that I felt people hadn't taken me seriously about the journey and Graeme responded "People will notice when you get out the other side of Nigeria." For some reason his comment irked me, besides the fact that Nigeria seemed a long way away.

I reflected on my first day. Stepping into the unknown is an experience that requires the determination to succeed and an ability to focus on how to forge ahead. While there are times when it is wise to retreat, if I had done so at any of the challenges I had faced that day I would have disappointed not only myself but also everyone who had faith in me. Worse than that though, it would have proven to all the naysayers that they were right and that I was too weak or foolish to achieve what I had set out to do... and *that* was not something I was prepared to concede – at least not so soon.

CHEFCHAOUEN – A DIFFERENT KIND OF BLUE

The next morning I was up early to witness my first African sunrise on this journey, which did not disappoint with another magnificent gilded array of colours. The Bells and I said our farewells, fully anticipating to meet each other again along the way since we would be heading down much of the same route. Regrettably, a few days later they had trouble with their gearbox and it would be almost a month before they were on the road again, by which time I was heading toward Mauritania.

My next stop was the legendary *Blue City,* Chefchaouen, renowned for its many buildings, stairways and towers painted bright blue. I had opted to take the scenic route to get there, which was indeed delightful; but the road, not so much: it was my first lesson in pothole-dodging!

The countryside was surprisingly lush. Morocco had always conjured up in my mind images of desert, sand, camels and the occasional oasis, but here it was green with rolling hills. The area was obviously influenced by the Mediterranean climate, and being winter now this meant that it was colder and wetter too. Donkeys were the primary means of transportation and used to carry unbearably heavy loads. These hard-working animals could also be seen on ploughs out in the fields, where even at the end of November they were tilling the soil in preparation for planting.

When I arrived in Chefchaouen in the late afternoon, the sunset was not far off and the clouds were threatening bad weather. I had trouble finding the way to the guarded parking where I would be staying, which was exacerbated by the fact that by the time I reached the city centre the rain had come and I was simultaneously met by rush hour traffic. As I inched along, men were knocking on my windows offering me parking, marijuana, companionship and various other deals, but all I wanted was for them to go away so that I could focus on getting to where I wanted to be.

I eventually found the parking area. I had missed it because it didn't look at all as I had anticipated: just a few taxis and buses parked inside a dirty compound with mud and rubbish everywhere. It was now almost dark and with the heavy rain I decided that it was too late to go and find somewhere else; and my shoulder was also giving me a lot of pain. I tried to find the guard but he was nowhere to be seen, so I just pulled in and parked next to another small overlanding van, which made me feel slightly more comfortable. I reversed in so that I could make an easy exit if necessary and put the keys where I could quickly grab them. These two habits would become my routine every evening.

It was now dark and sounds from the street and surrounding area were plentiful, including the call to prayer from the *muezzin* in a nearby mosque. I switched on my window alarms, closed the curtains to block out the disagreeable-looking world outside my van and cooked my first meal since breakfast, which I ate ravenously while listening to the rain pattering down on the roof. In this painted city I couldn't help feeling a bit blue myself: this wasn't at all how I'd envisaged my journey starting, parked amidst the mud and trash. I decided not to dwell on it and read my book before getting an early night, hoping that the next day would be brighter and I'd be in less pain.

The following morning I awoke and had a brief chat with my neighbours, a nice young Irish couple who were packing up and leaving to explore further. I had already decided on my course of action for the morning: explore the blue city on foot, buy some fruit and vegetables (I had not taken the risk of bringing any with me from Europe) and find something to help relieve my shoulder pain.

The parking compound looked even worse in the cold, grey morning light and the sky, although blue, was threatening more rain in the distance. I had checked the map before leaving and had an idea of the direction I needed to go, so I wandered through the narrow streets, stepping around puddles, trash and mud whilst avoiding taxis and street traders. After an hour or so of walking I found a few blue buildings, but mostly it was just an old town that had seen better days – as had I, I thought, with a brewing headache adding to the pain in my shoulder.

I knew I'd had enough of the day when the rain started again. I had not found the so-called *blue street* but I no longer cared because 'pain brain' had taken over. However, I was not done: I still needed the vegetables and a pharmacy. I had seen a small market on a muddy side street and bought some produce there. I was impressed with the freshness and how inexpensive it all was. The pharmacy I went into also had a kindly English-speaking pharmacist, who recommended a very good heat lotion to help soothe my shoulder. After traipsing back through the rain, the trash and the mud, I had never been so glad to be inside BlueBelle and made myself a well-deserved coffee.

Through one of the Facebook overlanding groups, I had been in touch with Laurie Heimbigner and her husband Bruce. I knew they were due to arrive in Morocco soon after me; having taken the ferry from Tarifa, Spain it was a short journey to cross to Tangier. They too were heading to Chefchaouen, so I had sent a message to let them know where I was and they were set to join me later that day. As I sat with my coffee, I wished I hadn't made the arrangement as I was truly not enjoying the compound, the town or the weather.

But as chance would have it, in the afternoon Laurie and Bruce sent a message to tell me that their large vehicle had been unable to get through the narrow streets to where I was parked, so they had opted to stay at a campsite on the other side of town. I saw this as a sign for me to leave: there was no good reason to stay where I was! At least the rain had finally abated. I locked everything down, got in the driver's seat, argued the fee with the guard (first lesson – always agree the rate in advance!), paid him just to be done with the argument and left. I had identified a proper camp a couple of hours drive to the south and hoped to get there before dark.

OUAZZANE – SIXTY AND THE HEIMBIGNERS

I arrived at the campsite just as the sun was setting and was guided to a spot on the paving next to an empty swimming pool. The area was clean and the hard surface meant there was no mud, so I parked up feeling I had made the right decision. I settled down for the night and enjoyed a peaceful sleep, only intermittently broken by the distant melodious call to prayer that is heard all over Morocco.

The next morning I was not in any rush as I had decided I would spend a few days at this location. I set about with some reorganising. Now that I was truly on the road, I had noted some items that would be better in the rear storage area and others that needed relocating inside. Whilst I was pottering around, I noticed a groundsman nearby and politely greeted him.

Parked outside the pool area were three huge motorhomes, and as the largest of those left I could not help but gawp. It was artic-sized – but even taller. I've seen smaller houses! As I watched, the driver loaded a Smart car into the 'garage' at the rear of the vehicle. It was truly a monster, and all I could think of was the challenges they would face with the road conditions, bridges and narrow city streets. I wondered idly too how much fuel such a monster consumed.

As I was gazing I noticed the groundsman to my right sitting on a low wall. He had obviously also been watching the scene but was now pointedly looking at me. Thinking nothing sinister of it, I smiled at him with a 'Wow!' gesture at the monster and continued to watch until it left. I returned to BlueBelle, and within minutes the groundsman had moved to the section of the garden directly next to my van and started asking me questions in French. I understood some of what he was saying but decided to decline answering him as I was feeling a bit uncomfortable with his proximity. Instead I told him politely in English that I couldn't speak French, but he persisted, his tactic being quite obviously: 'Pressure will change her mind.' I continued about my work, trying to ignore him when suddenly he appeared at my side with two pomegranates that he had picked off the nearby tree and proffered them to me: 'Gifts will surely change her mind!'

I was aware that it is considered impolite in Muslim culture to refuse a gift, so I hesitantly accepted them, not wanting to be seen as rude. Regrettably it seemed he translated this to mean that there was still a possibility of success – my error. I turned around to place the fruit in the doorway and it was then that he started getting a little 'handy'. He was a much younger man than me and had mistakenly assumed that my courtesy was an open invitation to my body. I was shocked, stepped quickly aside and gave him an angry look with a firm, "No!" I immediately tried to return the pomegranates, because certainly no fruit in existence could give a man these kinds of favours! At this he hastily backed down and stepped aside, realising that he had gone too far. I turned away to clean my side windows which the rain and dust had left in need of attention, but Mr Lusty immediately swept in and grabbed the cleaning cloth from my hands and started cleaning, telling me that this was not a woman's work.

He had now gone too far. Courtesy be damned, don't tell me I can't clean my own windows! I snatched the cloth back, told him firmly that this was *my* vehicle to do what I liked with, thank you very much, and he must please leave. I was furious and made no attempt to speak in French, but there was nothing about my body language, tone or look that left him with any uncertainty about my intent! He left.

When it comes to freeze, flight or fight I tend to have an overdose of the latter, and on several occasions during this journey this propensity came in useful.

Before leaving Europe, I had decided that I would spend a few weeks in Morocco. I felt it was important to find my 'Africa feet', get comfortable with being entirely on my own in a different world, settle my nerves and find a pace and routine that would benefit me in the months that lay ahead. There was a distinctive cultural shift between Europe and Africa and I didn't want to fling myself into this epic undertaking without taking a bit of time to reorient myself.

Earlier that morning I had sent a message to Laurie and Bruce to inform them that I had left Chefchaouen and was now just outside the city of Ouazzane. They too had decided to escape the rain and head further south to join me, and when they arrived later that day it felt like meeting old friends. They are Americans, hailing from Washington State, and were travelling in a huge Ford 550 truck they'd named Livingstone. Livingstone quickly became BlueBelle's bigger-younger-brother, and although we didn't know it then he would be of great help to her in months to come. The Heimbigners had been travelling for about a year: they had driven down through the USA and Mexico, then shipped the truck to Europe and toured there before taking the ferry across the Mediterranean to tackle Africa.[10]

The next day saw the sun rise on my birthday. A new year and a new me, that was the plan – and I had done it! I was sixty and I was in Africa! I had hit two milestones with one bird, so to speak. Or was that two birds with one milestone...?

On discovering that it was my birthday, Laurie made a beautiful impromptu card for me from a sheet of paper decorated with coloured marker pens, complete with a cut-out candle. I treasure it greatly and it has a memorable place in my journey book. That afternoon Laurie and I ventured into Ouazzane to find food supplies as I'd recalled seeing a market there.

We parked near the market and were immediately assailed by people wanting to look after BlueBelle, sell us their wares or simply show us around. I identified a man who looked trustworthy; I was always happier to pay for someone to keep an eye on my van than take the risk that something would happen to her. I quickly learnt it was best to make a deal with just one person and agree on a price in advance – or at least come to an understanding – before leaving BlueBelle. This prevented any unpleasant conversations later.

It was, for Laurie and me, a bit unnerving. Neither of us was accustomed to this new world we found ourselves in and we didn't understand the language or the customs – especially what was right or wrong behaviour for a woman in a Muslim country. An elderly man immediately seized the opportunity to be our guide, and although we insisted several times that we would be okay he persisted, assuring us that there was no charge and that it was his duty to help tourists. We eventually succumbed and followed him. (In hindsight, I think it would actually have taken us considerably longer to find BlueBelle on our return were it not for him.) We wound our way through the alleys of the medina, with the shops and stalls showing off their colourful wares amongst trays, boxes and baskets bulging with produce and everyday items; and all the while the strong scent of spice hung in the air.

---

[10] Find out more about the Heimbigners' journey at www.facebook.com/livingstonejournal

After purchasing some of the freshest and most exotic fruits and vegetables, dried figs and dates, nuts and spices, we wandered the narrow cobbled streets admiring the beautiful archways and doors. If Chefchaouen was the Blue City, this was the Green: there was a whole section with green painted buildings, green walls and a colourful stairway littered with a diverse assortment of cats. Eventually, and most gratefully, we were led back to BlueBelle with our edible treasures, tipped our guide and the parking guard and returned to the campsite. We felt quite pleased with ourselves at this accomplishment, small as it was. For me, it was a testing of the waters and a further building of my confidence by venturing out in this first African country of my journey.

That evening I was treated to a sumptuously spiced dinner in the camp restaurant by Laurie and Bruce for a perfect ending to a lovely day.

Welcome to the year of being sixty!

FEZ

A couple of days after my birthday, it was time to move on toward Fez. Before leaving Europe I had been contacted by Natasha, a young English woman who wanted to interview me for a five-minute film documentary of my journey. I thought she was mad: I couldn't understand her desire to make a documentary about me; but I had agreed and suggested that she join me for a few days on a short road trip. She thought that would be a great idea and we coordinated to meet in Fez.

Fez also held another plan. Some months before leaving, I had posted on several Facebook groups about my impending journey and a lady called Sahar had contacted me. We had become Facebook friends and agreed to meet when I came to Fez. I know many people despise Facebook, but to me it has been an invaluable tool that has helped me stay in contact with family and friends scattered all over the world, and also introduced me to some incredible people I would never have had the opportunity to connect with otherwise.

On leaving Ouazzane, I planned to take another scenic route to Meknes and then on to Fez. This time the road held up quite well and the route was very picturesque, taking me up into high hills that offered a breathtaking view of the agricultural patchwork quilt in the valley below. At its furthest edge I could see slopes covered in groves of carefully planted olive trees, and as I drove I passed workers walking along the roadside, so I waved at them and they waved back enthusiastically.

The steadily winding uphill climb did not bring out BlueBelle's best performance, and added to the regular stops I was making to view the landscape and take photos, I wasn't covering anywhere near the distance I had anticipated. I was also hot and tired as the air had become warmer and drier. The day was closing in and I realised that I might not make it into Meknes before the end of the day, so being considerably out of the way of civilisation, I kept an eye out for a wild camping spot to enjoy the fresh air and gorgeous landscape. The thing about wild camping is that you are facing the unknown and thus living an adventure, so it is both exhilarating and a little scary. Safety was always my first consideration, but sleeping out in unusual places – especially those that allowed a full view of the night sky with all the sounds of nature and nothing more – was irresistible.

As I neared the crest of the hill I saw a potential spot. Lying to the right, just before a sharp bend in the road and under a well-aged tree, there was a cleared section of ground with some large branches lying on the road's edge adding to the seclusion. It was perfect. I reversed in, allowing for a forward-facing exit, and opened my side door to let in some cool air. My view was of a small ravine with a trickle of water running down it and opened into the beautiful valley now far below.

A few trucks passed by without incident, and having seen no one around I felt at ease. I set about making a meal with the side door open and the front curtain and side net curtains drawn. Engrossed in my task, I suddenly heard a voice and looked up to see a man standing outside my door. I had nearly jumped out of my skin but now tried not to show my alarm. For a brief moment I was running all sorts of scenarios through my mind, but I quickly assessed that nothing was amiss in his attitude. It was too late to slam the door shut anyway, so instead of giving in to fear I opened the net curtain and offered a friendly greeting.

He asked me for something in French which I couldn't understand, and then indicated that what he needed was a match:

sign language worked just as well! Realising that I could help I smiled, whisked out my big box of matches from the drawer, took a bunch and handed them over. He accepted them gratefully and then motioned that he would be looking after me and I would be safe. Great, the last thing I wanted was to be in the middle of nowhere with a strange man 'looking after me' – and besides, I was certain that there would be a fee attached – so I just smiled and said goodbye. He accepted that I probably didn't understand, turned and walked along the road to the other side of the ravine and sat down under a tree. While I wasn't necessarily afraid of him, I also wasn't foolish enough not to keep an eye on him, but after about half an hour a truck stopped, picked him up and he was gone.

The sun began to set in a stunning display of golds and oranges and soon it was dark. I closed my curtains and kept my lights to a minimum for a while as I checked routes and thought about where I would go next. When I was done I stepped out to view the vast African night sky, all the more clear and beautiful there without any light pollution, and then headed back inside for the most peaceful sleep.

The next morning I decided that I did not feel like going to Meknes. One of the joys of being alone is the lack of any need to justify, debate, negotiate or compromise: I could do exactly as I pleased! The road back down the mountain was a lot faster and the scenery ahead would have been wonderful, except that a short distance from my camping stop, in the cool morning air, I found myself driving through thick mist that obscured my view until I reached the valley floor.

I was fast becoming used to the fact that before and after each city there was at least one police checkpoint, a phenomenon I would encounter hundreds of times driving through Africa. Halfway through the journey I began to wish I had started counting them from the beginning because it would have made an interesting fact to share, but I can only say that it would probably be an enormous number! However, I was prepared for these. Before departing I had printed off lots of sheets of paper that I had then cut into four strips, with each strip containing my personal information – full name, date of birth, passport number and expiry date, and so on – leaving blanks for information that would change with each country, such as my date of arrival. It was known as a *fiche* in French, and if I handed one to the police in Morocco they would usually not ask for more and let me pass. (Regrettably this only worked up to Senegal, and thereafter it was a never-ending impromptu Q&A session!)

I had earlier identified close to the medina in Fez a large parking area that was overlander-friendly and had a full-time guard (whom one would pay a fee). Being in a city I felt safer with a guard, both for the times I was away from BlueBelle and whilst I was in her sleeping. After passing the usual pre-urban police check I could see the impressive old city on a rise before me, with tightly packed buildings and the odd glimpse of mosque spires and domes. I was distracted by the view when I suddenly noticed, as I passed through a green traffic light, that I was being hailed by a man on a motorbike who was pacing me. I checked my mirrors, wondering if something was wrong with BlueBelle or my driving, but nothing was obvious. He appeared again beside my half-down window at the next traffic light. "Camping, follow me!" he shouted. I replied politely that I knew where I was going, but this did not deter him as he continued to insist that I follow him. The light changed and he pursued me for a way, still gesticulating at me. He became annoying and a real distraction; I had enough going on trying to follow the map and keep my eye on the traffic. At the next lights he reappeared, so I widened my eyes, looked directly at him and made a praying sign with my hands and then waved for him to leave. With a surprised look, he finally fell back. However, before I reached the next traffic light (there were several coming into the city) – yes, you guessed it, another guy on a motorbike started hailing me. This time I didn't look though, I just continued driving. I was starting to learn the rules of the African road!

My entrance into Fez was through a huge, ornate and very Moroccan-style gateway, and as I passed through I immediately spotted the parking area as there were two overlanding vehicles already in situ. The 'car park' was again just an empty plot of land on the edge of the town, but with the guard, I felt it should be safe. I enquired about the cost and he gave me a price which was more than I had seen in the overlanding app, so I disagreed. He shook his head: that was the price. I was now faced with looking for somewhere else or just paying. I decided that it was not worth driving about, but I was annoyed as I had the overwhelming feeling that I was being ripped off. I parked up and walked the kilometre or so into the town to find the medina.

(In hindsight I should have carried on: there was another parking area right next door and I'm sure the price would have dropped, but I was still only a few days into this new world with its different rules and protocols and had not yet strengthened my haggling skills. In the end I was proved right with the overcharge on the last day, when Bruce told me that he'd paid only half of what I had for a bigger van and two people! So I had it out with the guard, who made feeble excuses but received short shrift and my firm refusal to pay him for the last night. My instincts had been accurate and I started learning then to rely on them more frequently.)

If you hadn't already figured it out, I am unashamedly a feminist: I absolutely and without any excuse believe in the equality of women. I have never been 'looked after'; I have worked all my life; I have moved independently through the world, even when I was married; and I have stood up for women and against prejudice. These are the eyes I looked through when I walked the streets of Fez – and indeed most of Africa; actually no differently from anywhere else in the world. And at sixty I certainly didn't fool myself into thinking that every man in the world viewed me as a goddess. However, after an hour of walking the city all the cat-calling, the insincerely flattering remarks and the proposals of marriage started to wear me down and I took refuge in a café. The harassment did not end though, even while I was having my coffee, so I didn't stay long.

It was easy to understand that the men there were mostly of a different culture and belief system, but to be honest I wasn't wearing provocative clothing: just jeans, a long-sleeved high-neck t-shirt and a loose padded jacket. (I later started wearing an extra-large baggy cotton shirt and baggy pants, uncomfortable as they were, in the hope that this would put an end to it, but it did not.) There might be the odd man reading this thinking, 'Well, she should take it as a compliment'... but thanks, I'm just fine without the 'compliments'! What I did quickly learn in Fez was to be like the three monkeys: deaf, dumb and blind to any comment, advance, cat-call, whistle or compliment. I merely carried on as if the offender did not exist. I found that any hint of recognition – a look, a smile, any acknowledgement at all – ended up with my being pursued, propositioned, proposed to and generally harassed. I found it both exhausting and highly annoying.

Harassment aside, the medina was fascinating: a delight of smells, sounds, colours and buzz with every conceivable thing available, from cleaning products to food, clothes to hand-crafted metalwork. Hand-made leather shoes from Fez are also a popular buy as their tannery is world-famous. It was a hive of commerce among the dark narrow lanes within the city walls, a labyrinth that spread in all directions across the ancient well-worn cobbles. The danger of getting lost was quite real as my eyes led my steps from one fascinating sight to another.

The next day I found a taxi and negotiated a ride to the Blue Gate where Sahar would meet me. We greeted each other warmly and she then led me through the maze that is the old walled town of Fez and into her home, which to this day I know I would never find again. All I can tell you is that it was down a dark narrow lane with high buildings on each side, at the end of which there was an unassuming door that belied the treasure that lay beyond. The house was surrounded on all sides and relied on light from the top windows and the roof, which towered above its neighbours. It had various levels and each small floor served a different purpose. Narrow stairs wound around the side walls leading down to a basement kitchen, up to living and bedroom levels or higher still to a roof terrace with panoramic views over the tightly packed city and surrounding hillsides. The architecture was typically Moroccan, with beautiful wood-framed arches, colourful tiles and white-washed walls; and all of it spoke of a rich history.

It was from here that Sahar was developing her Moroccan vegan cooking.[11] For most Moroccans food without meat is incomprehensible, but Sahar is on a mission to show people that with the rich flavours available from a plethora of local herbs and spices, amazing meals can be prepared that are healthy, tasty and

---

[11] www.instagram.com/at_home_with_sahar

entirely animal-free. Having lunch with her I was privileged to experience both her wonderful cooking and her vibrant ideas.

As Laurie and Bruce were arriving in Fez the following day, Sahar offered to take all of us on a tour around the medina. My second visit gave me a much better idea of how large this market was and the mind-blowing variety of goods available. Sahar gave us some fascinating insights into Moroccan culture and traditions, and we certainly benefited greatly from having someone local to impart her knowledge and save us from getting lost.

A ROUND TRIP

It was now early December. I had been in Africa just over a week and was ready to meet Natasha to work with her on her mini-documentary. I had said farewell to Sahar as well as to Laurie and Bruce, certain that I would see them all again in the future. New friendships were well forged.

I was due to pick up Natasha in the afternoon from Fez Airport. I always prefer to be early for arrivals or departures, never knowing what might lie ahead; and of course with BlueBelle I was always at home so I could make coffee, sleep or do whatever I liked while waiting. Sure enough, no sooner had I left my parking in the old town than I hit a long queue of traffic. The road was a single lane in each direction, but some 'smart' people had decided they would make a third lane in the middle, creating further chaos. I should add that the edge of the tarmac was jagged and several inches higher than the dirt sloping away to the bush. Going off the edge would *not* be a good idea.

A small 4x4 had taken to the new middle lane and was jockeying annoyingly to pass me, but I kept close to the vehicle in front. At one stage an oncoming bus demanded that the 4x4 move aside, and the 4x4 came so close to me that he hit my wing mirror. The mirror was solid and I wasn't worried, but I was now fed up and felt it wasn't worth the hassle so I slowed down to let the 4x4 in. However, it appeared that *his* mirror didn't fare so well, and when he pulled in front of me he simply stopped. He got out of his car and walked directly to my driver's side.[12]

---

[12] I had a big sticker on the left rear of the van notifying people to be cautious as I was in a right-hand drive vehicle.

I didn't get out of BlueBelle, so with the added advantage of height I was looking down on him. I started with a polite, "May I help you?" and he replied (in very good English, without flinching) that I had damaged his car, and walked back to indicate that the wing mirror was no longer secure on its mounting but tilted at an angle. I looked back at him impassively, but he returned and this time accused me directly of knocking his mirror off. I told him that I was in the correct lane, that his driving was both reckless and illegal and that it was clearly his fault as *he* had hit *my* mirror. Still he insisted that I had hit him. The argument continued for a few minutes and by now vehicles were hooting their displeasure at his creating even more of a traffic jam.

I soon realised that this was going nowhere. but eventually he threatened to call the police. I knew I was not responsible for his recklessness, but in a foreign country overlanders are usually blamed anyway. However, I called his bluff. "Sure, you call them – I'll wait," I said breezily. Stumped, he briefly reassessed his strategy and then decided to carry on ranting. Although I continued trying to appear calm in front of him, I was getting close to severe annoyance. I looked him squarely in the eye and said, "I'm a sixty-year-old woman on a visit to Morocco. I don't know what you want or expect from me, but *you* hit *my* car and *you* should be paying *me* for the damage. Furthermore, I don't *have* any money, so if you think that I'm going to pay anything you are quite mistaken. So we will wait for the police – please do call them." I know what you're thinking: I'd resorted to using the excuse that I was an old penniless woman and a guest in his country. Yes, I was pulling out all the stops, but well, he did hit BlueBelle. He even showed me the mark on the back of his mirror that proved he had hit me and not the other way round!

Finally it must have sunk in that I wasn't budging, because as suddenly as he had stopped in front of me, he put out his hand to shake mine and said, "You are a woman and a tourist and I will leave it at that." I must admit I felt offended: somehow I was supposed to feel diminished by being a woman when I wasn't the one who had created this chaos?! However, I checked myself and tentatively shook his hand. He wished me a good journey but still had the audacity to remark, as he was walking away, "But you *did* hit my car." My shouted retort went unheard… and perhaps better that way. The drama thankfully over, I continued inching onward through the traffic as it became evident that a football match was causing the mayhem.

Despite the 'incident', I was still early to pick up Natasha and was pleased to find a shaded spot to wait near the airport. I had been so occupied with navigating the traffic and the drama that I hadn't checked my phone for a while, and on stopping I found a message telling me her flight was delayed and she would now land after dark. This meant that we would not be able to get to my first scheduled stopover because I had made the decision not to drive at night unless it was absolutely necessary. I occupied my time looking for an alternative campsite, but I couldn't find anything on the apps that wasn't too far away or in the opposite direction of where we were headed. While there was still daylight, I set off to see if I could find some somewhere to wild camp. I tried a garage parking area on the motorway, but there was too much traffic and it looked a bit rough so I drove a bit further on. However, when I passed through the toll booth on the motorway back to the airport, I saw a spot on the other side that would be perfect. It was a pullover in which a truck was already parked up, and it was far enough from the toll booth to escape the noise but near enough to it and the police station behind it for safety. The toll also ensured that there wasn't too much traffic, so I pinned the spot on my map so that I could find it later.

The flight from the UK eventually arrived at around one o'clock in the morning and by this time I was as exhausted as Natasha. I told her of our sleeping location and only then realised that someone not accustomed to my lifestyle might find it intimidating, so I reassured her that we would be fine until the morning. As she was taller than me, I decided it made more sense for her to sleep in my bed, out of the way, and I would use the shorter sofa. I warned her that the bed wasn't long enough for her, so if she wanted to stretch out she would need to do so diagonally, being mindful of the rear window and not push against it.

We both got some much-needed sleep and early the next morning set off toward the Atlas Mountains. With the planned three days we would not be able to make it all the way there, but I had worked out a loop route that would take us close and mean we could enjoy a different road back to Fez. We started with a discussion of what the expectations were on each side, and Natasha told me that as she had obtained a cheap flight she was prepared to pay for the fuel and our camping costs. I thought this was perfectly fair, since the camping and diesel wouldn't be more than €100 for the two nights. I had already filled my tank before leaving, so we would only need to refuel on the way back. I had also bought all our food for the trip, so it was certainly much cheaper than any holiday (including meals or tours) that she might otherwise undertake. I asked if she would share all her film and photographs with me if I gave her full credit for the use of them, and to this she agreed.

As we headed south of Fez the countryside kept changing, becoming ever more barren, dry and rugged with craggy hills and just the occasional lake. We took our time and stopped on several occasions for photographs and video clips and to take in the view. She also asked me to drive back and forth a few times within the landscape for some great footage that was regrettably never shared with me.

We arrived at our first campsite late in the afternoon and Natasha registered while I looked for a suitable place to park. The site was empty and I opted for a spot near the ablution block and washing sinks. Natasha wanted to do an interview so she set up her gear while I cooked a vegetarian meal. From the campsite we could see the Atlas Mountains in the distance, and nature's night-lights gave us a wonderful display, along with a generous almost-full moon.

The next day we rose early again as Natasha wanted to use the good morning light to do some more filming. It was bitterly cold so close to the mountains. We found an open field opposite the campsite with far-reaching views of the huge range – the perfect place to film. As she directed me, I could honestly say that being a photographer/videographer was certainly *not* a career I would be getting into, what with all the tedious work setting up, getting the right angles, shooting and re-shooting and finally editing it all together.

We set off again and the route continued to be fascinating, as from the previous day's rough and rugged hills we suddenly found ourselves driving through a lush green forest. There were signs to watch out for monkeys (although we saw none) and Morocco was providing constant surprises with the diversity of its landscapes. Our next stop was at an elaborate modern conference centre built in a traditional style, with camping places on a terrace above the buildings which afforded a splendid view. I cooked while Natasha set up for another interview.

It was early to bed, early to rise again as the next day we were returning to Fez. I indicated to Natasha that she needed to find the manager to pay for our night's camping, but instead, she headed off on a walk to find bread and take photos. The plan had been to have a quick breakfast, refuel and drive into Fez so that she could visit the medina; I reckoned that we would have enough time before her flight home. Breakfast was ready but Natasha was still missing, and on seeing the manager I decided to save the time and pay him so that we would have no further delay when we were ready to leave. I updated her when she came back, but she did not make any move to refund me; nor the refuelling later, which was also at my expense. It seemed that I ended up paying for most of this adventure.

The journey back took quite a bit longer than expected with lots of photographic stops. I could have dropped her directly at the airport, but Natasha wanted to see the medina, even if briefly. This was further out of the way and the city was full of traffic, nonetheless I sped along to give her an hour in Fez and then it was a mad dash to the airport to drop her off.

It was a stressful day having to drive to deadlines. I decided to return to a campsite outside Fez so that I could re-organise my home and find some semblance of order, having moved so many things around to accommodate an extra person. Living in a confined space can be disruptive when it is unorganised.

When I pulled into the campsite I chose a remote corner furthest away from the gate and restaurant, although most of the park seemed empty. As I was reversing into my desired spot, I noticed in my wing mirror that the left rear window looked odd; and indeed on checking I saw that it had been pushed out and was only barely held in by the rubber seal at the bottom. It was the window at the foot of the bed that I'd warned Natasha about. I was lucky that it had not come out altogether, which would have been a major catastrophe, however I was tired and the day was rapidly coming to a close so it was too late to do anything about it now. I would need to remove the window to fix it, but fortunately I had some experience of doing this when I was in Barcelona after I had replaced my other rear window following the burglary.

The next morning I foolishly decided to use the common Moroccan squat toilet in the ablution block. My choice turned out not to be so clever: it had rained the night before and the tiled floor was still wet in places, and in my effort to get up from a squatting position I slipped and ended up flat on my face, setting off my ankle and shoulder injuries all over again.

No time for self-pity, there were chores to do. Just because I lived in a tiny house it didn't mean that I was excused from the mundane. The first task was washing clothes (by hand) because the cool weather meant it would take the better part of the day for them to dry. Once that was done, and with my very painful shoulder, I started to manhandle my mattress out of the van so that I had better access to the damaged window. I needed to remove the beading, refit the window with its rubber seal in the frame and then reinsert the beading. On my own it proved to be a real challenge... but eventually I got the job done.

I was by now in a lot of pain, exhausted and very grouchy. This whole venture had cost me time, money and inconvenience; however, it was my own fault for not being firmer or clearer in advance. I never was refunded for the camping or fuel costs, or the money for the chiropractor that she promised after I told her about the window. Some six months later and after several requests, I did receive ten of the worst photographs I have ever seen of myself, but none of the video footage. A lesson to self: be clear about expectations and don't be on the losing end again!

THE CAPITAL, RABAT

The drive from Fez to Rabat again exceeded my expectations, the landscape varying with regularity and producing a new and interesting panorama around every turn. It was less green than it had been further north, but still not the desert I had been expecting. It was Sunday so the roads were quiet, making the journey even more enjoyable: less traffic meant I had more time to look around. Passing large swathes of rich agricultural land, verdant hills and the occasional unexpected lake, it felt like heaven.

I had been driving most of the day and at mid-afternoon I decided to stop at a service station on the motorway to get a cold drink and stretch my legs. Walking back to BlueBelle, I noticed that my left rear tyre was pretty flat. I was very concerned. I could not see anything obvious, but fortunately being at a garage I could get the tyre pumped up. I waited a bit and it seemed to be holding, so I decided to take the risk and drive slowly into a parking spot I'd identified on the outskirts of the city and decide what to do the next morning.

The parking turned out to be in an area of apartments still partly under construction and not far from the beach. The parking lot and many of the surrounding buildings were vacant and it seemed safe enough, so I took position near a corner where I was not so conspicuous.

The next morning I awoke with an incredible spasm in my left shoulder in addition to the constant pain in my right, meaning movement was limited and any I did make resulted in agony. It was probably the culmination of events over the past days that were taking their toll, yet I did manage to get out of bed and check the state of the tyre, which was frustratingly flat again. I took some tablets for the pain, burst into tears, had a big 'Woe is me!' conversation with myself and felt thoroughly miserable for a while. Finally I decided that the most sensible thing to do for the day was… nothing. There was no point in subjecting myself to further pressure: best to relax and not put more strain on my shoulders, because sorting the tyre or driving would do just that.

While I was sitting around, I decided to try to resolve the situation surrounding my Nigerian visa. I had come to learn that I should have applied for this in my 'country of residence', however I didn't have one because I had been drifting around for such a long time. I now needed to find out more. I was unequivocally informed by the Nigerian Embassy that unless I was resident in Morocco they would not assist me, so I then called the British Embassy and the woman who answered gave me short shrift. None of this improved my mood.

It seems ridiculous to me now that I had become quite so depressed about these seemingly small things, but I was not feeling well and adding another stressor to the situation had left me very low. I was also learning that worrying about stuff didn't resolve it and that my personal journey was as important as my physical one, so I capitulated and rested on my sofa checking routes. Later in the day, feeling marginally better, I took the short walk to the beach where I sat contemplating the sun set peacefully over the Atlantic.

In the morning I was relieved to find my shoulder much improved, mainly thanks to some small oval blue pills Laurie had generously given me in Ouazzane when she'd learnt of my pain. (I fondly call them my *Viagra.*) I pumped up the tyre with my little compressor and went off to get it fixed.

I arrived at a smart Ford garage and a young man came out with me to assess the problem. He called over a colleague who took off the tyre and carried it into the workshop. I had attracted the attention of a few more men who were now crowding around BlueBelle, one being a young man who was obviously from sub-Saharan Africa and had taken to translating for me as he spoke English well. It turned out he was from the Central African Republic. The mechanic came to show me a large bolt that was stuck between the treads and had been causing my slow leak. He advised me that the tyre had to be replaced and a gasp of horror escaped me as it was practically new, plus replacing one would actually mean replacing two to ensure optimum performance. I told them about my dilemma and said I simply could not afford two new tyres.

Seeing my distress the mechanic suggested he take a closer look inside the workshop, and not long after he returned saying that he had plugged the hole and the tyre would be fine (and it was, for the entire journey!) I was delighted and of course immensely grateful. I happily paid the €10 equivalent for their assistance, and with happy handshakes and waves I was on my way again.

Sahar (from Fez) had connected me with some of her networks and on reaching Rabat I set out to meet Heather, the wife of the Chargé d'Affaires for Canada in Morocco. She treated me to a lovely lunch and made me most welcome. I was interested to learn that the wives and partners of the ambassadors of the countries who had embassies in Morocco had joined together and formed *Cercle Diplomatique Rabat* to carry out 'good works'.[13] Heather's two gorgeous young sons had also initiated a similar programme for the children of diplomats, raising funds for specific projects of their own choosing. Apart from the charitable aspect, this allowed them to develop their leadership skills as well as their compassion.

Heather further invited me to attend the International Bazaar run by *Cercle Diplomatique*. Each embassy was selling products from their country of origin to raise funds for their aid projects and I very much enjoyed meeting the ambassadors, consuls and their staff from all over Africa. I was also graciously extended an invitation to Heather's Christmas party, whereupon I had to dig out my best clothes for an evening meeting dignitaries from the diplomatic community and presenting myself as the oddball adventurer.

Unfortunately Rabat did not have a campsite within the city itself, but I found parking near the beach on the outskirts where there were homes nearby and a guard who lived in a shack, whom I tipped for the comfort of knowing he was there. It was a much quieter location than being in the city centre and afforded wonderful sunset views over the ocean.

My shoulder was by now in serious need of attention. Heather was instrumental in helping me by recommending an osteopath, Ann, a talented French woman who fortunately spoke limited but better English than I did French. Having some long-term experience of chiropractors and osteopaths, I can honestly say that she turned out to be one of the best I have ever encountered. She manipulated my body from head to toe and frankly performed a small miracle. Shoulder injuries are often related to ligaments that take a lot of work to resolve, but while the area wasn't completely healed, the rest of my body was feeling so much better. That night I slept more soundly than I had for years, without tossing and turning every half hour as I had been since my sciatic episode. The next day I felt quite renewed and consequently much more grounded.

For my last evening in Rabat I went for a drive around the city and then found a nice beach location where I took some time

---

[13] You can find out more about them at www.facebook.com/CercleDiplomatiqueRabat/

out. As I watched the couples strolling along the beach and the children playing, I also noticed two Spanish motorhomes parked beside me with a man in one and a woman with some dogs in the other. I happened to catch their eye and we conversed for a bit, neither of us speaking the other's language; but often a willingness to communicate is all that's required.

For the past several years around November, Antonia had driven down to Morocco with her dogs to escape the European winter, stopping at different places on her way to Ouarzazate where campers from all over the world congregate to celebrate the New Year. She would remain there throughout the winter, returning to Spain in spring. This year she had brought her friend with her, although he was in his own camper. She told me firmly that she didn't want anyone travelling with her in her space and I understood that all too well. I admired her as she was some years older than me, but no less free-spirited and determined to live life on her own terms. They invited me to follow them to a place where they knew it would be less busy, secure and free. We parked ourselves in a row and they offered me some hooch, such as only those on the Iberian Peninsula know how to make. (It had a real kick, so I only had one!) I often say that language is no excuse not to communicate: I had the best time and Antonia and I are still friends on Facebook.

CASABLANCA WITH PASTEUR

A week before leaving Barcelona, while completing my final checks, I realised I had forgotten to get my Yellow Fever vaccination. The hospital there informed me I would have to wait three weeks before I could get an appointment, which would be too late, and a private doctor was too expensive; however I had read that I could get it done in Morocco at the Pasteur Clinic, so that put Casablanca squarely on my route.

Casablanca is dominated by the presence of Africa's second-largest mosque, King Hassan II, which stands on a promontory and towers over the city. The minaret was completed in 1992 and is a staggering sixty storeys high, with a laser light pointing at Mecca. I found a parking spot within walking distance of the mosque but also close enough to see and hear it. The parking was on the edge of a relatively poor part of the city, judging from the living conditions of the locals, and a vast contrast to the elaborate and decorative mosque only a hundred or so metres away. There was a guard who would be on duty all night in the parking and I was happy to pay him for the peace of mind.

I took the time before nightfall to walk across and view the mosque close up. I love these huge edifices that stand to the glory of a god: they add magnificence and splendour to a city and they are often sanctuaries of peace inside. However, I cannot help but question their enormous cost and what the money might otherwise have achieved. This mosque displayed classic Moroccan architecture with high arched doorways and magnificent carved wooden doors, with pillars and porticos covered with intricate mosaics in stunning hues of primarily green, blue and gold. Regrettably the building was closed, although being a mere woman I may not have been permitted to enter anyway.

The sun was setting when I left and I decided to walk around the area where I was parked. It was interesting to watch the everyday life of the locals. In tiny, cramped kitchens on the ground floor I could see large pots bubbling away, the women inside and in the doorways chattering and the children playing nearby whilst mamma cooked. Shops were open well into the night and the men could be found sitting in the cafés, smoking and watching football on the ever-present TV.

I decided to end my walk with a cup of the unique Moroccan mint tea with its delightful and refreshing flavour (I take mine with sugar). I started looking for a café but they were filled with only men and it felt quite intimidating, added to which I didn't feel like fielding the personal comments, which I'd still not become accustomed to. However, I decided that my desire for tea was stronger than my concerns so I chose one café, put on my 'I don't care' face and walked in, ordered my tea and found a seat. It was a bit like the scene in a western movie when a stranger walks into a bar and the room becomes quiet as everyone stares: I could feel their eyes interrogating me. But despite my concerns and their initial stares, they soon lost interest as they continued with their card games, television, or reading a newspaper. While savouring my tea I sat and wondered about their women. I was certain some might like to be relieved of the cooking and child-minding duties for a change and enjoy a cool evening sipping a mint tea instead.

I left the parking early the next morning to avoid the rush-hour traffic and found the Louis Pasteur Clinic, where I paid and waited and (a very efficient) thirty minutes later received a life-long vaccination and yellow card. In hindsight, I believe that having had my vaccination done in Morocco so recently meant that I experienced no issues at any of the borders further along my route. I'd heard numerous reports of people being harassed and detained with claims that their cards were not valid – probably just to extort a bribe.

Getting out of Casablanca to head to Marrakesh was another story altogether, as I found myself in the midst of the peak hour commute and the chaos that is Moroccan traffic.

MARRAKESH AND THE ATLAS MOUNTAINS

Having wild camped for several days, I decided to stop at a campsite just north of Marrakesh: a good shower was needed and laundry had to be done. My shoulder continued to be debilitating and driving made it worse, but resting it every few days seemed to help.

I heard some people speaking English and gravitated towards them. The husband was British and the wife German, but they lived in Mali and ran tours. The conversation soon turned to what vehicle I was driving, so the husband and I walked over to BlueBelle. He looked her over and commented that, while he'd like to see her a bit higher off the ground, she was a sound vehicle and I should have no difficulty if I was sensible. I was pleased to hear these words from a seasoned traveller who had experience of the local terrain.

After a couple of days sorting out my chores I headed into Marrakesh. I was first going to meet a woman my now-local network had introduced to me, who was doing incredible work with Down syndrome girls. After this I was to meet a woman from the USA who had converted to Islam, and finally I would visit a young couple who were running an organic farm south of the city using traditional environmentally-friendly techniques. I was particularly interested in women who were making a difference or had tackled change.

First I met Oumaima, a dynamic young woman who was the director and manager of the *Amal Women's Training Centre and Moroccan Restaurant,*[14] a wonderful non-profit initiative teaching and supporting underprivileged women in Marrakesh. They do amazing work primarily with Down syndrome girls, giving them valuable culinary and business skills and hence independent earning potential. I was incredibly impressed with the programme and with Oumaima herself, who has since gone on to new projects supporting disadvantaged communities and other entrepreneurs.[15] I expect to see much more success from her.

Next I met with an American woman, Lindsay, who had changed her life completely to follow Islam. I was quite fascinated to hear her story, as I firmly believe that 'you cannot judge until you ask the questions'. So I asked the questions and the answers were surprisingly simple yet impactful enough to show how she had redirected her life; and while I may not have made the choices she did, doubtless she would not have made mine. Her path was not an easy one but she seemed to be at peace with her decisions, and I respected her view and her reasons for the change.

My last appointment for the day was south of Marrakesh and I would be staying there overnight, but by now it was around lunchtime and I found myself weaving my way through the old part of the city. The traffic was manic, but the mania was not of the kind that you would find in London or New York: this was Africa. Here the mania consisted of multifarious taxis, scooters, buses, donkey carts, trucks and simply thousands of pedestrians. Adding to the chaos were the many roundabouts with people and vehicles jostling in from all angles... and hooting, lots and lots of hooting.

It was here in Marrakesh that I lost my European caution in traffic. It became very apparent that if I was to get on to a busy roundabout, there was no point waiting for a gap or for someone to politely let me in. I simply had to push forward and make my

---

[14] www.facebook.com/AmalNonProfit
[15] www.facebook.com/Impact-1011139309081109

own gap. It's a bit like life: if you wait around for something to come your way you may end up waiting a long time, but if you want to move on you need to push to get yourself ahead. This was why I was in Morocco, to get 'Africa training', and it all prepared me for cities like Dakar, Conakry and Lagos.

Marrakesh is considered the gateway city to the Atlas Mountains. It has an international airport and is very tourist-focused, but it is also a metropolis of great contrasts, with the old city full of narrow lanes, palaces and medinas alongside modern shopping malls and wide new avenues. For the short-stop tourist, it is well worth the visit as an introduction to the delights of Morocco. For the more intrepid traveller, I highly recommend going further afield.

It was notable that most cities and towns in Morocco had benefited from some infrastructure development, so that even the poorest town I passed through had a new or relatively new central meeting area, parks with seating or paved promenades with gardens all around. As I was driving I saw that most of these were empty in the heat of the day, but I expected that they would be well used in the cool evenings for the communities to congregate. Improving the quality of life for local people has a positive impact on tourism too, which is highly prized throughout Morocco. One of the first questions I was usually asked by the people I spoke to was, "What do you think of Morocco – do you like it?" They are enormously proud of their country.

As I drove east out of Marrakesh I saw the Atlas Mountains towering ever closer, and to witness a childhood history and geography lesson become reality before my eyes was incredibly exciting. I had always been truly in awe of these behemoths. In hindsight, I wish I had spent more time in the mountains viewing their grandeur and splendour, but sadly my budget was not unlimited and I still had a long way to go to get home…

I found Marrakesh Organics[16] behind a large old gate and was welcomed by Kenza and her husband. They showed me proudly around their land and demonstrated what they had done to grow wholesome organic crops for sale and personal consumption; how they were working with their environment and being eco-friendly

---

[16] www.marrakeshorganics.com

at the same time. They also ran courses for local people and international visitors, hosting, teaching, training and introducing them to their wonderful cuisine.

I learnt that Kenza was the victim of a racial hatred attack in Belgium some years before that had robbed her of her parents and brother. Fortunately, she was not home at the time or she would assuredly have been a victim too. Alongside all the work she does at Marrakesh Organics, she also advocates vociferously against racial hatred and raises awareness of how this devastates lives.

In the morning before departing I enjoyed the customary Moroccan breakfast of home-baked flatbread, honey, olives, cheese (which frustratingly I could not eat), juice and tea, all savoured whilst sitting on large cushions on the floor in Kenza's beautiful lounge-cum-meeting room – a truly traditional affair. Everything had been made by hand and I was shown how to dip the flatbread into different things to get different flavours. It was a wonderful start to the day.

I was then on the road again, and this time heading to a village in the foothills of the Atlas Mountains to view a project called *Education For All*.[17] Having a specific interest in the education of girls, I wanted to find out how this organisation tackled the issue here. Education For All works primarily with Berber girls from the High Atlas, who are predominantly Muslim. Were it not for this project, they would not be getting educated at all because of the distance to the schools from their remote locations; and also because the issue of modesty for girls means parents are reluctant to let them attend schools where there are boys too.

I misread the instructions on how to get to the project and bypassed the location by many miles, so I ended up driving into the Atlas Mountains towards Imlil, where I was rewarded by the most stunning landscape. The Atlas is made up of several ranges running from Tunisia across Algeria and down through Morocco, and the range I found myself navigating that day was the High Atlas. It was beautiful beyond words, with roads sweeping around the majestic mountainsides and passing wide ancient river beds where the clearest streams of water tumbled down over the well-

[17] www.efamorocco.org

worn rocks and pebbles. The mountains themselves were arid, grey and craggy, but as the road crept higher I saw pockets of forests where trees had somehow managed to find soil in which to take root. Then the road started narrowing and I came across multi-storeyed houses sandwiched between the road and the rock face, their occupants needing to practise the most extreme care when stepping out of the front door to avoid oncoming traffic. I observed many small wooden crates lying in stacks where space allowed, and I would later discover that there are apple orchards in the area that are harvested in the summer and the rich abundance of fruit sent to market. The people were friendly and always waved as I passed.

At some stage it became obvious that I was lost and so I turned around to head back down, the views of the valley and forests below being equally as breathtaking as on the way up. It was serendipitous that I had lost my way: the drive was magnificent and the landscape quite extraordinary. I was finally in the great Atlas Mountains, and I could never have imagined being blessed with such an incredible opportunity in my lifetime.

At the Education For All home, I was warmly welcomed and given a tour of the facility before being treated to biscuits and tea on the rooftop terrace, where I got to enjoy yet another wonderful view of the mountains. I heard how the home had started with just eleven girls, yet after thirteen years had won the trust of the Berbers so much that they received around two hundred applications each year. Regrettably they could only offer the handful of places left by the outgoing scholars. Nevertheless they had six houses that accommodated about a hundred and fifty girls, and the work they were doing to improve the status and quality of life for girls was hugely impressive. I learnt so much at EFA that I have applied since returning home.

ESSAOUIRA

After the High Atlas I drove down to the coast and Essaouira (previously Mogador), which has a rich and multi-ethnic past going back over two and a half thousand years to the time of the Phoenicians. It had been occupied by them, the Romans, the Portuguese and the French, and been used as a military base, naval docks and fishing port during all of this diverse history. The city was full of charm and still boasted some old buildings dating back several centuries. There was also a wharf where fresh fish was sold and many fine fish restaurants, a bustling medina, numerous art galleries and some beautiful beaches. Its campsite, however, must rank about the worst I've ever been in!

While I was feeling much better overall, I was still suffering with my right shoulder. I had been recommended to another osteopath in the town and had called ahead, hoping that he could continue Ann's good work. His technique differed from Ann's but he did provide me with one super tip that helped me throughout the rest of my journey, and that was to get some support for my right arm while I was driving. As it happened I had a spare cushion that I'd felt I might one day find a use for stashed under the passenger seat. It proved to be just the right height and a perfect fit between the driver's seat and the door to give me an armrest, which of course had been lacking on that side. This put less pressure on the shoulder ligaments and gave me much relief, especially on those days when I was driving for five or more hours.

After Essaouira my route headed ever south and took me through the striking hills and plantations of argan trees. Argan is a highly-prized oil that is obtained from the kernel of the tree and sold primarily in the western world for beauty, skin and hair care, but in Moroccan culture it is used much like olive oil to dip your bread into. The fruit of the argan tree is small and round with fleshy pulp covered by a thick peel. The pulp surrounds a hard-shelled nut that contains one or more oil-rich argan kernels, and it takes about forty kilos (nearly ninety pounds) of dried fruit to produce just one litre of the precious oil.

The mountain goats that live in the hills climb the argan trees and eat the leaves and fruit, distributing the seeds more widely and helping with the harvesting of the kernels. Argan oil is one of Morocco's main and most valuable exports, and the area under cultivation through which I was driving was vast and green as far as the eye could see.

I did stop along the roadside at a stall selling argan oil and local honey. The honey was deep amber and truly tasty and I purchased a huge jar that lasted me for some considerable time. I had it regularly in the morning because my first drink of the day was usually hot water and lemon, to which I added this glorious natural sweetener. If ever I was feeling ill or off-colour I would also eat a teaspoon several times a day, as honey has natural antibiotic properties amongst its many other benefits.

THE OASIS

If you're near the Sahara then you *must* visit an oasis – or at least see one up close. I arrived on Christmas Eve in an area where oases are dotted around the landscape and began looking for a campsite with WiFi where I could stop for a few days. I needed to do some urgent work for a client, which demanded a high-speed internet connection. Data in Morocco is pretty cheap, but the 3G/4G signal varies widely and WiFi was usually better when I was able to find it.

The first campsite I reached was firmly closed with no one at all in sight. I found another not too much further on that also boasted on its write-up that it had WiFi, but I was concerned by the roads leading up to it which were mostly sand. BlueBelle made it through OK, however when I arrived the man at reception was offhand and informed me that there was no internet available, leaving me annoyed. It was too late to find another site, so I opted to stay the night and do some repairs on my window which was still giving trouble.

The campsite was small with only five parking spaces in a long narrow space, but it had a pleasant open lounge area they called the *kasbah*, basic ablutions that were at least clean, and hot water, which was unusual. The restaurant was not open but I was offered the menu as I could order a take-away, but it was more than I could afford so I declined and returned to BlueBelle. The tall date palms provided some nice shade, but the ground was littered with fruit that had fallen from the trees and attracted hundreds of flies and bugs, so I swept away as many as I could from my spot. There was one other van in the camp belonging to a Swiss couple.

I have motor-homed my way around parts of Europe (mostly Portugal) both wild camping and also using paid campsites, and I know a bit about the travellers who frequent these: some people love the solitude and some need to talk to everyone in the camp, and the Swiss woman here was the latter. As I unpacked some tools and started quietly working on the back window she took to walking past my van, to and from the kasbah, back and forth, stalking me to get my attention by slowing down as she passed.

My attention, however, was focused entirely on fixing the window before it got dark so I ignored her. Eventually though I could no longer take the pacing, so I looked at her as she passed again and as expected she said "Hello" and I responded in kind, knowing this would start a conversation for which I had no appetite. I admit I was being grumpy and I should have continued to ignore her, however the conversation went as follows:-

Her: How long are you staying?

Me: Only one night. I'm looking for a campsite with WiFi and this one doesn't have it.

Her: But there *is* internet...

Me: I have no mobile signal and there is no WiFi here.

Her: But there *is* internet...

Me: Well, I don't even have one bar.

Her: How is that possible? We have internet and we also have an American card which has internet!

Me: (*thinking, Well, lucky you!*) That's great, but I'm on Orange and I have no signal at all.

Her: That's just not possible!

Me: (*my irritation level rising*) I've been working with the internet almost since it began. I build websites for a living. I have been online for many years and I know what a signal looks like and I don't have one. However, I'm very glad that you do.

She seemed to appreciate my direct tone as much as I appreciated her assuming I was dumb, so we politely left it at that and she was not to be seen again.

My again unsuccessful attempt at fixing the window (not aided by my irritation on various levels) meant that I gave up, packed my tools and ladder away and set up for my usual drink on my step before making dinner. While I was doing this a large, portly man seated himself in the kasbah and started talking on his phone. Obviously he had internet too, I thought miserably, although I still had none.

At one point he looked up and noticed me sitting on my step minding my own business and clearly saw this as an invitation. He sauntered over (I am being kind: it was more of a tumble) and asked me in French if I would like to have a cup of tea with him. As I've said before, I had learnt not to give men encouragement of *any* kind, even if they thought I was being rude. Perhaps this gentleman was just being polite, but I was too tired and grumpy at this point to fend off another person so I replied, "No, thank you. I don't speak French." (Trying to navigate my way through a conversation in a language I could barely master was beyond my ability that evening.) Astounded, he asked me (again in French), "You don't speak French?!" and I answered (still in English), "No, I don't, but thank you and enjoy your tea." I was learning by now that short replies were usually accepted as understanding and long replies in English confused them, so then they tended to leave me alone. However, this one was regrettably persistent: "The owner speaks English and we can go and see his restaurant and garden." So I repeated, *"No, thank you!"* with a courteous but very firm tone. Thankfully at this he gave up on me and my grumpiness and at last I got some peace.

HAPPY CHRISTMAS!

It was Christmas Day… but it could have been any morning. I decided to move on. I wished the Swiss couple season's greetings as I drove out, silently hoping our paths would not cross again.

Fortunately my invaluable iOverlander app[18] was available offline and I had sought out a new destination. I passed a town with an incongruous modern French supermarket, and because Morocco is a non-Christian country the store was open. On entering I found it very odd to hear a Christmas jingle being played on the sound system and see the aisles sparsely decorated with baubles and tinsel, while outside the sun was shining brightly and it was already up to twenty-five degrees Celsius. Over the previous weeks I had thankfully not observed the manic consumerism of Europe, the over-buying of 'stuff' that was often

---

[18] www.ioverlander.com

discarded as quickly as it had been acquired. All I wanted for Christmas was… WiFi.

Shopping done, fuel topped up, I was on the road again. The landscape was scattered with oases for a while before it became drier, sandier and rockier the further I headed south. At the turnoff from the tarmacked main road to my intended campsite, I found myself on a horribly rutted track. It sounded like everything inside BlueBelle was smashing to pieces as things were bouncing about, leaving what I had thought to be secured spaces to fall randomly in the aisle. I wondered if I would make the eight-kilometre drive in one piece. I was only about a kilometre and a half along and my head was hurting from the bumping and noise, when ahead I noticed a patch of what looked like sand and decided that a steady pace should see me through. It didn't look too intimidating.

My technique failed and resulted in an obligatory sand stop. Yes, we were well and truly stuck. I naively thought to myself, It's OK, I'll just dig myself out of it, but it was midday and very hot. I was miles from the campsite and a good walk back to the main road and since there was no one around digging seemed like the only option. I quickly realised, however, that sand has a nasty habit: a bit like water, when you move it to one side it just seems to flow back to its lowest point. I was ill-prepared and had no idea how to deal with this situation, so I started to panic. I gave myself a brief but stern talk: "It will be fine, I can do this. It isn't the end of the world, and if all else fails I can sleep here. I have food and water and I'm not going to die." Good talk, Dot!

I decided – strangely I had a signal, out there in the middle of nowhere – that I should look to see what YouTube suggested. I was sitting in the shade of the driver's seat with my dash fan blowing on me and the internet was slow, when suddenly I heard an out-of-place sound from the otherwise silent landscape… and as I looked up, a 4x4 sped past. I leapt out of the van, waving my arms frantically in the hope that they might see me; and indeed they did and reversed towards me. Three guys and a young woman jumped out to greet me and I was even more delighted that most of them spoke English. They quickly assessed my situation, reversed up behind me, tied a strap on to my rear bumper and pulled me away. Within minutes BlueBelle was free from the sand, as easily and non-dramatically as that!

They were Basque (from northern Spain) and were holidaying at the campsite I was heading to. They wanted me to continue there with them, but assessing the road from all angles I realised that even if I made it to the campsite (which my rescuers confirmed had WiFi), I would at some point need to come back this way and would likely get stuck in the sand again. I decided to return to the main road and head further south to my alternative destination, so after a quick photo call we wished each other well and were all on our way again with only twenty minutes' delay!

They had been a godsend. This was my first experience of what I fondly came to call 'Africa Roadside Assistance' (ARA)[19] and I was grateful beyond words. ARA 1 : DB 0

THE SAHEL OR EUROPE?

I had reached the edge of the Sahel, the semi-arid transition between the Sahara and the Sudan savanna to the south, and ended up at Tan-Tan Plage in a campsite on the beach where I finally found the WiFi and electricity I sought. My converter[20] had given up the ghost a couple of days before, so even though my solar was working I couldn't convert it from my solar-charged battery, and that in turn meant I couldn't charge my laptop. I took some time to investigate the problem and discovered that the converter seemed to have burnt out... but where on earth was I going to find another? I was very kindly permitted to sit in the camp's restaurant and use their electricity, which meant I could charge my laptop and do some uninterrupted work to earn some much-needed money.

The campsite was in reality a large plot of sand with a few palm trees dotted about, a beach some fifty metres away and basic but adequate ablutions. It was filled with European motorhomes

---

[19]Africa Roadside Assistance is a name I coined on my journey. In the vast majority of Africa there is no official roadside assistance and consequently people help each other. There was seldom a time when I was stuck that I waited more than fifteen minutes for aid and there was always someone around to lend a helping hand. Tipping is customary as a way to offer thanks and of course I gave whatever assistance I could in return, but this system was much cheaper, faster and more convenient than I have experienced anywhere else in the world. I also met some amazing people this way. To keep track I have noted these incidents as they occur.

[20] Also referred to as an inverter or transformer, basically it converts electricity from 12V DC into 220V AC.

and the odd overlanding vehicle. The motorhomes were big, white and shiny from the men cleaning them constantly, while my BlueBelle was now looking like she had been through a sandstorm. For a moment I forgot where I was: I could have been in a Spanish campsite in autumn when all the Europeans come down to avoid the harsher northern winter. Commonly they are pensioners who are not only escaping the cold weather but also saving money, since the cost of living is much lower in these southern climes. They are dubbed 'silver swallows' because they fly where the climate is more tolerable for the winter and back home again for the spring.

The silver swallows around me here were in two camps: the French and the Germans. They had come all the way to Morocco with their satellite dishes atop their expensive (often €100,000+) motorhomes, with scooters or quad bikes in internal garages or enclosed trailers. These additional smaller vehicles meant that the swallows were mobile without having to move their giant homes-on-wheels. I noted that the smaller vehicles were used primarily to go into the village for groceries, to race along the dunes, to take their wastewater and toilet containers to the septic tank (few of the silver swallows used the local ablutions, preferring their own pristine internal environment), or to convey full bottles of water to refill the on-board tanks. These jobs occupied the old men for most of the day, and when they were not doing all these 'chores' they were cleaning their vehicles (only for them to be covered in sand again within seconds of course). Surrounding their small patches of temporary 'territory', they installed windbreaks or pitched tents: all the joys of home away from home on the edge of a desert. Living in a van I truly appreciate the comfort of having all your things with you, but somehow all of that seemed to me quite bizarre there in the Sahel.

What I love about Africa is that people greet you with true sincerity, however in this 'little Europe' my greetings were met with reluctant responses and frequently with disdain, possibly because I was driving a British-registered van and spoke English… or perhaps because I was a woman on my own..?!

I had progressed well with my work, and with 2019 approaching the staff suggested I might like to join the camp dinner to celebrate the changing of the year. I could not think of anything more horrific than eating a meal I could barely afford with people who had made no attempt to be civil; I couldn't face being in the campsite any longer. I decided I'd rather be in the middle of nowhere and planned to leave early on New Year's Eve and see what I could find in the way of a wild camping spot.

WESTERN SAHARA / MOROCCO

The formerly-known Western Sahara is now the Moroccan Southern Province and is an area that has endured much hardship. It was once ruled by the Spanish, and then upon their withdrawal it faced conflict with Mauritania and Morocco who both wanted to occupy the area, primarily for its rich mineral resources. Mauritania has since pulled out, nevertheless the province remains in strife as the Polisario Front continues to seek self-determination. There is an obvious increased military presence as there is still fighting on the Eastern border; tourists are advised to stay out of the area. The region is mainly occupied by the Sahrawi people but also Tuareg, Berber and other tribes, along with the many Moroccans who now live there.

Whilst in Morocco I had been cautioned by a few people – mainly Europeans and including a Dutch journalist – not to cross through the province (although I cannot say how many of them had actually driven in the region). The problem was that if I did not cross here I had no options other than via Algeria, so I decided to take my chances. I had done my research, which showed that the dangerous area would be to the east where a large fortification berm had been built to prevent incursions. I, however, had my route planned close to the coast.

There was of course no official border, but there were two large police checkpoints within a few hundred metres of each other which seemed to signify that I had entered the region. The first checkpoint requested the usual *fiche*, which I obliged in providing, and I was waved along. At the next checkpoint I was asked the usual questions by the policeman and thought I had passed by without event, when a supercilious ranking officer came out of the small hut and shouted something in the local language to the officer attending me. He approached me with a swagger and asked to see my passport, which was unusual as the *fiche* usually did the job. I presented the notarised laminated copy of my passport but he insisted on my *actual* passport, so this meant rummaging around in my bag to get it out. While I was thus occupied, he started with the questions in a suave tone: where was I going, why was I alone, where was my husband? (a conversation I became accustomed to over the months). On receiving the document, he checked all my details and began addressing me by my full first name.

He continued with the conversation, all the while holding on to my passport, and I was becoming quite concerned wondering where this was going. My responses became less friendly and curter. He seemed to think that I was an interesting proposition and eventually asked for my phone number, but I responded that I did not know my local number and anyway once I was over the border it would no longer work. He considered my reply and proceeded to ask me if I was on Facebook. I was still new at this 'men have no boundaries with women' idea and my discomfort was growing by the second, but I heard myself saying yes. He then asked if my Facebook profile was the name in my passport. This was my opportunity to ditch the guy, so I lied and said yes again. OK, he replied, he would send me a friend request on Facebook and I *must* accept it. I nodded enthusiastically, at which I was handed back my passport and permitted to leave.

I drove off with a relieved "Shukraan,[21] merci" and got away from there as fast as I legally could. Then I proceeded to have an earnest conversation with BlueBelle: "How dare he?! Who did he think he was, using his position to harass me?!" And like the best of friends, she listened in silence and with great empathy. I had not felt threatened as such, but I was very uncomfortable with the exchange and it took a while for me to calm down. I baulked at the thought of what women there had to deal with daily.

Throughout Morocco, with the exception of Rabat where there was a greater international influence, women were mostly dressed in simple colours with long skirts or dresses, high necklines and scarves over their heads; however, very few were covered from head to toe. As I entered the southern part of the country though, the dresses became more colourful and flowing

---

[21] 'Thank you' in Arabic

with lighter-weight fabrics and more of the women had face veils, usually an extension of their headscarves or shawls. As I was driving through one village I noticed a lovely girl, obviously young from her size but wearing a head covering, and she stared at me as I passed. I'll never know if I read her eyes correctly but I think they said, 'Who is this woman driving a van, with no covering at all and wandering freely in the world of men?' She was probably married, being so covered, and in that fleeting moment when our eyes met I tangibly sensed the difference in our worlds and felt sad for her; and perhaps she felt sad for me, or envious...

As I drove onward and further south, the landscape became markedly drier. There was much more sand and a wind blowing offshore from my left, and this constant pressure made driving tiring as I had to grip the steering wheel tightly to keep from being pushed off the road. I was on the lookout for a place to wild camp so that I could enjoy New Year's Eve in peace, however the landscape was flat, sandy and lacked any sizeable vegetation or rock to shelter behind. I tried to identify a good place as close to dusk as possible because it left less opportunity to be spotted; and I also knew that under cover of night out in the middle of nowhere, BlueBelle would fade into the dark and be near invisible.

The only notable structures were cell towers, which had walls around them and were likely occupied inside with guards; and besides most were in the midst of sand, making them impossible for me even to access. It was now dusk and the sun had set, but with a word to the Universe to please not let me down, I finally saw one tower that had potential. I drove around the ochre-coloured walls to the rear where it provided some shelter from the wind and... bonus: I had a sea view!

With no one in sight, I opened my side door to listen to the sea and the sounds of night falling. I was on top of a steep cliff and the waves could be heard crashing on the rocks below. I didn't want to risk taking my one bottle of Luxembourg *crémant* through Mauritania (no alcohol was allowed in this strictly Muslim country), and so I decided that it was fitting to drink it now in celebration of all that I had achieved over the past year and to toast what lay ahead. I made some dinner and I must say the *crémant* went down very smoothly. I had been driving all day and didn't manage to see midnight, but I was totally content in my bed, in my van, in the middle of nowhere, with a new year of exciting opportunities and adventures in front of me.

The drive continued southwards and with it came a new challenge: that of the sun rising more or less on my left, crossing the horizon directly in front of me and continuing its descent to the west on my right. I was in full sunlight behind the windscreen for most of the day and it was stifling. Opening the window meant the wind took every opportunity to blow sand in and it was already up my nose, in my eyes and hair, between my teeth and irritating every orifice. The wind and sand continued to batter the left side of the van and I needed to maintain my firm grip on the steering wheel to keep BlueBelle on the road, adding strain to my right shoulder despite the cushion. The worst thing was the number of large trucks passing in the opposite direction, obviously accustomed to the road and driving at some speed. As they passed me the impact of the elements would treble and at times it was all I could do to keep from being buffeted off the road by the sheer force of it all. I wasn't having much fun.

You will recall that BlueBelle's smiley radiator grille had been stolen in Barcelona, and since then I had been forced to duct-tape the right front indicator light in place to stop it from falling out. However, the tape was no match now for the Saharan wind and sand. Three times I heard the light fall off as I was driving, forcing me to stop, pick it up from the road and tape it back on; but eventually the desert won and I lost it once and for all. This was a major concern: I'd heard tales about the police in some African countries finding any opportunity to fine a visiting vehicle, added to the fact that it wasn't safe to continue my journey without one. The question was how was I going to find a replacement in this remote area? My next main stop would be Dakhla and I would look for a solution there, but I held little hope for this town in the middle of nowhere.

Dakhla is built on a peninsula and as there were no listed campsites I was looking for somewhere to wild camp. I had read that there was a popular spot on the lagoon, but when I arrived there in the late afternoon I could not believe what I saw: the area was packed with European campers and motorhomes, parked edge to edge and getting free water from a single tap (I did not dare ask where the toilet waste was going!) It looked like a posh squatter camp on wheels.

I drove in and drove out almost as quickly. The beach was filled with people and it seemed more like summer in the South of France – definitely *not* my scene. I decided to try an alternative place on the other side of the peninsula and on arriving there I saw an overlanding vehicle I had seen in Tan-Tan which belonged to a German couple. I parked and approached them to ask what the site was like and they told me they had been there a night and had not been disturbed. Excellent news. I watched the locals surfing as the sun set over the ocean, turning the entire vista a fiery golden orange, and then the waves soothed me into a calm and untroubled sleep.

Early the next morning, the first order of business was to find a car parts shops and see if I could get a new indicator light. The iOverlander app had indicated a reportedly reliable place so I decided to start there. I was early, but still not seeing any life in the shop so at 8.00 I called the owner, who advised me he was on his way. After half an hour a young lad – I wouldn't have rated him more than fourteen – unlocked the door and went inside, however the shop remained firmly closed. After another half an hour's waiting, my patience was up and I knocked on the door to ask the youngster about an indicator light. He had been joined by two more boys, of a similar age. As usual, communication was successfully accomplished with pointing and gesticulating rather than the use of any actual language, my French certainly not extending to the words for vehicle parts.

One of the lads nodded, left and walked across the road, returning about ten minutes later with *exactly* the right assembly. I could not believe my eyes and, even more shocking, the cost was exceptionally low, so with my enthusiastic agreement they set out to fit it. Within thirty minutes my indicator light was fixed, looking brand spanking new and working perfectly. I was ecstatic! I paid my bill, tipped the boys, bade them a joyful farewell and headed off. I never did see the owner of the place, but it made me realise how we tend to dismiss young people, and yet if we give them a chance they can surprise us.

My journey continued south. The wind and sand were my constant companions but I have to say the landscape was spectacular: vast open spaces with few landmarks, just the windswept plains, occasional eroded hills and rock formations before me and to my left, and the cold blue Atlantic Ocean to my right. I passed through a rocky area where some creative soul(s) had balanced numerous stone stacks, which added an interesting diversion to watch them teetering in the wind.

The land, far from being dead, was full of life when I looked closely. I found an area with dragonflies in abundance and left pondering how they survived in that parched environment. Small succulent plants displayed blotches of colour on the creamy sand: yellow here, orange there, pink, lilac, a splash of red – all of it signifying life; and occasionally a patch of green indicated the presence of moisture underground. It all told of a time when there was plenty of water in the region, perhaps millennia ago, and I wondered what had changed to turn it into a full-on desert. The Atlantic remained visible away on my right, but here the continent sat high above the ocean with steep cliffs denying access to it. My mere words cannot do justice to this immense landscape and no photograph could properly convey its splendour. It left me in awe of this planet, its beauty and its great diversity.

My constant challenge was to find enough time to relish the scenery while still focusing on the road and the destinations I needed to reach before the day ran out on me. I also realised that I had to stop taking so many photographs. There was so much that was remarkable, but each sighting meant I needed to find somewhere to stop and park, unbuckle, move my cushion armrest and seat, get out of the van, take the photographs and enjoy the view, then get back in the van, seat, elbow cushion, seatbelt. It was becoming challenging, and I eventually took most of my photos through the front or side window while I was driving. If I had taken the photography more seriously, I would have been on the road an awful lot longer!

On my last day in Morocco, due to my late Dakhla departure and the wind continuing to slow me down, I had to find somewhere to spend an extra night as I didn't want to cross into Mauritania late in the afternoon. Again the challenge was to find a secluded spot in the ever flatter landscape with increasing amounts of that thing I dreaded – sand. Added to this the mobile towers now all had a military presence and didn't feel like a viable option.

Finally, just as dusk fell, I saw it: a rocky outcrop where the ground was compacted with tracks, suggesting I may not have been the only person to use it. I reversed in as close to the rock as the sand would permit, allowing for an easy departure should I need it. I was still visible to oncoming vehicles, but I knew that once the sun set we would be almost invisible. With the quickly fading light I seized the opportunity to take a closer look at the surrounding plant life, then cooked myself a meal and enjoyed the splendour of another African sunset before darkness fell, allowing only the stars to tell their stories.

Despite reaching the Moroccan border early the next morning, there were already queues. The building looked new but like no one had bothered to finish it, with holes and wires randomly poking out of it and trash everywhere; and there was not one sign to indicate where to go first. I parked and walked towards the nearest queue, smiled and greeted the men (no women to be seen at all) and joined the back, hoping it was the right place to be. After a moment I was pushed to the front by an officer, and I guessed it had something to do with either my age or my gender. I was motioned to put my passport through a slot in the window and I obeyed, although I could not see a human on the other side. My passport disappeared but mere moments later popped back out of the slot. I looked at the officer, confused, and there ensued some shouting between the man inside the box and the officer standing with me. The passport went back in and emerged again a few minutes later. It seemed I had passed immigration!

Next to clear BlueBelle, I was directed to join a queue that was very slowly heading towards a booth, but after forty-five minutes I had moved only a few cars' lengths forward. Perhaps I was in the wrong place. There were no signs, no arrows, no information: how did anyone know what was going on? I got out and it was revealed that BlueBelle had to be X-rayed, and around the corner from where I had been waiting there stood an enormous hanger, within which there was a large truck with a cumbersome machine attached to it. This was the X-ray machine and the truck drove back and forth to enable the X-ray to be taken. Seemed like overkill. What did they think I was smuggling *out* of the country… guns?! Anyway, I was eventually given the all-clear to exit.

I was a little sad to leave Morocco. It had been easier than I had imagined and my time there had helped build my confidence. I had met some amazing people and driven through extraordinary landscapes, some of which I'd never considered I would be able to view with my own eyes. I would not hesitate to recommend it and I hope very much to return one day.

Chapter Two – Mauritania

3 January 2019

After leaving the Morocco border it was onward to Mauritania. To my horror, as I approached the exit road to no man's land between the borders I was faced with two exceptionally long lanes of mostly large trucks, with people, cars, wooden trolleys and litter scattered everywhere. This was the queue *into* Morocco *from* Mauritania. However, the two solid lanes meant that there was no lane for me to use. No one was moving out of the way and they were all so tightly packed that my options were either to wait for a clearing, which the vehicles coming behind me would not appreciate, or to try somehow to drive around them. The predominant issue was that the side of the road offered little space before sloping steeply down to... sand!

I had to try. It would mean two wheels on the tarmac and trusting that the other two stayed on the harder part of the roadside which lay several inches lower, so I would be driving at an angle and with BlueBelle's height I was nervous of toppling over. I worked on the semblance of something I would regularly apply throughout the journey: *velocity and determination in a forward direction achieves results*, a strategy I came to call 'the Dot Effect'. Gripping tightly on to my steering wheel I set off. I was dreadfully tense. Sweat was dripping off me and I kept hooting at people in my way because I feared that if I slowed or stopped I might not get going again – or worse, would simply topple over the edge. Nevertheless I made it, with much swearing and cursing in between. I won't exaggerate: it was only a few hundred metres, but it could have been twenty kilometres from the way it felt!

Before me now lay well tarmacked road and I breathed a great sigh of relief... but too soon. A short distance further and there was no more road – nope, no road at all, not even a track; just uneven slabs of worn and weathered grey rock and sand. The rock had been slightly smoothed with the traffic, but it still looked more like an off-road obstacle course than any kind of proper thoroughfare. I stopped to look at it and truly could not believe my eyes. There must surely be some *real* road hiding somewhere? I was feeling aghast that I had to cross this when a 4x4 came belting past me in the direction I knew I must head.

I realised it was either turn back here or continue. Again I took a deep breath, and apart from the velocity and determination lesson there was another I had learnt, and each had its own specific application: this one was *slow and steady wins the race –* or, in this case, would hopefully get me to the other side. Retightening my grip on the steering wheel and whispering some words of encouragement to BlueBelle, I gently accelerated.

It was the longest two and a half kilometres I had ever driven. I can't tell you how long it took me, but it was one of those experiences when time slowed to a crawl and every second felt an aeon. Halfway through this ordeal, I stopped by a man standing outside his (non-4x4) car and asked him if he was ok. His response was, "I'm just taking some photographs, but I have never seen such a road!" I tried to smile in agreement, and after he assured me he would be OK I continued. In trying to recall the details of that section of road, I can only say that it is a blur. I remember swearing and cursing, sweating, panicking, focusing on and making decisions for every metre in front of me... and I still have no idea how I managed to avoid the sand and navigate the uneven slabs of rock in my amazing two-wheel-drive van.

It was some while after this drive that I found out the importance of sticking to the 'main road'. I thought at the time that the carcasses of vehicles I had seen abandoned in the desert had simply failed to make the crossing, but it turned out they had gone off-road and hit landmines. In hindsight, I believe that at this part of my journey it was a very good thing I had not known this. I had enough to worry about without hidden explosive devices.

When I eventually got to the Mauritanian border post I parked and took a moment to breathe deeply. It felt like I had held my breath for the entire two and a half kilometres and my hands were still shaking, but I wasn't sure if it was from the adrenalin or the fact that I had been gripping the steering wheel so tightly. I was trying to gather my composure when BlueBelle was suddenly surrounded by Arab-looking men wearing turbans and all talking at the same time. With my window as usual half-open, hands were thrusting SIM cards and cash at me and fixers were touting to 'assist' me. I had to get moving quickly or I realised that, like flies to food, there would be more coming.

I picked up my folder with my papers, put on my cross-body bag and stepped out into the melee with a determined 'Don't mess with me!' look. I had decided not to use a fixer,[22] after all I had managed Morocco without too much issue. The 'flies' buzzed around, shoving things at me all the time. I gripped my folder tightly, clipped my keys on to my belt loop and put them in my pocket (as became my habit). I was wearing jeans, a shapeless long-sleeved shirt and a scarf in case I needed to cover my head. I was now entering a Muslim country where it was reputed that women should be seldom seen and never heard.

I was directed to the first building where I presented my passport. The official spoke to me in rapid-fire French, but I did not understand as I was still attempting to regain my composure after the drive and feeling a little overwhelmed. He shouted for someone outside and a young man in a yellow hi-vis safety vest came in and spoke to me in excellent English. His name was Ahmed and I was most grateful for his appearance.

Ahmed actually ended up being my fixer and, to be honest, the comparatively small amount of money that I paid him was well worth it for the difficulty I would have had without him. I did insist on keeping my passport on me and I was thankful he didn't argue with this, although he did suggest that it would all go faster if he could take it and attend to some things while I was attending to others. But I remained firm: the passport stayed with me.

I had no idea what the first office was for but I was given the nod to continue to Immigration. Here I was directed to stand by the wall opposite the men behind a queue of three local women. One of them, much older than me, had obviously been waiting a long time and was getting annoyed because she kept shouting at the official security guard. I was the only white woman there and with my blue eyes and blondish hair, I confess to feeling 'well observed' by the growing number of men in the other queue. I decided to use my scarf and pulled it over my head in keeping with the other women.

---

[22] Someone who smooths the way

We were all waiting behind one door through which people were randomly let in, but by my count not as many let out, which worried me. After some forty minutes the women were directed to enter the room. There were five of us by now: a very beautiful woman had arrived after me and been escorted to her place by her clearly much older husband. (I did wonder how that marriage had been set up as the old man didn't look like much of a catch!) On approaching the door the beautiful woman started to scream for her husband, insisting that he come into the room with her, but the guard was having none of it. After a few moments of everyone shouting – the woman, the husband and the guard – the husband reluctantly stepped back and we were all allowed to enter the room.

The room was dimly lit by just one power-saving bulb hanging from the middle of the long ceiling and barely illuminating two desks standing side-by-side, both with new computer screens on them. The windows had been covered in newspaper and brown paper so that no one could see inside – or out. Coming from the bright Sahel light outside it took a while for my eyes to adjust to the dimness, but eventually I saw two men behind the desks: one stern-looking in a suit and sitting very upright, the other, more casual and relaxed in both manner and clothing. There were also two local men and two young European men waiting by the wall. (So much for separating the women from the men; I still don't understand the logic!)

Nonetheless we women were now queuing to get our biometrics taken (photo, iris scan and fingerprints) at the desk on the far side with Mr Suit. Whilst waiting I couldn't help but overhear the two younger men speaking Portuguese, and as I understood one of their comments I replied in my little-used Portuguese. They were surprised to hear a stranger speaking their language so far from home and we started to chat across the room. By now I was happy for any diversion. My turn for the biometrics came, all the necessary information was captured and I was released to join the queue at the next desk. As I walked across, in burst the beautiful woman's husband and refused to be thrown out. I decided it looked safer and much more interesting to chat with the friendly (and yes, rather handsome) Portuguese guys, Hugo and Luis.

They turned out to be charming young men who ran a company called *Hostel on Wheels*[23] in Portugal. We were quietly chatting away when a funny comment had me burst out laughing. I have one of 'those' laughs: it is not discreet but loud and spontaneous, and often people will say, "I knew you were around because I heard you laughing!" Mr Suit, sitting behind his desk, flashed me a stern and disapproving look, and without thinking I clapped my hands over my mouth like a naughty child and apologised profusely. I then switched tack and smiled at him with all my charm, hoping they didn't jail women for guffawing. Everyone else in the room started to snicker – it seemed to be contagious – and I did see the hint of a smile crossing Mr Suit's lips as he turned away, gathered his composure and returned to his work with a straight face.

Hugo and Luis finished up their business and next it was my turn. The visa fee, which I paid in euros, was tossed into a drawer already overflowing with cash, my passport was quickly stamped and thrust back at me and I was dismissed. I'm certain they were happy to be rid of such a troublemaker! Blinded by the bright light outside, I happily identified Ahmed who had been waiting patiently for me. He took me to the next building for my TIP[24] and then to get a SIM card. (I learnt always to ensure that the card worked before I left.) Next, insurance – costly since I was only there three days – and finally I exchanged some euros for Mauritanian ouguiya. The money was confusing since they had lopped a zero off the end of their currency and it was now seemingly more valuable, although there were posters on the walls to confirm that what they had done was quite legitimate. I thanked Ahmed and tipped him, grateful for his having guided me through it all.

Hugo and Luis were also about to depart so we said our goodbyes, exchanged Instagram account details and hoped to meet again further down the line. They were not going as far as I was, but their route was more or less the same. A quick selfie was

---

[23] www.facebook.com/pg/hostelonwheels/services/
[24] A Temporary Import Permit (TIP) is mandatory for vehicles in many African countries if you do not have a *Carnet de Passages en Douane*.

photo-bombed by one of the guys selling phone cards, and with his turban he added a touch of the exotic to the scene.

Finally, I was on the move again and skirting the grand and vast Sahara. The nights were cold and the days hot, and I was most appreciative not to have travelled there in the middle of summer. It would have been utterly unbearable.

SAHARA

Mauritania – officially the Islamic Republic of Mauritania – is a country that sits on the western edge of the Sahara, the world's largest hot desert, which stretches across the African continent from east to west and is larger than the entire United States of America. Its name is derived from the Arabic word *sahra* which simply means 'desert', so to avoid tautology we just need to call it 'the Sahara'.

The only good road I found in Mauritania was a stretch of about fifty kilometres running into the capital, Nouakchott. The rest were either badly potholed or full of sand, which made them very challenging. Progress was slow, however I was getting excellent bad-road-driving practice and quickly developing my 'pothole slalom'[25] strategy. It soon became evident that there was as much diversion via sand as there was actual road, which had me worried. I was still thinking with my Europe-driving brain, so when I saw two diversion lanes I immediately assumed that I should be driving in the left-hand lane without properly evaluating the situation. I realised too late that this was more sand than road and soon I was stuck – again.

I had not seen much other traffic since the border so I wasn't certain of getting any help soon. I got out to assess how badly I was wedged. It didn't look too bad, but I'd learnt that persistence in trying to get out meant my tyres just sank in deeper. At this point, I had not yet discovered the power of deflating my tyres.

As I came around to the left side of BlueBelle, I noticed in the lane I should have taken an old low-slung black Mercedes approaching at some speed. My first thought was that if *he* was able to drive the road in that vehicle then so should I (although he

---

[25] The ability to manoeuvre around potholes without needing to brake every few seconds

was probably better versed in sand than I was). I must have made an interesting sight in the flat beige landscape with BlueBelle standing out like a beacon and me in my baggy blue pants and white shirt. The Mercedes came to a halt and out poured eight men in long loose shirts and flowing robes, who proceeded to walk over the sandbanks towards me.

I have to confess there was a moment when I thought, this can go either horribly wrong or perfectly right. I took a deep breath and employed my Strategy #3: Attack is the best form of defence – and pulled out my gun… No, just kidding! Remember, I didn't have a gun. However, if this was another country on another continent, it could easily have gone that way. No, I employed the courtesy attack and shouted and waved, "Bonjour, merci, bonjour!" The driver approached me. "Ten euros and we will get you out," he said in French. Sounded like a deal to me.

He shouted some orders to the others and they lent their shoulders into the back of BlueBelle while the driver of the Mercedes got into her driving seat. I didn't think to argue with him, although I guess he could have driven off in her and left me standing on the side of the road. But *this is Africa* and I was confident that it would be fine.

I had brought my phone with me and as I had nothing else to do I decided to commemorate the moment with a photograph; however, one fellow in a blue t-shirt, white flowing robes and a turban was trying to engage me in conversation. It seemed he was not going to demean himself by pushing but instead decided to stand in front of the scene. I tried waving him aside but he was not budging: he was determined to be front and centre of the photo, so eventually I gave up and took the shot with him in the spotlight looking positively regal. It turned out to be one of the best photos I've ever taken.

Van pushed out of the sand, money paid (still cheaper and faster than any breakdown service anywhere) and I was off, back on solid ground again and determined to avoid anything that looked too sandy. Africa Roadside Assistance had won again! ARA 2 : DB 0

With all the delays at the border and then getting stuck in the sand, I was now running dangerously out of daylight and loath to wild camp in this desolate landscape; there was nowhere secluded enough. I also dared not stray off the road for fear of sand and there was no rock or tree to hide behind anyway. While BlueBelle blended into the dark in most places, here with a background of white sand she would stand out like a swimming pool in the desert. I had to make it to a little town called Chami, where my app had told me I should be able to park at the *gendarmerie*.[26]

The land was scattered with a few small shacks of varying descriptions and in places I could see the Atlantic off to my right. Thankfully the harsh wind had died down a bit but there was barely a person in sight among the endless sand. From time to time, usually near the makeshift villages, I saw a couple of donkeys and pygmy goats wandering around looking for morsels of vegetation. Some people might have found it mind-numbingly dull, but I was noticing the shifting hues and textures of the desert. I had previously assumed that it was all beige sand, but I was wrong. It was rich in colour when you cared to look, from whites, greys and silvers to oranges and dull reds, and from fine to coarse-grained sand to the occasional rock: the majesty of nature.

I reached Chami just as the sun was greeting the horizon. I had only a short time to find my parking spot for the night as it would soon be dark and I'd noticed no street lights, and there were only sand roads to the police station at the far edge of the town. I found it and pulled up outside a large gate and walked to the guardhouse, where two men were asleep on the floor and one was sitting next to them. In my shockingly bad French I asked if I could park for the night and was directed to the main building. As I walked through the sandy yard a man came out and I asked him the question again. He indicated that it would be fine, so I asked if there would be a price and he replied that all he needed was a *fiche*.

I drove into the compound, a little concerned how potentially unsecured this place was, because a part of the wall was missing and other sections seemed to have been reclaimed by the desert. Nevertheless it was a police station, so I should be OK. I parked, handed over my *fiche*, graciously thanked everyone with a smile and collapsed in my van after a more than eventful day, wishing there was a glass of wine or a gin and tonic somewhere that I

---

[26] Police station

might have forgotten (Although I'm not sure that drinking at the police station would have been a clever thing to do in alcohol-free Mauritania!)

THE ESSENCE OF NOUAKCHOTT

Early the next morning I headed out through the open gate and onward to the capital city. I had set myself a new rule: when I hit half a tank of diesel I would start looking for a fuel station. I probably had enough to get to Nouakchott but didn't want to risk it. There was a station on the way out of town, but being so early it was still closed so I decided to wait. A grumpy young man came out of the office, still tucking in his shirt and zipping up his pants and looking decidedly sleepy.

As I turned to look at the fuel pump I noticed that it was labelled *essence*. Was that petrol or diesel? I had no idea as I had not come across this description before. I looked across at the pump attendant, already used to the fact that in Africa you hardly ever get to pump your own fuel.[27] Mauritania is a French-speaking country (along with several local dialects), so I made my best attempt to ask him, "Diesel? Gazole?" (as it is sometimes known). He responded, "Oui", although I wasn't at all comfortable that he had understood me; but after repeating the question a further three times, I succumbed to his superior knowledge. I filled up with a half tank of *essence* and off I set to Nouakchott.

Amongst the ramshackle homes, the rubbish on the side of the road, goats eating plastic and donkeys munching on cardboard for the lack of anything else to eat, there was not a blade of grass, a bush or a tree to be seen. I passed a market of sorts but with very little in the way of wares. I've seen plenty of poverty in Africa, but this was a level of poverty I had never before encountered.

Surprisingly, a short while after leaving Chami the road improved significantly. It was tarmacked, with no diversions and only the occasional pothole: a real road – in truth, the only real section of road I experienced in Mauritania – and it saw me into the capital city. Even more astounding, the entrance to Nouakchott was a dual carriageway, although the driving skills of

---

[27] When I moved to the UK twenty years ago, it took me six months to overcome my fear of filling my car after a lifetime of never having done so!

the locals were somewhat haphazard. It also actually looked like a city, complete with shops and buildings and wide avenues. I was surprised and impressed after what I had seen until then, which had set my expectations quite low.

I arrived around lunchtime and arranged to meet Rob, a Dutchman who had set out to drive around the world on his motorbike. (I lost my first husband in a biking accident and so I'm not really a biker fan, but each to his own.) Rob and I had been in touch on a Facebook group and I had made contact with him since we seemed to be heading in the same direction, although it seemed unlikely that we would meet as I was some days behind him. I thought I had missed him by a day, but trouble with his motorbike meant that he was still in Nouakchott.

I sent him a message as I entered the city, and knowing where his guest house was I drove in that direction. He came out to greet me when I arrived and invited me to join him for tea. We spent a good hour chatting about our travels and experiences thus far and he expressed serious concern about the roads (which were assuredly worse for him than they were for me!) He asked whether it would be like this throughout Africa, and while I had no idea I certainly understood his concerns. I told him that there would surely be challenges ahead, but if he wasn't getting a feel for it there was no shame in turning back and trying another part of the world.

When foreigners come to Africa, and especially when they venture off the beaten track, they bring an expectation that the continent is just a poorer version of where they are from but with more melanin. This infuriates me. Africa is Africa and you'll either love it or hate it, and I always recommend that people immerse themselves in a new culture, because when you do so you'll have the experience of a lifetime. Rob had various unrealistic expectations of Africa and was having trouble adapting, but I kept telling him to relax into it: TIA![28]

During our chat I raised a topic that had been bothering me since the morning: what was *essence*? He had a grasp of French and replied coolly, "That's petrol" and a curse escaped my lips. I told him what had transpired and then started to research online

---

[28] This is Africa!

what the implications were (although I had nonetheless driven with half diesel and half petrol for a quarter of a tank without so much as a hiccup). My research indicated that a vehicle like BlueBelle could handle it, but there might be implications for the diesel pump, the seals and other smaller parts. The last thing I needed was any of those packing up in the middle of nowhere so I decided to have the tank properly emptied and refuelled, which of course would additionally cost me about three-quarters of a tank of wasted fuel. (I now know that I should have simply continued adding diesel and she should have been fine. That 20/20 vision thing really isn't helpful!)

Rob spoke in French to the owner of the guest house and he arranged for one of his staff, who spoke a little English, to accompany me to the garage to get it sorted out. I put out my hand to shake his in thanks but he ignored me, leaving me feeling rather stupid. He didn't acknowledge my hand at all, nor offer even a hint of any emotion. It slowly dawned on me that being a devout Muslim he would not shake hands with a woman, much less an infidel. There was nothing impolite about his demeanour but hand-shaking was not going to happen. So although it does annoy me not to be recognised as anything other than a 'mere woman', as my Greek friend George often says, "What to do?"

We set off and I was directed to a sand patch filled with vehicles and parts of vehicles and vehicles in parts, and on the one side there were shacks with people living in the most basic of conditions. I parked between some vehicles that looked like they had been abandoned. My translator went off and I sat back, thinking it was unlikely that anything would happen quickly. Some time later he returned with, I assumed, a mechanic and his young helper, who grabbed a piece of cardboard lying in an ocean of trash, shoved it under the van and disappeared. While I knew they would not understand my words, I was going to make darn sure they understood my meaning. I motioned them to stop, brought their attention to me and told them to be *very* careful: this was my baby and they should take *extremely* good care of her, I added with a stern look, wagging my finger and emphasising (with a dash of humour) that if they were not careful I would 'take care' of them. I know I must have looked ridiculous, the only old woman with a van within miles, telling off a bunch of Muslim men… but we are all human, and I've learnt that getting people to smile and connect with me usually gives a better result than being haughty. My translator conveyed the message but they were already laughing at me and smiling their reassurances.

With the fuel tank removed, the contents were decanted into a variety of containers and from the colours it was obvious that there was a mix of diesel and petrol. I did have occasion to question how was it that I have driven vehicles since I was seventeen years old and did not know until then that diesel is blueish and petrol is yellowish! I took out a new fuel filter from my stock and had it fitted; I felt it was a precaution worth taking. It all took time with the initial negotiation and the to-ing and fro-ing, but I was not on a tight deadline. While the work was being done I chatted to the men – only one woman was in sight, sweeping her shack – and they were polite, friendly, had a laugh and found me most bizarre.

A dirt path separated us from the shacks standing cheek by jowl on the sand before me, thrown together with whatever could be claimed from the environment: bits of wood, metal sheets, an odd door that was now not being used as a door. I watched the woman chasing some goats that were eating pretty much anything, including plastic. Children with books and backpacks were returning from school, and I could not imagine the discipline it would take in this environment to live and learn and strive to get an education, especially as a girl.

The tank was refitted and enough diesel added to allow me to get to the fuel station. The repairs were not expensive and, thanking everyone with a wave, I departed in a healthier BlueBelle. I decided to fill up before reaching the guest house as I planned an early start to Senegal the next day and it would be one less thing to worry about in the morning.

When I got back to the guest house I was permitted to park in the driveway for the night. Rob had been tending to his bike and we agreed that we were both hungry and should look for a place to eat. We plumped for an Indian restaurant just a short walk away and during dinner decided that we would travel together to the Diama border post into Senegal. We also agreed to keep this to ourselves: everyone we encountered seemed to be 'in' on the scam because we were constantly interrogated with an unusual degree of interest. The Rosso and Diama borders into Senegal are renowned for their corruption and I had been stressed about crossing for a while, so I hoped that with a man present I might have a better chance. I was later disavowed of this notion.

When it was time to leave Rob said that he would lead using his TomTom, and I set my phone too so that I knew where I was going in case I lost him. I wanted to change some euros before getting to the border as I was now low on cash, so we stopped at a garage to try our luck. While the pump attendant couldn't help, another customer was prepared to offer a reasonable rate which I accepted. Rob did not have any cash on him so I gave him some, concerned that if something happened or we were separated he should not be without means.

Finally, we started to make our way out of Nouakchott. Rob took a different route from the one I had, but believing his device to be superior I put my phone aside. I noted with alarm that the streets were narrowing and the area, if it was possible, was becoming even poorer. There was often only one passable lane with people, cars, donkeys and mounds of trash on one side or the other. Rob was having little trouble on the sandy lanes, but I was struggling since I was much wider than he was and had slowed to a crawl to get through the mayhem. Just what I needed: more white-knuckle driving. As I started wondering if we would ever manage to get out of this ordeal we broke out on to a wide road and Rob pulled over. I followed suit and took a deep breath as he walked across to me. "Wow, that was quite a route out of the city!" he exclaimed. Exasperated, I responded with, "Yes, you really know how to show a girl a good time!" I should have paid more attention as it was not the last time his GPS or directions would lead me astray.

The roads heading south were appalling, with bad sections of tarmac interspersed with rutted sandy diversions. I decided that Rob should go ahead as I was creating too much dust, and behind me he would end up eating it – literally. We fell into an easy routine.

WETLANDS ON THE EDGE OF THE DESERT

The road turned from bad to worse, with again more diversions than road and all of it in scary amounts of ridged sand. Rob was having increasing difficulty holding his bike steady through the powdery terrain, while the corrugations had me believing I wouldn't have a single glass or mug left intact. It gave a whole new meaning to 'shake, rattle and roll' and our progress was painfully slow.

We had hoped to make it to the border in one day, but after too many hours of teeth-rattling and bone-shaking I knew that it wasn't going to happen; and frankly, I'd had enough. There were times when Rob would take a fair lead and then stop some way up the road, and I would find him having a smoke break, allowing his engine to cool down as the slow driving was overheating it. On one of these breaks I told him that I didn't believe we would make it to the border that day, but he countered that he was sure we would. I had been watching how much distance we were covering and how much was still ahead and the numbers said it was unlikely at the pace we were holding. Nevertheless we continued.

In the late afternoon we unexpectedly entered an area filled with foliage. For hundreds of kilometres I had seen nothing but rock and sand and there was something about this greenery that delighted my soul. It consisted mainly of grasses and shrubs and stretches of water, and these were the wetlands that lie on the Senegal River, the border between Senegal and Mauritania. I grew up in a dry, drought-ridden area of Zimbabwe, and while I can admire deserts, they are not my preferred habitat. I was struggling to keep my eyes on the road ahead as I marvelled at the beautifully altered landscape, utterly fascinated by the plants and diverse birdlife.

We were pretty much in sub-Saharan Africa and I knew how quickly night falls there after the sun sets. It was now only an hour or so before dark, which had me concerned as I was still quite sure that we would not make the border in time. When I next caught up with Rob he was taking in the breathtaking sight of flocks of shimmering pink flamingos, their long legs standing in glittering patches of water for as far as the eye could see. I stopped, got out of the van and breathed. Yes, this smelt like sub-Saharan Africa. It smelt of earth and water and something unmistakably like home. I stood drinking in the view and the plethora of birdlife, listening to their calls as the chorus of frogs and crickets joined in to announce dusk.

I decided I was going to stop here for the night. If Rob thought he could make the border before nightfall he was welcome to try, but I wanted to enjoy this moment, this piece of Africa. As though the Universe was inviting me to stay, I turned around and there, cleared out of the reeds next to the road, was the perfect parking spot. Rob readily agreed. He too was tired of the dust and the road. He needed to set up his tent, but with sunset coming and all this water I knew that an awful beast would arise and make a meal out of us both: the dreaded mosquitoes would soon come to devour us. I also sensed he was nervous about the number of wild warthogs he had seen wandering about, so I suggested he sleep on the floor of the van. It was long enough to accommodate his full Dutch height and seemed a more practical solution.

Before anything, I had to tidy up BlueBelle. I replaced all the items that had fallen into the middle as a consequence of the bumpy roads, and then I did some dusting so that I could cook us a sand-free dinner. Rob remained outside taking photographs and learning to delight in the warthogs. Few vehicles passed us but when one did I waved and smiled, the usual surprised looks turning into great big white-toothed smiles and waves back. We ate our dinner, swapped stories and fell into a dead sleep after the challenging day's drive.

Just before sunrise, I awoke to the sound of thousands of birds welcoming the day – one of my favourite sounds and the best alarm in the world! Breakfast, coffee, van check and we were again on our way. However, we were soon halted by a checkpoint and it turned out we had been unknowingly in the Banc d'Arguin National Park. Having already driven through it – albeit unwittingly – we still had to pay the charge, but word had reached them of our parking overnight so we had to pay an additional camping fee. We had no idea if this was right but we knew we would not be permitted to continue without paying. I hadn't exchanged a lot of cash so I negotiated down the cost of the camping and scratched together enough to get us both through, adding a few euros to sweeten the deal.

The main road was now so bad that cars had created a secondary route some metres down an embankment and we joined this. At one point Rob headed back up to the top road, but I decided that the lower one still looked fine and carried on. However, I began to doubt that decision when I saw that the few vehicles around were on the road above me. The explanation for this became clear when the lower road simply ran out, leaving me with the only uncomfortable options of turning around on the narrow track or climbing an exceptionally steep incline to the top. Although 'uphill' isn't BlueBelle's best feature, I once again employed the Dot Effect, my theory that Velocity + Determination = Result. I reversed a little way to get some speed up and told myself firmly: Let's get this done!

Well, BlueBelle positively aced the incline. I felt like a stunt driver as we came flying over the top and bounced on to the road, certain I would have no glassware left! Rob was already at the border and had taken it upon himself to find us a fixer. (I wasn't planning to use one as getting out should have been easy.) He came over to inform me and I found myself a little disturbed by his making-decisions-for-me approach as I didn't feel we knew each other that well. I asked the fixer to give us a moment since I preferred to discuss the strategy before tackling this. I thought the price we had been quoted was too hefty, but Rob informed me that *he* would handle it and I should let him do so. While I had earlier thought that being in the company of a European man would make my crossing easier, I had not guessed that I was going to be mansplained to or treated like a helpless, hapless woman. As you can imagine my annoyance was growing, so I ignored him and instead called over the fixer and negotiated a reduction for the two of us. It was a grudging compromise because it was more than I wanted to spend – or even believed was necessary.

There was still the matter of my vehicle to negotiate. The Senegal border posts on the Mauritania side are full of corruption and there was a lot of anecdotal evidence that cars older than eight years must pay a fee of €250. Everyone knows that this is illegal, but some smart guy had all the border officials and government turning a blind eye to the practice. The money disappears into many private pockets, it seems.

I tried to negotiate but Rob was taking the fixer's side and it wasn't helping. I was stupid and succumbed to the pressure: I was stressed and tired and afraid I might harm someone. So I got the fixer's assurance that he would see us through to the other side and Rob and I each paid our share (in euros); but while he also wanted my €250, I firmly informed him there was no way he was getting it until I got all the paperwork and a receipt.

Although it was an expense I could have done without, the fixer took our papers and headed off to sort out our immigration and vehicle exit… and we did not have to show our faces at a single office. This is how corruption thrives at borders: with ramshackle posts, no signage and a bit of chaos keeping things just enough out of kilter for it to be unnoticeable. Later I would come to 'boss' these border posts on my own without paying bribes and using only the occasional fixer.

Chapter Three – Senegal

6 January 2019

We were eventually permitted to cross the bridge from Mauritania over the Senegal River. The fixer assured us that he would meet us on the other side but we never did see him again! On the Senegal side the post was almost deserted but there were proper, clean buildings and a semblance of order that I had not yet experienced. Immigration went smoothly, but at customs my van papers were not dealt with by any of the officials. I was told to wait outside. It would take some time as the person responsible was not at the border on a Sunday and the paperwork would have to come from Saint-Louis, thirty kilometres away.

The 'fee' charged was the bane of any overlander crossing that border in an older vehicle without a *carnet*[29] and those refusing to pay it had sometimes been held up for days. Occasionally someone managed to negotiate a reduction but mostly people just paid up. While we all knew it was a scam, there seemed to be no way of stopping it.

Rob paid €15 for his motorbike, which only served to add to my annoyance. He had no reason to stay and I told him he should continue to Saint-Louis, however he offered to wait with me. It was mid-morning and I returned to BlueBelle to make some much-needed coffee. While we were drinking it a man came over to talk to us. He spoke English well and I learnt that he was a history teacher in the nearby village, so we fell into a discussion about African history – a topic I am quite passionate about. We were inside BlueBelle and engaged in deep in conversation, with me loudly and passionately expressing my views.

Rob was standing outside and I suddenly noticed that he was gesticulating at me to calm down. But *never*, since time immemorial, has a woman 'calmed down' when a man suggested she do so! Of course I ignored him and continued the discussion,

---

[29] The *Carnet de Passages en Douane* is a customs document required by a significant number of countries around the world, which identifies a motor vehicle or other item/s of value and allows the traveller to temporarily import these items without having to leave a cash deposit at the border.

but clearly still of the opinion that he needed to silence me, he then *verbally* 'shushed' me!! Although I managed to restrain myself from other actions, I'm certain my blue eyes were ablaze with fury when I advised him, "If you don't like what I'm saying, feel free to leave!" and continued talking to the teacher, who gave no indication that he was threatened by either my views or my passion. I was beyond exasperated that a man I had known for less than forty-eight hours was taking it upon himself to 'manage' me in public!

After about two hours my papers arrived and everyone turned a blind eye as the transaction took place outside the government offices. I checked everything carefully before paying the 'fee', but all I received was a letter on a computer-printed letterhead from some man who ran a rally in Senegal. I sighed and walked back to the van.

Leaving the border and its experiences behind me, I smiled to myself as I drove along. I was now in more familiar territory in sub-Saharan Africa, where the people were a variety of rich dark-skinned tones and there was a sense and rhythm that felt like home.

Rob had a contact, whom I shall call 'The Frenchman', who had informed him that the road to Diama was fine (although as we now knew, it was far from it). This man also reported that the road to Saint-Louis was *not* good, and so I was fully expecting something horrific, which fortunately did not transpire. I wasn't having much faith in this Frenchman and his assessment of the local highways and byways.

The decent road condition meant that we made good progress until the police checkpoints started in earnest. I watched Rob driving through each one of these without so much as a look from any policeman, but upon seeing my beautiful BlueBelle they were apparently compelled to stop us. The conversations took place in French, although I was still not making much progress with the language. Each stop took at least ten minutes and, throughout Africa, went mostly like this:

Police/Army/Immigration/Customs: Bonjour. (Good day)
Me:　　　Bonjour (*and I would hand out a TIA card*). Bonne année! (Happy New Year) Pardon, je ne parle pas Française, je suis Zimbabwean, la

lingua Zimbabwe Inglais (Excuse me, I do not speak French, I am Zimbabwean, the language of Zimbabwe is English) (or something like that)

Police: Zimbabwean?

Me: Oui. (Yes)

Police: Zimbabwean? (*with greater emphasis: had they not heard me?*)

Me: Oui.

Police: Zimbabwean?!! (*now with utter incredulity*)

Me: Oui!

Sometimes the discourse continued with questions like, "How is that possible, there are white people born there?!" Frequently though, I was greeted with a smile and a "You are African!" which always delighted me. Then followed the request for my van papers or my passport. I only handed out certified laminated copies – good thing too since the number of checkpoints I went through meant that any loose sheets would have fallen apart by the end. Since the papers presented were, of course, for only me, it was at this point that it usually occurred to them that I was travelling on my own:-

Police: Seule? (Alone?)

Me: Oui.

Police: Seule? (*with greater emphasis, like I hadn't understood*)

Me: Oui.

Police: Seule??! (*again with incredulity, and seemingly always in threes*)

Me: Oui!

What now tended to happen was a cross-questioning on where my husband was and why he wasn't with me, and I would offer that I was widowed. (Being both widowed and divorced I felt that the former would have a better outcome than the latter, however I now don't think that it mattered; just that I wasn't married!) The officer concerned would then show overt interest in accompanying me and looking after me: he would drive for me, I should not be alone, I must have a man… I would laugh and firmly say, "No, thank you!" to the offers, and tell them there was only room in BlueBelle for one person – me!

This conversation and variants of it occurred regularly. I don't think I recall a day on the road when I wasn't asked at least twice – and sometimes up to ten times – until I got to Angola when it almost stopped. At first it annoyed me intensely but after I while I just learnt to have fun with it. The conversation often ended with, "Do you have a gift for me?" or something similar; they seldom asked directly for money, but the implication was clear. I had great fun with these questions too, coming up with a variety of silly, serious and downright irreverent answers as I gained confidence in the encounters.

After three such stops on the road to Saint-Louis, I found Rob parked up under a tree having a smoke. He asked me where on earth I had been. "Police stops," I replied. "But I haven't stopped at one!" he countered to my annoyance. I started to sense a hangry man and yes, he agreed he needed food. It was hot though. I was tired and I was not prepared to cook, so I suggested we continue further along the road to see if we could find a restaurant.

In a small village we spotted a simple roadside place with chairs on a little veranda. Rob stopped so I pulled over too. We now had the challenge not only of understanding the local French patois but also of understanding what food was on offer, since the names of dishes were only in the local language. The women serving were equally frustrated and instead invited me to go to the back to see what they had. The 'kitchen' was a very basic affair that would not have passed even the most rudimentary of health and safety regulations in Europe. There were big old worn cooking pots on gas plates holding different types of stews, and I understood that one was chicken, another was beef and the third was goat. I ordered the beef for Rob and the chicken for myself, each with rice. I figured that if the locals were surviving the cooking, we would too.

I returned to Rob. He asked about the food so I told him it looked fine and I'd ordered him the beef. He seemed satisfied. I knew that if he had gone to the kitchen himself he would have had a fit and insisted on leaving and driving to who knows where, and a hangry man is not great company. I smiled sweetly, omitting any mention of the state of the 'kitchen'. The food arrived and actually it tasted very good, albeit spicy hot, so a cold beer accompanied our meal.

SAINT-LOUIS

Our destination for the night would be a popular campsite south of Saint-Louis, and as I had been accommodating, cooking and paying for Rob, he offered to pay for the night at the campsite including a meal – and of course, I graciously accepted. Getting there took some time. There were road works and Rob's now-becoming-annoying GPS had taken us in loops, so I eventually did what men are incapable of doing: I stopped a local to ask for directions.

Bearing in mind that I had been driving almost non-stop for five days since leaving Tan-Tan on New Year's Eve, and the driving had required my full attention and been physically demanding due to the state of the roads, exhaustion was now impacting my mood. I was hoping that the campsite would be suitable for a couple of nights to get some well-earned rest and catch up with myself. The location was nice enough and the views from the shore of the Senegal River were lovely, but the ablutions were basic, the camping terrain was sandy, the staff were aloof to the point of rudeness and the cost was unexpectedly high. This last had Rob complaining: obviously he'd thought he would get away with a bargain. I offered to pay for myself, but to be fair he did honour his word.

A shower to wash off all the layers of dust was my first stop and then to the bar for a quiet drink and to enjoy the scenery. When I arrived at the bar and enquired about dinner, I was informed that we would dine at the big table with the 'boss' and there were no food options, a set menu would be served. The last thing I felt like was making small-talk with strangers.

Dinner was a bland affair – our lunch on the street had been far more appetising – but the company was more distasteful than I could have imagined and took matters to a whole new level of irritating. The owner was Swiss but had lived in Senegal for many years, and his blond-haired teenage son, who had a very high opinion of himself, was having an argument with his father (which, thankfully, I did not understand). The boy was seated opposite me and had a surly look on his face throughout the whole meal. The daughter was a lively young dark-skinned girl who, when she wasn't jumping up and down on her chair, was asking me rapid-fire highly personal questions which I eventually declined to answer. The father finally reined her in but only after I gave him a 'Control this child please!' look. Throughout all of this Rob was chatting away in French to the owner. He did politely try to get him to speak English to include me but failed. I could see where the son got his manners.

I excused myself early and returned to my van, where Rob found me a short while later. I thanked him for paying for the camping and the meal but told him I would be heading off in the morning as I had no inclination to stay any longer. I would go into Saint-Louis to organise insurance, cash and a SIM card and then head on to Dakar. Rob agreed that staying wasn't on the cards for him either, and since he needed to take care of those things too, he would join me.

The historic town of Saint-Louis is built on an island and full of colonial buildings that would exude plenty of charm if it weren't for the eye-watering amount of litter and neglect. What should have been beautiful waterways were instead trash-filled channels, the majority of it plastic. This was the first painful example of a constant eyesore throughout most of the countries I visited and it hit hard. Not only was the view shocking but there was a nasty stench too.

The iOverlander app directed us to a place where we could sort out our insurance, and since we could purchase a policy covering all the ECOWAS[30] we would not then need to buy insurance on a country-by-country basis, saving us plenty of time and money.

Rob had managed to withdraw some cash and was tasked with purchasing the insurance since I had not had any luck with the local ATMs. I tried several before going into the banks to enquire, but without an account there they wouldn't change cash for me either. I was out of options. Dismayed, I returned to the insurance office where Rob was finalising the paperwork. He

---

[30] Economic Community of West African States, a union of fifteen countries located in West Africa

handed me my papers, insisting that I check every detail – critically important of course, but something I'm horribly bad at. He had paid for both of us and I promised to refund him in Dakar, where I hoped to have better luck.

Our last stop was the mobile phone company to get a local SIM card with data. We had to verify our identity with our passports and they took copies. Then they set up the cards on our phones and we were ready to go, insured and reconnected to the world. All I still needed was cash.

LAC ROSE

Some time before leaving Europe and while researching my route through Africa, one of the first things I'd noticed in Senegal was a lake called Lac Rose on the Cap Vert peninsula which I really wanted to see. I had determined that it would be a logical place to use as a base to commute into Dakar, where I would arrange my visa for Guinea. Rob again needed to go through the same process so he agreed to join me for a few more days. Our destination was a campsite near Lac Rose.

We agreed to take the longer route to the camp since reviews on the app had mentioned that the shorter route was very sandy – and as you know, neither of us did well in sand. I decided after leaving Saint-Louis that it would be best if Rob and I met at a specific spot on the main road just before the turn-off to the site, as this way we could each drive at our own pace.

It was a good idea to drive separately. I was enjoying the freedom again and not having to be concerned about keeping up with the motorbike. The heat, however, was insufferable, and all the more unpleasant because it was accompanied by high humidity. I was mighty grateful for my dual dash-fans, and as the roads were tarmac it was fine to keep the window two-thirds open. In the afternoon I found myself weaving my way through a busy town, and whilst focused on traffic I missed a turn-off and had to go some distance before I could turn around… and then my phone battery died and along with it my map. I was in a horrible muddle. The phone would clearly need some time to charge, so I stopped to ask for directions and eventually, through heavy rush-hour traffic, I inched my way out of the city and back on to the Dakar road.

Having been so delayed, I was concerned that Rob was already waiting for me. I had no money and no phone and I was stressed. After a while the phone had charged sufficiently to switch back on and, to my great relief, the map told me that I was not too far from our meeting point. I sent a WhatsApp message to Rob that I was on my way, but when I arrived Rob was nowhere to be found and there was no response to my message. A few minutes later, however, a message popped up: Rob had been delayed too, by a police check, but he was on his way. He had also spoken to his friend The Frenchman and was assured that we should not take the pre-agreed route but the one we had in fact eliminated the day before. I was annoyed at the change of arrangements, but arguing over WhatsApp wasn't easy and he again assured me that The Frenchman knew the recommended route well and could be trusted.

In hindsight, it was at this point that I should have stuck to *my* plan, to my own gut feeling and to the route I had determined, and allowed him to follow The Frenchman's recommendation – which would take us several kilometres back down the road I had just driven.

To go meet Rob I had to turn BlueBelle around in the small side street and get back on to the now busy and narrow main road. I used my side mirrors to reverse, but when I pushed BlueBelle over the 'kerb' (for a wider turning circle), what I couldn't see was that it was just a concrete kerb block with nothing behind it. As I found my axle wedged on the block and a wheel spinning uselessly in mid-air, I cursed.

At this juncture, a kind man came to my aid from across the street and asked for my jack. He was joined by another man and the two seemed determined to use the jack on the bodywork to lift the rear of the vehicle so that we could put something under the tyre to give it traction and enable me to drive off the concrete.

I, however, was determined that he did *not* put the jack under the bodywork. I was grateful for their help but I knew that the body was not going to support the full weight of the van, so I kept pulling the jack away while they kept telling me it was fine. This conversation was of course all taking place in French, but I clearly understood when I was told – in that charming way that some men have – that they knew what they were doing and that, as a woman, I should step back. Step back, like heck!! In no uncertain terms I told them, "NOT ON THE BODY!" using every possible gesture and tone of voice to make myself clear. I was sweating profusely. A crowd was gathering and I was trying to keep my eyes simultaneously on the van and on the guys helping me. I managed to message Rob to ask him to PLEASE come to help me.

It wasn't long before he arrived on his bike and parked it next to BlueBelle. As he walked towards the van I turned to follow him and passed just millimetres too close to his exhaust, burning my right calf on it. "Darn!" (That's the politest expression I shall use here.) It hurt like heck but I ignored it. Priority number one was to get my van back on the road. With the presence of another man suddenly everyone was listening to Rob, and with some creative application of rocks and stones we eventually got BlueBelle off the concrete block. Borrowing some more money from Rob I thanked and tipped the helpers and apologised sheepishly for shouting at them. ARA 3 : DB 0

I followed Rob back to the route that The Frenchman had recommended. Still in a mainly residential area, we turned off the main road on to a dirt track. The day was closing fast, we still had some distance to go and we were both overheated and tired, none of which helped. It quickly became evident that Rob was having great difficulty with the terrain and his bike had gone down several times. I was managing slightly better because I had a higher vantage from which to discern the least sandy route; and four wheels.

We continued struggling through the sandy track for some distance. It was now twilight and Rob took a turn off the road. It looked wrong to me but I had not set navigation so there was no way to check. As I followed he was just a few metres ahead of me and I watched him get deeply stuck in the sand. With such poor light I could not properly assess the way ahead either, and before I knew it I too was stuck. We realised (too late) that his GPS had lagged and indicated the wrong turn. Thus far I could seriously have done without his GPS – or The Frenchman's questionable aid.

We found ourselves in a narrow residential street and within a few minutes everyone from the surrounding houses, men, women and children, had come to help dig BlueBelle out of the sand. I was trying to reverse her but she lacked the power. They were all shouting for me to give her more but she just didn't have it. Rob decided he could do better and took over the driver's seat, but he too failed and more digging ensued. Eventually, after one big push with everyone putting their shoulder to her, Rob succeeded in freeing her; but as he reversed he hit a tree, and only later did I notice that it had broken off a section of the shower pipe on the roof.

Rob's bike came out with just a few guys helping him. I still had no money so Rob paid the chief spokesperson who would, he assured us, share it with the rest of the community. It was now fully dark and having lost faith completely in Rob's GPS, as well as being concerned about getting stuck in more sand, I was more than happy when the spokesperson offered to come with us to the campsite. He would be my passenger and guide, with Rob following. I was concerned about his return but he was quite content to walk with the bonus he'd received in directing us. ARA 4 : DB 0

Some eight or so kilometres further, driving in the pitch dark on wide sandy roads, we found a campsite. It didn't appear to be the right one but by this stage I was certainly beyond caring. It was a hotel, almost empty, but they agreed to let us park in the parking area for free if we had a meal in the restaurant. Sounded like a great deal to me if I didn't have to cook! There were no ablutions for us, just a shower by the swimming pool and a toilet at the restaurant. I had my own toilet so all I needed was some way to wash off the dust and sweat of the day.

I'm really not a swimmer but I was so overheated and covered in sand that I got into my swimsuit (I don't recall the last time I used it), showered off the worst of the grime and sweat first and then stepped into the pool. It was chilly at first but soon felt like heaven and I spent quite some time relishing the cool water. In hindsight though, that marvellous swim was the worst thing for my leg burn, which I had entirely forgotten about in all the drama that had followed.

Rob decided to sleep outside rather than pitch his tent and it was certainly warm enough. It had been quite a day.

The next morning after breakfast I decided that I wanted to find the original campsite I had intended to stay at with its better facilities. Rob agreed so we headed off. This site was better: it was set a bit further back from the 'road', the ground was sandy but there was some shade, and it had a nice dining area out in the open with a pool and pretty fair ablutions.

Lac Rose lies about thirty kilometres north-east of Dakar and gets its name from its gorgeous pink colour, which is due to the algae that thrive in the high salt content of the water. The lake was also the original starting point of the famous Dakar Rally. I had very much been looking forward to seeing it, but my leg deteriorated so much that I was unable to walk the few kilometres to get there, so I asked Rob to take me on the bike. Instead he walked to the lake by himself early one morning before I was up, and returned to tell me, in great detail, all about it.

DAKAR

A visa for Guinea was the one thing we both needed and Dakar was the place to get it. Many of the reviews on the app advised avoiding driving into the city under any circumstances: 'Take a taxi but DON'T drive!' was the consensus. However, I felt less comfortable with taking a taxi than I did in my van, so Rob accompanied me in BlueBelle and we headed into what was, thus far, the craziest city traffic I had ever experienced.

On leaving the camp Rob had designated himself navigator and of course had brought his untrustworthy GPS with him. We found ourselves on a very modern and lovely motorway: fresh tarmac and no potholes or sand. For some reason though the three lanes were packed edge to edge, resulting in four lanes of traffic; evidently few rules of the road were being observed. It was here that I became adept with my hooter while crawling through the traffic, dodging motorcycles and taxis and joining in the general cacophony.

The capital of Senegal, Dakar is a wide sprawling conurbation that is home to an estimated three million people – triple the number quoted in 2011 and now representing nearly a fifth of the country's entire population. This exponential growth was one factor that I had noted throughout Africa, and with more people migrating to the cities, the infrastructure just cannot cope with the sheer increase in numbers. Indeed I fear that the projected doubling of the African population within the next thirty years, alongside the continental and global impact this will have, is something governments seem to be ignoring.

Anyway, back to Dakar. First I needed cash – desperately as I had not had any since Mauritania and I needed to refund Rob and pay for my Guinea visa. I tried the banks and the ATMs, but again not one would give me money. Eventually I became tired of walking around in the dust. My burnt leg was hurting and the heat was again intense. I suddenly had a brainwave: I could send myself cash from my credit card via Western Union (these outlets are everywhere throughout Africa). The fee was higher in comparison but it would get me out of my current predicament. Rob thought it was a great idea and asked me to draw some additional cash for him too. Once sorted I was back in business. I reimbursed Rob for the meals, tips, insurance and SIM card and he transferred the additional amount into my bank. Fully funded, we headed to the Guinea Embassy where we were promptly attended to and advised to return in two days.

Next stop was to get our vehicle permits extended at the customs office – a ridiculous system which only permitted a short stay when issued at the border. This was a particular drama with much to-ing and fro-ing, handing over numerous copies, going to one office where papers were filled in, then being sent to the next office where stamps were issued, finally back to the first office for signatures, and eventually the extensions were granted and we could leave. All in all it proved another lengthy, inconvenient and bureaucratic process that allowed for corruption and the collection of additional funds – and certainly not tourist-friendly.

Our last stop would be a supermarket. Rob decided to stay with BlueBelle so I took his shopping list with mine. I included in the purchase some cold beers for Rob as I was sure this would keep him content for the return journey, but in retrospect this may have been an error on my part. I decided to forego the alcohol since I would be driving, and by now we were approaching peak-hour traffic heading out of the city.

Our return to the campsite should have been simple. It was mostly motorway, but again I was on the road later than I hoped and the sun had set, meaning there were only minutes of daylight remaining. I noticed that we had passed through one more toll than we had on the way in and started to suspect that we had overshot our turnoff. Indeed the cold beer had distracted Rob: he had been making jokes and singing along to the music and not watching the route. By the time we got back to the right turnoff it was fully dark and his GPS took us along sandy roads. I was stressed at the prospect of a repeat performance of the other day, however thanks to the stalwart BlueBelle and some careful driving we made it back to the camp without incident. My driving skills were certainly improving, even if the navigation frankly sucked!

Stopping over in campsites wasn't just sitting around eating and drinking: there were always jobs that needed to be done. I had to get rid of the ton of sand inside BlueBelle and effect some small repairs. The rutted road in Mauritania had dislodged some of the brackets on my seat that would need to be retightened, and there was the inevitable mounting pile of dirty clothes in the laundry bag. I also had to fix the broken shower. (Rob had implemented a solution but it didn't last long and remained a problem for the entire journey.) For his part, Rob needed to repair his panniers as they had taken a beating with all the falls, although they had thankfully saved his legs from the full force of the heavy bike. Luckily for him I was fully equipped with a rechargeable drill, drill bits, screws and precious *Sikaflex®*,[31] all of which I made available and which he used liberally.

Hugo and Luis (from the Mauritanian border) sought me out at the campsite and I did enjoy reconnecting with them. Their girlfriends had flown into Dakar to join them and they were all going to spend a few months exploring the west coast, so we spent a lovely evening by the fire chatting.

---

[31] A multipurpose product that is both glue and silicone, sealing and holding while still remaining flexible

Black Civilisations Museum and Hospital

The return to Dakar to collect the visas was in separate vehicles. Rob had decided to move on, whereas I wanted to spend a night in the city before heading out. We again agreed to go at our own pace and meet at the Guinea Embassy a little before our 11.00am appointment.

I opted for the coastal route, which I hadn't driven yet, and was rewarded with an excellent clear road that took me almost right into the city. Despite the metropolitan traffic I made good time and had found a parking spot near the embassy by 10.30. I couldn't see Rob but wondered if he had perhaps parked in the narrow street by the side of the embassy. I walked down it but he wasn't there, so I went to wait in the relative cool of the building. As I entered, the man who had assisted us a few days before beckoned me into his office. He immediately handed me both passports and said goodbye, so I checked the details and all seemed to be in order. Outside I looked around again for Rob, who still wasn't in sight, so I returned to BlueBelle. He would surely see her and find me.

It was well after 11.00 before Rob arrived. He had taken the motorway route and hit traffic. As I handed him his passport he was thoroughly shocked that they had given me *his* too, but I reminded him that, despite missing the appointed time, he now had both his passport *and* his visa, so what was the problem? He, however, could not reconcile himself with this turn of events. "TIA!" was my response.

While we were travelling together people frequently assumed that we were a couple. This seemed to horrify five-years-younger Rob and he spent a lot of time explaining to people who we would undoubtedly never meet again that we were not 'together'. I think the fact that the embassy had just assumed he was my partner probably horrified him more than anything else!

I had two things on my to-do list for the day. One was to find a replacement converter for my solar charger (although I didn't hold out much hope), and the other was to visit the Museum of Black Civilisations which had opened just weeks before. Rob was originally going to leave the city once he had his passport, but on hearing my plans he decided he wanted to see the museum too and offered to help seek out my converter.

I asked some locals and we were directed to a long street jam-packed with electrical, mobile phone, computer and technology shops. We decided to trawl the street and meet at a fuel station midway, Rob being able to get through the traffic on his bike a lot faster than I could in my van. I tried a couple of shops I spotted along the way, but they only had very large or heavy units and I was starting to feel a little despondent. At the fuel station Rob said he would check a shop across the road. He went in, re-emerged a short while later and then disappeared around the corner, returning after some minutes with a perfect converter! It was quite reasonably priced so I snapped it up, pleased as punch and very grateful for his help.

At the Museum of Black Civilisations[32] I asked if we might park in their courtyard and the guard was very obliging. The museum had opened just a few weeks before and was constructed on a large patch of ground with a theatre at the other end. Both were grand, modern-looking buildings and very eye-catching, with the museum's curves apparently recalling the architectural styles of traditional homes typical to southern Senegal. Entry was free. The museum aimed to showcase 'black' or sub-Saharan Africa, chronicling the history, art and culture of the entire region – which it must be said is as immense as their ambition. In the press statement I had read about the opening, Dakar was setting itself to be the cultural capital of the region.

I valued the fact that such an undertaking had been started. Promoting and raising awareness of the rich pre-colonial history and cultures of Africa is integral to a better future. This exhibition, however, was all in French, so it automatically excluded the majority of potential English-speaking visitors who are the continent's larger contingent, and thus sadly it did not feel truly pan-African. The museum contained various artefacts from a number of the sub-Saharan countries but was far from comprehensive and to me lacked details of the incredible African history I so passionately sought. I had hoped to be viewing some

---

[32] www.mcn.sn

of the great pieces I had seen in European museums; even the incredible Natural History Museum[33]in my home town of Bulawayo was a shining example of how to display local history and culture. I confess, here in Dakar, to being torn between admiration and disappointment. Nonetheless it is a start, I hope with time it will improve, I would still recommend it. The art section in particular exhibited some of Africa's wonderful talent, bold and colourful and representative of her vibrant peoples.

After an hour and a half we had completed the tour and, with my leg painfully throbbing, we returned to the courtyard. I checked my phone and saw a message from Mary in The Gambia, my next stop after leaving Senegal. We had connected via a Facebook group and she had invited me to park up at her home there. While Rob was checking his bike and I was waiting to say goodbye to him, I decided to call her. During our chat I mentioned the state of my leg: it was looking and feeling grim, and Mary recommended that I should have it seen at the hospital in Dakar because this would be better equipped than the one in The Gambia. Rob finished his bike inspection and was keen to get going, so we said our farewells and he headed off further along the coast while I went off to find the hospital.

The streets were full and I had to park several blocks away before I finally found a spot, so slightly nervously I secured BlueBelle and limped off to the emergency area. I wasn't at all sure where to enter but a kind man escorted me to *Urgences*.[34] I eventually found myself in a small office with someone who spoke only French, but he understood well enough when I took off my bandage and revealed a wound that was not looking at all healthy. The burn, despite all my attention to keep it clean and tended, had not responded well and was now angry and weeping.

I was instructed to wait for another doctor, and while doing so three members of staff thought I would make good sport for their afternoon entertainment. They spoke in French and the local dialect, Wolof, and although I did not understand all their ridicule (which appeared to be primarily for not speaking French), being a student of non-verbal communication I quite clearly got the

---

[33] www.facebook.com/naturalhistorymuseumzimbabwe
[34] Accident and emergency/ER

message. I responded simply by smiling and saying to them, "You can make fun of me as much as you like, I'm just here to get my leg fixed." Sadly, ignorant people can be found everywhere.

I was briefly seen to by a doctor who directed me to go 'over there' for attention. I had no idea where 'there' was and asked, but his brusque response prevented further enquiry from me. Luckily a nearby guard came to my rescue and offered to escort me. I joined a queue and when I got to the front realised that I needed to pay before I could receive treatment. The woman at the window babbled something at me really fast and there was no hope that I could understand her French, so I begged her pardon and asked her to repeat it slowly. She gathered that I was English-speaking because I understood the response quite clearly: "English! You don't speak French?!" I smiled and apologised again but she merely scoffed and said something that the tone indicated was rude. She thrust a piece of paper at me and waved me to the next window, where I would have to pay. At this window the mood was the same, and I received my receipt and was again waved in a general 'over there' direction. The queue was pressing me on so I asked another guard outside where I should go, but his response was also 'there'. Did no one understand that I had no idea where 'there' was?!

I eventually found my way to a small waiting-room with several people in it. One man had severe burns on most of his arms and head, another was lying on the bench moaning in pain and in the corner was a woman looking particularly miserable. I considered that the chance of being seen quickly was unlikely.

Happily though my wait was short and I was directed into a side room where a young woman took off my bandage and inspected my leg. She was Moroccan, very kind, and doing an internship at the hospital assisting the duty doctor. She spoke English and we enjoyed a chat about her country. When the doctor did arrive he inspected my leg, although I'm not sure he noticed *me* at all as he neither greeted me nor spoke to me before proceeding to write a prescription for bandages, antiseptic and a tetanus shot. The young intern informed me that I would need to purchase the items and return with them before I could be treated.

My tetanus was still valid and I assured them of this, but the doctor was having none of it. He sternly told me that I needed an injection as he thrust the script into my hands and packed me off to the pharmacy. Again the directions were not evident and it was more by good luck than good judgement that I eventually stumbled upon it.

The woman behind the window looked at the script, shoved it back at me and directed me to another window a block further along (which did not say *Pharmacy*). Despite my polite smile and greeting, the man behind this open window grunted at me and rattled something off, again too fast for me to understand. I apologised and asked him to repeat it slowly, at which he also took it upon himself to berate me for not speaking French and further asked me why I did not speak the local language, Wolof. By now I was sore, tired, hot and losing my patience: it had been over three hours since arriving at the hospital and I'd had enough of the rude and unfriendly attitudes. In rapid-fire English I responded, "No I *don't* speak French but I'm *trying* to communicate and certainly I don't speak Wolof either because no one in the entire world speaks Wolof except the people here and how would that be of any use to me when I get to Zimbabwe?!" I'm sure he didn't understand most of it, but he surely understood my tone and the flash of my angry blue eyes. At this point he refused to assist me at all and directed me to get what I needed at the pharmacy on the street outside. Now I really was mad! In language that was neither French nor Wolof, I told him to do rude things to himself, snatched back the script and left.

I limped out of the hospital grounds to find the pharmacy I had passed on my way in. On the way there I gave thought to the fact that if the only thing the doctor was going to do was clean the wound and bandage it, I could do it myself; I was not prepared to return to that ill-mannered place. I was by now even more angry, hot, tired, sore and frustrated, and when the woman at the pharmacy enquired what I needed I immediately burst into tears. She was kind and spoke English and I managed to briefly outline how rudely I had been treated, grateful for a friendly face at last. When she relayed the story to the other pharmacists and customers, who were now wondering what on earth had happened to me, they were all horrified and apologised profusely. The pressure was instantly released and I returned to the task at hand.

I bought antiseptic and some extra bandages, knowing that my first aid kit was well enough equipped to manage anything else.

As I shambled back to BlueBelle I decided to leave Dakar immediately and make my way to The Gambia. I'd had quite enough of this area. It was late afternoon and I hadn't given much thought to where I was going, other than the general notion of heading toward the next country on my journey. I just wanted to get out of the city as quickly as possible, so I plotted a route and started driving.

Getting out of Dakar proved not too difficult, but one of the cities further along had me stuck in peak hour traffic right as the sun was setting. I couldn't find a place I would consider safe enough to park overnight, and so my options were to stop in an uncertain area or to keep driving in the dark until I found somewhere suitable.

I truly did not like driving in the dark. In my right-hand-drive van I was on the wrong side for the oncoming headlights, which always seemed to shine directly at me. I used a trick I'd used before, which was to find a large vehicle such as a bus or truck that would block the worst of the oncoming lights, and then, if they were driving steadily, I would hang behind them just close enough to avoid being blinded.

I kept asking the Universe to deliver a good parking spot. By 9.00pm I was giving up hope, but at least the traffic had calmed. My route told me I had to turn off the main road, and as I slowed down to turn I heard singing coming from a church on the corner. Churches were often good places to park, but although I looked carefully I could see no parking area around (probably because few of the parishioners owned cars and so would mostly walk). I did see a low wall with a slight indent, giving me protection to the side and partly behind. It felt right and I quickly reversed into the space. I was off the road and I hoped close enough to the church to put the fear of God into anyone with dubious intentions; and BlueBelle's stealth hue would do the rest since there were no street lights. Once settled, I fell into a much-needed sleep.

At first light I was up, feeling quite refreshed, and on my way before the locals appeared to start their day. The morning was crisp and clear and as I crossed a wetland I was treated to a glorious sunrise, with the still water reflecting the fluffy white clouds and the morning light changing like a prism from inky lilac to dark orange to golden yellow, before tentatively revealing the bright blue sky as the sun quickly rose. I opened the window and took a deep breath of fresh African air: I was feeling relieved to be out of the city and back in the beautiful countryside.

Before long I had reached my first ferry crossing of the day, over the Saloum River at Foundiougne. I joined a queue of taxi buses piled high with goods precariously tied on to their rooftops. Only one of the three ferries was working so I could do nothing but wait. I welcomed the opportunity to go for a walk and watch the brightly painted carved wooden fishing boats being paddled on the river, as they had done for millennia, with the early morning light gleaming across the water through a sprinkling of stark white clouds. I know that many people scorn this ancient way of life, but on hearing the loud happy voices and deep laughter of the people, I couldn't help but think that I would much rather be here than in the stifling morning commute to work in any European city.

It was impossible not to notice a big new factory on the side of the river bank with several Chinese people wandering around inside a high-fenced yard. I wondered what they were there for. Their presence was usually indicative of some commodity they were harvesting, and I later believed this to be a fish processing factory, such as the one I would soon learn was devastating the local fishing economy in The Gambia.

Boarding the ferry was hair-raising and meant driving over loose, uneven metal plates that bridged the gap between the ferry and the dock and made a loud clanging noise as I passed on to the deck. I smiled and waved at the staff who looked at me with shock to see a lone woman driving a van, where here too only men were around. We were loaded up tightly packed together, BlueBelle looking decidedly small next to the top-heavy fully-loaded vehicles all around her.

A crew member approached me with a life jacket, thrust it into my hands and indicated that I must put it on. I was still in European 'Health and Safety' mode: when you are given a life jacket, you must don it without question. I naively believed that everyone else would be doing the same, but it was only after leaving the dock that I looked about me and noticed that I was the *only* person wearing a life jacket… yet there was an unused pile of them under the nearby stairs. I had no idea if they considered that I needed the extra safety measure because of my age, that every precaution should be taken with any international visitor, or that perhaps I just looked like I couldn't swim.

After disembarking I continued to the border, where I was immediately mobbed by the usual fixers, money-changers and SIM card sellers. I had enough trouble remembering everything I needed to do while keeping an eye on my keys, papers, bag and so on, but with a crowd around me I knew that I was more vulnerable – especially being alone. With my confidence growing at every stage of my journey, I now gathered my things and, before winding up my window, informed the mob that everyone should move away from the door. As I got out I waved everyone away and told them I would deal with each of them after I had taken care of my papers. I wouldn't be rushed or harried so most wafted off to the next opportunity. The empowerment felt good!

A young man who had originally offered to change my money decided instead that the fastest way to get my attention was to help me. He directed me to immigration, which was remarkably swift and painless, and then to customs for the van, again expedited in very little time… and suddenly I was free to leave. I returned to BlueBelle and, as good as my word, dealt with each person in turn by politely declining all their services.

Chapter Four – The Gambia

12 January 2019

Passing through a simple barrier, within twenty metres I was in The Republic of The Gambia – and speaking English!

I had fallen into the routine of greeting everyone in the vicinity with a smile and a "Good Morning, Hello, Bonjour!" – whatever was appropriate. This immediately helped people see me as friendly and the response was almost always warm. I was often drawn into conversation and in the 'normal' course of life it might have felt like wasting time, but I loved these encounters. This was, after all, one of the reasons for driving: to have the opportunity to engage with local people. Africans also tend to laugh freely and loudly and I found myself fitting back in with ease.

The Gambia, the smallest country within mainland Africa, is bordered on three sides by Senegal and is situated on both sides of the lower reaches of its namesake, the great Gambia River. It is less than forty-eight kilometres at its widest point and has a coastal region on the Atlantic where the river meets the sea. The country has a population of approximately two and a half million. The Gambia River originates in Guinea and is one of the most navigable rivers in West Africa, and as such has long been the source of trade and fishing, the primary occupation and food source for locals. I was to learn that a Chinese fishmeal factory on the river had devastated the local fishing industry because they use huge nets, as they do elsewhere, to scoop up every conceivable fish. As with most Chinese projects, the companies bring all their skills and experience with them and only employ locals for the menial tasks, thereby adding little lasting value to the regional economy since they take whatever they need and then ship it to China for further processing.

I would see this trend throughout Africa, whether it was mining, forestry or fishing: all the continent's natural resources are being pillaged. It is surely the fault of short-sighted, mismanaged, greedy and corrupt governments, who are filling their own pockets and flagrantly selling out not only their people and nature but also the future generations who will reap the bitter harvest. The allure of Chinese money turns African politicians into a semblance of the three monkeys: deaf, dumb, and blind to any consequences.

At the border post a rotund official took it upon himself to 'look after' me, and in hindsight I think he did so to make me pay for a visa that I didn't need. I should not have doubted myself. I eventually learnt that asking for receipts was a good way to tell if I was being taken for a ride or not, but in this case I trusted the man helping me because he was in uniform. Another lesson learnt along the way...

I left the border and was on my way to the ferry that would cross the Gambia River and take me to the city when I came to the usual police checkpoint. A portly officer checked my papers and advised me to buy my ticket before arriving at the ferry port, and then told me he could arrange one. I had read somewhere that the ferry could be a crush of people and vehicles so I entertained his offer. He gave me a price that seemed rather steep and I reluctantly agreed. He then suggested that I drive him back the way I'd come, but there was something about the man that I did not trust and, policeman or not, I was not putting him in BlueBelle. I told him I would sort it out myself, but Officer Fatty hastily assured me not to worry, he would organise it. Still highly dubious I parked to the side and watched him flag down a taxi.

Whilst he was gone I took it upon myself to investigate the price of the ticket and, as I had expected, it was considerably less than he had quoted. I had only given him half the money he had demanded – which was still more than the ticket price – so I figured that this would settle the matter. By the time he returned I was a touch tetchy about being ripped off, but also cognisant that he was a police officer who could give me trouble further down the road. I thanked him, took the ticket and looked at it, but I could not discern a value on it. I showed him my findings on prices of tickets and told him that I wasn't a fool: I would take the ticket, he could keep the extra money I had already paid him and that would be that. But he then had the audacity to ask for *more* money for his time and trouble (and the taxi fare, which I was certain he didn't pay for), so I told him either he could refund me the whole amount or we would consider it a deal. As with most conmen, he then tried to redeem himself as honourable and said he would grant me this 'favour', and of course he was happy to help me. I smiled politely, said goodbye and drove off, happy that I was learning to trust my instincts with these wily officials.

At the ferry port I did indeed encounter the anticipated mayhem, and once again only one ferry was running so the queues were endless. However, this ferry was much larger. My leg was hurting and the heat and humidity were not helping matters. I joined the queue, trying to ascertain what I needed to do and where I should go before getting out of my van. Within minutes a man came to my window offering to help, and since I was in English-speaking territory, communication was so much easier. I smiled and thanked him, but I was fine.

The man insisted that he would help me and I sensed something was going on, so I was wary but still pleasant and polite. I felt that Officer Fatty was somehow connected to this guy and, sure enough, he gave himself away by calling me Dot before I had introduced myself! Nonetheless opportunity was a two-way street, so I asked Mr Helper where I needed to go. He told me to wait and within moments someone was at my side, checking my ticket and wanting to inspect my vehicle. By now Mr Helper had some friends hanging around him, so I locked my driver's door and went to open the side door, upon which one of the friends said, "You are safe here, you don't have to worry about locking." Of course I knew then that I *did* have to worry, so I cheerfully responded, "I'm an old woman and it's a habit. I'm sure you would agree it is always better to be safe than sorry." This quite disarmed him. The brief inspection done, I was put in another queue and told I would be on the next ferry. Well, so far so good. Perhaps Officer Fatty was being helpful after all.

I found the people of The Gambia very friendly. They understand the value of tourism there, but with the prolific sex-trade in the country they did seem to think that every single man or woman was obviously 'looking for a good time'. When travelling through the country I steered clear of the beaches where most of the illicit activity took place. I was getting enough attention already and was tired of fending off the constant propositions.

The wait for the ferry was going to be a while, so I employed Mr Helper to go and find me a SIM card. When he returned I put it in my phone and ensured it was all working before I paid for it, and now at least I had data. I also tipped him a small amount and he set off to find more generous prey. So far it had paid off to get my ferry ticket early, despite the higher price. I hadn't had to move away from BlueBelle, who was always my first priority, and nor did I have to compete in long and disorderly queues.

In front of me was a taxi van, as usual fully loaded on top and inside likely to be twice the number of people than it should carry. With it being so hot, some passengers were standing outside it. I had noticed that the women were dressed in tight, bright, colourful and immaculate dresses, often with a matching headpiece, whereas I was gloriously attired in my oversized khaki shorts and t-shirt, dripping with sweat, a bandage on my leg and looking quite dishevelled.

When we needed to move forward in anticipation of the ferry's arrival, I saw that all the passengers had started pushing the taxi, which seemed to be having some battery or starter issue. As it came to boarding I saw that the ferry's ramp was at a slight incline, causing a problem for the people pushing the van. They clearly needed more manpower, and while I had until now just been watching, I suddenly realised that I too could be helping. I jumped out, locked the van and took position to push. The looks were incredulous, but I smiled broadly and said, "Let's get going!" ARA 4 : DB 1

TENDING THE LEG

The ferry delays had cost me time and once again I was annoyed to find myself driving at sunset, trying to find the campsite where I had chosen to stop. If I'd been earlier I would have gone to find Mary, but it was late and so I opted for the more impersonal accommodation. The sign for the campsite had seen better days and driving back and forth in the dark I kept missing it, and on top of this one person had directed me to entirely the wrong place. Nevertheless it was a welcome sight of order and tidiness that greeted me upon my entrance when I did finally reach the camp. In the morning I saw numerous pieces of paper stuck to walls and doors about what was permitted and what was not: it turned out the owners were originally from Germany!

When I'd left Dakar I had been tending my leg twice a day, but it wasn't healing. I decided that I would need to stop and give it closer attention until it improved, lest I risk a serious infection which would cost me more in money and time. I hoped that I could make that stop at Mary's house and I left camp to find her. By now I had become accustomed to the fact that the main roads were tarmac and the side roads were all dirt and/or sand, but I was becoming less afraid of the sand roads as I learnt how to handle them better.

Mary hailed from Australia and was very much into West African music. She had hurt her knee hours before my arrival and was barely able to walk, although she didn't think she needed medical attention. I soon learnt that her personal life and relationships probably did need some attention, with two Guinean ex-husbands, one who was living with her and not at all in good health, the second who had made a baby with a neighbour, and a third local Guinean man, Lamin, who was intent on becoming her next husband. I didn't care about her personal life, but I was quickly getting the gist that she was a woman with issues. Amidst all of this she was, according to her, running a business managing musicians to ensure that they were paid properly for their gigs, since local performers tended to receive poor remuneration from hotels and event organisers.

When I arrived mid-morning I hadn't yet eaten. Mary suggested that her friend Lamin go and buy breakfast, so I gave him money to get everyone something from a local street seller. I had no idea what might come back, but I figured with breakfast he couldn't go too far wrong. When he returned I was given a short baguette with several round things on it in some sauce, and was told that the contents of the roll consisted of mashed cooked beans rolled into small balls and deep-fried, covered with an onion and chilli relish. At first I was quite dismayed by what I saw, but I confess that, while I'm not sure it had much nutritional value, I quite enjoyed it!

We spent the day at Mary's home: she was nursing her leg and I too was now nursing mine. BlueBelle was parked outside in the dusty street in the full sun and had to remain there because she was too high to park in Mary's garden with its low-hanging trees. This was not ideal for me as a hot BlueBelle makes for a hot bed and I would be spending the night in the street, which meant keeping my doors closed.

I was sitting with Mary when I received a cryptic message from Rob, in Dutch, saying the equivalent of "Bloody bank!" I asked him what was up and eventually he replied that he was having issues accessing money. His bank was offline and he was trying to transfer to himself via Western Union, as I had done in Dakar. His message showed me that he was in quite a state and in desperate need of funds, with which I naturally empathised, knowing how I had felt in a similar situation. I asked if it would help if I sent him some money, and with obvious relief he replied that it would and he would repay me as soon as he could access his bank.

I sent the money and forwarded a screenshot of the payment and the associated fees so that he could refund me appropriately. He organised the refund the next day but failed to repay the fees, which rather annoyed me. I tried to make light of it and sent him a message pointing out his oversight and that he owed me several beers to make up for it, to which I received neither apology nor response.

That night I bought dinner for everyone in the house. Mary's leg was no better and I convinced her to let me take her to the hospital in the morning. She vacillated about going because she was learning to play the *kora*, a complex twenty-four-stringed West African instrument, and was due for a lesson in the morning; but I felt it was essential she get treatment. I told her it would be best to get to the hospital early in the morning rather than waiting until midday (added to the fact that driving about in the heat of the day in a city wasn't my favourite activity), to which she eventually agreed. I retired to BlueBelle parked in the street and listened to the sounds of drumming and singing well into the early hours.

I woke before sunrise and the street was silent. As the sun rose at around 7.30 I saw the odd person walk by, but then, as if by some pre-arranged plan, on the dot of 8.00 it seemed that every door, gate and garage opened and all the adults and children poured out into the street. The African people are not known for their quiet conversations and the air was suddenly filled with the sounds of chattering and laughing, shouted greetings across the street and children giggling. The day had begun and I smiled to myself, sitting in bed in BlueBelle, drinking my lemon and honey and watching the world go by.

By 9.00 I had everything battened down and went to see if Mary was ready to leave for the hospital, however she had meanwhile decided that it would be impolite to put off her teacher and so had decided to go for her lesson instead. I was annoyed on several levels but breathed deeply and told her that I would be in BlueBelle when she was ready.

Eventually, just before midday, we departed for the hospital – which turned out to be some considerable distance away. When we arrived I had luck on my side as there was a parking spot not far from the entrance. I supported Mary inside, through the triage queue and on to another waiting area. This all took a couple of hours, so it was then well past lunchtime and I was hot, hungry and thirsty. I offered to go to the street to find some food. It would be a good distraction from all the complaining and martyrish behaviour that Mary was demonstrating.

In the street I found a woman with large pots of food, a common sight throughout West Africa, and I felt confident about choosing her as several men were waiting to be served. I'd learnt throughout my travels that if the locals frequented a place, then it was usually a good bet. I didn't know what I was buying as I had no idea what the local dishes were, but I was recommended a fish dish made with palm oil and served with rice. The men I had been chatting to while I waited had proposed it and I reckoned that if it was local then Mary was sure to be okay with it. I bought some bottles of cold water too and returned to the hospital.

Mary was still in the queue, speaking to a large man with dreadlocks in typical Rastafarian head gear. His name was Respect, a name he quite lived up to with his gentle manner and deep bass voice. He had been hit by a car the day before but hadn't been seen as the queue had been too long, so he was back now for treatment. I gave Mary the food and the water, but as soon as she opened the container she began complaining… and complained, and complained, until I got so annoyed that I told her I was happy to give it to someone else if she didn't like it. Her response was to grudgingly start eating. My patience was wearing thin and with the humidity and heat my leg was throbbing, telling me that I should be somewhere cooler, resting it and changing the dressing.

While I waited I couldn't help but notice that people came to the hospital as they would to a picnic: entire families arrived, bringing with them food and drink and laying out blankets in the grounds. They were well-versed in the amount of waiting required.

At the end of the afternoon Mary was eventually seen. She argued with the staff about what the issue was and the quality of her care, which was of course limited by a lack of resources. They advised her that she had torn a meniscus in her knee and should keep it immobilised for two weeks. They applied a large instant plaster splint and told her to give it a while to set, and I went off to fetch the van while she was wheeled to the exit.

By the time we got home she had almost entirely removed the splint because she said it was uncomfortable. By now I felt like I had wasted the entire day and I was very cross with her, so I dropped her off in the company of her various men and told her I was going back to the German campsite. My leg was now extremely sore and the wound oozing and I needed to spend time tending to it, which I did not want to do in the dusty street outside. I left with no thanks for my time, effort, fuel, cost or trouble.

I returned to the campsite where all was quiet, bar a French couple who I had been parked next to the day before. It had been ten days and the burn was getting worse, not better, so it was time to be sensible and not delay self-care any further. I promised myself that I would remain at the campsite until my leg started to heal properly, realising that if I did not stop and give it all my attention I would certainly regret it.

I didn't have any antibiotics in my first aid kit and I had already seen the state of the local hospital, so I had to come up with a plan. My nephew had made me several litres of colloidal silver to take on my journey. I had experienced the benefit of this after cutting my leg in Barcelona, and treating the gash with the 'silver water' had healed it beautifully.

This recent wound was about eight centimetres wide and five high, and to ensure that the area was as clean as possible I had to start by carefully picking off with my tweezers all the dead skin cells that were the cause of the infection. I then introduced hydrogen peroxide, an antiseptic, and finally some iodine; I pretty much threw everything I could at it. Finally I wet the wound well and some gauze with the colloidal silver and put on a bandage it to secure it. Over the next few days I regularly spritzed the gauze with the silver water to keep it moist.

It seemed counterintuitive to keep a burn wet, but nothing else had helped so I committed to this. Determinedly I tended to the wound and after three days it had stopped oozing and was definitely improving. I then started adding aloe vera to the final dressing to accelerate the cell regeneration. By day five the wound was starting to close up and, best of all, because I was using the 'colloidal silver cure' there was no scab. I find wounds heal much more cleanly using it.

A couple of nights into my enforced stop, I heard the distinctive sound of Rob's motorbike drive into the camp. When he saw me he expressed surprise that I was there, but I was surprised that *he* was surprised since I'd told him where I was a few days earlier when he messaged to reimburse me! He set up camp a bit further along from BlueBelle. I kept to myself as I knew he thought that I was romantically interested in him, and I was intent on clarifying that notion.

One evening I went to the camp restaurant for a cold beer and found Rob and three other Dutch guys already a few sheets to the wind. They were complaining loudly, and when I asked what the issue was it was evident that they required more beer but the lady serving was nowhere to be found. I informed them that the lady on duty was Fatou and if she wasn't at the counter she would be in the compound just behind the restaurant building – but, "Not to worry boys, I will call her for you." On hearing my call she was there in no time, but at the sight of her one of the 'boys' immediately demanded rudely, "Three beers!" I was taken aback. Perhaps this was acceptable in their local bar, but here it was downright rude. I corrected him: "It is 'Three beers, *please*'. You may be in Africa, but that's no reason to forget your manners!" I don't think they liked me so much after that, but Fatou had the hint of a satisfied smile on her face that was unmistakable.

The local beer, Jul, was very pleasant to a not-really-beer-drinker like me, so I ordered one and told Fatou to add it to Rob's tab. When he objected I reminded him that he owed me at least five of them in return for the Western Union fee he had failed to repay, but the response was muttered and ungenerous. I decided I would just have the one and not seek further recompense from him as it seemed to aggrieve him so much to honour his debt. It was a stark reminder to be more cautious about who I helped.

I broke a tooth just after arriving but managed to get the names of a couple of dentists. Luckily one of them was able to fit me in the next day and I found the practice in a nice office block. But when I entered I could barely hear the receptionist because the sound system was blaring out gospel songs. I managed to shout out that I had an emergency appointment and was instructed to take a seat, but after thirty minutes no one had moved and my head was starting to hurt from too much fire and brimstone preaching, interspersed with gospel music at decibels that were surely illegal. When I approached the receptionist and asked how much longer the dentist would be he didn't seem to know, but after expressing my displeasure and sitting back down with a scowl I saw him go to enquire. Not long after that, a woman who seemed to be midway through her treatment was thrust out of the consulting room into the reception area and I was permitted to enter.

The dentist was a tall, slim, bald man dressed in whites that looked more reminiscent of Muslim attire than Christian. He gave me a friendly greeting, inspected my broken tooth and announced that I would need root canal work. This was definitely overkill and I told him clearly that I did *not* need a root canal, just a filling. To be sure he understood, I added that I was only passing through and would not have time, or money, for such work.

He remained insistent until I asked how much the root canal would be and I gasped out loud at the cost. No, I told him clearly, I did not have that kind of money. I was driving to Zimbabwe and I would rather spend that on educating girls! At this point he started telling me all about his philanthropic work and then asked me if I was a Christian. (How was I to answer that without lying?) "I am a God-fearing person," I replied. This satisfied him sufficiently that he said he would do my filling free of charge! I now felt bad and offered to pay, but he still declined and gave me a temporary filling which lasted until I got to Namibia. The Universe did work in mysterious ways…

My route back to the campsite in Serrakunda, a sprawling urbanisation with a rich tourist sector around the beach but shockingly poor everywhere else, took me through the 'real' city. As I drove along I was assailed by the most disgusting smell. It came from an enormous open dump and there were dozens of people, mostly children, picking through the trash, and cattle wandering about eating heaven only knows what. It was deplorable and I was dismayed why nothing was being done to resolve this. I could only imagine how much of it was ending up in the beautiful blue ocean just a few hundred metres away.

On my last night at the camp I decided to treat myself to a restaurant-cooked meal. It was my second favourite time of the day, the late afternoon/early evening, and the street I was walking down to reach the main road and the restaurant was like all side streets with red dust, gouged and grooved. It was busy with people walking home from a day's work and women sitting around their fires cooking dinner next to the dusty roadside. One looked up at me. I smiled and she waved while the others peered at me suspiciously.

As I passed a patch of green (rare here) I heard the early evening crickets summoning the night, that little bit of nature that would not be suppressed despite the surrounding urbanisation. I turned on to the main road where a metalworker was busy forging a gate, the clanging of the metal mingling with the sounds of a carpenter sanding a piece of wood by hand while he sat on a magnificently carved bed frame, one of many displayed on the roadside. The background music was provided by the constant stream of taxi buses and motorcycles hooting and beeping whilst weaving in and out of each other, stopping and dropping or picking up, creating a chaotic pattern. From the taxi buses there was always some young fellow hanging perilously out of the side door, shouting out a destination and waving at passers-by to find one more customer to squeeze into a van already bursting at the seams.

An old man on a cart pulled by a sad donkey clip-clopped past me carrying bags of who-knows-what to who-knows-where. Every now and again I would see a cluster of schoolchildren shouting and laughing, dancing and jumping on their way home. As I continued down the road I heard a sports commentary belting out of a small shop doorway. It seemed to be coming from a radio and the tiny space inside was filled with men laughing and shouting encouragement. The street traders sitting under sun-worn umbrellas were selling phone credit, vegetables or sweets, their smiles always bright in response to mine.

Two men ahead of me were shouting at each other and it was escalating: one hit the other in the face and then picked up a rock, obviously meaning to throw it. I was unsure whether or not I should intervene, but as I was considering doing so I noticed that locals were shouting at them and several men were walking towards the fighters to dissuade them from further fury. The community aspect of African society means that people will get involved in such a situation here, whereas too often in the Western world they would merely walk on by.

I eventually reached the restaurant, The Kingfisher,[35] which had come recommended and was run by an excellent chef and his wife. Their background story interested me. Many years before, a British couple had come to The Gambia and forged a strong friendship with a local family. The couple, Paul and Heather, returned every year and helped the family with the education of their children, and one of those children had gone to catering college in England and become a chef. It was he who was now producing delicious meals here at The Kingfisher.

Paul and Heather were here now and while I was sitting chatting to them on the restaurant terrace and enjoying a cold Jul beer, Rob appeared. We all greeted him but I didn't encourage him to join us. Shortly after this I ordered my meal and left the couple to go and find a table to sit and eat, but the few they had were all taken and there was nowhere else to sit but with Rob. Karma gave me some instant feedback for my rudeness and I had no choice but to ask if I could join him.

Our conversation was pleasant enough and the meal delicious. As we walked back to the campsite together he asked my advice about how to resolve a situation. When he was at the

[35] www.facebook.com/pages/category/Restaurant/The-Kingfisher-Bar-Restaurant-1598557143753521/

border he had, once again, run out of money and then didn't have sufficient funds for the ferry, at which point a local man had given him the necessary fare. Now Rob wanted not only to repay him but also to give him a gift, but he wasn't certain what would be suitable. I gave him my opinion and he snapped at me, saying it was a ridiculous idea; it seemed he had already made up his mind. Yet I noticed some days later on his social media that he had done exactly what I'd recommended.

I was done with his kind of crazy in my life. The next day, with my leg on the mend and having accomplished my objective, I said farewell and hoped that I would not be seeing Rob again further down the road.

MANGROVES OF THE GAMBIA RIVER

I had discovered a community initiative on the banks of the Gambia River surrounded by mangroves, and since I'd never seen mangroves before, I was intrigued. As I drove out of town I noticed the extreme poverty of the country, with donkey and cart being the primary mode of transportation outside the city, large trucks dashing their way around and the occasional dead donkey at the roadside being feasted on by wakes of vultures.

On my way to the Tumani Tenda Eco-Tourism initiative,[36] I was abruptly brought to a halt by a policeman remonstrating loudly at me as I passed. It seemed I had overlooked a police check, so I reversed back to him. The burly officer asked me in a stern voice why I had driven past without stopping, so I apologised and said that I had not seen him or the 'police station' (to be honest, the well-worn building was not one of note). He asked where I was going but I couldn't remember the name and I didn't want to take out my phone to find it; I like to keep my profile low. I did the best I could to pronounce what I recalled the community to be and he gave me an entirely different name, but I didn't think it worth the debate so I nodded: yes, that was the place. He asked, "What do you have for me today?" I still had calendar cards so I offered them out and some of his colleagues also took one. He then suggested, "Coffee would be nice too."

---

[36] www.tumanitenda.co.uk

(Right, like I'm just going to stop on the side of the road here and make you all a cup of coffee because I'm a mobile restaurant?!) I smiled sweetly and replied, "I'm very sorry but I was too hot and tired to get groceries before I left town. I'm hoping that they'll give me some food when I get to where I'm going – the food here is very delicious!" He laughed, and when I asked if he would like to see my van papers he replied no, I could go. I drove away but had to ask myself what that stop was for. Was it just to see if he could get something? Certainly there was no other reason that I could discern.

Shortly after that I turned off the road towards the eco-camp and drove down a dusty track through what seemed to be a village, with a few huts and a large number of big leafy mango trees, providing not only cool shade but undoubtedly in the season a plethora of lovely juicy fruit. I passed a school complex; I loved seeing that children were receiving an education! The end of the road was announced by a view of the river and the camp, and since there were no demarcated areas I parked under a mango tree that would afford me good shade and a beautiful view of the river and the mangroves.

There was a large construction, square in shape with a half-metre high wall around it and pillars at regular intervals to support the thatched roof, leaving the majority of the sides open. In the intense heat I could only imagine that closed spaces would also be hot spaces. Between the pillars there were several hammocks and the inner circle was furnished with benches and a bar area. This was the social and gathering space for locals and visitors. As I approached I saw weathered fishermen repairing fishing nets and women sewing, all seated around an old sewing machine.

I was greeted by a friendly woman in a colourful long tight dress and a headdress of wrapped fabric, as was common throughout West Africa. She introduced herself as the person in charge and apprised me of what was available in terms of meals and tours. I had my mind set on a dugout river tour of the mangroves: it would be all I could manage on my budget, but when would I ever get to do such a thing again?! I was introduced to my tour guide, Alim, who would later that afternoon take me out on the river.

I am not a water baby. I like my feet, or tyres, firmly planted on the ground, so going out on water always makes me a little nervous. I was also worried that I might be carried away by the anticipated swarms of mosquitoes, so despite the heat and humidity I covered up well with closed shoes, full-length jeans and a vest covered by a flimsy long-sleeved top. With my guide in just a pair of shorts and a vest I must have looked ridiculous, nevertheless I wasn't taking any chances.

I was seated in a dugout canoe that must have been quite old because it had chunks missing from the front, and it was clear to see that it had been carefully constructed out of a single tree. My guide pushed us out on to the river and I must admit I felt a thrill at being on the slow-flowing current. There was something about being in a dugout on a great river that afforded a completely different view of the world.

I picked up one of the paddles and offered to help out Alim, who seemed surprised, but I had found the feeling of gliding through the water and directing my way quite blissful; plus I like to be in the driver's seat! It was late afternoon when we paddled away from the camp towards the mangroves. From afar they looked like shrubs with their feet in the water, but on closer viewing I could see the tangled roots more clearly. There was an eerie feeling about them, as though they had legs and could walk away at any time.

My guide pointed out the oysters that attached themselves to the mangroves and thrived there. They were picked at low tide (meaning there was no need to cut the mangrove roots) and usually boiled several times before they were ready to eat. The shells were collected in a mound and eventually ground into a paste, which I was informed was used for decorating homes.

While we drifted amongst the mangroves it was evident that this was an important eco-system not only for fish and shellfish but for birds too. I saw many of them flying across the waterway before me and heard their songs as I drifted by on the calm channel. I was delighted beyond words to see a few forest kingfishers, close relatives of the woodland kingfisher I knew from home; and this was also the bird depicted on my favourite Gambian beer, Jul. They are brightly jewelled in the most magnificent azure blues, and when you see them you just cannot believe the glory of their colours.

There was a magic that lay within the mangroves, with their peculiar shaped roots and thick green foliage forming a natural barrier to the rest of the world, blocking it out and creating a pristine natural space that emanated peace and tranquillity. It was heavenly to experience this calm, disturbed only by the gentle swoosh of our paddles dipping in and out as we glided through the waterways, and my occasional gasps of wonderment.

Alim decided it was time to return and so we navigated our way back towards a glorious African sunset that transformed the blue sky and white clouds as the pinks dissolved into deep red-oranges and then to lilac and purple hues, announcing that it was time for night to descend. As we paddled into the open waterway leading to the camp, the gorgeous sunset was still visible to my left while a full orange moon was rising to my right.

It was the most perfect end to the most perfect outing and I took the time to reflect for a moment. I was happy: the kind of happiness that filled me from the tips of my toes to the top of my head and swelled my heart… and I hadn't felt like that for a very long time. It was evident to me how much nature restored me and how, the further I moved away from it, the more I lost something of myself – perhaps because I forgot I was part of nature too.

I spent much of the next day relaxing under the mango tree, watching the mangroves and contemplating life. Regrettably there was no way to walk the shores of the river as the vegetation was thick on either side, the main transportation being by dugout canoe to the various villages dotted along the river. In the afternoon I went to the social area to buy a cold drink and met a young couple from Ibiza, the Spanish island renowned for its tourism and clubbing. He wore very skimpy shorts and sometimes a thin vest reminiscent of the seventies; she wore a skimpy bikini covered with barely-there shorts and a flowing see-through top. I care little what people wear, but I was dismayed at their blatant disregard for the local culture and customs. The camp's website requested that guests should make themselves at home, but with the only specific limitations being to respect the environment and to be modest in dress within this Muslim community.

After two days in this idyllic place it came time to move on to an eco-village that I had arranged to visit. By morning I was packed and ready to leave but I had not yet heard back from my contact, Sanna, and I didn't want to spend more money at this camp. I decided to wait a while for his message and drove to get a better signal near the main road, where I parked up in the shade of a lush mango tree. A white woman in a car approached me and stopped to ask if I was okay, so we had a chat and she offered that I should join her for the evening. I could park in her yard too. It sounded like a nice idea. She was on her way out but would be back in a few hours if I was happy to wait. I didn't mind at all and it sorted out my indecisiveness.

When she returned I followed her to her home, a modest local house consisting of two round huts adjoined by a central kitchen. She had decorated it in her own style in a mixture of continental European and African. Her name was Annelies and she was a Dutch film producer and actress who spent the winter months in The Gambia and the summer (wet) months in the Netherlands. She shared stories with me of life in The Gambia and her adopted family, which was a sort of mutual adoption since she lives on their property and pays their land taxes and supports their children with education. We enjoyed a very pleasant evening together and I spent a peaceful night in her yard.

ECO VILLAGE

I had been told that Kiang Eco Village was supporting women to be self-sufficient and so I thought it would make an interesting stop. Sanna eventually messaged to finalise arrangements, however there was some confusion and we ended up in different locations. After I'd been waiting three hours, he finally caught up with me and directed me to the village.

I arrived to find that all the ladies had their very best dresses on: I think they thought I was some sort of celebrity! It must be said, though, that the women seemed always to be elegantly attired in bright and colourful full-length dresses, usually quite tightly fitting. I wondered how they managed in the heat to stay so clean and tidy as it was certainly proving a challenge for me. Typical of any African village, the children were drawn to the new and the different like bees to honey and they crowded around BlueBelle and me, delighting in everything that I did. From smiling at them to shaking their hands, it all added to their curiosity about someone living in a van. I was introduced to a great many people that day and I knew I would never remember all those names, but I smiled and thanked them all for welcoming me so warmly.

Within minutes of arriving a baby was thrust into my arms, and I reacted as you do when a ball is thrown at you: the automatic response is to catch it. I cannot recall the last time I held a baby; I tend to avoid them. I don't know what to do with them and certainly changing a nappy would make me flee. In my experience babies, like animals, can usually smell my fear and will start screaming, but this sweet little girl, the latest-born of the village, remained asleep in my arms. It was a great privilege to be given the newest member of the community to hold and I tried to show the proper respect for the honour, whilst simultaneously looking for someone willing to take her off my hands.

They had prepared breakfast for me and, despite it now being almost noon, they went ahead with the meal. I was invited into a small dimly lit room with a tiny window, where I sat with three men on a variety of low stools and we were each given a spoon. Breakfast was served in a single large metal bowl and was some type of semolina with a good helping of milk poured over it. I was not too concerned about sharing the bowl – a common way to eat in West Africa – but the milk… I have an intolerance to all milk products, which set my sinuses off in such a way that within hours I am choking so badly that I find it hard to breathe. It is a dramatic and unpleasant experience.

I was stuck. If I declined the meal it would appear an exceptionally rude gesture, but if I ate it I would have to survive the consequences. In for a penny in for a pound… I took my spoon and, trying to minimise the amount of milk I consumed, ate slowly and in small amounts so as to dupe my hosts, but their constant encouragement to eat more told me they were on to me. There was one upside: they took the baby so that I could eat!

After 'breakfast' I was to be shown the gardens the women had established and was advised to drive behind them so that they could direct me. I told them that if they were walking, I was walking; and besides, BlueBelle would never have made it along the narrow dirt track. I walked several kilometres and deemed the exhaustion I felt fair karma to balance all the sitting and driving I had done thus far. The women frequently commended me for being so strong, yet there were many older than me, doing more labour than I will ever see in my life.

The gardens were impressive, with each woman having an allocated plot within a larger area of rich fertile soil on the river's flood plain. However, whilst their production was good, they were primarily growing the same crops as each other and all the other traders I had seen lining the sides of the roads – tomatoes, onions, and potatoes. The answers they gave to my questions showed a huge enthusiasm to succeed, but they were much in need of practical knowledge about planting, growing and water management, and the business principles of product diversity, meeting market demands and optimising profitability.

Whilst walking around the gardens I was given various produce by the women working in the field, and as my arms filled I was allocated a young girl to carry my loot in a bucket atop her head. In Africa almost everything is carried by women on their heads and obviously the training started young. This girl was no more than about nine, I guessed, and she shyly responded to my grateful thanks for her help.

It was in a conversation about compost that I got the lesson that I was meant to learn there. At one point I noticed a small pile of ash and soil and asked what it was, and their proud response was 'compost'. Surprised, I asked why it was burnt and they replied that they always burnt the compost before they added it to the soil. Whilst not being a gardening expert, I had successfully made my own compost for several years and understood that the process required bacteria and worms to break down the organic material. Whilst adding ash to the mix separately was certainly a good idea, burning the precious earthworms and killing the bacteria seemed ridiculous. I asked them to explain but they just looked at each other confused. No one knew the reason. "This is the way it is done," came the eventual reply.

At this point I told them that it didn't seem right and they needed to check Google for details of how to properly make compost, but again I was met with blank gazes. One of the men reached out with his phone and asked, "Can you tell me how to do that?" …but it was just a mobile phone, not a smartphone. How privileged was I, that I thought everyone had a smartphone and knew how to use Google! It was a humbling exchange and I now had to explain that it couldn't be done on his phone. They told me that a man in the village had a smartphone but the data was costly to them.

And there it was…

The world is truly connected: we can find anything we need to know about anything we choose to pick on Google, but in Africa the majority of people cannot afford to buy a smartphone, let alone the data, both of which are of course necessary to find all the information that would solve so many of their problems. In the rest of the so-called 'civilised' world, we happily discard our old smartphone for the newest latest model without a thought, while the 'dark continent' remains in the dark because they cannot even afford one. In a land where mobiles are plentiful and the primary form of communication, this was an indictment to every single greedy network provider who makes huge profits off the back of each African user, but won't solve the issue of bringing real access to the people.

Soon after that, it became evident that they saw me as someone who might give them the assistance to raise funds or bring them funds to support their community. They had to repair two of their three water pumps; they wanted to extend a section of their land for eco-tourism; and they needed to employ a teacher and buy basic supplies for their local school. This was the plight of many a village in Africa, where there was a willingness to improve their lives but no idea how to self-sustain and grow without the financial support they had come to expect from the rest of the world. I now needed to explain that I had not come with a cheque book to help them, I had come to learn from them, to experience their success; but suddenly I realised that it was I who was teaching them. I felt a bit like an imposter, seemingly there under false pretences – although not of my making. However, I agreed to connect them with people who might be able to give them advice on how they could diversify their crops and optimise their yield.

By the time we'd finished the tour of the gardens and their intended site for an eco-camp it was late afternoon. I was tired and the walk, heat and humidity had all taken their toll. I was mobbed by children and women on my return and used the opportunity to take photographs, which they were all delighted to participate in. I found it was always best to obtain the permission of anyone you wished to photograph in Africa, as without doing so you could find yourself in serious trouble – or, at the very least, a tongue-lashing from an angry subject. There are African cultural and religious reasons for women and children not wanting their photograph taken and it is best to respect these. If the subjects do agree they may in return ask you for money, but it is usually a token and an exchange.

I asked if I might park at the village for the night as it was too late to be finding a camp with sunset on the horizon. I declined their offer of a meal as they had already prepared the special welcome breakfast for me earlier, and with all the gifts I had received it did not feel right to me to further impose myself on this poor community, no matter the honour they were willing to bestow. In Muslim communities any guest is a blessing and must be treated well, regardless of the sacrifice to themselves.

The real challenge for me was all the children who wanted to hang around, look inside the van, chat with me and touch everything. By the end of the day I was a grouchy old woman who was exhausted, hot, sweaty, dusty and unsociable, and all I wanted was to take the bucket of water that I had asked for and wash, then make some coffee and put my feet up. After what I deemed a suitable amount of time socialising I bade them good night and closed my door. I would rather have left it open but the curtain alone wouldn't have stopped their friendly intrusion and I really did want to wash in privacy!

I departed early the next morning, waved off by those who were up; a number of the women were already tending the gardens. I was armed with a list of things I must send them by email: how to make compost, the benefits of moringa,[37] a contact for processing their chillies, the name of an expert for eco-

---

[37] also known as the drumstick tree: www.en.wikipedia.org/wiki/Moringa

growing… it was the least I could do in return for their warm hospitality.

It should be noted that I surprisingly survived the milk I'd consumed without any ill effects. Probably it was fresh from the cow, or perhaps even a goat, but it did lead me to wonder how I had escaped the usual consequences…

My next stop was not far from the village in the grounds of a scout camp. In the dusty parking area under a shady tree, I started organising myself for the next country. I had quite a lot of dirty washing from the previous few days and it was getting in the way. I should add here that it became imperative to ensure that my clothes were the right way round when packing them away: on several mornings I had dressed in the dim light before sunrise and later found myself wearing things inside out!

HOW MANY BORDER POSTS IN A DAY?

I was heading next for the Republic of Guinea – or Guinea (Conakry), as it is sometimes referred to – and my only way out of The Gambia was to pass through Senegal again. I planned to make the journey in just one day, which meant passing through four border posts – pretty ambitious for Africa, but I was going to give it a go. I had already decided to forego Guinea-Bissau after reports that the roads were very bad going into Guinea (Conakry) and the visa costs were mounting with still so many ahead.

I plotted my route and set off early to give myself the most time to make the crossings. I so enjoyed the early morning drives when the air was cool and fresh and the sun displayed its rich palette using the sky and clouds as its canvas. This was the beginning of a new day – and a full one.

There were the usual police checkpoints, some of them very close together, which always messed up any time estimates. The policemen were jovial, as I had found most of the Gambians to be, and one of them quizzed me about where I was going and asked me where the 'boss man' was. I responded, "I am the boss man." This seemed not to go down so well and he proceeded to instruct me that there are men and women in this world and we must work together. I wasn't sure what that had to do with the situation at hand, nevertheless I responded with a laugh and informed him, "In this van, *I* am the boss man!" He countered with a big belly laugh and allowed me to proceed. There was much to be done before women could be equal in Africa.

Driving along I suddenly noticed a large billboard for girl's education. In 1998 former Gambian president Jammeh had mandated that the right to attend school is a basic human right, making primary education in The Gambia compulsory and free, so I was intrigued. I had already passed the billboard when I realised what it was promoting and I caused some traffic chaos (me, for a change!) as I reversed to get a better view. I found my phone and took a couple of photos of the board through the passenger window – not great shots but I wanted to remember it. As I turned to face forward though, there was a uniformed man with an automatic weapon standing in front of my van. It seemed that with my attention on reversing back through the traffic and the cars and taxis all hooting at me, I had missed the armed officer standing at the gate to the property. Now what?!

He came round to my window and enquired what I was doing and I replied that I had seen the billboard and wanted to remember it. He asked if I knew that the ex-president's property was behind it and that I was not allowed to take photos, so I explained that I didn't know whose property it was, I was only interested in the billboard. He insisted on seeing the photos on my phone – for security he told me. I reluctantly showed him – he did have an automatic weapon, after all – and on seeing the pictures he insisted that I delete them. I complained but he looked at me and shifted his weapon slightly on his shoulder as if to remind me that *he* was the boss there, so I reluctantly acceded. Annoyed, I could not resist having the last words as I departed and shouted out of the window, "I could probably see more of the property on Google if I wanted to!"

I had come to see that the roads between country border posts were not particularly good, but I thought I had been doing well on fairly decent terrain until I turned towards the first border crossing and saw a red dirt road. I knew what lay ahead: red dust and sweat. Not an attractive look!

It was a Friday. I arrived at the border and saw a building to the left and a parking area to the right, but there were no other vehicles and lots of space to park (no markings though). I pulled up alongside the kerb so that I could drive straight off when I'd finished, grabbed my papers along with my bag and walked over to the building. A man in civilian clothes approached and informed me that I must move my car. When I asked the reason why, I was instructed to park at an *angle* to the kerb to allow for other vehicles. There was no point arguing so I parked as required in a manner befitting an expected mad rush.

In the building there was a short but disorderly queue so I enquired where it ended. In Africa, the notion of a queue is confusing: often people do not stand in an organised line but might be sitting or standing elsewhere or conducting other business in an entirely separate room from the queue. I would get into trouble if I berated someone for pushing in when they, and others, would assert that this person was indeed in the queue. It was confusing and frustrating but I had learnt to ask first. In this instance I was directed to an office behind me where I had to report first.

On entering I greeted all present with a bright, "Good morning!" A few men were sitting in chairs to the right of the room and in the far left corner was a desk with one man standing in front, and behind it another man in pure white cotton. I could see that this was the traditional Muslim long loose shirt with pants underneath. I took a seat on the right.

The queue moved quickly. I gathered that the man in white was the customs official and would clear my vehicle, although it must have been casual Friday because he lacked any semblance of a uniform. It was unusual to deal with my vehicle before immigration but who was I to argue. He asked for a document from my entry into Senegal but I didn't have it with me as I had only brought the Gambian documents. I had to return to the van to find it, perplexed as to why it was required, though fortunately I had put all my border papers together and it was easy to locate. I was quickly back to the official who seemed satisfied. We exchanged pleasantries, he stamped my papers and retained my entry paper into The Gambia – but not before I'd photographed it, not knowing what they were going to ask me for at the next border.

I returned to the first office to find that the previous queue had been dealt with, leaving the room nearly empty. As I approached the desk a man came up beside me and asked for my passport. He was dressed in jeans, a shirt and a thin windbreaker with a baseball cap on his head. Ha! I had been warned about these people: you gave them your passport and then they held it hostage until you paid them for its return! "Why do you want it?" was my defensive question, accompanied by one raised eyebrow and a 'Don't mess with me' look.

"I am an immigration officer." I looked him up and down and responded, "Really? And how am I to know that? The man over there is behind the counter and wearing a uniform, so why should I believe you?" (I added this with a smile, just in case he *was* an immigration officer.) He presented his credentials, the other officers behind the counter smirking. "Thank you," I replied graciously, adding, "As a woman on my own, when a man comes to ask for my passport without any uniform or identification, how am I to know who he is?" An officer behind the counter nodded his understanding but pointed out that the windbreaker had IMMIGRATION written on the back. I suggested that he should therefore approach people back-first, which made everyone chuckle and immediately dissipated the tension. I received my stamp and returned to BlueBelle, who was still totally alone but correctly parked.

On the other side of the boom barrier was no man's land. I continued along the red dust road which was full of villages, and I wondered if they knew which country they were in or whether they just continued to live as they had done for millennia, without the concerns of colonially imposed borders. It was some distance before I reached the Senegal border post and it was now lunchtime. Hoping for a quick stop I handed my papers to the one official present. I was back to attempting to speak French when he advised me that the document for my vehicle had expired. Darn, I had not even considered this and it would have been impossible to extend in The Gambia. I would need to buy a new TIP, just for the few hours it would take me to pass through Senegal on my way to Guinea. That was going to hurt.

I begged, pleaded and sighed. I didn't have any CFA francs with me and would need to go to the nearest town to get money, so I didn't know what to do. I explained that I was on my way to Guinea and on a tight schedule, but he could not assist me and told me I would have to wait until 2.00 for the boss to return. It was now just after noon and a two-hour delay would seriously impede the likelihood of my making Guinea by nightfall, so I continued the drama of the poor old crazy woman about to burst into tears. I'm not sure if he'd had enough of me or actually felt sorry for me, but eventually he took a new TIP form, rewrote the information but extended the validity by twenty-four hours, signed, stamped and handed it to me, and stamped my passport. I could not believe my luck! I profusely thanked and blessed him and hurriedly trotted out of the building. (And for those who are wondering, no, I didn't pay him a bribe.)

This was why I loved Africa. Amongst all the mayhem and chaos, there was also room for humanity and the simple understanding that I was not going to cause an international crisis. This would *never* have happened in any Western country.

Two border posts down, two more to go…

At the nearest town I stopped to top up with fuel, but I needed local currency first as no one took credit cards. Finding a working ATM was essential. I found one with a short queue that was obviously working and joined the line. Next to me was a guard in a small cubicle eating his lunch from a large metal bowl. I smiled and greeted him and in return he smiled and proffered a spoon for me to share his bowl of rice and sauce. I thanked him sincerely but lied and said I had just eaten. I didn't have the French words to explain that I need to get the cash and run so I could cross another two borders, but I very much appreciated his hospitality.

At the fuel station I took the liberty of checking my route with some locals. As usual, there were only men to ask and I needed to know which of two routes would be better. One was considerably shorter but it was a dirt road in uncertain condition and would mean that my speed would be much slower, added to the fact that at this stage in my journey dirt roads still held some level of concern. The alternative route was longer but would be on tarmac. The question was how many men would it take to agree on a route? I was soon surrounded by about a dozen: employees at the fuel station, customers and a passing cyclist, who I guessed was just curious about the gang of men around a lone woman, all speaking and offering opinions to each other. (Notably, two other customers, white French men with local women, looked at me condescendingly and paid no attention.) Consensus was not reached about the condition of the dirt road, but after listening to the men debate I quickly decided not to run any risk and opted for the longer tarmac route. While it was fun getting everyone's participation and assistance, I did need to get going, but I can say that the friendliness of the people of south-east Senegal redeemed their country somewhat in my experience.

The Senegal exit border was relatively uneventful. Three border posts down and it was late afternoon as I entered the no man's land before Guinea. There was again some considerable distance between border posts and I believed I had arrived at the next one when I saw a new building, well laid out with plenty of parking and signage; but weeds were poking through the pavers and there was not a vehicle or soul in sight. I suspected that this was not the actual border post as I saw no booms preventing my onward journey, so I drove on.

Within a few kilometres I arrived at a... place: I don't know what to call it other than that. It was a higgledy-piggledy group of shacks and the odd concrete building, with trash everywhere and goats and donkeys roaming freely. There were some vehicles and motorbikes but no signs, and I felt like I'd arrived at the local market rather than a border post.

I pulled up near the first string (which acted as a barrier) a little before 6.00pm, and seeing a group of men I asked where I needed to go. They indicated a small office with three more men outside, two sitting and one standing. I walked toward them and greeted them with a "Bonjour" but only one of them, wearing a military-looking uniform, responded. The other seated man and the one standing were in conversation. I assumed that this seated man was the person I needed to address since the man who had responded to my greeting offered nothing more, so I decided to wait for further instruction.

The seated man was in his late thirties and wearing what looked like silk pyjamas, the traditional long shirt and loose pants of the Muslim people but this time made of a light grey silky fabric. As the standing man left, Pyjama Man thrust out his hand and asked for my papers. I smiled and handed him what I thought he needed, but without warning he started shouting at me in French. I was completely taken aback and had no idea what he was saying and my face must have reflected my surprise and confusion. I trotted out the usual apology about not speaking French and that I was from Zimbabwe, but started to understand that I was being berated for not greeting him. I responded that I *had* greeted everyone when I arrived and looked to the army officer for confirmation, and fortunately he nodded. However, Pyjama Man continued shouting at me.

If there is one thing I hate it is being shouted at for no reason. I asked why he was shouting at me and the army officer, who seemingly spoke some English, replied, "It is because you are an Anglophone."[38] I was shocked, but before I could respond Pyjama Man thrust my papers back at me and declared that it was after 6.00pm and they were closed so I should come back tomorrow! I was quite shaken. I had not planned for this, and I was now faced with having to stay in this ramshackle place for the night. I asked where it was possible to park my van and he pointed to a large empty plot across the way where I saw a couple of trucks parked. It was directly within his line of sight.

I went very quickly from shock to anger. I took my papers, thanked him politely, said a short goodbye and without further ado I turned around and, belying my inner state, strode confidently back to BlueBelle. When I reached her I breathed deeply. I decided that I did not feel safe there and *definitely* didn't want to stay anywhere within Pyjama Man's view, but where should I go? The only way I could go was back in the direction of the Senegal border, where I recalled a very pleasant man at a boom barrier and a clearing nearby. As I drove down the road I saw ahead of me the new building that I had originally mistaken for the border post. Perhaps I could park there since it wasn't as far to drive.

I pulled into the entirely vacant area and parked the van at the far side of the main building. I was not visible from the road in either direction so I believed no one would even know I was there. I did a walkabout to check and the coast looked clear, but as the sun was now setting the mosquitoes were starting to attack. I locked up, switched on all my window alarms and made sure I knew where to go if I needed to get out. I fell straight into bed,

---

[38] Someone who speaks English

exhausted but determined to rise early in the morning to get through the final border.

I might have failed to cross all four border posts but I still gave myself a pat on the back: in Africa, three in one day was quite an achievement!

Chapter Five– Guinea (Conakry)

26 January 2019

At 11.00pm a van alarm went off, and I woke from a dead sleep having to take a moment to comprehend what was going on. I carefully got up to make the minimum amount of movement or noise and grabbed the baton that was always tucked into my mattress. It was the alarm on the side door of my van and I pulled the curtain back slightly to switch it off. It was dark inside so I had the advantage that I could not be seen, but there was enough moonlight outside to make the world visible as I looked out to see if there was anyone around. I crept round the whole van and looked out through all the windows… but I couldn't see anything, so I reset the alarm and sat for a moment to see if there would be any further development. As I waited I realised that no matter what happened I no longer felt safe and I would probably not be able to return to my much-needed sleep; and my intuition was also telling me to move. I grabbed my keys from their night location, jumped into the driver's seat and drove off.

I decided that the closest and best place to relocate would be at the border, believing that by now everyone would be asleep. As I approached I switched off the van lights and glided in behind a few large trucks now parked on the side of the road, obviously also waiting to cross in the morning. It looked deserted and quiet and it felt safer there: the truck drivers were probably sleeping in their trucks too or nearby, so that would suffice. I checked the alarms, returned to bed and fell fast asleep, knowing that I had an uncertain day ahead.

I awoke before sunrise and reviewed my route for the day over a coffee. Then I washed in my little sink, dressed, picked up my papers and walked across the road to Pyjama Man's office. The 'village' was quiet, the only sounds being the crowing of roosters and a few goats browsing the trash. I stood waiting in the cool morning air and watched the sun rise over some low hills, a sight I never tired of seeing. I took the moment to appreciate that I was about to enter my fifth country – provided Pyjama Man had no more antics up his silky sleeve.

A guard appeared and asked why I was standing there. I felt like saying, "I'm shopping for the latest fashions", but I wasn't sure he would understand my irony; and I was at the border, for goodness sake! I smiled and politely informed him that I was waiting to be admitted to enter Guinea, and he nodded and walked off. A moment later a motorcyclist approached from the Guinean side. The guard took his papers, walked into the 'office' and within minutes returned and handed the papers back to the motorcyclist, who manoeuvred his bike around the string and rode off. I looked directly at the guard, my eyes wide in question as to how this had happened so easily for the motorcyclist and yet I was still standing there. My wordless message had obviously been received because he approached me and asked how I got there, so I told him by van. Again I felt like asking if he thought I'd walked from Dakar, or perhaps come by donkey... but instead I contained myself and pointed to BlueBelle hiding behind the trucks. I was instructed to fetch her and park where I had been standing.

As I parked up, a man in full uniform and cap and looking very professional came up to my window. I did not immediately recognise him, but it was Pyjama Man. He asked where I had been: did I return to Senegal? I replied in half-French, half-English that after his rebuke I did not feel safe and went to park elsewhere. I don't think he fully understood me – or indeed cared – because he had already turned and beckoned me to his office. The uneasy feeling about him remained with me, despite his affected charm.

The interior of the office was dark. Against the right wall stood an ancient wooden desk hailing from some colonial time, with two mismatched wooden chairs in front of it, and to the left there was a sofa that still had a pillow and a sheet draped across it, looking like it had been used as a bed. Pyjama Man indicated for me to take a seat as he pulled out the now-border-obligatory large black book with red binding wherein my details would be written, never again to see the light of day. Whilst he was scribbling he reiterated how worried he was about where I had been, but I believed that the only thing that really worried him was that something might have happened to me to cause an international incident, or that I had reported his behaviour. However, the *real* bombshell came when he told me that I should have stayed with him and he would have kept me company in his bed! My mind simply did not grasp what he was saying for a moment, but when it did dawn on me I was certain that I had a look of utter horror on my face. Fortunately he was writing and didn't notice.

I hid my sense of outrage, realising that any attempt at schooling him on better behaviour would have been futile. He struck me as decidedly untrustworthy and volatile and I did not want to deal with any consequences. Instead I smiled and responded in a firm voice that I was quite content alone in my van, thank you. My mind meanwhile was saying: Finish writing and let me get out of here and as far away from you as possible!

His parting words to me were that he looked forward to my invitation to Zimbabwe, as it was a place he would very much like to visit. I smiled and replied, "Sure", knowing that it was never going to happen. I was surprised that he did not ask for my personal details; nor did he offer me his. I guessed that he was merely testing me… or perhaps this was all just a game to him. I coolly responded, "Merci" and left.

After I'd passed through the string barrier there was a distance of about ten metres before another string blocked my route, a clear indication that there was another office for me to report to.

I got out of my van to look but there were no signs and no clearly defined buildings. I went to one shack and was directed 'over there', but it took some time before I found the open building – with no windows and no doors – a few metres behind some other buildings; a sort of hide and seek for visitors. There I was told I didn't need a TIP for BlueBelle. "But I do," I protested. "No you don't, you're a tourist," I was told. I tried insisting several times for a document of some sort but they kept repeating that it was not at all necessary and eventually I gave in, though reluctantly. Next I was directed to a building I had passed earlier where another ubiquitous big black ledger was completed, and then another. I was never sure why the same information needed to be written down so many times. Thinking I was done I got back into the van, but just as I was about to depart a man came running towards me shouting that he wanted my Yellow Fever card. I sighed and was escorted to *another* office so that he could sign my details into *another* big black ledger.

I was allowed to continue, but within a few more metres there was a third string barrier. I was again obliged to get out, this time to visit the police station where my details were *yet again* written into *two* black ledgers by *two* different officers. The officer that I'd greeted the day before at Pyjama Man's office entered and, knowing he spoke English, I asked him about the TIP and whether I would have any difficulty at the police checkpoints ahead if I didn't have one. He too assured me that it would all be fine, that I merely had to tell them that I was a tourist. Still, I couldn't shake the concern.

At last my details had been written into every conceivable big black book, the drama of the border was over and I was on my way. I did not manage to change money nor buy a SIM card, so I determined that the first town I found would be a necessary stop for these and to fill up with fuel.

The first police checkpoint I encountered was not far from the border and I was asked where I was coming from. (I had not seen any other roads crossing from anywhere else and the only tarmac road I'd seen was this one, so where did they think I had come from?!) I announced firmly, "I come from the border and I am a Tourist"... And it worked! They merely checked the laminated and notarised copy of my passport and let me proceed.

It was evident that Guinea was an exceptionally poor country – or, let me rephrase that, the *people* of Guinea were poor. Their currency notes were mostly in the hundreds and thousands, in shocking condition and of such little value that it required handfuls to buy the smallest thing. People in the rural areas lived in mud huts with no access to water or power; few of the villages had water pumps and usually I saw women and children carrying water from the river and collecting firewood from the surrounding area. I also found that I could tell how poor the people were by how much trash I saw. In deeply rural Guinea it was mostly clean and plastic-free, an indication that they could not afford packaged goods. However, at markets and in towns the trash was again a heart-breaking sight. All too often it would be piled on the side of the road and burnt and the stench was often overwhelming, especially from the plastics.

In the first town I reached I saw a mobile phone provider shop and parked right outside. It was still early and the security guard outside the shop told me he would look after BlueBelle. As usual I was grateful she was under someone's watchful eye and less likely to be broken into.

I asked in the shop if they would accept euros but they did not, so I asked how I could get money changed as I had not seen any ATMs. Not a problem, they said: remember this was Africa and pretty much all things were possible. The owner made a call, asked me to take a seat in the waiting area and within fifteen minutes a man arrived with wads of cash. His exchange rate was acceptable and the deal was done. Armed with a wad of local currency I bought a SIM card with data and then I bought some bread and fruit at the market around the corner and gratefully tipped my car guard. Finally I topped up with fuel. I found that all of this took a big chunk of my changed cash but felt sure that I would be able to draw more at my next stop, Boké. Replenished on all counts, I was ready to rock 'n' roll!

HELL'S HIGHWAY

Shortly after I had set off again I turned off the reasonably tarmacked main road heading east and noticed that there were an unusual number of tyre and vehicle repair shops at the junction, as well as numerous trucks parked up by these. I considered that this was obviously a very busy road, but it served as a warning of a different kind. I was in a good mood and ready to tackle the day when suddenly the tarmac stopped and a deep ochre-red dust road appeared... and it was in the worst condition I had seen – ever.

For the next two whole days I drove that two hundred kilometre stretch of road, which I came to call 'Hell's Highway'. The misery of the red dust was compounded by the heat and humidity into one of the worst experiences of my travels, but it was also one that taught me an immense amount about driving and handling BlueBelle. In retrospect, I believe it prepared me for the rest of my journey.

The 'road' put us through a rigorous test of different terrains all in one stretch. A particular surface condition could either continue for kilometres or be short and interchangeable, from tyre-shredding striated rock to small stony patches, corrugations, sandy sections, face-powder-fine dust, potholes and gullies. I started off thinking that each new surface was better than the last... but ended up hating them all.

The gullies were an exceptional challenge. Trucks had gouged deep ruts into the dirt, probably during the rainy season when the ground was soft. I was grateful to be there in the dry season as I wouldn't have stood a chance in the mud. I had seen numerous tankers and heavy-duty lorries drive like lunatics up and down that road and some of the gullies were as deep as a car. I had to be extremely cautious that I didn't get stuck on the raised mid-section. While BlueBelle has a higher clearance that most vans, it would not have been nearly high enough.

On one occasion, in a particularly messy area, I had stopped to check my options and decided that each side of the road looked as bad as the other. Oncoming traffic could be predicted from the dust clouds that announced their approach, so I decided to stop and watch which route the locals would take. They were understandably more familiar with the road and it would help me to plot my course. It was also preferable to wait and avoid driving blindly through their dust.

The first vehicle was a car with three men in it, one very large, and as they drove through I waved and they waved back. Behind them an old ambulance conversion came at equal speed and... Bang! It ground to a halt midway, stuck solid on the higher mid-section of road. They were going to need help and I was not going to be able to do much. I hooted, stopping the taxi that had just passed me, and we all got out of our vehicles and walked over to the ambulance. It was evident that it was stuck pretty fast and being loaded to the brim added to the problem, but they were not inclined to offload the goods to give it better clearance.

There I was, a lone white woman in the middle of nowhere with five French-speaking local men, and I understood them better than they did me! The question is how many men would it take to get this vehicle unstuck?

Their first idea was to put foot to the floor to push through, but I argued that they should reverse since forward had got them into trouble in the first place. The taxi driver ignored me and boldly got into the ambulance driver's seat, revved the engine and accelerated. To be fair, he did manage to move it forward by about five centimetres… and now the vehicle was well and truly wedged. Everyone was shouting at him, obviously telling him he was an idiot (that thought had occurred to me too). He got out of the ambulance, whereupon more shouting ensued and in a huff he walked off to sit under a nearby tree to ponder his contribution to the mess.

Their second idea was to push the vehicle sideways over the mid-ridge. I was totally unable to comprehend the genius of this idea: with the middle of the vehicle stuck and the sides of the tyre tracks being so steep, there just wasn't any leverage to make this happen. I told them as much, shaking of my head, but still they ignored me and set about trying. I gave up; there was a distinct lack of common sense here. I turned around and walked back to my van, but I could feel the men's eyes boring into my back.

The only passable way now was the other side of the road, which had gullies even deeper than the side the ambulance was stuck on. I braced myself and started inching BlueBelle along one side of the gouged tracks. This meant that her wheels were on the sloping sides of a gulley, so I needed to keep her firmly in line to prevent her sliding one way or the other, the result of which would have been trouble of an entirely different type. It was only about ten metres but it felt like so much more. I knew the men were watching me but I paid no attention and just coached BlueBelle to see me through and not make *me* a victim of their rescue efforts too.

Once I had reached the other side, I aligned BlueBelle with the rear of the ambulance and reversed until I was only a metre or so behind it. I got out and with pointing and gesticulations told them I would tow them out if they had a rope. Some kind of strap appeared and we were tied on. I gave the driver strict instructions to reverse at the same time that I was going forward, but to take great care not to run into me when he was free of the ridge. These instructions were all in sign language, but the guy got my meaning clearly when I demonstrated that if he did hit my van I would punch him… and everyone laughed. Haha, they thought I was joking..!

However, it all went according to plan and within minutes BlueBelle had them free. I got out to remove the strap, but it was now impossible to untie the knot so we had to cut the strap off with a knife. I warned the driver not to try to take the same route again but to drive on the sides of the gulley as I had because I wasn't hanging around to pull him out a second time! He nodded, although I'm not sure he understood, but I bade them "Bonne journée"[39] and left.

So how many men *did* it take to get this vehicle unstuck? None – no, none. It took one woman and BlueBelle! ARA 4 : DB 2

I still have that piece of strap on the end of my van and think of this incident often. And I still wonder what they said after I'd gone...

An hour later I came across a man sitting on a log near his truck and looking most dejected. I stopped. The traffic had dwindled in the late afternoon and I always feared what would happen to me if no one stopped when *I* was in need. I asked what his problem was and he told me he had run out of fuel and had no money, so he couldn't even hail one of the passing taxis. Unfortunately he was travelling in the opposite direction to me so I could not take him along, but I asked what the taxi would cost and then gave him the small amount of money that would help him catch one. His grateful response and broad smile assured me it was the right thing to do. ARA 4 : DB 3

I was still new to this type of driving, never going above second gear and having to make a decision at every metre of the road: did I go left, did I go right? There were no 'right' sides of the road; just road that needed to be conquered. My progress was slow, and with an average driving speed of only twenty-five kilometres per hour the two hundred kilometres took me the better part of two days. With the slow pace under the searing African sun, BlueBelle frequently overheated and I had to take regular breaks in the shade just to cool her down. It was reassuring that people often stopped to ask if I was OK.

With the sun getting low on the horizon on the first day of Hell's Highway, I was nowhere near any civilisation. The dense vegetation made it impossible to get off the road to find a place where I could park privately, and I didn't want to wild camp as

---

[39] "Have a good day" in French

there were regular warnings of bandits in Guinea. It now seemed standard after a day on the road that I would be overly hot, dirty and tired, so I decided that one of the villages along the way would have to do. As dusk fell, I pulled into a settlement that had a large, dusty open space with football goals on either side, with a track off the road and on to the side of the 'pitch'. I noticed villagers milling about as they do at the end of the day, tidying up and preparing meals.

It is always advisable to get the permission of the chief if you want to stop in a village, just as you wouldn't park in someone's yard without asking first, so I stopped to ask a woman with a baby on her back and a bucket on her head if I could speak to the chief. She clearly did not understand me and called over a man to come and help. He told me it would be possible to park but didn't indicate that I could proceed. It was clearly time to negotiate.

The man had noticed the two mobile phones on my dash behind the steering wheel, one for navigating and one for photos, and when I asked him how much it would cost to park he nodded that one of them would suffice. I laughed and said no chance! I told him I could pay a small amount and handed him some local currency. It wasn't much, but there were no ATMs for the foreseeable future and I needed to keep some cash in reserve. There was no way of knowing what lay ahead and I didn't want to be stuck like the man I met who'd run out of fuel earlier that day. However, Mr Phone said he needed three times the amount I'd given him, so I told him I didn't have it and asked for my cash back. He clearly didn't want to part with the cash so reluctantly agreed that I could stay and then directed me where to park up. I wondered after if I should have paid more, but all I needed was a parking spot; and frankly it was more money than he would make that day from anywhere else, so I remained firm.

I had no sooner pulled on the handbrake than I found a large crowd around me. I had parked next to a grass fence, knowing that when night fell BlueBelle would disappear into the darkness, adding to our safety. Mr Phone was watching me like a hawk and I was uncomfortable with his look, so I moved my phones into the space between the seats, out of sight, and made the decision to stay in the van. I always drove with my doors locked and everything I needed was in BlueBelle anyway. I remained in the driver's seat while I greeted all the people who came to see this strange phenomenon parked up next to their football pitch. I shook hands with everyone who came, including all the kids who wanted to shake my hand over and over. I realised it was probably the first time they had touched a white person.

It was getting dark fast so I made my excuses, telling everyone I was tired and must rest. I wound up the window, waved goodnight, closed the curtain and set about to give myself a much-needed wash from my sink before grabbing something simple to eat and collapsing into my bunk.

The night was quiet and I slept the sleep of the utterly exhausted.

Having gone to bed early I naturally awoke early. I tidied up, gave myself a cursory wash, made coffee (it was too early to eat) and was dressed and ready when the morning light arrived. As I climbed into the driver's seat I noticed Mr Phone standing a short distance away. I couldn't tell if he had been watching all night or if he was waiting for something else, but I smiled my "Thank you" and waved goodbye as I drove off to face Hell's Highway once more.

The air was still cool but I knew that by mid-morning it would again be searingly hot. I would try to cover as much distance as the road would allow. The drive was made more taxing by the early morning sun casting shadows across the road from the trees next to it. It was difficult enough to assess any changes in the terrain, but the dappled light and shade made spotting hazardous potholes and other obstacles a real challenge.

My next adventure arrived when I was faced with three ghastly parallel road options, one having been unmistakably forged by divers unable to pass the deeply rutted other two. I stopped to take stock and patiently waited for vehicles coming in the opposite direction to see how they fared.

The first to emerge was what I call a 'city 4x4' which had opted for the far-right track, but I could see that this route was narrow and very sandy, and the tree around which the vehicle had to manoeuvre was too low for me to pass under. The next was a car taxi which took the far-left track, and as he passed me the driver indicated that I should go this same side – although it was too deep and dusty for me to see exactly how he got through. The next vehicle was a tall, fully-laden truck with an equally full trailer. He too took the far-left track and I watched him pass through this gorge with awe, his cab and trailer swaying precariously from side to side. The driver looked calm and I applauded him enthusiastically and gave him a big thumbs-up as he breached the end. My reward was a bright white grin and a nod of acknowledgement. I doubted his boss ever realised the real condition of the roads his driver had to travel.

The way was now clear and I had to make my choice, so I got out and 'walked the groove' to decide my route through. Back in BlueBelle I steadied my nerves and gently eased her forward, once again balancing on the edges of one of the ruts and holding my breath until I got to the other side.

It was handling this road and at this stage, above all others, that stood me in the greatest stead for all the roads I would still have to face, both physically and emotionally. I learnt not to panic and that slow and steady wins the race.

In the intense heat of mid-afternoon I spotted a mirage shimmering ahead of me. Could it possibly be that thing I had left behind so very long ago, tarmac..? Yes! Glory hallelujah!! I could see it, could almost feel it, smooth and comfortable under BlueBelle's wheels… but I was so distracted by the vision that I failed to see the police checkpoint. I was jolted abruptly to a halt by a piece of string across the road, barring me from reaching that anticipated smoothness.

"Bonjours" were exchanged and I announced clearly that I was a tourist, expecting no further trouble. Regrettably this time it didn't work. The officer insisted on seeing my papers and then instructed me to get out of the van and go to the office to get a visa. Off to the side of the road he indicated a roughly constructed open-sided shack with a counter at the front and several police officers enjoying the only shade for some distance. I gave pause: I was sweaty, exhausted and filthy with red dust, and I could see the tarmac ahead; and besides, I *had* a visa.

I waved my papers and informed the man clearly that I already had one and that I had just come through the border a couple of days ago, so why I must get out of the van? However, I quickly realised that this wasn't going to be resolved quite so easily. I was ordered to bring my passport – not a copy – so I grumpily and frumpily got out.

One ranking officer asked me in a gruff tone if I had come from Burkina Faso, and was I carrying guns? I decided that they must come across a lot of gun-toting old women like me in Africa as this seemed to be a recurring question! I repeated that I was alone, adding that I had not been to Burkina Faso, and there ensued some consternation and discussion in the local language. What followed were the usual questions about my being alone, with several of the officers then volunteering to accompany me, be my driver or marry me. I politely answered all their questions and equally politely declined all their offers. I further clarified the matter of the visa by showing them the sticker in my passport and the entry stamps. The officer in charge proceeded to carefully check each page of my passport but still seemed dubious about my presence. There was some shuffling of papers and gestures, which I thought might relate to the fact that they were looking for someone coming from Burkina Faso... or perhaps they were merely trying to figure out how to con me out of some money... but they eventually decided that I could leave. My papers were returned and I was allowed to proceed, so I smiled, thanked them and returned to BlueBelle where I could focus on the nice smooth tarmac road ahead.

The road ahead, however, was far from nice smooth tarmac: it was full of potholes. I still counted my blessings that it was only potholes though and that I'd finally found fourth and even occasionally fifth gears. It wasn't long before I hit civilisation again and what I came to call the 'grand melee'. This was a common sight when entering an urbanisation of any size. It would start with a vision of trash, followed by a swarm of scooter taxis weaving all over the road as though there was no one else using it. They had the nasty habit of overtaking on both the left and the right, which was very unnerving! Vehicles were parked at random and people walking everywhere and there were often donkeys and goats picking through the day's waste. I had to find a way through this obstacle course without hitting any of them – or the trading stalls. I dreaded the sight of this, but by now I had learnt to use my hooter like a local which, due to BlueBelle's unusual appearance, always drew attention. Slow and steady was again the only way through.

One of the rules in Guinea is that you must drive in closed shoes and not open sandals, so despite the heat I kept my sneakers on. Several policemen at checkpoints had already peered into my van through my driver's window, not only checking my shoes but insisting on seeing the other compulsory items – first aid box, warning triangle and hi-vis vest. The irony was that I had seen a great number of vehicles broken down on the side of the road where the drivers had used branches as an indication that there was trouble ahead; but I had yet to see any warning triangles!

When I reached Boké I knew that I was entering a city because the traffic increased and so did the western-style buildings, many of which had seen better days. My order of business was to find cash and fuel and then the museum where I hoped to spend the night – perhaps two nights to recover. The museum was owned by relatives of Lamin, whom I had met in The Gambia, and it was his idea for me to visit it.

The property was pleasantly located on the banks of the Rio Nuñez river and consisted of a once impressive double-storey colonial building in a large courtyard with four smaller buildings at each corner. Built in 1878, it had been a fort and former Portuguese slave outpost, and its basement contained sinister interrogation rooms which had borne witness to the so-called 'tough interviews' that the colonial administration subjected on those who became skirmishers in Senegal. The museum boasted a few old but highly interesting artefacts from the different cultures and ethnicities of the region, alongside some ancient colonial photographs of men in pith helmets with their slaves. The building, artefacts and photographs were all in poor repair and sadly few people there could give many details about the place or its exhibits; but with some judicious investment the museum could be a real gem.[40]

I was warmly welcomed into the grounds by one of Lamin's brothers, followed of course by the curious children and then the inquisitive women. I invited the women inside BlueBelle and they

---

[40] This video gives a good view of the museum:
https://www.youtube.com/watch?v=QbC0QMiECcY

were completely mesmerised by her interior, amazed that I had everything necessary for living inside a van. I was given a brief tour of the grounds by Ouseman, a local wood craftsman and musician who had use of one of the corner buildings as a workshop; all the corner buildings seemed to be rented as offices and shops. He spoke more English than the others and was tasked with helping me.

After all the hubbub of my arrival I asked if there might be a tap for me to take some water to wash with. A short while later a woman carrying a bucket came over to me from the direction of the river, and I immediately realised my privileged view in assuming that there would be a tap on the property! The water looked clean and cool and inviting, although because of its source I decided that washing would be all I could safely use it for.

But first I had to chase the children away. They had been watching my every move and, despite my drawn curtains, I wanted some extra privacy. They reluctantly left but started sneaking back within minutes, tugging at the main curtain so much that I had to resort to closing the sliding door. Privacy is not an African concept and they find it strange that we desire it.

I used the bucket to wash, saving some of the water to wash a few 'smalls'. Washing from the bucket quickly became easier than washing in the van's little basin, since wastewater from the basin would empty into the greywater (disposal) tank, which far too soon would need to be removed and emptied. The heat also quickly made the greywater smell and I only had limited eco-chemicals for this and the toilet. Using the bucket meant I could simply throw the water away, and I usually chose to water a plant with this as it didn't contain any toxic chemicals.

My hair was stiff and strawberry blonde from all the red dust from the road and it left the water a strong pinkish colour! After my wash I did a quick dust-down of my bed, wiped the countertops and swept the floor, hoping that I'd disposed of the majority of Africa which had found its way inside the van. By the time I was done it was dusk, and after saying thanks and good night to my hosts, I returned to my bed and a sleep of the dead until the dawn roosters announced the start of the new day.

In the morning I was invited to visit the local craftspeople, but had to convince them that I could not buy anything with my limited space; and besides, the crafts were very similar to those I could get in Zimbabwe. The highlight of my day was to be invited by Ouseman to a practice session he was having with two of his fellow musicians. Down a zig-zagging walkway towards the Rio Nuñez I found a clearing with some basic bench seating, and there, entertained under the shade of the trees by singing, African drums and a kora, I felt totally at home.

CONAKRY

After two nights at the museum it was time to head to Conakry, the capital of Guinea, which sits on a peninsula amidst a number of waterways. As much as I dislike big cities I was obliged to go there to get visas for both Côte d'Ivoire and Ghana.

Despite several checkpoints with the usual interrogation about driving alone and needing a man, the road was fair and the surroundings interesting now that I had time to look about rather than focus all my attention on the road. Guinea has a wonderful variety of landscapes and was greener than any country I had seen thus far on my journey, with regular evidence of intact areas of tropical rainforest. The route to Conakry revealed frequent road construction and mining, all being conducted by the Chinese, and I came to learn that the huge new highway I passed was being built to facilitate the extraction of bauxite.[41] The highway, however, would not benefit traffic to Conakry itself, but rather directly to the port from the mine, thereby facilitating the extraction.

There would not be one African country that I passed through that did not expose the same approach by the Chinese, whether it was extracting minerals or logging. They also built compounds and shopping districts especially for 'their people', and they were notably rarely seen out and about, almost as though they were not really there. It was worrying evidence of a new form of colonisation, something I had hoped would never again impact the continent.

I found myself in Conakry just after lunchtime, and saw that the city had taken the grand melee concept and expanded it into

---

[41] A mineral used in various petrochemical industries as well as in the production of aluminium

something that more closely resembled grand chaos. The circulation was again a mix of everything on two to four wheels or two to four legs, and included donkey carts, bustling pedestrians and traffic that would rival the UK's dreadful M25 at peak hour – but without any of the discipline or road structure. The roads themselves were appalling: where there was tarmac, it was deeply potholed or just non-existent and filled with large quantities of sand. There was also all the hooting. They hooted when you were in the way, when you were not moving fast enough, when they passed you, when they were irritated; and in addition, there was the constant toot-tooting to pick up people in both formal and informal taxis. In other words, it was constant. I eventually joined in. It was a great way to get rid of road rage and I found myself easily matching the hooting frenzy.

It took me three hours to reach my destination, a small guest house on the coast called Les Palmiers.[42] I parked up in the yard and walked to reception, and as I entered I saw through the large glass sliding doors a glorious green palm-filled garden with a gazebo, a terrace, a swimming pool and a view of the beach. After all the long days in the dust, it looked like heaven.

The options for parking in the city were few and far between and this one had seemed like the best. I asked what the rate would be to park in their yard and use a shower and the man at reception explained that I would have to pay for a room, the cost of which was way beyond my budget. On hearing my gasped response he advised that I speak with the owner, so while I waited I ordered a much-deserved icy-cold beer, my first in many days.

Ismael, who runs the establishment, came to meet me and he was truly a stroke of good fortune. I explained to him who I was and what I was doing, and somehow he was immensely impressed and insisted that I meet his mother. He offered me a very reasonable rate to park in the yard and use a shower in one of the rooms, since they were not full at that time, and he generously included breakfast too. In return I also offered to pay for a meal each evening while I was there. We had a deal – still on the expensive side for me, but the bonus of home-cooked food made it very attractive.

---

[42] www.pensionlespalmiers.com/

Conakry was a noisy city and the loud music from the beach and the consistent hooting made it difficult to rest. It only fell quiet in the early hours between 2.00 and 4.00, and the sudden silence would often wake me!

The next day Ismael introduced me to his mother, Mrs Ghussein. French by birth she had come to Guinea many years before and married a local man, but sadly he was murdered by Sékou Touré's government, leaving her a widow with two young children. She had bought the house, which was then on the outskirts of the city (hard to imagine now) and set it up as a boarding house for business people and international visitors. It proved a successful venture and grew so that there were now two additional buildings and a total of about twenty rooms. The woman had great stories to tell and I was impressed by her stamina, considering the challenges she must have faced; yet she was still going strong in her eighties.

Ismael further extended his kindness by taking me to the Côte d'Ivoire (CDI) Embassy and also introducing me to a friend who could help with my Ghana visa. When Ismael drove me into Conakry for the first visa the city was too chaotic for words, but it afforded me an opportunity to look around rather than having my attention on the traffic and the road. My CDI visa would take a day and only then could I apply for my Ghana visa.

I stayed at Les Palmiers for a few days, using the valuable WiFi to catch up on news and friends. Whilst there I met a lovely French-Canadian woman whose husband originated from the Caribbean. They lived in Paris, but Marie Hélène spoke excellent English and gave me a respite from hurting people's ears with my appalling French. She was in Guinea conducting research on female genital mutilation and how best to try to prevent this widely implemented practice, which is unbelievably harmful to women but also deeply culturally embedded into rural society. I very much admired her and her passion for the work, and she was great company and a brilliant translator.

One morning at breakfast in the garden gazebo, I found Marie Hélène chatting with two Frenchmen, solar engineers with *Electriciens sans frontières* ('Electricians without borders') who were about to return to France. The organisation raises funds and then offers to fit solar energy solutions to hospitals, clinics and schools. I was excited to hear of such a project, however I was concerned that, like so many European-implemented projects, alongside their honourable efforts to 'give people fish' they were not also 'teaching people how to fish'. Marie Hélène found herself in the middle of my direct questions and their reticent answers, but she calmly translated everything.

The Frenchmen responded that it was too difficult to find people to train or who already had the skills. My exasperated retort was, "Well they don't have the skills because you come and fit things but don't train anyone!" Once again a project was doomed to failure, not because African people cannot be taught – in my experience, they were very keen to learn and to understand – but because others cannot be bothered to teach. Consider the millions of skilled African people in Europe and elsewhere: to say that in Africa they cannot be taught is nonsense! The reluctance was to take the time to teach people and, since there was no desire to push beyond their own limitations, the cycle remained. Needless to say it was a brief conversation before they felt the need to flee my verbal onslaught to pack for their trip home.

With the return of my passport, complete with CDI visa, Ismael introduced me to Felix, a very kind and gently-spoken Ghanaian who helped me through the Ghana visa application. This necessitated a form being filled out by hand in quadruplicate, and four passport-size photographs (I only had two) with some additional photocopies. Acquiring the extra photos and photocopies was an interesting experience. Felix knew where to get them done and so we took a taxi back into the city. It all looked the same to me, with people on the streets in front of shops selling a variety of goods, often under worn umbrellas that had seen much sun and many rainy seasons. However, on closer inspection the corner I was directed to was different. Right there on the open pavement (or what was left of it) there were any number of copiers, photographers, printers and photo-printing machines. Cables and wires ran both along the ground and up in the air, connected heaven only knows how to heaven only knows where. It was all one big print and copy shop – outside.

My photographs were taken on the street corner with a cloth draped behind me and swiftly printed, while another fellow made the photocopies, equally as fast and proficiently, and all at a reasonable price. When I first saw the chaos I had this deep feeling of it not being 'correct', my indoctrination into 'good and proper' being the measure; but experiencing this surprising efficiency in amongst the bedlam, I could not help but revisit my notions of 'correct'. The people of Africa have very little and are often maligned for being lazy and lacking initiative, yet they are amazing at providing what the customer wants, regardless of whether or not they do it in a 'proper' shop. The vast majority cannot afford rent, and so they turn to the streets where they do whatever they can to make a living – as they have done for millennia.

People are often quick to condemn the street traders and hawkers that line the streets selling their wares. I, however, applaud them. They are not waiting around a corner trying to mug me; they are not stealing my car or my belongings, breaking into houses or robbing banks; they are trying to earn a living – and, believe me, out in the sun in that heat and humidity, on their feet for many hours a day, it is not easy.

With the visa application completed and paid for, I had to wait until the next day for it to be issued. I returned to the guest house and bumped into two motorcyclists who were heading back up to Europe and departing for Guinea Bissau the next day. One was Italian, Enrico, the other a Romanian, Marco. Enrico had met Marco en route and they had travelled together for most of their ride through West Africa. The amazing thing to me was that Marco was deaf and mute.

Marco was an astonishing guy. He could lip-read English and had successfully traversed many parts of the world on his motorbike and ridden through Africa five times. On his travels he visited schools and societies for the deaf, and in the African countries he brought books and stationery to the schools, as well as a large dose of inspiration, by demonstrating to these children what is possible for a deaf person to achieve with the will to do so.

Expecting to collect my Ghana visa the next day, I had planned to leave early in the morning to pick it up and then drive to meet a new contact in Conakry, Ibrahim. He was a musician who also ran a night club and I had been told he would have a place for me to park for the night before I made my way to Côte d'Ivoire. With this plan in mind I checked out of the guest house, but then the embassy advised me that my visa would not be ready until the next morning and so I headed off to meet Ibrahim. The mid-morning traffic was better than normal and I decided to drive around to see some more of the city on my way. The people were really friendly and while I was stopped in traffic or at traffic lights I had some good chats with other drivers and the street hawkers. Overall though, I found Conakry a heaving, chaotic city. There were too many people for my preference, with a population at that time estimated at two million and growing, all crammed on to a narrow peninsula.

It isn't hard to see why so many conurbations in Africa are bursting at the seams. In the rural areas there is very little other than subsistence farming, chopping wood and collecting grass (which will be sold for much less than it can in the city). The city provides more opportunity; and yet I believe that the people live in greater poverty, all for the hope of a better tomorrow. However, the governments of Africa are failing to drive the economy because they won't improve the infrastructure, leaving the cities with bad roads, poor utilities and atrocious communication. Instead they fill their pockets or remain completely ineffective, leaving their countries to be pillaged by savvy foreigners and sink further into decay.

I arrived at Ibrahim's night club and was somewhat surprised to see that the only parking was right next to the club beside the street – but it was free and just for one night, I told myself. I was warmly welcomed by Ibrahim who introduced me to his apprentice, a nice young man with long dreadlocks who was learning the art of *djembe*-making. The djembe is a rope-tuned skin-covered hand drum carved out of a single piece of wood, the hollowing out of which is made with a special curved knife, while the exterior is decorated with traditional designs. The degree of hollowing defines the sound that the drum will make, for example a soprano or a bass. I was treated to a wonderful performance on a completed drum, all done on the side of the street in the dust where there was once a pavement, amidst the people and cars passing by. No need for pomp and ceremony: music in Africa is played whenever the mood takes them!

Inside the night club it was air-conditioned, and it was a great shock to my body to find myself suddenly so cold. While I'm not normally a fan of air-conditioning, I have to admit it was a welcome change from the oppressive heat outside. I was introduced to a friend of Ibrahim's who was impressed with my travels, but added that he would not want *his* woman to be so adventurous. I couldn't help myself: "Of course not. You want your woman to stay at home, wash and iron your clothes, cook your meals and raise your children so that you are free to do whatever you like!" – and he agreed with me! Aaargh!! What hope for a better life do the women of Africa have? The door would surely never be opened for them by a man like this! I know some will say that the women are happy – and I'm sure that some are – but in my time I've met a sufficient number of women of all nationalities to know that there are many whose lives revolve around husbands, children and home chores, but who long for something different too.

The night club started up in earnest and the music and lights were all too much for me at that late hour. I politely excused myself with the truthful explanation that I needed to be off early in the morning after some food shopping at the market. However Ibrahim would not permit me to go to the market on my own and said I must be accompanied by the drum maker, so I agreed to meet him in the morning. In bed I sought my earplugs: with the noise of the traffic and the night club next door, it was my only hope for a modicum of sleep.

Early the next morning I was taken on a walk to the market, where I was very glad that my escort spoke English. Communicating was a challenge because the vendors mostly spoke one of the twenty-four local languages. I realised that while the variety of produce available was greater in the city, the prices were higher than those on the rural roadsides. I got some papaya, oranges, potatoes, onions, aubergines and tomatoes. Eggs were taken from a tray and packed in a plastic bag, and sugar was scooped out of a big sack into a smaller plastic bag. I yearned for the return of paper bags.

Ibrahim was still fast asleep when I returned and I gathered he wouldn't rise until late morning, so I asked the drum makers and crew who hung out at the club to send him my best wishes and waved farewell. I collected my passport from the embassy and started looking forward to getting out of Conakry after almost a week of incessant noise. Before leaving the city, I fuelled up and then faced three hours of heavy traffic before I finally found the countryside.

I breathed a sigh of relief when I saw more nature than concrete and the hills and mountains rose gently to surround me. This was much more my 'happy place' than in any city. It would still be almost a thousand kilometres until I reached the border with Côte d'Ivoire, and I wondered what roads awaited me...

I passed through several checkpoints and again my footwear was checked, as were the other Guinea requirements of a hi-vis vest, fire extinguisher and first aid box. I was becoming more accustomed to the fact that I needed to pass through police checks whenever I entered a province, and sometimes there were additional army and immigration checks too. I never understood the reason for all of these but tried to approach each one with a smile.

In the afternoon I came to what looked a little like a border post. I had decided to bypass Sierra Leone and Liberia and drive through Guinea to Côte d'Ivoire, but signs were few and I wondered if I hadn't mistakenly turned toward Sierra Leone. However, it soon became obvious that this was a more elaborate provincial check, which meant that they were making it worth their while to be there.

I was duly stopped, whereupon I informed the guard that I was a tourist, as I had done countless times before. Usually, after some polite conversation, I had been allowed to drive on, but this particular young officer didn't seem to know what to do with a 'tourist'. He called over an older short bald policeman with a sly look in his eyes, who started a debate with me through my window about my TIP – which of course I did not have and had not thus far needed. I replied calmly, "I am a tourist", but he didn't care and continued to blurt out French that I didn't understand. I repeated that I was a tourist and he motioned me to pull over to another location, which I did, but still the argument carried on. The more annoyed I got, the less French I used[43] and the louder I

---

[43] That's really a joke because I never used much French!

shouted. Looking back I believe this was all a ploy to get a bribe, but he was out of luck with me.

Eventually Officer Crook, tired of getting nowhere with me, took the laminated copies of my papers from my hand and stalked off. He didn't do anything with them: he merely walked across to a shack, sat on an old chair and continued chatting to his mates. I figured he was thinking that the waiting would make me nervous, but he was in for a surprise: I was quite ready to spend the night there if necessary! One of the great freedoms of being an independent traveller was that it was really hard to make me feel pressured. Instead I relaxed, pushed back my seat and drank some water, all under his watchful eye. (I had fortunately made a point of parking under a shady tree.) A little while later another policeman came to ask me what was up and I again explained that I was a tourist but that the officer (motioning in his direction) would not let me go. He nodded and walked over to Officer Crook where some discussion ensued, and not long after that Officer Crook returned in a leisurely fashion to give me some more of a hard time. I didn't budge. "Je suis touriste" was all I kept repeating, until finally he worked out that I was not conceding and didn't give a damn whether he made me wait or not. His stubbornness was no match for mine and, exasperated, he handed my papers back to me and with a dismissive wave walked away.

I'd wasted considerable time due to Officer Crook's shenanigans and would now not make the stopping point I had in mind, but I was not prepared to overnight at the checkpoint. There were no campsites or other suitable places within any sensible distance that I knew of, so I was on the lookout for a good spot. I had again planned my cash poorly. All the money-changing into different currencies was messing with my bad math, and after paying for the shopping and the fuel I didn't have much left on me; but I felt confident that there would be an ATM on my way... surely..?

I travelled through some stunning countryside, the rainforest looking more and more lush and beautiful the less interference I saw from man. There were a few small towns and many rural villages, but no ATM and nowhere I would have liked to park up for the night. As the rainforest thickened there were fewer and fewer clearings coming off the main road – and most of those were to villages; I'd done that before and didn't like it. I also wanted to find a location as close to nightfall as possible so that I didn't give myself away by being too noticeable. I was having no luck at all and I was already driving with my lights on, although fortunately there wasn't much traffic. As I approached a bridge over a small river, I noticed a slight clearing on the right. I stopped, and since it looked both far enough off the road and sound enough underfoot for BlueBelle, I reversed in. By now it was dark, so I shut everything up and fell into bed with a snack.

I must mention that I didn't always drop into bed and sleep. There were days – when I had time and wasn't depleted by the heat and driving – when I composed posts to update my followers, mended clothes (I was rapidly losing weight and most of my pants needed taking in), and watched repeats of the movies I had copied on to my external drive. And when signal and data allowed, I enjoyed the occasional WhatsApp call with some close friends.

I was going through some messages on my phone at about 8.00 when I heard something outside and noticed a light. I closed my phone and listened. There was no further noise, so I quietly got out of bed to look through one of the windows and saw a motorbike parked to one side. At the same time someone knocked on the driver's window. My first thought was that thieves probably wouldn't knock; but then came a second knock, so I peeked from behind the curtain and saw a middle-aged man standing there. He called out and I pulled back the curtain, opened the window a crack and asked what he wanted.

He proceeded to tell me that I could not park there, so I told him, "I'm fine, please go away." He informed me that he was a policeman and that there were bandits about and I was not safe, so I reiterated, "Really I'm fine, please go away." Then he told me that there was a hotel just the other side of the bridge and I would be safer in their compound. I replied that I had no money for a hotel, reiterated that I was fine and queried how was I even to know he *was* a policeman? He continued by insisting that I follow him and I realised I was not going to win this argument. The possibility of sleeping safely in a compound was also rather appealing so I agreed to follow him, but cautiously.

Indeed not fifty metres after the bridge there was a wall with a gate and a sign that identified a place that offered rooms, food, and music (although thankfully there was no music!) We were let in by the gate guard and Mr Policeman called for the owner and introduced me. At this point I got out of the van to greet him and say that I was sorry but the man claiming to be a policeman would not let me park outside, but anyway I had no money, I couldn't find an ATM and therefore I couldn't afford to stay. The owner immediately verified that the man was a policeman and kindly replied that it was no problem, I could stay there for free. With grateful thanks I parked BlueBelle out of the way.

Despite all the discussion about not having any money, I did actually have a small amount; I didn't want to risk driving about without any at all. Before he left Mr Policeman came to my window claiming that I must pay him. I reminded him that I didn't have any cash and if I did I would have to pay the owner of the hotel, but he insisted that I must pay for his fuel (really? But he had earlier said he wasn't far from home...) or at least for some food, because he was hungry (well, so was I!) Eventually I gave him 20,000GF (less than $2) and told him it was that or nothing. He took it as a win and left.

In return for the host's kindness, I posted his hotel's location on iOverlander. There was very little accommodation available for some distance in this area and I felt it might be of use to someone... And it so happened that it *was* useful to the Bell family, who stopped there and had a great time with the owner and enjoyed "the best chicken and chips" they had ever eaten. So I felt that, in part at least, my debt was repaid.

BAIT AND SWITCH

I had no idea that my departure at sunrise the next morning would bring mixed blessings. As I drove through the hotel gates I found that I was at quite some height up a mountain, and below me stretched a beautiful green valley filled with ethereal patches of mist that were gently filtered by the rising sun. It was one of those sights that words cannot justly describe. I was surrounded by the verdant mountains, looking upon the road winding down before me into the hazy valley. The air was fresh and cool and the only sound was the call of birds.

With more mountains, however, came more winding roads, and overtaking the large trucks was proving a challenge. As I've said, BlueBelle isn't at her strongest up hills, so I had to consider carefully before starting any overtaking manoeuvre; plus as she is right-hand drive and I was in a left-hand drive country, it meant cautiously pulling quite far out to see what lay beyond the vehicle in front. Someone in a LHD once berated me for driving a RHD as it was "too dangerous on overtaking"; however, needs must and I learnt many tricks. First and foremost was patience. Secondly, being seated on the right meant that on a right-hand bend I could get a better view past the vehicle in front of me to see what lay ahead. It was also important to keep enough distance to view the road but not so much that it slowed me down when overtaking, and eventually I became an expert at it. My last tactic came about by chance and worked effectively for much of Africa.

Getting from A to B is expensive for locals who don't have jobs or cash and they often catch a ride on the top of huge trucks. This is, of course, a risky business and they are known to fall off, sometimes with grisly consequences. On one occasion, whilst I was patiently sitting behind one of these trucks and seeking my opportunity to pass, one of the 'passengers' whom I had waved at earlier noticed my attempts and realised my problem. He then acted as a lookout to see when I could pass and waved me on when the road was clear. This was very handy and so much safer and easier for me.

So from then on, whenever I came up behind a truck I would wave at the guys on top, and inevitably they would look to see what type of unusual vehicle was behind them, smile widely and wave back. I would then gesticulate to indicate that I was trying to pass and needed their assistance, and after a couple of these gestures they would quickly catch on to what I wanted to do. Eagerly they would wave at me to wait and then, when the time was right, motion that I might pass. From their high vantage point they had a great view of the road ahead and they never let me down, always waving and smiling as I hooted my thanks. Only once did a guy refuse to help me.

I had no success finding an ATM but there were Western Union shops aplenty, and since I needed fuel and the money to pay for it, despite the fee this was again clearly the only option.

By now I was fed up with always having too little cash, and I considered that if I drew enough now I could change the rest at the border so I would be set for Côte d'Ivoire. I had no idea when I might find the next opportunity. At one WU shop I was paid out several million Guinea francs, mostly in small denominations and most of them dark tatty notes barely holding together. As I needed diesel I asked the shop owner where I could find a fuel stop, and he indicated that the route out of Kissidougou would be best. This town would stay uncomfortably in my memory as the only place in Africa where I got conned... and it was my own stupidity that got me into trouble.

In Guinea, as in many African countries, the black market for fuel was immense. There were not enough outlets for those living in the rural areas, and in some instances there was not even enough fuel outside the main cities. Long distances between stations exacerbated the problem, meaning that vehicles (mainly scooters) serving as taxis in rural areas would be using as much fuel to get fuel; hence the thriving black market. I had noticed that when a tanker arrived and the fuel had been decanted into the station, within hours the pumps were empty as people arrived in droves to fill every conceivable type of container. Motorcycles and scooters were laden down with yellow plastic canisters filled to the brim, and taxis had containers strapped to their sides once the boot and seats were full. Thereafter the only place to buy fuel was from the side of the road in mostly wine-sized bottles which had been standing in the boiling sun. I did wonder how safe this was, and yet scooters, motorcycles and cars were regularly seen filling up by the bottle.

Having had issues in Mauritania with fuel, I regularly had concerns about the quality I would get in this part of the continent; however after several fuel stations were found to be empty I was becoming worried. I pulled into what looked to be the last station in town and was again advised that there was no fuel. I was on a quarter of a tank and believed I had enough to make it to the next big town... but what if I didn't? I hadn't yet bothered to fill up my jerry cans, which proved a mistake.

As I was pleading with the pump attendant at this Total garage, a man appeared at my window and told me he could sell me some diesel. Wary, I looked at him and replied, "No, thank you," but he persisted. I hesitated and then asked for the price. Oddly it was the same as the pump price and I considered that there seemed nothing to lose, so I agreed. "Please bring me twenty litres of diesel," I instructed him, feeling that this would give me enough to make the distance, but if the fuel was sub-standard it would do BlueBelle little damage. He told me I had to drive around the corner to get it and I just laughed. I was *not* going around any corner to get anything: he could bring the fuel to me or there was no deal! He reluctantly agreed but told me I would have to drive off the station forecourt, which made sense.

Under the watchful eyes of the pump attendants, I moved the five metres or so off the forecourt and got out to unlock my diesel cap. As always I left my purse in the van and locked my door behind me, taking no chances. Although I was surrounded by men I was not concerned, but I now realise that they were chatting with me to distract me while the contents of a twenty-litre container were being poured into my tank. After what felt like too short a time they announced that they were done, but when I looked at the container and saw that there was still some fuel inside I told them, "I want all the fuel I'm paying for, thank you!" and they continued to pour. I was still not suspicious when a large well-built man walked from the station toward me, shouting aggressively in French something about paying for the fuel.

Now as you know I *hate* being shouted at and I immediately turned full on to face him, put up my hand in a STOP gesture and told him, "Stop shouting at me!" in a loud and firm voice. He kept it up for a few more seconds, and when I looked aside to ask someone else why the large man was shouting at me, I turned to find that he had vanished as suddenly as he had appeared. The man filling my tank again announced that he was finished. I still had a feeling that this was far too quick but the evidence was a now-empty container. Something didn't look or feel right though, and I was left perturbed.

As I got back into the van, the man who had initially approached me at the station started harassing me for the money. I told him he would get his money and to stay calm and wait. This rushing tactic was to keep me off balance and not allow me time to think. I discreetly counted out the amount owed and handed it to him, whereupon he swiftly counted it, thanked me and walked off.

I started to reverse out, but as I pulled away I saw that no more than five litres had been added to my tank. I was instantly furious, both with them and with myself as it dawned on me that I had been the victim of a 'bait-and-switch'. My mind was working at a rate of knots. I had two choices: either I could go back and give them a piece of my mind, which would almost certainly result in no change to my current status – I doubted I would see the fuel or the money; more likely they would simply flee and I would never be able to find them, added to which I was a lone woman here and didn't know how many were 'in on the game' – or I could carry on, nurse my wounded pride and just curse them for their wicked deed. I opted to carry on.

It took me many miles before I could release my fury at my stupidity and let the whole episode go. It could have been a lot worse of course: I could have paid them a higher rate, or asked for more fuel; at least here I had moderated my loss, which was only about $18. It seems so little, writing it down, but it was about more than the money.

The good news was that a few towns further along I found a fuel station with fuel, and at last my panic was over. Not too long after that I came upon a resurfaced road with a new sign saying something about being installed by the EU. I blessed them frequently. It was a pristine road with no potholes, well-painted lines, signs to indicate bends in the road and stop signs at village crossroads. It was a work of art. I was so entranced that I ended up on a longer route, deluding myself that this road would last forever.

THE CROWN JEWELS OF AFRICA

What was most interesting about my drive – and indeed my whole journey through Africa – was my observation that where there were good roads, the villages were perceptibly better off. They were cleaner and looked just that bit better organised and more prosperous. The villages with proximity to a road had easier access to transport, and that meant being able to take produce and wares to neighbouring villages or nearby markets. It became clear that roads and prosperity were inextricably linked: just think how roads expanded the Roman Empire.

As I drove along this particularly lovely road (how easy I was to please now!) I had more time to look at my surroundings. The rainforest too was pristine, lush and green, varied and dense, and occasionally there were small clearings with bananas or sometimes pineapples. It was all extraordinarily beautiful. We no longer see what we have lost in nature due to human impact, but I saw the evidence when I compared the huge empty spaces of agriculture, mining, deforestation and human habitation with the identifiable remains of what used to be vast areas of virgin rainforest. Africa is huge and it has been abused by so many, not just its native cultures.

As evening approached I knew that I was not too far from Guéckédou, where I had identified a place to securely park for the night on the other side of town. The sun was close to setting when the inevitable tragedy happened. The beautiful road ended – abruptly – and there was a police checkpoint to announce it. I was about fifteen kilometres from the city, and after the checkpoint the tarmac became so appallingly rutted and potholed that it almost made me want to turn back; but it was already nearly dark.

The grand melee was the first thing I ran into in the dark. It was hard enough to negotiate it in the light of day, but I had another five kilometres before I would reach my stop for the night. As if it couldn't get any worse, the potholed tarmac disappeared and I found myself on an even worse stretch of road. I had to inch my way into slow traffic across a bridge that could only still be standing by the sheer determination of will. The traffic was worsened by the fact that a truck, which I assumed had been driving in the opposite direction, had broken down in the middle of the 'road' and now looked abandoned. There were also dozens of traders encroaching on to the 'road' with as many pedestrians viewing their wares, leaving almost no space for vehicles to pass. I had to hoot and hoot for people to get out of the way. Having a larger-than-average vehicle, I needed the extra room so that I could get by safely without killing anyone.

A man, obviously annoyed by my hooting (or by me), came up to my window and began shouting that I was being rude. I shouted and gesticulated back: with the truck stuck to my left and the people in my way on my right, what the hell did he think I should do?! He looked around, thankfully realised my problem and started telling people to move aside. Finally there was movement and I was most grateful. I inched past the broken-down truck, bouncing from side to side through the gullies and potholes. However, after finally clearing that mess, a little further on there was – of all things – a traffic light. The sight of it seemed so ridiculously out of context... but of course it was not working since there was no electricity!

I turned left, once again manoeuvring my way around parked vehicles and hoping that I had left the worst behind me. I had not. The 'road', which continued for the next several kilometres, was an uneven dirt track that had been gouged out of the ground next to the original tarmac road, itself now so broken and potholed that it was easy to understand why it was no longer used. I crawled along in the dark, my headlights struggling to discern the best route.

I breathed an enormous sigh of relief when I finally arrived at my destination, a large hotel set in enormous grounds but seemingly empty. Eventually a man appeared in his vest and informed me that, despite the vast grounds, I had to take a room at an exorbitant rate. I firmly told him that I didn't have enough money for a room, but I could offer him the going rate for a place to park out of everyone's way; and if that was not OK I would go back out into the night and carry on driving to the next place. Fortunately he accepted my offer and showed me where I could shower. When I laid eyes on it, I thanked him and forced a smile in the full knowledge that it would not be used by me under any circumstances: it had algae, dirt, slime and who knows what all over the bottom of the walls and the floor! My bucket would suit me fine, and in anticipation I filled it from a nearby tap.

After I'd had a cursory wash and got into bed, I reviewed my day. Had I taken the shorter route I would not have seen those glorious rainforest views; or experienced the beautiful road and imagined what Africa might look like if governments invested in infrastructure; or felt the incredible lack of concern that a town can have about its state. I revelled in the memories of those images and my newly-honed bait-and-switch skills. However, before I fell asleep the rain came and I lay in bed worrying about how it would affect that awful road outside.

It rained for several hours and I awoke to silence. That meant there was no traffic, and no traffic in an urban area meant something was wrong. I lay in bed feeling decidedly depressed at the idea of facing that road after the rain. However, by the time I did hear some traffic and decided to leave, I found that the heat of the African sun had dried out all but the deepest puddles.

There was still some considerable distance of dreadful road before it became 'normal' again: tarmac but with many potholes. Our average moving speed was about eighty kilometres per hour – not very fast, but the constant braking and speeding up again was wasteful, not to mention tedious. I soon developed considerable skill at the 'pothole slalom', cruising between and around the craters without needing to step on the brakes.

My experience in Conakry had taught me to buy fruit and vegetables from the side of the road beyond the towns and cities since it was substantially fresher and cheaper. I had started to see avocados being displayed in the customary metal bowls along with an array of other produce, and I couldn't resist. I eventually found a safe spot to pull in and asked (in my limited French) how much it would cost for a single avocado. The woman told me it would be the equivalent of about 50c, so still thinking with a European head I was happy to take three avocados plus a large papaya, which was the same price. I handed over a bag for her to put my goodies in, but to my astonishment she poured out the contents of the metal bowl – about eighteen avocados of varying sizes. It then dawned on me that I was purchasing the *entire* contents of the bowl for 50c! Holy guacamole!!

Before I was landed with three times the amount I already had, I quickly adjusted my order to ONE avocado and three papaya, since I didn't want to reduce the original order price. The lady obliged and I took my bag and handed over the money, whereupon she immediately asked me to wait and tried to give me another three more papaya as a *cadeau* (gift). I was quite content that I had paid a fair price for my fruit so waved at her, "No, no," but she was insisting and heading toward me with said gift. Refusing to add to my loot I smiled, waved and shouted a sunny

"Merci!" as I drove off. The generosity of the African people that I encountered was a joy and a blessing.

I was heading for Nzérékoré, the second-largest city in Guinea. The region is known as *Guinée forestière* or Forest Guinea, and has the reputation for being the most beautiful area of the country. I had only seen a small corner of this friendly republic so far but I could certainly agree that it was quite lovely, with more vast swathes of pristine rainforest and great glorious mahogany trees towering majestically above the emerald landscape. Once again the early morning drive was cool and fresh compared with the ever-increasing diurnal heat, and rich with the glorious burnished orange hues that nature presents in Africa to announce the new day.

As soon as the sun rises, the women and children are about the task of collecting water. The women were in beautiful, long and often narrow traditional print dresses with turbans of differing styles and often a baby on the back; and each woman had a bucket on her head and one in either hand. Out there, every litre counts. The children were all carrying buckets too, sometimes by hand and sometimes on their heads. I marvelled at their stamina: water is heavy. Many were in their school uniforms doing their chores before their often long walk to school. They were joyful little beings, chattering and playing as they went along, not complaining about their lot in life but merely living in the moment.

There were no surprises or unanticipated stops along my way and the drive was not too taxing, so by early afternoon I was in Nzérékoré City (which felt very different from Conakry) and navigating my way to the Catholic Church, where they allowed overlanders to park in their secure grounds for a donation. The grounds were large and I parked BlueBelle under a tree, appreciating the little shade it had to offer, and caught up with messages on my phone.

I had seen on the West Africa Travellers' Facebook group that a Chinese-Canadian woman was overlanding West Africa by public transport: now *that* was challenging! We had been in Conakry at the same time but on opposite sides of the city and we had different routes planned; however, I was sure we would soon cross paths. Over and above the fact that she was travelling by public transport, she had unfortunately had her phone stolen some weeks before and was only online with her laptop – and then only when she had WiFi. I really didn't think I could manage without my phone and access to the internet!

I was sitting on my sofa with my 'air conditioning' on (aka a 12V dual-fan blowing hot air around) and enjoying the view over a nicely-manicured green lawn. My sliding door was open but my net curtain was drawn, (a) for privacy and (b) to keep flies and mozzies out. I heard a strange noise and looked up, and just a couple of metres from my door a woman came into view pulling a standard size suitcase and carrying a travel bag. She had on a dress and a hat and her dark hair was arranged in a long plait down her back. I instantly knew who she was as I recognised her picture from Facebook and I shouted out, "Rowena!" She stopped, turned around to look where the voice had come from and beamed, calling out my name when she saw me step out of the van.

We were both very surprised to have found each other at this place. She had come a few days earlier than anticipated as her other accommodation had not worked out, so it was a bit of serendipity. It was a Thursday and I was planning to cross into CDI the next day because I wanted to try to catch up with Chloe, from West Africa Travellers, before she left on a business trip. Meanwhile Rowena was planning to head off to see the chimpanzees at Bossou[44] on Saturday but hadn't yet figured out how to get there. After she'd settled into a room, we walked along the street to find food and a cool drink and spent the time catching up and sharing experiences.

I went to sleep but woke at about 3.00am with a voice in my head saying, Chimpanzees – will I ever get the chance to see them again in the wild? I'm dashing off ... but I could be going to see chimpanzees! The voice was right: I love the nature on my continent and often call its wildlife the 'crown jewels of Africa'. They are partly what makes Africa so precious, and knowing that in the next ten to twenty years there could be none left of many species... well, that would be a calamity of grand proportions. I decided there and then that I wanted to see chimpanzees – in nature, where they belonged. In all my route planning I had totally

---

[44] www.greencorridor.info

missed the review of this place, so it seemed that Rowena had been the prompt I needed.

Having grown up in a country where wildlife was part of my surroundings, I had been fortunate to see Africa's 'Big Five'[45] quite often (and so much more), but I had taken it all for granted: it was just... always there. It was only when it was *not* there that I realised how much I missed it and how immensely privileged I was to have had such experiences. So instead of leaving the next day, I told Rowena of my decision and offered her a lift, sorting out her how-to-get-there issues. She was naturally delighted and we decided that an early departure the following morning would be best to avoid the more intense heat later on.

I spent most of that day resting up, not knowing what roads were ahead of me. I planned to go to see the chimps in the morning and would continue to the border after that; while Rowena had decided that she wanted to return to Nzérékoré to attend church on Sunday, so I would drop her on the main road and she would find a taxi back.

Early the next morning I took a shower in Rowena's room and, fresh and clean and raring to go, we headed out of the city and on to Bossou. The drive started quite well, but when I turned off the main road at Lola I found myself once again navigating an often deeply rutted red dirt track. (Fortunately it was still dry season or we would not have made it.) We passed through several villages and, as usual, I waved and greeted people as we drove by.

The Mount Nimba Nature Reserve covers a vast area very close to the border with Liberia and CDI. Soon we arrived at a cluster of buildings of the *Institut de Recherche Environnementale de Bossou*[46] (IREB), from which the chimpanzee tours started. The buildings had clearly been there for some time but were well maintained and sat nestled in between hills and rainforest. We were met by the director, who informed us that the entry fee was the equivalent of $50. While this was a lot of money to me, I really wanted to do this. Rowena, on the other hand, was only prepared to pay the equivalent of $20 from

---

[45] the Big Five game animals of Africa are the lion, leopard, rhinoceros, elephant and Cape buffalo

[46] www.greencorridor.info/images/green-corridor/education/Pamphlet-Bossou-Nimba_2005.pdf

her budget, so I offered to pay the difference as it seemed ridiculous to have come all this way and not do the tour. She declined at first, but after some discussion she agreed she too would do it.

However, it turned out Rowena did not have the correct shoes. While we were discussing the matter, we were joined by an American woman who was researching at the facility and about to head out into the jungle for the morning. She happened to have the same shoe size as Rowena, and on hearing our dilemma offered her the loan of a spare pair of boots. I had extra socks for her so we set off to see the chimpanzees!

The pressure is on between wildlife and humans: encroachment, poaching and hunting take their toll alongside the clearing of natural habitat for agriculture, and as these all increase, so the animal numbers plummet. Already most African people have never seen any large wild animals, just their cows, goats and donkeys. I fear that future generations of Africans too will mourn the loss of our great crown jewels, but by then it will be too late…

The IREB project takes fifty percent of the funds received from tourism and gives it to the local village, providing them with an income to ensure that they do not seek to use the reserve land for farming, poaching or hunting. This demonstrates to the people a reason to preserve the local wildlife and its environment. The remaining fifty percent of the funds goes to supporting the Institute, enabling ongoing research into preserving the chimpanzees in their habitat. This was true conservation and addressed the issue sensitively and creatively, so I was more than happy to give them my money.

Before the tour began we were asked to sit and wait under some trees on several benches, some already occupied by local men. The guides and trackers would be called from the village to come to take us out. I greeted everyone as I sat and one of them spoke good English, so I asked him whether he and his colleagues were there doing research. He replied that this team was replanting trees in the Nimba Reserve, a joint project between the United Nations and the Guinea government to restore the natural habitat of the chimpanzees and their food sources. I was impressed and inspired and commended them on being part of the solution.

It was now mid-morning and here, next to the dense rainforest, the humidity was intense and the sun unrelenting, yet I was wearing socks with my closed trainers, full-length jeans, a short-sleeved t-shirt and a long-sleeved denim shirt over that. You may ask what on earth was I thinking? Well, I was thinking bites: with my record-breaking appeal to all things that nibble, I wanted to take every precaution. At the guest house in Conakry, I had briefly spoken with a woman who had been to one of Guinea's reserves and she had the most appalling insect bite marks all over her arms and neck. I was determined to show as little skin to those pesky bugs as I possibly could, so the full body armour and closed shoes were essential. It's a jungle, people!

Our guides arrived, one for each of us, and two trackers who took their scooter up the path and would then start tracking towards us. They were all wielding machetes and I felt a bit like Stanley or Livingstone as I walked into the dense vegetation behind my guide. I was very excited!

The light dimmed as we entered the rainforest, the dense foliage filtering out the sun and the humidity intensifying. The forest floor was layers deep with damp leaves, twigs and branches – none of which presented a problem until it came to climbing or descending when everything slipped and slid underfoot. Fortunately there were plenty of roots and vines to hang on to, but as the angles steepened I was having more and more trouble staying upright. My trusty guide, Manu, was a short young man whose invaluably strong hand supported me numerous times and prevented me from gliding unceremoniously down the slopes. His familiarity with this environment was evident and, despite not speaking each other's language, he smiled at my (often rather blue) exclamations. He also patiently waited as I frequently paused, taking a break from watching my feet to ensure that I looked around me to absorb fully the magnificence of the environment.

After an hour and a half of lots of jungle but no hint of a chimpanzee, we stopped to take another break. Manu disappeared (I assumed to take care of a personal matter) and Rowena and I were chatting. Her guide, Boniface, was on the phone with the trackers again; they had been in regular communication throughout our trek. Suddenly, from out of the forest we heard a hooting that was definitely not a bird. I looked at Boniface, my eyes wide in question, and he nodded in response. They were not far away! Manu reappeared and we spent at least another fifteen minutes walking. We were on reasonably level ground but the path became more overgrown, indicating that people had not passed there recently. The machetes did their job and cleared the way with ease.

As we moved closer we were joined by the trackers, who guided us beneath two young chimpanzees high up in the trees, swinging and chattering to each other. My heart skipped a beat in awe and tears filled my eyes. I was watching wild chimpanzees! The chimpanzees, however, were not quite as happy to see us. One of them scampered over to the top branches of a tall tree just metres in front of us, plucked a dead branch from the canopy above and threw it in our direction.

Rowena was taking photographs and it was a few seconds before I realised that the missile-thrower's aim was pretty accurate. I shouted at her to get down as the branch sailed just centimetres above her head, hitting the ground behind her. A nervous laugh escaped us all. The chimpanzees in the area are renowned for their use of tools and this one had done an expert job of confirming that! We moved along the path slightly to see if we could get a better look at both the youngsters, but our friend procured another branch and this time the team hurried us back along the path – just in time because the next missile would almost certainly have hit one of us. The trackers decided we should continue along another path, leaving the angry chimp to his friend.

A little further along there was a group of three. It was obviously a family, judging from their size: a momma, a baby and a very big daddy. They were seated on the ground tearing leaves off a shrub and munching on them happily. It wasn't easy to see them as the forest was so dense, and when there are babies in tow it is advisable not to get too close. We watched them for a while until the guides told us we should return to the camp, which fortunately was not too far away. Beautiful as the experience was, I was certainly ready to head back as every piece of my clothing was soaked with sweat. The hike had been more exercise than I'd taken in a long time.

I was in a daze of excitement after such an incredibly profound experience, but I remembered to tip the team and thank them most effusively, and they keenly participated in some group photos. I also spoke to the manager and the director, expressing my sincere appreciation of their work. They told me that the chimpanzees do sometimes disappear when they need food, but they always seem to return to a specific hill which faces the Institute, named Chimpanzee Mountain by the locals.

The next most important thing was to drink lots of water in an attempt to replace what I had lost. Then I changed out of my drenched clothes as Rowena returned the boots and, somewhat sadly, I waved goodbye as we returned to real life.

Back at the main road in Lola we looked for a bus or taxi for Rowena, but although it was now about noon on a Saturday, extraordinarily there was not a taxi in sight. Usually there were hundreds of them, but when needed not one! Rowena spoke to some people loitering outside a building and I went to ask some others when I noticed a nice new white 4x4 hurtling towards us.

There's not much to stop a fast car like an old woman standing in the middle of the road frantically waving it down. This belonged to a Chinese man with his driver, so I asked if there was any chance of taking my friend back to Nzérékoré. Although they were not going there, they kindly offered to help her out, so Rowena bundled into the rear cab and waved goodbye. Along the way she had said how much she admired me driving on my own, but at this moment I had to admire *her* getting a lift from strangers in the middle of nowhere. I hoped I would see or hear from her again...

I was off to the border. The heat was incessant, as was the sweating, so I drank more water. Soon I was enjoying a drive through what I can only describe as a cathedral of bamboo. I had no idea until then that bamboo was indigenous to Africa as well as Asia, but I would become familiar with the sight of it in various rainforests. Here it grew densely on each side of the road, its long branches bowing overhead to create a magnificent vaulted green canopy.

Unfortunately the greenery did not last and the road turned into another red dirt track. The Chinese were building a new highway from the border towards Nzérékoré. This meant that my route was taken up by the new road under various stages of construction and, along the sides, tracks in varying stages of *de*construction that were masquerading as the diversion. I was grateful that it was Saturday, with likely fewer large aggregate trucks on the road than normal. I cursed them as they hurtled past me, kicking up tons of red dust.

The border was quiet and I was out of Guinea without any of the drama that I'd had coming in, just the usual, "Are you alone/why are you alone/I will come with you" – to which my replies were, "Yes/because I want to be/no thank you, I'm happy on my own – less trouble". Their retort to this last reply was usually an assurance that they *wouldn't* be any trouble, and my retort to that was, "Men are *always* trouble. They want cooking, cleaning, ironing and looking after: much easier for me to just look after myself!" The entire conversation was light-hearted and always taken with a laugh and a smile. It made the whole process much more pleasant, especially while waiting for the obligatory recording of my details in the obligatory big black books.

Chapter Six – Côte d'Ivoire (Ivory Coast)

8 February 2019

I had been warned that the Côte d'Ivoire border was corrupt and could present problems, so I was on high alert. But I was also learning to relax and take it as it came, with the security of knowing that if they wouldn't let me through I could always stay in my van. I had food for a few days and enough water, so I didn't have to stress. My approach had become: smile, make a joke and don't look intimidated.

There was a building at the CDI border – an upgrade on my entry into Guinea! I greeted a variety of men loitering on the veranda, some in uniform, and went to have my passport stamped before customs. I knew that a TIP was free but I would only be able to get it in Man,[47] still a few hours' drive from the border; and it was now gone 2.00. I was directed to take a seat in an office, where they proceeded to tell me that I had to *pay* for my TIP. I understood them fully but thought, OK, let the games begin… and replied that I didn't speak French so I couldn't understand what they wanted. I was told to wait, while off they went to see if they could find someone to speak English with me. It seemed they were determined to catch this fish.

I sat back in the seat and looked around the dingy office with its broken chairs and drawers. In time I was approached by a uniformed officer who thought that if he spoke to me slowly in French I would understand him better, so I just smiled and shrugged. A while later another man arrived, this one not in uniform, who started the discussion in basic English about how I needed to pay to get my TIP. When I replied that I *didn't* need to pay he insisted that I did, and this went on for some time until I realised that this was not changing anything. New tactic: "I don't carry money with me when I'm travelling and I wasn't expecting

---

[47] Pronounced *mã*

to pay." That foiled him and he left the room, perhaps thinking he would let me stew. I smiled to myself.

By now I had been there an hour and was mentally readying myself to spend the night. I did have an ace up my sleeve though. Chloe from West Africa Travellers had told me that if I ever had trouble I should get in touch, as she had an official contact who was trying to curb this corruption and would be able to sort it out. Nevertheless I was sort of enjoying seeing where this conversation would go.

Mr Corrupt returned and again pressed me for money, so I reiterated that I didn't carry cash: being a woman on my own, I told him with great seriousness, it would be unwise of me to do so. (I should have been an actress.) He gave this some consideration and then told me that if this was the case then I needed to have an escort into Man and I only had to pay the escort's return journey (inevitably the price he would have charged for a TIP!) It was time to get tough, so I immediately told him that it was out of the question on several levels. Firstly, I was a woman travelling alone and I was not putting a strange man, no matter his position, in my van with me. Secondly, my insurance wasn't going to cover me if I took a passenger (that was a big fib, but he was trying to get a bribe so gloves off). And lastly, I was quite capable of finding my way to Man and the required office without an escort.

He was taken aback by my sudden change in mood and elevated his insistence that I needed an escort. I sat back, gave this some thought and looked at the clock on my phone: 3.30 on a Saturday afternoon. I leaned forward and spoke quietly.

Me:	So if I take your escort, I have to take him to Man?
Mr Corrupt:	Yes.
Me:	I drive slowly so I probably won't get there tonight, but if I do will the office be open?
Mr Corrupt:	No.
Me:	Is the office open on a Sunday?
Mr Corrupt:	No.
Me:	If I have to spend a night on the way and a night in Man waiting for the office to open on Monday morning, what will your escort be

doing? Is he going to watch me and sleep outside my van? If he really *is* an escort, then he has to see me to the office, right?

Mr Corrupt was now well and truly stumped. Game up, and I knew I had the advantage.

He took a few minutes to realise he now had no further cards to play and then came up with the story that he would trust me to get to Man by myself and pay for my TIP. I assured him, with the most demure of smiles, that it wouldn't occur to me *not* to have the correct papers, because I knew that the police checks would catch me. He reluctantly let me go, but not before warning me, "You must pay at the office!" I smiled pleasantly and thanked him for his kindness, acting like I was completely unaware of his ruses for a bribe.

I smiled and waved at everyone sitting outside, including all the men who had interrogated me, and I was soon happily bumping down the road. The road conditions worsened, slowing me down considerably, and the day was fast running out, but I had pinpointed a 'hotel' on the outskirts of Danane and was hoping they would let me park in their compound.

MAN

It was dusk when I arrived in Danane and I pulled in to my destination just off the main road. It was a hotel/night club/bar and within the compound there was a parking area, which included two broken-down vehicles and a lot of trash – not ideal, but it would have to do; anyway when I was inside BlueBelle I was oblivious to the world outside.

I asked to see the manager, who didn't speak English, but I managed to get across that I just wanted to park, not to take a room. The look on his face told me he thought it rather odd so I responded with my best smile, sweaty and bedraggled as I was. He offered a price and while we were negotiating I noticed that they had food, so I added that I would buy a beer and something to eat. The price settled, he directed me to a counter and I ordered chicken and chips (the universal meal), a soda to hydrate and a cold beer to enjoy. After all my adventures of the day, sitting back and relaxing was a blessing; and while it cost me a whole $10, I considered I deserved the break – although after splashing out on the chimpanzees I would need to be extra careful about my daily budget for a while.

As usual people were curious and the lack of understanding privacy persisted, so it wasn't long before I had a few young men sitting at my table. One of them spoke English and was full of questions. I always tried to answer what I could without giving away too much as I never knew who I was speaking to. It was just a matter of balancing my personal security with being friendly and engaging with the local people. If I had been a man I could probably have been less wary and more relaxed, but with all the proposals and innuendos I felt the need to strike a more conservative role.

My beautiful dusty BlueBelle was safely parked between the broken cars and trash, some of which had been shoved aside to accommodate me, but I was not concerned. I had something cool to drink and food I hadn't had to cook; I'd seen chimpanzees in the wild; and I'd beaten Mr Corrupt at his own game: all in all it had been quite a day! And as I nestled in my bed and heard the big metal gates being locked for the night, my eyes closed and I slept like a baby.

I reached Man on Sunday and located my parking spot, a Catholic Church conference facility run by the Bishop of Man. They wouldn't let me just park up without accommodation so I took the cheapest room: it was affordable and had a shower, however I opted to sleep in my van as that would be more luxurious! The shower was located on an enclosed veranda but there was also a basin in the room that I used to wash a few clothes. The toilet block was 'interesting', and as usual I was happy to have my own facilities.

On Monday morning I looked through my checklist: change my Guinea francs (GF), which I hadn't been able to do at the border because there were no money changers; buy a local SIM card; fill up with fuel; and of course get my *free* TIP. I had already paid for my accommodation, hoping that I could continue on my way to Yamoussoukro when I had everything done.

The first problem was that no one would change my GF. I drove around to several of the banks and tried the usual haunts of taxi and bus ranks looking for black market traders, but no luck. I needed the cash to do the rest of my chores so I eventually succumbed to using the ATM, but I only managed to get a small amount of money. My credit card was prepaid and my tactic was to put in money only when I had to draw it out, leaving a small balance – good security too. I needed a SIM card though to transfer funds to my card, and only then could I withdraw the cash to buy fuel. I had been going around in ever-decreasing circles, but luckily the small amount of cash I had drawn was just sufficient to buy a SIM card and some data. I successfully transferred funds and went back to the ATM to withdraw more cash, still in possession of 1.5 million GF (approximately $150).

My last stop was to get my Temporary Import Permit. I arrived at customs with all my papers and copies and held my breath to find out what came next. Despite it being almost 9.30, the TIP office was still not open. Phone calls were made and I was asked to wait, which I did patiently while watching the comings and goings. Soon after 10.00 the secretary arrived, and I was instructed to complete a form as she captured my information on a computer. Then I had to see the boss, but he was busy so I waited some more. It doesn't help to be impatient in Africa. Like bureaucrats worldwide, *they* were in charge here and getting irritated wouldn't achieve anything. Finally though I got to see the boss and he carefully reviewed my papers. I said nothing but what was required, waiting to see if anyone asked for money. However, no request was forthcoming and my paper was signed. I returned to the secretary who had to enter some more information into the computer before I was given a TIP print-out... and that was it. Put that in your pipe and smoke it, Mr Corrupt!

By now it was late morning and I was exhausted from all the toing and froing, so I decided to return to the conference centre and stay another night. Once there I took the opportunity to relax and ready myself for whatever adventures lay ahead. I was learning that driving-and-doing had to be balanced out with stopping-and-relaxing.

YAMOUSSOUKRO

An early departure was required the next day. The map told me that it was only three hundred and sixty kilometres to

Yamoussoukro, but of course it would take me more than the estimated six and a half hours at our limited speed. A long day of driving lay ahead, but the road into the capital was not good...

I was no sooner out of Man than there was the customary checkpoint and I was, of course, stopped. I gaily produced my shiny new TIP and passport copy, and after the usual quizzing I was about to leave when an officer approached me and asked me in French to take someone to Abidjan. I feigned not understanding but he persisted, and since I wanted to get going I responded that, as a woman, I regretted that I could not take a strange man in the van with me. He took a moment to consider, then stepped back and nodded in understanding and let me go. Being a woman unfortunately affected many of my decisions, but my safety and comfort had to come first.

Yamoussoukro was the birthplace of the first president of CDI, Félix Houphouët-Boigny, who ruled for more than three decades until his death in 1993. During this time he developed the city into the political and administrative capital. Most people think that the port of Abidjan is the capital, but this is the business centre where the majority of economic activity takes place. It was Yamoussoukro, located in the middle of the country, which officially became 'the capital in the jungle'. It had a much more contemporary, open feel than most capital cities I had visited thus far, being laid out in a modern grid. It also boasts some remarkable sights: the one hundred and fifty-eight-metre high Vatican-inspired Basilica of Our Lady of Peace, the tallest Christian church in the world; the seven-storey House of Deputies convention centre; the impressive Grand Mosque; and the vast President's palace, which wasn't visible and sadly is not open to the public, but which has a crocodile lagoon nearby with an interesting back story.

After his death President Houphouët-Boigny was buried inside the palace grounds, guarded by an artificial lake and the city's sacred crocodiles. It seemed that the caretaker of the crocs, a Malian called Dicko Toki with the same nickname *le Vieux* ('the Old One') as his late master, was much admired for his work. During his forty years of service he fed the crocs daily with around thirty kilograms of meat in a sort of public ceremony and gave each of them authoritarian names to which they responded, such as *Chef de Cabinet*, *Commandant* and *Capitaine*. The crocodile has a mythical role for the Baoule people of the area, of which the late president was a member. On the last day of Ramadan in 2012, the elderly Dicko was seen to stumble on his robes and fall, and the nature of the crocodile being ever-present, *Chef de Cabinet* saw his opportunity and dragged the man swiftly into the centre of the lake. The grisly event was of course filmed by visitors and widely reported. On my visit, however, there was no evidence of crocodiles and the palace next door looked quite deserted and not very sacred at all.

I took up 'residence' at a local convent where they had rooms to rent and some conference facilities. Here though I only had to pay for parking and I'd found a spot under some leafy trees which brought about a welcome coolness. I was also permitted to use the staff shower, which was clean and in perfect repair. (I can honestly say that in my wide experience of monasteries and convents, the ones run by women were much cleaner and better maintained... just saying!)

It had now been several days and I had not heard from Rowena, so I was concerned whether she had been able to make it across the border; I had not seen much transport on that road. I decided to message her and surprisingly found that she too was in Yamoussoukro. She'd had to endure some long waits and a few changes, but she had made it. Her hotel was more expensive than where I was staying so we agreed to meet the next morning and I would relocate her to the convent.

Sadly my rendezvous with the chimpanzees meant I missed Chloe, but she had put me in touch with Paul, a local entrepreneur who also ran a restaurant where I had a delicious conversation about Africa and a quite magnificent meal. The next day I picked up Rowena with her suitcase and bag – which, incidentally, she lets no one else carry for her – and we decided to go for a drive around the city to see some of the sights I mentioned. When we had finished, rather faster than we had anticipated, we returned to town and I spotted a café – an unusual sight. I had been craving a fresh coffee (one that I didn't have to make) and a croissant for weeks, and we were both excited by the find. I parked out front (not very legally but I took my chance anyway), and in a civilised fashion we sat inside in the cool building.

We caused quite a stir, a white and a Chinese woman in the middle of town. As Rowena liked to say, "We are exotic creatures here!" As usual I greeted everyone with a friendly "Bonjour" and went to view what delights there might be on offer. Happily a variety of croissants were available, and they were so delicious that I ordered some to take away to enjoy the next morning on the way to Abidjan.

ABIDJAN

Rowena and I departed early. The drive was pleasant along a dual carriageway with a mostly decent surface. Obviously the route was important for commuting between the two political and economic centres.

Côte d'Ivoire clearly places a high emphasis on cultivation, because I saw only small pockets of rainforest. Plantations of bananas, palm oil, coffee and cocoa were all in evidence, and this production must have been why CDI was noticeably wealthier than Senegal or neighbouring Guinea. It is also the largest producer of cocoa in the world, although very little is processed in the country to add to the value chain.

It took us the whole morning to get to Abidjan. I was driving at the usual speed despite the improved road conditions and by the time we reached the city it was terribly hot and, if possible, even more humid. Rowena already had her accommodation sorted but we could not find it on the map, so she eventually opted for a taxi to take her on the last leg. I didn't see her again, but we remain in contact.

Meanwhile I had been invited to stay with a Dutch couple, expats who had recently arrived in CDI. We had connected on the West Africa Travellers group, with my ability to speak (although not write) Dutch being an easy connecting point. They were interested in my travels as they hoped to explore the region in greater depth.

I was a little early to meet them so I decided to take a drive around the city. Abidjan is built on a lagoon and is surrounded by waterways and bridges, and it looked every bit the twenty-first-century metropolis but with a touch of Africa thrown in, where the old and new, rich and poor mix. Overall I was impressed.

I hadn't realised that my hosts were in a gated community in a 'posh' part of town. The drive over there was interesting: many of the streets were lined on their verges with nurseries where the locals were selling the most gorgeous plants, the tropical climate ensuring that they were exotic, colourful and very, very lush. Realising that I had no gift for my hosts, I bought them a pretty white bougainvillaea.

The capacity for strangers to connect with me throughout my journey and take me into their homes was immensely humbling. Duncan and Klaartje were wonderful hosts and they insisted that I stay in their house with its excellent air-conditioning (which for once I was very glad of!) It would be my first night out of BlueBelle in Africa, which felt slightly strange. But to be perfectly honest, I had accepted the offer of hospitality mainly because I had put my kettle on my bed that morning (I hadn't yet found a secure place for it) and it had fallen over, soaking the bedding and mattress.

The room they gave me was spacious, with a large double bed and my own sparkling shower and toilet, all with the bonus air-conditioning. It was heavenly. My plan was only to stay a couple of days, but then they offered me the use of their washing machine and that was a luxury I just couldn't pass up. I was mightily tired of washing clothes in a bucket!

Klaartje had recently had a baby to add to the little boy and girl they already had, and to make life even more challenging in their new country they had taken on a lovely Labrador puppy just days before. In exchange for food and their hospitality, they welcomed my advice on how to look after their new fur baby. Having been a dog trainer for ten years in a previous life and a dog owner for forty, I knew a bit that could help them. As they were still a young couple I also realised that they might benefit from some non-child time together, so I offered to babysit one afternoon on the weekend and they grabbed the opportunity (but took the baby with them, which was probably a good idea!)

I was sad to eventually leave this wonderful little family – not to mention the bed and the lovely shower – but it was time to get moving; and I never regretted getting back into BlueBelle with all my things exactly where I needed them. I still hoped to get the

1.5 million GF changed before I left town, and it had been suggested that I try the airport.

Inside the airport building there was nowhere obvious to change cash, so I asked around and was recommended to speak to some guys hanging about the information counter. I greeted them and set out my requirements, whereupon there was some humming and hawing and they offered me a rate that would mean a forty-five percent loss. It was just unacceptable so I laughed and told them, "I'd rather eat it than give it to you for that!" and returned to my van and left, still a millionaire in currently valueless Guinean francs.

GRAND-BASSAM

Grand-Bassam was on my route to Ghana and looked like an interesting place to explore. Once the colonial capital of Ivory Coast it is a UNESCO world heritage site, and being on the coast it had lovely palm trees all along the beach. The town was filled with once-beautiful but now crumbling nineteenth and twentieth-century French colonial-style buildings, most beyond repair.

The old Governor's house, however, was in reasonable condition and now home to the Costume Museum, so I decided to stop by and have a look. The building told of an age of colonial grandeur, but in contrast again the old sepia photographs of men in pith helmets hinted at the brutality and contempt of the time. The costumes on display were those of local tribes along with accessories and weapons, and there was an interesting section demonstrating different tribal hut constructions. There were a variety of buildings around the main house, obviously former kitchens, servants' quarters and laundry rooms but now put to other uses.

One of the outbuildings housed craftsmen selling a variety of wares, including carved wooden statues, beaded jewellery, colourful fabrics and small painted masks. Most interesting to me were the masks. They were known as 'passports masks' and were once sewn on to a piece of clothing or carried in a small pouch and used as a form of identification. For example, the people of the region would carry a small mask in their own particular tribal style and, when travelling out of Abidjan would show it as evidence of their origin. The masks had a mystical and spiritual side to them and were also believed to protect the traveller, and I found their history quite fascinating.

I would have spent more time exploring Grand-Bassam but there was regrettably nowhere suitable to stop over. Chloe was planning to open a hostel-cum-guesthouse for overlanders and backpackers, The Elephant's Nest,[48] but it wasn't ready then.

After Grand-Bassam I went further down the coast in the direction of Ghana to stay at a lodge and restaurant in Assouindé that Chloe had again recommended I visit. The road was lined with tall willowy coconut palms and I felt like I was in a tropical paradise, but it was unnaturally hot and there was definitely a storm brewing. I arrived at the Hotel Jardin d'Eden,[49] which was set right on a pristine beach with grass umbrella stands and loungers under them. It looked like a glorious place to have a truly get-away-from-it-all holiday. I asked if I would be permitted to park in their grounds overnight and they were happy for me to do so, without charge, if I ate in their restaurant just across the track. Food for parking was always a good exchange: it allowed me to pay for a meal but not feel guilty about the cost.

The restaurant was gorgeous. Seated inside a large open-sided building with a thatched roof, I was in heaven, with WiFi and cold beers too. I arrived a little after lunchtime, but it was no problem for the kitchen so I chose a local fish dish. They said it would take a while, but I was happy to wait: I had WiFi and that meant I could occupy myself. When the fish finally arrived, accompanied by delicious fries and plantain, it looked magnificent, fresh and tasted amazing. It was a big meal so I took a doggy bag for the next day. Any day I didn't have to cook was a bonus!

It was late afternoon by the time I had finished eating, but before settling into BlueBelle and hiding from the inevitable mosquitoes at dusk, I decided to take a walk along the beach. The storm was getting closer: the sky was quickly turning black, the dark clouds illuminated by angry flashes of lightning, and the smell of rain came with the wind that precedes a storm. It was

---

[48] www.facebook.com/elephantsnests or www.youtu.be/2-mR8zZgpxA
[49] www.facebook.com/jardinedenassinie

quite splendid – and on top of that, the mosquitoes would probably not be out on such a night. I made a little video that I uploaded on to my social media, and soon after that I had to run for shelter as huge raindrops started to fall, swiftly followed by a full-on African deluge.

Chapter Seven – Ghana

19 February 2019

Although each border post experience had been distinctive for one reason or another, I can honestly say that getting out of Côte d'Ivoire was so easy that I don't even recall it. There was, however, a marked change in road quality as the road to the Ghana border post was a wonderful dual carriageway. No man's land wasn't too far and as I approached the checkpoint I started mouthing my "Bonjour" before suddenly realising that I was in another English-speaking country.

At the checkpoint I was asked the usual questions – why was I alone, where was I going? – but after a while the questions became more relevant and I was asked if I had a *carnet*. When I answered that I did not, I was instructed to wait around the corner. There was some shouting in the local language, a fellow came trotting along and one of the guards (who had already proposed to me) (and been declined) told me that this man would take care of me. He was wearing a Tourist Assistance hi-vis vest, similar to my fixer in Mauritania, but I couldn't quite get to the bottom of who employed him or how I seemed to have landed myself with a fixer again. When I asked him what I should pay him he said that he couldn't ask me for money but would welcome anything I could afford as a tip.

Immigration was our first stop, but when they saw that I was without a *carnet* they would not stamp me in until I had clearance for the vehicle. Ghana had become quite sticky about allowing vehicles in on a TIP, so I already knew this might be a challenge. Mr Helpful asked me for as much information as possible about my journey and what I was doing, so I explained that I was only passing through Ghana, that I was Zimbabwean and on my way home, and all about Kusasa, my non-profit for girls' education. Armed with my business card, my passport (I'd become better at assessing people and trusted him enough to give it to him) and my certified copies of van papers, he led me off to find the head honcho. Most of the conversation took place in the local language, interspersed with the odd question directed at me which I answered politely,

I was directed to fill in some TIP forms and then wait, so I occupied myself by chatting with the guards and some of the other people waiting. It was early and already hot and I was starting to get thirsty. I had seen some people walking about with drinks so I went off to find where they came from. The best option seemed to be small plastic bags of water – annoying as the plastic was everywhere, but they kept cold when they were frozen. The cost was negligible – probably why they were so popular – but I only had a small amount of cash in Ghanaian cedi from the few CFA francs I had changed at the CDI border. I bought several bags of water (it made for not having to ask for change) and handed them out to the people sitting around me. Never hurts to throw some goodwill into the equation when you're asking the Universe to help you out.

After about an hour the head honcho appeared and wanted to inspect the van. He proceeded to give me a lecture about taking care driving a right-hand drive vehicle in a left-hand drive country, but I assured him that over the past year I had become well acquainted with driving on the 'other' side of the road. Finally he seemed satisfied and I was permitted to go and pay the TIP fee at the small bank cabin around the corner of the main building. Having done so, my papers didn't take much longer... and voila, I had a TIP – rare as hen's teeth in Ghana! I completed immigration and was all finished. I expressed my sincere gratitude to Mr Helpful and tipped him well, certain that his persistence had swung the deal for me. The whole process had cost me €20, a bargain really!

After the nightmare of Hell's Highway and Conakry, I had known that I was tired and would soon need a 'holiday' from my adventure. I was feeling the strain and wanted to catch up with myself, so I had decided to stop for four or five days and do nothing – no driving, no planning, no traffic, no uncertain roads or border crossings; just rest and assimilate my experiences thus far. I had looked for a place I could go that would meet these needs, and while I'm really not a 'beach person' I had decided that by the sea there was always the chance of some breeze to cool things down. I had also opted for English-speaking Ghana so that

I wouldn't have to tax my brain attempting to speak French. With all this in mind I had found Hideout Lodge,[50] a gorgeous rustic place on Butre beach about ten kilometres from the nearest town of Agona. They welcomed overlanders to park there and it wasn't too far from the CDI border.

I had seen warnings of a speed checkpoint soon after entering Ghana but thought it was more of a 'corruption point'. I always kept one eye on my speedometer anyway. During a quick check of the map for my turnoff I had momentarily taken my eyes off the road, and no sooner had I looked up again than I saw a policeman waving me down. Infuriatingly, I'd missed that one important sign to reduce my speed, so there I was, pulled over again. The plain-clothes officer showed me his badge and informed me I had been speeding, but when I objected that it was unlikely, he claimed he had a reading on a machine. He told me he would write me a ticket and I would have to report to the nearest city to attend court and pay the fine. At my protestations that this would be impossible, he interjected that I could pay him to settle the matter. The game was on!

I told him I had just come through the border and spent all my money on my permit, and now I was on my way to Accra, the only place I could access more funds. He claimed not to believe this but I continued to assert my poverty, and eventually he proposed that I give him whatever I had in my purse and he would call the matter settled. Luckily I only had a single cedi in my main purse pocket (I failed to show him the other funds I had in the back), so I opened my purse and handed him the note, at which he laughed uproariously. He then asked how I was going to get into Accra with no money, so I explained that I had sufficient fuel and food on board my van. Shaking his head he told me how much I reminded him of his grandmother, warned me to be careful and sent me on my way.

Still chuckling at my good fortune I sailed along the tarmacked road, and before the turnoff for the coast I spotted a garage with a shop where I hoped I would be able to acquire some cold water and maybe a few beers. It was the usual garage shop and the prices were not too high, but as I neared the checkout I

---

[50] www.hideoutlodge.com

saw some Hunter's Gold, a South African cider that I really enjoy and hadn't had in about ten years. Coupled with the fact that the beers in Guinea and CDI were nowhere near as nice as Jul in The Gambia, I decided to splash out on a few cold libations amongst my other purchases. I pulled off the main road and started looking forward to the evening, when I would be sitting on my step overlooking a beach, drinking my favourite cider and pondering why I reminded the plain-clothes officer of his grandmother...

ON THE BEACH NEAR LONDON BRIDGE

As I'd anticipated, the road to the lodge was a dirt track, though fortunately in not too bad a state – well, relatively speaking based on my experience thus far. I was having some directional issues since online navigators were not always that reliable in Africa and I often had to use my common sense instead of just following them. This wasn't the first time it had led me astray, but now there were so many tracks and makeshift roads that it was hard to figure out which was the right one to take.

I passed several oil palm plantations on my way and saw many bunches of the fruit piled up on the side of the road. I must confess I had been quite ignorant about this crop before I arrived in West Africa. I found out that the oil that's extracted from the fruit is naturally a deep red because of its high beta-carotene content, and because it is also packed with sterols and vitamin E it is considered very healthy. This oil is not to be confused with palm *kernel* oil that is extracted from the kernel of the fruit and then highly processed, or coconut oil that is drawn from the kernel of the *coconut* palm. The red palm oil is cold-pressed and used for cooking in a great many of the local dishes.

The navigation told me to turn left and I found myself driving along an ever-narrowing road through one of these oil palm plantations. I passed a few workers with machetes so I smiled and waved like I knew where I was going. However, about half a mile further on I decided that this didn't feel right and I was not actually going in the right direction, so I made a tricky turn around and returned along the same track. One of the men I had passed was near enough the track to talk to, so I stopped, greeted him and admitted I was lost. He agreed and indicated the way I should go.

Eventually I found a sign for Hideout Lodge. I had noticed with some concern the amount of red dust on the road leading to the lodge, which would most assuredly turn to mud if it rained: something to keep in mind. My faith in persevering paid off when I came upon a view of a beautiful palm-lined beach, with the rustic lodge complex to my right, an open parking area to my left and not a soul in sight. I took a deep breath, relieved and grateful to be here at last. It was time to catch up with myself and my many new experiences and rest my still painful shoulder. Welcome to my holiday!

I spoke to the staff and was permitted to park in the parking area and use a shower for a small fee, once again after convincing them that I did not need or want accommodation. They assured me that the guard at night would look out for me and there were also meals available and cold drinks, so I was all set. I parked with my sliding door facing the Atlantic Ocean, took out my awning and settled in for the evening. There wasn't much shade but the Harmattan was in full force, masking the sun to a large degree.

The Harmattan is a north-easterly trade wind that comes at this time of the year and which I had first encountered in CDI. It originates in the Sahara and fills the air with fine particles of sand, enough to form a haze as far as the eye can see, making the sun less intense but the heat more oppressive.

The beach was reasonably quiet, with the exception of some schoolchildren who walked down a nearby path on to the sand. As usual they found me fascinating but were thankfully chased away by the attending staff, so I could keep all my doors open without concern. The beach led to a local village and people passed each way across the sands in the early morning and the evening, their commute an envious one. But for me, other than the odd person passing, I was left to my own private beach lined with swaying tropical palm trees. I only took one dip into the ocean during my stay: there was a strong rip tide and I'm neither a great swimmer nor fond of salt water and beach sand. The continuous sound of the waves and the palm fronds were soothing and only occasionally did the wind whip them up enough to wake me.

When I arrived there was again a full moon. It had been a month since I was in The Gambia and much had happened since then, so I took the time to reflect on my journey thus far whilst I cleaned, fixed and sorted at a leisurely pace. After a couple of hours working it was too hot to continue, so there was nothing to do but relax and nap. Each day I took the time to enjoy my early morning coffee on my step while watching the passing parade, and my cider each evening as the sun set and cast its last shot of colours across the hazy sky.

The staff found me an oddity, appearing only occasionally to take a meal or buy a cold cider or soda, and when they found me outside they would stop by to chat from time to time. In Africa the people live in close proximity and pretty much know everyone else's business, added to the fact that their family is usually an extended one; so a woman who chose to be alone and left to her own devices was unusual and stimulated their curiosity.

One chap came by to offer me a coconut, and with swift chops of the machete he removed the green skin (this variety was the most common here) and cut a hole in the top for me to drink the sweet juice. Once I'd finished he took it back and deftly chopped it in half so that I could eat the soft pulpy flesh, quite different from the hard inner meat of the hairy brown coconut.

One morning as I watched the school procession to the village, I saw a young boy and his sister looking at BlueBelle and then noticed hesitant moves in our direction. They hadn't seen me as I was sitting behind the net curtain, which afforded me a degree of privacy and helped keep the flies and mosquitoes out (the latter unfortunately with limited success). A little concerned, I stepped out from behind the net to ask what they wanted but they scampered away. It was only when I turned around that I realised that an empty plastic bottle I'd put next to the step while I was cleaning had been blown by the wind to the edge of the car park and caught their attention. I was often asked for my empty plastic bottles, so although I hated buying them I knew that passing them along meant that the locals could use them to carry water, the children at school and the women working in the fields. I felt a bit embarrassed that I had misconstrued their intent; however, I rectified the matter the next morning and when they passed I held out the bottle. They looked at me with trepidation until they realised that I was actually offering it to them, whereupon it was excitedly taken, with a hope and a prayer from me that it wouldn't end up in the ocean...

I was sitting outside under the awning one afternoon when a group of men passed by and one, in his late twenties, came over and started chatting to me. It all started quite politely but soon deteriorated into a conversation about how God had put me in this place expressly to meet him. (Flatter himself, much?!) Mr Proposition made several mentions of God's intent and references to the fact that I was a 'fine-looking woman'; but he must have thought I wasn't picking up the hint because he then elaborated that he could be my 'friend' and keep me company in a less than platonic way. Maybe there's something wrong with me, but I'm just never flattered by this kind of pick-up – even at my age! I assured him that I was not looking for any kind of anything, thank you, and he should be on his way. He eventually realised that there was to be no 'action' of any kind and left, but not before clearly explaining where he lived and how I could get there by simply walking along the beach. Perhaps Mr Proposition figured that I just needed time to think about it…

A couple of days before leaving I decided to try to top up my supplies without having to drive the horrific road, and was informed that the village by the river mouth just up the beach would be my best option. I had been so lazy, with the oppressive heat, humidity and Harmattan playing their part too, that apart from the occasional short stroll along the water's edge I had not gone far. So early in the morning I set out to find data scratch cards, bread and eggs, enough to keep me going until it was time to leave.

I took off my sandals and walked, as all the locals did, along the shore; there was no other road or path to the village. Already there were men busy at work threading fishing nets, repairing and laying them out on the lagoon side of the beach closest to the river mouth. I came across an assortment of small buildings on stilts, to survive the high tides I guessed. They were painted blue and white, with one exceptional building that was called Johannesburg House. It made me smile and I had to take a photograph of it for my niece, who lives in the city of that name in South Africa.

As the beach curved away to the river mouth, a vision appeared before my eyes and I could not believe what I was seeing: it was a bridge – but what kind of bridge? As I neared it I saw a few locals walking across and I stopped to observe. The bridge was made of planks of wood, which at first sight looked like they had been salvaged from a boat wreck, such was the state of them: uneven in depth and width but all strapped together. The arrangement rose unevenly over the river mouth, reaching a sharp peak before descending on the other side. It was a unique and innovative construction, the like of which I had never seen before.

I found out later that it is known locally as London Bridge and used to have a lifting section in the middle allowing boats to pass, but a storm had torn it apart (perhaps this was why the planks were so uneven). The bridge had been rebuilt and they had decided on a 'more practical' peaked construction which allowed the boats to pass under it freely.

Whilst dubious about the safety of this structure, I decided that if the locals were traversing it regularly it would be safe for me to do so too. I took a few steps and the whole thing wobbled underfoot, so I took a firm grip on the rope strung along the side. I had been so focused on my balance that I had not noticed three young men approach me from behind until they too stepped on to the bridge.

If I thought it was wobbly before, when they joined me the whole thing took 'bouncy castle' to a new level! I shrieked at the increased movement, having only just gained a modicum of ability to handle this novel walkway. They apologised profusely and politely asked if I was OK, and I declared that I was more shocked at the sudden bouncing. They all laughed and told me that this was why it was also called Dancing Bridge. Thanks for the dance, guys!

I eventually reached the other side and on to solid ground, where small houses sat cheek by jowl next to each other, most without fences and with people, goats and chickens traversing freely between them. There were lots of children, many in uniform, going off to the school somewhere beyond the houses. Shopping facilities took the form of a variety of basic stalls selling sweets and vegetables, but I had not yet seen bread or eggs.

No sooner had I managed to orientate myself off the bridge than Mr Proposition from a few days earlier hailed me. My first thought was, "Oh no!" However, my next thought was, "Aha, a guide!" He seemed surprised that I remembered him, but it wasn't every day I was so thoroughly propositioned by someone who thought I was sent by God! When I asked, he courteously led me to the place to buy eggs (I would never have found it amidst the warren of shacks), and from there to a lady who baked bread, and finally to someone selling data vouchers for my mobile. All shopping done, I thanked him and he started to walk with me back to the bridge. It seemed he intended to follow me – and without doubt he would consider it encouragement if I allowed him to do so – so I thanked him again and said I would be fine from there, shook his hand, smiled and quickly walked off before any potential negotiation on the matter.

The Harmattan had been persistent throughout my stay and after several days the haze became tedious. However, shortly before I was planning to leave for Accra it was suddenly replaced by a beautiful blue sky and some large clouds, which looked foreboding. Remembering the dust road coming in I checked the forecast, which said rain and thunderstorms were imminent. Whilst I had hoped to stay at least another day, I decided not to tempt fate and instead leave my little palm beach haven to continue my journey. My break had been thoroughly enjoyable and I felt ready to tackle the next phase; and I'd also decided to take more regular small breaks to sustain my energy.

I had arranged to meet up again with Mary (from The Gambia). Her knee had not healed and she was being sent to the capital of Ghana, Accra, for expert advice, and I had offered to drive her about whilst I was in the city. Accra would also be a good place to get my oil and filters changed and have the brakes checked as they were feeling a bit 'off'. BlueBelle required and deserved some TLC too.

I worked out that I would need three night stops before reaching Accra to match Mary's arrival. My first stop was back along the tarmac main road, but before I could reach it, as predicted the rain arrived. I decided to pull over to wait for it to pass rather than continue in the deluge. The countryside traffic in Ghana was much more intensive than I'd endured in previous countries, and adding rain to crazy motorists just didn't make for relaxing driving.

It is worth noting that Ghana is an oil-producing country and the President of Ghana has set out a programme to increase transparency in the oil trade, so while there was still much talk of corruption locally, from my experience of other African oil-producing countries there was one significant difference here: there were fuel stations aplenty – and a host of brands I had never heard of before. The encouragement for local business people to start their own chain of fuel stations was apparent, so fuel was also comparatively inexpensive.

My parking spot for the night was at a hotel, where I was shown a narrow, seldom-used lane to access the front lawns near the swimming-pool. My shower and toilet facilities were by the pool and adequate enough to clean and cool down. The hotel was on a high ridge above the ocean and my view was actually better than those of the rooms. The agreement was free parking if I ate in the restaurant, so as you know by now, that was deal done.

The restaurant was positioned behind the hotel and the menu quite expensive, but I chose the cheapest thing that I deemed I might like, a local dish called Red. This consisted of deliciously cooked and spiced onions and tomatoes with black-eyed beans, accompanied by fried plantains. It was superb and sadly the only time I managed to try it, as every time I was in a restaurant after this they had always sold out, attesting to its popularity.

The rain was intermittent and my night peaceful, and only enhanced by the pit-a-pat of raindrops on the roof. I had been contemplating staying an additional night to get some more of that Red for my next dinner... until the wailing woke me at 5.00am. It started with one person on a speaker, who was joined shortly after by the muezzin from the top of the mosque; and then one by one several others joined in and the competition was on to bring people to God, all of them shouting at the top of their lungs. However, it was such a cacophony that it was impossible to make out a single word! This lasted two and a half hours and only then started to simmer down, but even my trusty earplugs could not totally block out the sound.

In Ghana I found that religions were practised publically and loudly: it seemed that just about anyone possessed by 'the spirit' would take to the streets, Bible in hand, and start shouting and waving it around. Often this preaching was performed through loudspeakers with a microphone (where did they get the electricity at the side of the road?) or sometimes using a megaphone, but all too often it was just shouting. Most of the messages that I did manage to catch were of hell and damnation. Well, I can attest that being stuck in traffic next to any of these evangelists blasting their message felt like exactly that!

By 8.00 I had had enough and prepared myself to move out. I had decided to camp at a spot in the popular city of Kokrobite, and fortunately the rain had abated and the sun was out. The closer I got to the city, the heavier the traffic, with the usual taxi buses stopping at random, dropping and picking up passengers. The fuel stations increased in number so filling up wasn't going to be an issue here; however, the decision on which brand would provide the best quality proved challenging since I had identified at least twenty different brands along the way.

I turned off the main road and it was a sandy, muddy and potholed track that led me to the place I was looking for, Kokrobite Garden,[51] but once through the gate I arrived in a small parking area with a lush, colourful and exotic garden. This little place had a charm all of its own: much of the furniture was made of mud or concrete painted in rich colours and placed in a garden that could only thrive in the hot, humid conditions of the tropics. There was a round, open-sided building with a thatched roof and fans overhead to keep the air moving, and this was the eating, drinking and sitting area. It also had the bonus of electrical points and WiFi, so all in all, after a hellish start to the day, I had found heaven. I decided to spend two nights there before my next stop, Accra.

ACCRA

The city of Accra was not as crazy as Dakar or Conakry; there were more tarmacked roads for starters. At this stage I wasn't sure where I would be spending the night: again the city didn't present easy solutions and I'd planned to scout out options later in the day. I went directly to meet Mary who was with Fatou, a young woman she had almost adopted some years before, but it had fallen through when Fatou's mother remarried and came into better circumstances. I liked Fatou immediately: she had a

---

[51] www.facebook.com/kokrobitegarden

demeanour about her that was kind and sweet. Mary, however, had lost none of her complaining ways over the past month and wanted me to take her to find another accommodation she had identified as the one she was in was not acceptable.

I loaded up the luggage and ladies and set off to what turned out to be a guest house near the beachfront, La Paradise Inn.[52] There was a small but lovely garden with shady outdoor seating, a plunge pool and a small restaurant. The owner Donna and her husband Victor were a lovely couple. Donna was British-born but of Ghanaian heritage and on inheriting the family property had turned it into a guest house. She greeted us as we entered, and when she heard that I was still looking for a parking spot invited me to park in front of the property wall where there was a full-time guard. Sounded like a plan to me, so in return I agreed to buy meals and drinks from their restaurant.

Mary and Fatou got settled into their room and I went off to find a mechanic. Through various contacts I was recommended to use Eli, who arrived later in his van filled with tools and oils and his 'guy'. I detailed what I thought needed attention: oil change and new filter, new fuel filter, new brake pads and a general check of the vehicle underneath. He gave me a price which I agreed and he said he would return the next day.

The next day I delayed my plans and waited and waited, but by mid-morning and after several unanswered calls Eli eventually messaged me to say that he would come "later". I blew my own gasket. I left him in no doubt that if he did not come that day he should not bother coming at all. He appeared within the hour.

The brakes were first to be checked, and indeed there was nothing left of the pads. Eli needed to go and purchase new ones and came to ask me for money to buy them. I was rather surprised as I'd asked him to give me a parts-inclusive price, but I had no option really but to give him the extra cash. (Oh, how I hate mechanics!) He disappeared for almost two hours and I was becoming less and less impressed. When he finally returned he replaced the brake pads and, to be honest, they lasted an inordinately long time under less than desirable circumstances.

---

[52] www.laparadiseinn.com

Whilst under the vehicle he spotted some fluid on the rear axle: it seemed the gasket had sprung a leak (or whatever it is that happens to a rear axle gasket). He drained the oil, removed the bottom section, cleaned it, put on some glue stuff which he assured me would work as well as a gasket (I was dubious, but it has actually lasted), and finally changed the oil.

When it came to changing the engine oil, he fiddled about but then decided he didn't have the correct size spanner... and neither did I. In hindsight, I can recommend any travellers to ensure that you have the right size spanners for your vehicle – and probably all the men are slapping their foreheads saying, "Well of course!" And my response to them is: If I've never fixed a car, how was I supposed to know that?! But certainly a 13mm and a 17mm spanner would have come in very useful. Anyway, some half-hour later the bolt was still not loose and Eli started claiming that it had been too tightly fitted.

Finally, fed up with his tinkering under the van and having a sense that whatever he was doing was simply making it worse, I told him to leave it, negotiated the price down and paid him for what he'd done. Even the guards and staff at the guest house were shaking their heads at his work by this time! I was not filled with the utmost confidence, but at least my rear axle wasn't leaking and I had brakes again.

It was the end of the day by the time all was said and done. Mary and Fatou returned from a visit to one of the markets and it wasn't long before Mary was complaining about the WiFi and the cost of the rooms and food. I turned a deaf ear.

The next morning I was up early as usual and went into the garden to appreciate the cool; the sun was already on BlueBelle and making it uncomfortable inside. I was joined by Fatou while Mary was still sleeping and we spent some time chatting and laughing over a coffee and breakfast. It was mid-morning when Mary joined us, continuing with the complaints about anything and everything. I was really getting tired of it, so I said to her in the nicest way I could muster, "Please stop complaining about everything." She immediately lashed out at me with a tirade, shouting at me about how I had been picking on her and being nasty to her for no reason whatsoever.

I couldn't believe my ears. I held myself back and asked her to stop shouting at me but she continued, so I told her she was speaking nonsense. (Of course arguing with a person with psychological and emotional issues is pointless: I had done it in my marriage for the better part of twenty years without it changing a thing.) I certainly did not deserve to be spoken to in such a way, so I turned to her and said, "Mary, I'm done. Enjoy the rest of your stay, but I have nothing else here" – to which her reply, and the final straw for me, was, "Good riddance!"

After all my years of tolerating people's bad behaviour toward me, I had only the year before promised myself that I would no longer pick up other people's garbage but would leave it with them, where it firmly belonged. I felt I had done all I could do for Mary with the very best of my intentions… so I left it at that.

I smiled at Fatou, apologised and said I would see her later, paid for my meal and returned to BlueBelle. I went out for a tour of the city, which I had planned to do earlier but I had waited in case Mary and Fatou wanted to take a drive with me. That was now firmly off the cards!

Accra has a rich dynastic history which was unfortunately hard to find, and being a Sunday, many places were closed. I drove all around, got lost in a very poor part of town, saw the old slave forts and admired the grand Independence Arch. I'm often asked if I visited the slave outposts but I could not bring myself to do so. It was again a city of contrasts, with street traders and trash next to shiny modern shops and restaurants. I can't say exactly why I had great expectations of Ghana, but regrettably Accra did not quite meet them for me, although it was one of the first African countries to have gained independence from the colonialists and the first in sub-Saharan Africa.[53]

I took a drive down the coast and, finding a beach bar-restaurant, I decided to stop for a drink and a snack. As I sat overlooking the palm-lined beach and great ocean beyond, I couldn't help but think, "Here I am in Ghana, in Accra!" Never,

---

[53] It should be noted that fifty-two of the fifty-four states and island nations that make up Africa were colonised.

when learning African geography at school so many years ago, had I thought that I would one day be sitting where I was!

On my return to the guest house, Fatou came to bid me farewell as she and Mary were relocating to yet another hotel, and we happily exchanged numbers so that we could stay in touch.

My chores in Accra included applying for my Gabon visa and finding a way to fix the screen on my main phone, which was broken and causing me issues with navigation. In fact two of my phones had broken screens and one had a burnt-out battery too; I was currently using a not-so-good third phone. I was grateful that at least I had brought all these phones with me on my travels, but now I was running out of options. Again Chloe from West Africa Travellers had kindly put me in touch with a friend who would help me find what I needed – or at least try.

In the city I arranged to meet Hamza of Ghana Nima Tours,[54] who took me to the 'tech' section of the city. Here there were literally hundreds of street traders and shops selling every conceivable mobile phone, part and accessory, new and second-hand – not just the cheap ones, but Apple and Samsung phones too. Computers, laptops, printers, cables, headsets: you name it, all could be found there... except a new screen or a battery for my specific phones! It was a hive of activity and I stood out, yet I felt neither threatened nor intimidated and was constantly greeted with friendly smiles, hellos and only the odd look of shock. We left, regrettably without what I needed.

In the meantime I'd heard from Guy, a Luxembourger who had been motorbiking through various countries, most recently in Malaysia. He was currently in Ghana and was soon going to ride back to Europe, thereby heading in the opposite direction to me. We had been in touch via the overlanding group and he was prepared to take my Guinea Francs that I had been struggling to get rid of; and as luck would have it, he was at a hostel not far from where I was.

Guy was staying in the Sleepy Hippo hostel[55] and they kindly allowed me to park overnight in their driveway without charging me, so I spent the money I had set aside for this eating in their

---

[54] www.facebook.com/GNTours
[55] www.facebook.com/thesleepyhippo

restaurant and having a drink with Guy. We had a great chat about many things. He had been in Ghana for several weeks waiting for his motorbike, which he'd had shipped from Malaysia, and during his wait he had toured some of the inland areas I was heading into. His motorbike had been at customs for some time and he couldn't get them to release it, so I gave him some ideas on how to manage the situation (and happily he got it out within a couple of days). I shared some route and border information with him too. Sadly, I discovered much later that he came down with malaria in Western Sahara and eventually had to be evacuated back to Luxembourg.

LAKE BOSOMTWE

I opened the hostel gate early the next morning and headed out. Early mornings in a city are for the early birds, but African cities never seem to sleep and there were already well-dressed men and women heading off to work. The air was cool and it was still relatively quiet, with only a few taxi-buses about doing their usual thing.

I was very pleased with myself to be on the road and heading north out of the city by 6.00. Already the rush hour traffic coming into work was heavy, and as I neared the edge of the city the oncoming lane of the dual carriageway turned into a parking lot. In Accra (and several other cities) there was a crazy traffic system, whereby if you joined a dual carriageway heading in the wrong direction, you would have to drive a considerable distance before there was an official U-turn point between the traffic islands allowing access to the direction you actually wanted; and all of this happening in the fast lane. It was one of the most insane designs I'd ever seen.

I had seen no directional signs to tell if I was heading the right way and for some reason it felt like I needed to turn. I believe I was affected by 'queue hypnosis', that zombie-like state when you see a queue and you join the end of it. That is how I ended up in the queue for the U-turn, with concrete barriers on either side of the road preventing me from changing my mind or doing anything other than contemplate the likelihood of getting stuck in the city-bound traffic. The idea of being paralysed like that over several kilometres – and heaven only knew for how long – had me thoroughly annoyed with myself.

I saw some police up ahead, chatting and not doing much else, so I guessed that the traffic jam was something that managed itself. I eventually succeeded in pulling up to them out of the way of the other vehicles, smiled, greeted them and started expressing my frustration at my error. My next question was how did they think I could best get to where I needed to be? Their response was initially most unacceptable: I would have to join the inbound traffic and turn around several kilometres further along. I was mortified: it would take hours.

One officer took pity on my obvious distress and suggested that I could conduct a (probably highly illegal) manoeuvre by crossing the oncoming traffic, driving up the hard shoulder in the wrong direction, crossing the traffic again and then turning into the lane which would take me back on to the road I needed to be on. I smiled ruefully and asked, "But how will I ever cross this traffic?" There was some shouting to a couple of officers on the other side of the road and one suddenly deployed himself to stop the oncoming vehicles.

And so I managed to cross the traffic to the opposite side, manoeuvre myself off the tarmac on to the dusty hard shoulder, slowly drive up alongside the oncoming vehicles and then back up on to the tarmac, where another officer was waiting to stop the traffic again so that I could cross back to access the lane feeding into the outbound side. Whilst it was all quite challenging, I was back on track without having to sit in a queue for hours on end, so with a broad grin I shouted my thanks out of the window and waved at all the police officers, delighted to be on my way again. I had to smile. It was a unique experience and I can proudly boast of having stopped the traffic in Accra!

My chosen route would take me up the western side of the Volta, the river that dominates Ghana, to get to the country's biggest game reserve, Mole National Park. From there I planned to drive across and around the river and down its eastern side to make my way into Togo. My first stop was to visit Lake Bosomtwe, Ghana's only natural lake, which lies within an ancient impact crater. The lake is about eight kilometres in diameter and lies between Accra and Kumasi.

I was again relieved to get out of the city. The countryside was becoming greener and more contoured, very pleasant but for the constant burning of grass. I encountered this practice pretty much everywhere on my journey and nowhere more so than in Ghana, with the fires creating a huge amount of smoke that hung in the air, especially on oppressive Harmattan days. I struggled with the effect on my sinuses which were affected by the hours, if not days, of breathing in smoke; and I could imagine that for the local people, particularly the children, it would surely have a negative impact. There was nothing about the 'bush burning' practice in Africa that made sense to me.

My drive that day was broken by about ten heavily-armed police checkpoints, and considering that I was only covering about two hundred and fifty kilometres this was much more frequent than usual. I was always polite and pleasant and this was mostly reciprocated... with one exception. As usual, I stopped on request and a young man with an automatic rifle slung in front of him came over, shouting at me, and started yanking my door handle. Shouting, as you know by now, was not a good way to start a conversation with me. I greeted him through my half-open window and asked him please to stop pulling on my door, but he continued by shouting that I must open it; and then he was joined by a female officer who insisted I get out of my van.

Nope, not happening. I smiled at them, ignored the request and instead thrust my folder of documentation into the male officer's hands. This had the desired effect of him releasing the door to start investigating my paperwork, so I then engaged in some conversation to distract them.

After answering the universal questions about where I was from, why I was alone, where I was coming from, where I was going to and why I was in Ghana at all, he had calmed down. However, the woman officer who had joined him was now intrigued that I lived in my van and she wanted to take a look inside. I wasn't particularly in the mood and I'd wasted enough time already, so I said they could peak behind me to see the inside but I wasn't opening up: this was my home and I liked my privacy. They accepted my answer and, after a quick look inside, let me continue on my way.

I was relieved to turn off to the nature reserve of Lake Bosomtwe, where I had to pay a one-off entry fee. The road down gave an example of what Ghana must have once looked like, with rich rainforest and a diversity of greenery that was now only found in small pockets like this. I could see the lake glinting in the distance, but keeping my eyes on the twisting road was a priority. There were times when I wished I could let BlueBelle do the driving and I could just enjoy the scenery!

I passed through several villages on the way. The homes were right next to the road with ladies cooking outside, and I tried to go slowly so as not to churn up too much dust to spoil their meals. As usual a wave and a smile elicited a reciprocal response and these small exchanges with local people – strangers – always warmed my heart and made me smile all the more.

Soon I arrived at Wildwin Resort.[56] To my right was an expansive green grassy area flowing down to the lakeshore and a large, whitewashed hotel-looking building up to my left. On the edge of the grassy area there was an outbuilding that looked like a bar, so I pulled into a space off the track and went to find assistance.

I discovered that the bar was also a restaurant serving cold drinks and food: good to know. I asked about being able to park up and they welcomed me to do so for a small charge, and I could park wherever I liked on the grass since it seemed I had the entire place to myself. I was given the use of the shower in an empty room, located in the hotel building a stiff walk up the rise. I chose a parking spot near some trees offering a little shade and only a few metres from the lakeshore, so that I could listen to the gentle lapping of the water. It was much more to my liking than the crashing ocean waves.

The lake had many wooden canoes, similar to the ones I'd seen in The Gambia, and the men were frequently out and about fishing the lake and throwing nets. I guessed that fish was a staple food for the locals. The lake sparkled and shone and there were a variety of birds visiting from the surrounding trees, with larger ducks and herons strolling and feeding along the shoreline. Sunrise and sunset across the lake were magnificent, and when

---

[56] www.wildwinresort.com

231

there was no breeze, the high hills around the edge of the crater were perfectly reflected in the water's mirror.

Being able to open my doors and not worry about keeping a watchful eye on everything was a pleasure I always had to forego in the cities, and BlueBelle was well overdue for an airing. The usual chores of washing and tidying done, I even found time to read a book that my niece Ursula had given me about a woman and her dog driving around the USA. As a dog-lover I was reminded how much I would have loved to bring a dog with me, but I had been right not to as it would have been exceptionally difficult in the heat.

I had been in discussion with Ursula about joining me for a short part of my journey. At the age of fifty-one she was taking a well-deserved twelve-month break from her career and was intent on adventuring, and I couldn't think of a better way to spend a gap year! She needed to decide when and where to connect with me, considering my route and flexible timing. The main stumbling block was still whether I was going to be able to get that valuable visa to cross into Nigeria.[57]

MOLE NATURE RESERVE

Having much enjoyed my short stay at the lake, I felt my energy returning and was ready to continue my journey. As usual I headed out early in the morning and made my way north. En route I passed Kumasi, the renowned capital of the Ashanti Kingdom with a rich history, though sadly I didn't find much evidence of this. However, I did find a shopping mall – a real mall with big brands that I recognised from South Africa. It was an opportunity I couldn't pass up. My first stop was an all-purpose store to get some odds and ends for the van that I was running short of, and I also had my eye out for one specific piece of equipment: amongst the long list of things I *should* have known I would need on my journey was a tow rope. I'd not thought about it until I'd helped the guys out in Guinea, but the Nigeria-Cameroon border road was looming and I feared it might be essential.

---

[57] You may recall that I should have applied for this in my country of residence.

I found a comprehensive supermarket where I was able to stock up on canned goods, which I could store easily, and lastly there was a shop for the mobile network provider I was using. I had been struggling to get reception and was finding it infuriating; ironically I couldn't even get a signal in the shop! It took a while, but eventually they adjusted their system setting for my account and that seemed to moderately improve things. I can honestly say that having experienced my fair share of them, internet and mobile providers are the same useless bunch all over the world.

I had been pondering about visiting a Kente cloth-weaving community not far from Kumasi, but reports were that the road was not great and I was enjoying the good tarmac roads far too much. I found myself dawdling around the shopping centre since I was, unusually, undecided... and then the Universe in all its wisdom delivered exactly what I wanted. Down one of the mall 'avenues' were two men, one putting pieces of cloth on a table and another sitting at a loom. Incredibly, he was weaving strips of Kente cloth – the real thing, not the cheap printed variety. No need to go and find it: here it was right in front of me!

Kente cloth is a traditional Ghanaian fabric made by hand-weaving strips of silk and cotton. In days gone by it was the royal and sacred cloth of the Akan people, worn in times of great importance and then only by kings and the nobility. The name Kente comes from the word meaning 'basket' in the local dialect and reflects the geometric configurations, and Ashanti folklore includes a story about weavers inventing Kente when they tried to replicate the patterns of Anansi the spider. Each of the vibrant colours and designs has a special meaning, and today these intricate fabrics, woven mostly by the men, are used for clothes, ties, bags and even shoes.

Andrew was the man weaving and the speed with which he did so was incredible. As his hands and feet all moved like lightning, in the shifting coloured threads I saw a pattern swiftly emerging. It was mesmerising to watch and I barely managed to tear myself away to shoot a brief video for my Facebook followers. His friend John then showed me the delightful smorgasbord of finished fabrics with their gorgeous colours and patterns, describing to me what each one meant: there was Knowledge, the Wise Woman, the Dignitaries (I chose a piece of this one) and many more; I lost track of all the references. They were normally sold in packs of three, about one and a half metres wide by two and a half metres long, but the price was beyond my limited means. I negotiated for a single piece that I now use as a tablecloth and it delights me to see the vibrant hot orange mixed with the deep azure blue and hints of red and white.

After spending more time and money than I should have, I was very pleased with my loot (although still without a tow rope!) I drove into Kumasi, trying to find the museum, but ended up in the great morass of markets, people, taxis and traffic, until the heat overwhelmed me and I decided that history would be passed up this time. I did spot some odd statues but they were located where it was nigh impossible to stop and photograph, so I resigned myself to moving on. It was also getting late: my dawdling had meant that I wouldn't make it to the game reserve that night and there was no other identifiable place to stop, so I again needed to seek out an alternative.

As I drove along through the lush green fields and more areas of grass burning, I noticed dark clouds brewing ahead and realised I was driving directly into them. It was surely going to rain: the scent of it hung heavily in the atmosphere; but the question was how hard? The answer came a lot sooner than I had hoped and in the late afternoon it bucketed down with such force that it was impossible to see more than a metre ahead. Again I was more worried about the reckless overtaking that I had witnessed and the odd animal that might be on the road.

I saw a fuel station still under construction and pulled up under the cover over the pumps to wait it out. It seemed it was never going to abate – certainly not in time for me to move on – so I had to come up with a plan. The service station was a possibility and I decided I could sneak around the back of the main building and be out of the way. But then I spotted some guys working inside and went to ask them about parking. They were finishing up for the day and would shortly be leaving so suggested I should ask the old night guard when he arrived.

The night guard was late and it was already getting dark. I figured that saying sorry rather than please would be the better option so I parked up behind the main building. But when he did arrive he didn't mind at all, and so I said I would pay him in the morning. The rain persisted through the early part of the night and I was pleased that I had decided to stop rather than press on.

In the morning I gave the old man a tip and some bananas that I would never get around to finishing, both of which pleased him, and I was back on the road again. It was interesting to note the time shift as I was driving further east across the continent, with the sun rising earlier in the morning and setting earlier in the evening. The morning air was fresh and cool and the rain had settled the grass fires. I loved those early mornings: they were the only time that I wasn't soaked with sweat, and of course I knew that by 10.00 the furnace would be fully on again. I turned west in the direction of Mole. It had been many years since I had been to a game reserve and delight in the presence of Africa's crown jewels, so I was very much looking forward to it.

The road was a good one, running through several villages which (annoyingly for me) meant speed humps on both entry and exit and sometimes two or three in succession. It was slow going. Occasionally a hump or two went unnoticed until I was virtually upon it, causing some low-level flying experiences. There were also noticeably a few pedestrian crossings, an oddity there in the middle of nowhere. I was amazed when I saw them: this was hardly a high-traffic thoroughfare!

There were not many women with white-blonde hair and blue eyes driving around in vans on their own and it seemed to be a scary sight to some people. On one occasion I had just gone over a speed bump, beyond which was a pedestrian crossing. To my left, two women carrying big metal bowls on their heads were about to cross, so as I was going at minimal speed I stopped to allow them to pass. My vigilance at pedestrian crossings comes from my time in Portugal, where if I failed to stop I would be severely berated by the crossers, especially the little old ladies who were fiercely intimidating. However, on this occasion the women were busy chatting, and when I stopped and waved them to cross one woman looked at me and with alarm, dropped her bowl on the ground and legged it in the opposite direction, while the other stood immobile, staring at me wide-eyed. Clearly no one was going to cross, so I shrugged and continued on my way.

Some way further I again had to slow down at the humps and passed some very young children. As usual I smiled and waved at them, and two of them again went scampering in the opposite direction as fast as their tiny legs would carry them. I was quite bemused as I continued on my way: "Beware of old women driving blue vans!" seemed to be the warning message.

I arrived at the reserve and after I had found the reception area and settled the campsite fee, I was shown to a scrappy campsite with poor shade, a broken viewing deck, lots of dust and only one shower and toilet that were barely worth using. All that plus staff who were distinctly lackadaisical. Thus far I was underwhelmed.

The one upside was that there was a motel within a short walk from the camp, which had a good viewing platform overlooking a watering-hole, cooked food and that most vital thing that had become my obsession: icy-cold drinks. There were a variety of visitors from a range of countries, and I befriended Amanda and her mother Dorothe from Germany and Mitja, a guy from the Baltics whose name I kept getting wrong but who was a very nice young man and quite forgiving. There was also another distinctive German couple, the kind of people who really should not travel: they were complainers, and I had the misfortune to have them in my group on the early morning walking safari.

The safari began with a walk through the staff compound before entering the main reserve, and as no one was talking and we were not in the bush yet I began informally chatting to the guide, asking questions about the reserve and telling him of my experiences with nature parks in Zimbabwe and Botswana. It seemed that this was annoying the German couple, because as we were waiting for someone in the group to catch up, the man aggressively stepped in between the guide and me and said, "If the rest of us can get a word in to speak to the guide..!" I was shocked at his aggression: all he had to do was ask a question himself; but I smiled a smile with a hint of sarcasm as I replied, "By all means!" (Well, he did seem to be asking my permission.) The funny side of this was he then struggled for a few seconds to figure out what he was going to ask, and finally came up with an inane question about whether the staff on the reserve lived in the houses we were passing. I stifled a laugh lest I should incense the man further.

He continued to posture and pout and his wife also gave me the nose lift and head turn, indicating that she found me most distasteful. They were so out of place in the easy-going way of Africa, yet apparently they came annually. I guessed they now felt they owned a part of it, but I didn't know how the locals tolerated it. The man also proved himself to be completely insensitive by making it his mission to walk directly in front of several of the group who were videoing two elephants playing. Most of the other people found the couple equally annoying, and thus they found themselves sitting alone at breakfast after the walk.

Our guide was regrettably ill-informed about his surroundings and had to be prompted to identify – or even notice – tracks or answer questions about the local flora or animal behaviour. Having grown up with a nature reserve only a short drive away from my home city and having frequently visited Hwange National Park in Zimbabwe, as well as several game reserves in Botswana, I consider myself not an expert but nonetheless experienced. This young man was disappointing, because a good guide can transform the ordinary into the extraordinary.

I spotted the tracks of porcupine, mongoose and some antelope, but the only animals we saw were dung beetles and three bull elephants. Seeing elephants again was exciting though: they are such odd creatures, their size so intimidating and yet they tread the earth so softly with those flat, round, cushioned feet. I don't usually find the bulls as interesting as the maternal groups, however two of these bulls were relatively young, and being clearly comfortable with the daily walking tours and tourists, they pulled out all the stops to make our walk entertaining. They dusted themselves with sand and scratched themselves on trees, and the younger one skilfully played with sticks like they were marching batons and then threw them in our direction. We were told that it was one of his favourite tricks and were warned to stay back: wild animals are unpredictable and can be very dangerous, no matter how playful they look.

By the time we retraced our steps to the lodge it was seriously hot, so the rest of the day was spent relaxing. In the evening I went on a game drive with my new friends and I must say we had a wonderful time. The German couple didn't come.

Wildlife is best seen in the early mornings and late evenings when it is cooler: this is when the animals are seeking water or shelter and so are generally on the move. The game viewing at Mole was challenging, with many small shrubs and trees obscuring the view and making it difficult to spot the animals. In southern Africa, more savannah allows for better sightings. We did see a variety of antelope and some birds but not much more. The evening drew to a close as we sat on the viewing platform with the baboons around us, enjoying the colours of the sunset and the arrival of the night sounds. I so cherished these warm nights without needing a jersey, with the low lighting and most beautiful starlit sky and the crickets and night birds providing the musical backdrop.

TOP OF THE VOLTA

I had bid my new friends farewell the night before and moved out in the morning. The campsite was so uncomfortable that it was not worth staying longer and the game viewing had proved less than rewarding. My next stop would be at the top of the Volta River in a city called Tamale, considered the capital of the north. It wasn't far away, so I slowly drove back over the humps and avoided panicking the locals by *not* stopping at the pedestrian crossings.

The road remained in good condition. I was impressed with the roads in Ghana: they were not too potholed, well signposted and more orderly than I had experienced thus far. A glaring difference between the former British and French colonies was the infrastructure, which seemed better developed in the former and therefore lasting years longer than that in the latter.

It was now unbearably hot: the humidity remained high but the heat was even more intense. The Harmattan seemed to have cleared, but I wasn't sure that this improved things and I was struggling to cope. Due to my intolerance to dairy products (which mess up my sinuses), ice cream was out of the question; however ice lollies were not. I found one called Fandango – really just orange-flavoured ice and sugar in a plastic tube, but they were heavenly. I would buy two at a time and devour them to take my mind off the heat. They not only made me feel cooler but also boosted my sugar levels. (I confess: I'm a sugar addict!)

I found the guest house I had chosen away from the centre of Tamale in a suburb with a few houses and dirt roads with lots of sand. It was quite an unremarkable location; however Dawadawa Lodge,[58] named after a large shady tree in the middle of the yard, was a pleasant surprise. It was a nice clean place with an open seating area serving cold drinks and snacks and it also had decent WiFi. The Dawadawa tree is known locally as the 'African locust bean' and a powder is produced from the fruit and popularly added to cooking. I was offered a bottle of it, but while it looked interesting I have to say that the name put me off buying it! I later discovered that it was apparently good for reducing hypertension and improving sight, so perhaps it would have come in useful.

The next morning would take me along the eastern side of the Volta to a school that had been built for a village further down the river. I was in a good mood as I set out early, missing the traffic… but then it happened, again; I should have learnt by now never to take the road conditions for granted. Ahead I saw dust – lots of red dust but no tarmac. It was at least not too rutted but it was bumpy and uneven. The Chinese were building another highway too and that meant lots of big aggregate trucks hurtling down the dusty road and throwing up more of the ghastly red stuff.

I put on my headscarf. I had been moistening it and placing in my neck to cool me down as I drove, so now I wet it thoroughly and put it on as a face mask to help cut down on the amount of dust I had to breathe in. It had become a useful trick.

What I had hoped would be a quick drive that day turned out to be slow going and I was beginning to reconsider my options. There were also a fair number of checkpoints impeding my progress – unusual for a dirt road. Since I hadn't escaped one thus far without being stopped, I had taken to pulling up at every one I saw. One official was very surprised to see me stop, relaxing as he was under the shade of a tree, and he just waved me on. At another there was the usual signpost but I saw no one around, and after a couple of other vehicles passed me I carried on too. I needed to figure out where I could make my next stop if the road

---

[58] www.facebook.com/DawadawaLodge

continued to slow me down, and since the cities were few and far between I pulled in at a half-built garage and parked up in the shade of the roof over the pumps to review my route.

There appeared to be no stopping options on the usual app so I resorted to Google Maps to find hotels. I had my driver door open to increase the air circulation when a man on a motorcycle stopped next to me. I looked at him suspiciously and he returned the favour. He asked why I was parked there, so I explained I was just resting in the shade: was that a problem? It wasn't, and we got chatting for a bit. He owned a franchise for fuel stations with his uncle and they already had several operating under their brand. This one was taking longer to get the paperwork finalised, hence they had stopped work until that was resolved. I found it all highly interesting, although I wondered how they managed to make a profit when I had seen so many empty forecourts.

I set off again, but not fifty metres away there was another police checkpoint so of course I stopped. The armed officer immediately approached my vehicle, peered inside and behind me and abruptly started questioning me about who was with me. I looked surprised and replied I had no one. "Where are they?" he continued. I still had no idea what he was on about and replied as much, but I was instructed to get out of the vehicle as I had apparently passed through a checkpoint without stopping. Puzzled, I insisted that I had stopped at all the checkpoints.

I was hot, dusty and mightily irritated that I had to get out of my van and play some ego game. By this time another officer was closely inspecting BlueBelle's exterior. I was taken down a steep slope off the road to the shade of a tree and quizzed again about why I'd not stopped at the checkpoint. I repeated that I had not, but was secretly starting to suspect he meant the one that I had passed through with no one there. He dialled a number on his phone, muttered something in the local language and then thrust the phone at me. I looked at him. "You must speak to the officer." Seriously…?!

Me: Hello, sir.

Officer: You did not stop at the checkpoint!

Me: Sir, I have stopped at *all* the checkpoints but at one of them there was no one there.

Officer: I was coming but you drove away before I could get to you!

By now I realised he was *never* going to admit that his lazy ass was snoozing in the cool of some hidden shade and therefore unseen by me. In order to get this over with, I acted contrite.

Me: I apologise, sir. I stopped but I did not see you, and certainly I did not see you approach and so I continued, but I am here now and I apologise that I missed your checkpoint.

He continued berating me and I reached the end of my rope.

Me: Well, what do you want me to do? Drive back to where you are, wherever that is, in this heat?! I've apologised, I get it, I was wrong – so what do you want me to do?!

A brief silence on the other side, then:

Officer: Let me speak to the officer.

I handed back the phone, there were further mutterings in the local language and the call was ended. I was instructed to bring all my papers so I climbed back up the slope to my van to fetch them. My mood was certainly not improving but I was trying not to get myself into deeper trouble.

Back with the other officers, questions ensued and were followed by a brief recounting of my journey and discussions around being a brave woman and having "the balls of two weak men". (Personally, I thought two giant's balls really, but who was I to argue with two weak men?!) I was then quizzed about the tracker in my van. The tracker (and its associated stickers) was to help avert theft; the fact that the thing hadn't worked since Morocco is another story.

Officer: So, they are watching you by satellite?

What? Did he think I was a CIA spy or something?!

Me: No! The tracker is so that if anyone steals my van I can find the offender and kill him! (OK so a bit over the top, but it was getting tedious now.)

What then transpired was a lecture about how I should turn the other cheek and should not murder anyone.

Me: They take my van, they are thieves, breaking the commandments and the law – so I will deal with them on those terms and there will be no cheek-turning about it!"

At this point they all laughed nervously.

Me: You just think about it, boys..!

And with my papers in hand I walked off waving goodbye, leaving them to wonder if I was a smart spy having just escaped their clutches or merely a crazy woman. I hoisted myself back into BlueBelle and left.

The eastern side of the Volta was much less developed, leaving more visible rainforest with the exceptionally tall and elegant mahogany trees always towering over the landscape. The little mud hut villages were peppered with more modern concrete block buildings and the usual goats roamed about in gangs on the road, sometimes unwilling to give anyone else right of passage.

The only place I'd been able to identify to stop was a hotel, which on the Google satellite image didn't appear to have suitable parking for me, but I decided to stop there to ask about any other place in the vicinity. The Gateway Hotel[59] was just outside Nkwanta town, and when I arrived I had managed to drive two hundred and forty kilometres and was thoroughly dusty; I could feel it in my hair, returning it to that strawberry blonde colouring. At the reception I was greeted by a middle-aged man to whom I explained that I had been driving all day and needed a safe place to park, but since most of their parking was under netting and too low for me to get in, was there anywhere nearby? No, came the response, but he could offer me a room. I explained that I was driving through Africa and that I needed to watch my money so I could not afford the room. We discussed my travels for a bit and then he came to view BlueBelle.

I was concerned that it was getting late and I would need to find a place soon, so I asked him again if there was anywhere he might suggest. He looked earnestly at me and said, "Park there, just outside the reception area." I couldn't believe what he was saying. I checked but he confirmed that it would be fine and there was also a night guard, so I asked how much I must pay and he simply nodded and said, "It will be fine, just park there." Again that wonderful African hospitality saved my day! I parked and

---

[59] www.facebook.com/Gateway-Hotel-1784143941640647

returned inside to press my luck, as I hesitantly asked if it was possible to shower. He nodded kindly (my need for a shower being quite obvious) and took me to a dormitory block and its ablutions, where I washed out the strawberry blonde and the dust of the day with the added bonus of being able to cool down before bed.

As usual in reciprocity I frequented the hotel restaurant, where that night I ordered a couple of cold drinks and a delicious meal of okra, aubergine and chicken which I devoured greedily. I had a daily routine of coffee in the early morning (lemons now being scarce for my previous lemon and honey), breakfast at around 10.00 before it got too hot, and dinner before it got too dark, while throughout the rest of the day I just consumed copious amounts of water; so by the time it came to dinner I was usually *very* hungry – unless I needed to cook of course!

I took advantage of the secure compound with its night guard and slept with my side door open and the curtain drawn; it was just too hot to close myself in. I had done this in a few places already, especially where there was security. It may sound risky, but the heat was overwhelming and I only did so when I felt it was safe enough.

WLI FALLS

My return to the dreaded dust road was early and the sun was just peeking up, but with the smell of the cool air on the earth it was still my favourite time of day.

Having considered the heat and the terrible road conditions, I decided I would forego my planned stop further south as the longer travel time so far meant I would have to cut short my stay there. Instead I turned east toward a smaller border post that would give me access to Togo. My decision also gave me a few days to relax before crossing the border as I had to wait for my Togo visa to kick in, plus I was feeling fatigued again. Navigating the non-tarmacked roads required constant vigilance, and whilst I was OK with the driving and had become accustomed to long hours in the seat, add into the mix the heat and humidity and it was all taking its toll.

The map had identified two possible routes, but when I saw an actual sign (it was so unusual to find signposts on dust roads) to Wli Falls, which I knew was near the border, I followed it hoping to avoid the town ahead. However, I now found myself driving down a narrow, uneven and much bumpier dirt road: had I just gone from the frying pan into the fire? Admittedly I didn't have to contend with any aggregate trucks heading back and forth churning up dust; but worse, it looked like it had rained in the area, so I prayed that the road ahead was navigable and not a mud pit.

I was stressing about the road conditions when a taxi bus came hurtling toward me in the opposite direction, and as he saw me he started waving frantically for me to slow down. My first thought was that he was warning me about the road conditions, so I stopped and he pulled up too just past me. The driver climbed out of the bus and trotted over to me, as usual to the wrong door (thinking I was in a LHD), so I waved him across to my side. Smiling widely he greeted me and quickly announced, "I love your car, I want to buy it from you!" It took me a moment to understand that this was the reason he had waved me down and I had to smile!

This epitomised the very soul of Africa to me: the people are happy and enthusiastic, with a great zest for life. I tried to imagine someone waving me over in Europe and saying the same thing, I'd think they had come out of some asylum and would hasten away in fear of my life; and if this had been the USA, I may have been terrified of him shooting me – or me shooting him. But this was Africa, where we express our emotions more freely and love interacting with people.

I responded to the driver that BlueBelle was not for sale, but he insisted that he wanted my van because it was a good, solid, excellent vehicle. I was quite certain she would have been instantly transformed into a taxi bus, hurtling down these roads daily! I replied that it would be impossible to sell her as I was driving home to Zimbabwe and without her I couldn't get there, so of course this led to the conversation about where I was from and why I was driving alone. He insisted I gave him my telephone number in case I *did* decide to sell her when I got to Zimbabwe (probably without any knowledge of how far away that actually was). I replied that I didn't have a number – certainly I didn't know my Ghana one – but he insisted I find a piece of paper for him to write down *his* name and number, and handed it back to me with the firm reminder to call him about the van.

I did get to ask him about the road conditions and he replied that the route was fine (by his standards, not mine!) and that it would be no problem getting to Wli.[60] Relieved, I wished him goodbye and we shook hands. His name was Samson and, just like that, all the stress of the road disappeared and I was left with a great afterglow of the warmth that the African people exude. They can take a joke, they smile so readily and they love being social more than anything. Finding the pleasure in such small exchanges kept me smiling for many miles. It was people's natural desire to share their warmth that made me all the more keen to soak it up; and by doing so, bit by bit the sadness of my troubled heart started to melt away.

I was now driving into the rural heart of Ghana. There were more rustic mud hut villages instead of concrete buildings and of course the usual women and children carrying water. As I was slowly driving along I saw five men walking down the opposite side of the track, all of them elderly, but what made them mentionable and memorable was the fact that they were wearing traditional togas in beautiful African print fabrics. It was an impressive sight. I stopped a little way before them, just wanting to admire their poise and style. One of them came over to me, thinking I was having some problems and might need their help.

I had not thought this through; I merely wanted to appreciate seeing them. The man greeted me in the style that I had often encountered, "Hello, you are welcome." It took me a while to realise that in the local languages they have a greeting, "Akwaaba" (often with a different spelling), that literally means 'you are welcome', and so their greetings were directly translated into English. I came to find it charming and always made sure to show my appreciation for their kindness. I told him that I found them all to be so handsome in their togas that I had to stop and admire them, and he smiled shyly and, in the most excellent English, thanked me for the compliment. When I asked where

---

[60] pronounced 'vlee'

they were from he informed me that they were the chiefs and elders of some villages "down the road" (in Africa this means a fair distance away): they had been attending a meeting in a neighbouring village and were now heading back home.

I asked if I might take a photograph of them, so he called across to the others, who looked at each other slightly bemused but nodded their consent. They proudly stood together as I took their picture and then they asked me where I was from and were even more surprised by my answer. When we said our goodbyes I offered my respectful thanks to both them and the Universe for the encounter as we each continued on our different ways.

The approach to Wli displayed impressive foliage-covered mountains looming above the trail and the lush rainforest became denser, which of course meant increased humidity. The town itself was small, with shops and restaurants of a local standard as well as signs for lodges and campsites. I noticed a sign indicating that the border post was a short distance from the town – good to know as my camp lay only about half a kilometre away. There were warnings on the camp reviews NOT to arrive on Mondays as they were closed and would not open up under any circumstances. Fortunately it wasn't a Monday, but it should have been an indication of what to expect. I arrived, the gate guard let me in and I stopped in the parking area. He advised me that the owners were out but would return soon.

Mrs German was the first to get back and she came to greet me coldly. She confirmed that I could camp, and although the charge was expensive by my standards the place looked clean, plush and well organised; it would have to do for the few days I needed to kill before my Togo visa came into effect. I had to register inside the main building and agree to the many terms and conditions that were typed up next to the registration book. There were also pieces of paper stuck everywhere with instructions on what could or could not be done and how, when, and where it could or could not be done. German precision did not fit easily into relaxed African tourism.

However, the lush gardens provided a distant view of the lower waterfall, a beautiful tall cascade tumbling down the side of the mountain and surrounded by dense green rainforest. I was permitted to park on the lawn under trees which would offer some morning shade, but I would have to spend the afternoons in their covered outdoor restaurant area to escape the worst of the heat.

Mr German seemed more amenable than his wife and chatted to me when he arrived back from a trip to Accra. He was very impressed by my journey and we enjoyed a brief exchange until Mrs German joined us and started complaining about the staff. I couldn't bear the demeaning manner in which she was speaking about them, so I excused myself.

I took the next couple of days to catch up on chores, rest my still-nagging shoulder (which had not appreciated the days of difficult driving) and tend the constantly irritating thing in my elbow which I believed to be a thorn...

The Wli Falls, the tallest in West Africa, are known to the locals as *Agumatsa*, which means "Allow me to flow" in Ewe, the language spoken in Togo and south-eastern Ghana. There were two distinctive sections, both of which could be hiked, where the lower fall would take about an hour to reach and the upper fall up to five hours. However, neither of these was on my list of things to do since walking anywhere in the heat was a challenge I was prepared to forego. One morning I left at 8.00 to walk to the village for some phone credit and bread rolls, and by the time I returned I needed to drink two litres of Agumatsa water to replenish my reserves! I contented myself with enjoying the gorgeous fall views from afar, listening to the sounds of the local birdlife and observing the pineapples growing in the garden: a peculiar plant indeed.

Chapter Eight – Togo

17 March 2019

On Sunday, a day earlier than my visa indicated, I decided to take my chances and depart for Togo: I was uncomfortable with the attitude of the camp owners and the general ambience of the place. The worst that could happen was that I'd have to spend the day in no man's land, but with BlueBelle that didn't present a problem.

It was 7.30am when I arrived at the border and I was expecting to have to wait, but the staff were already present and I was told to go to the open covered office. I did so with my folder of papers and within ten minutes I was all done and driving through no man's land to Togo.

One of the smallest countries in Africa with a population at the time of around eight million people, Togo – officially the Togolese Republic – is also one of the narrowest mainland countries in the world. It was initially colonised by the Germans but transferred to France after the First World War, and gained its independence in 1960. During the height of the slave trade in Africa, Togo found itself at the centre of what became known as the 'Slave Coast'. Today it relies on agriculture and the mining of rich phosphate deposits to support its economy, but poor leadership and political unrest have consistently impacted the country's ability to prosper.

It wasn't too far before I reached the Togo side of the border, and because it was early on a Sunday there was only one fellow present in a small building. He stamped my passport, opened the ubiquitous big black book to immortalise my details (giving no credence whatsoever to the dates on the visa) and I was in. BlueBelle, however, was another story. The officer who normally issued the TIP was not there and I would have to drive some unspecified distance to find his office.

The road from no man's land wound steeply up the side of a mountain and I was grateful that there was little traffic. Staying on my side of the road was a challenge as the bends were so sharp, and to make matters worse the surface was only occasional patchy tarmac with long muddy stretches in between. The views were gorgeous but the road kept me from fully appreciating them. I stopped and took a few photographs at one section where I could at least see the traffic in both directions, but none of those did justice to the vast green landscape before me.

The customs office turned out to be considerably further than the first fellow had said and I was starting to worry that I might never find it, but at last there was the roundabout and the turnoff he'd described. I found the police station and was informed that I needed to go a little further down the road (but of course not before they had asked where I was from and why I was alone).

When I finally reached the customs building it seemed they had used the last of the receipt books. In hindsight I'm not sure that it wasn't a ploy; and who knows where the cash would have gone… But blonde as I am, I wasn't leaving without the receipt in case I was required to present it at some checkpoint later on. I established that they did have other receipt books, so he would just have to go get one. I smiled sweetly at him and went to make myself some coffee while I waited.

As I walked back to BlueBelle I noticed that a small 4x4 van had parked behind her and a young couple were walking toward the office. I guessed they also needed to admit their vehicle, so I told them as I was passing that they would have to wait for a receipt and they thanked me. Whilst I was making coffee, the young man came over to introduce himself as the woman was still in the office. I offered him a drink and we chatted about where we were from and where we were going and shared some of our experiences.

His name was Anatole, hers Marion, and they were French. They have a huge following on their YouTube channel *Les Marioles Trotters*[61] and this was how they made their money to travel. They had plans to go to Kpalimé, a popular nearby destination in Togo, whereas I intended to see what the inland area of Togo held and so was heading east and then north to Atakpamé. We would both ultimately make for Lomé on the coast, where we would be able to get various visas for the way ahead, so we agreed we would probably cross paths again there.

---

[61] www.youtube.com/channel/UCW-dQeNiTp8vSwHQpwdSHPg

I eventually received my receipt along with my TIP document and remembered to pack up the coffee things before I left. I can't even begin to count the number of times I'd forgotten to stow something away or strap something down. You'd have thought that after three and a half months on the road it would be done without thinking; but no, it happened frequently – my kettle being the victim too many times! I had also started looping my bungee cords into strategic hooks to keep doors in place, as I was yet to find latches that prevented them from opening all the time on the bumpy terrain.

As much as I had been challenged driving up the mountains, it naturally came time to drive down them, and fortunately the road was less steep and winding and allowed me a better chance to view the lush valley below. I reached the town of Adeta and went straight to find a SIM card and some more cash since there had been no one changing money at the border. I still had some CFA from Côte d'Ivoire (it is also Togo's currency), but thought I would need a bit extra because I'd learnt that few places took international credit cards. I parked in front of a suitable shop, not wanting to let BlueBelle too far out of my sight.

I entered, somewhat apprehensive about having to revitalise my appalling French after a month of speaking English, and waited for the customer in front of me to finish being attended to. As I stood there I received some uncertain looks: they had obviously not seen many of my kind around there. When my turn came I greeted the attendant, and as I was speaking to him a man came into the shop complaining loudly to no one in particular about a vehicle being inappropriately parked near the corner. He was certainly making his point known, and since it was obvious that the vehicle was BlueBelle, his passive aggression was directed at me.

I didn't have the words in French, so I looked at him and told him in plain English that I had just arrived in his country and needed some help; and sorry, but I didn't know the local etiquette of parking. He clearly hadn't expected to be challenged and within a moment of comprehension he replied to me in English, apologising and explaining that he would take me to the shop next door where I could be assisted.

Indeed I managed to exchange my cedi for CFA at a reasonable rate and buy a SIM card with data. Back outside I spotted an ATM so I could now draw more CFA from my credit card. The essentials done, I was on my way.

Togo immediately impressed me with the cleanliness and order I noticed. The roads were well paved with good signage, people were polite and the regional authority had billboards every few kilometres informing about litter, AIDS, childcare and other social issues. It all seemed to be working, from my brief observation. However, the area was flat and quite unremarkable so regrettably my hope for more of the splendid rainforest I'd seen in the highlands came to nought.

As it was Sunday the roads were very quiet. I reached Atakpamé about lunchtime and went to check out my parking for the night at the local Catholic church, which had accommodation attached to it. I noticed the large open parking area which would suit me fine; but a shower... well, that would be a bonus. The attendant advised that it was possible to park, but for a shower I would need to pay for a room. I managed to negotiate him down on the rate when I explained that I wouldn't be sleeping in the room, something he had a little difficulty grasping, but eventually we agreed on a price and I was happy.

I set off to find some fruit and vegetables in the open market but it was impossible to park within any proximity, and leaving BlueBelle any distance away gave me concern about her safety – after all my entire life was in there. As I was driving about I saw a sign for the 'Luxembourg Hotel' and under it another sign read 'Restaurant and Bar'. It felt serendipitous as I'd lived in Luxembourg for several years, so on the spur of the moment I decided to go and take a look.

Weaving around the back of a block of buildings I found the small hotel, and just opposite there was a bar with an open shaded terrace. I decided that I would treat myself to a local beer (which came in a very large bottle and wasn't great, so I ordered a lemonade to turn it into a shandy) and chose an unknown-to-me chicken dish with plantain. The 'chicken' was a road-runner chicken and I'd usually found these to be tough, regardless of the cooking, but I was hungry and didn't have to cook so my fussy level diminished considerably.

Meal over, I returned to the church grounds and found a nice big shady tree some distance from the road. I opened my side door, pulled the net curtain into place and lay on my sofa catching up on messages and making some posts. The very large beer got the better of me though and I soon fell asleep. I have no idea how long I slept but I dreamt of people singing... No, wait a moment... people *were* singing – right outside my door! While I was trying to re-orientate myself and work out why they were there and why they were singing, I realised that I had parked under the tree where the church choir practised before Sunday mass. The practice was clearly going to go on for a while, but nice as it was it felt like they were inside my van. The beer had also given me a headache, so I drove off to a different tree where there was less likelihood of disturbing people; or being disturbed.

Night began to fall and I moved the van again to a spot outside the administration building, where there was a guard, and went to take my shower so that I was cool enough to sleep. I was always grateful for my little USB fan and my 12V dual fan as I kept one or both of them blowing on me throughout the sticky night – the next best thing to air-conditioning in my small space.

The next morning I departed early, but not before having availed myself of another cold shower. I still always made sure I paid up the previous night so that I could leave without disturbing anyone and drive in the coolest part of the day. I had done some more research and decided against going further inland as the reviews were mixed and I didn't want to risk being disappointed; and I was also tired.

I decided to find a place by the sea in the hope of a hint of a breeze to relieve the oppressive heat. Chloe had again made a recommendation of a place on the beach just outside Lomé where I could stay while I waited for my Gabon visa, which would be cheaper to buy in Togo. It was odd but visa prices varied depending on the country where you obtained them, and once I was wise to this I started to plan my applications accordingly.

Overlander's Disease

Driving into Lomé, a city of less than a million people and quite spread out, I passed by a huge modern dock area with many trucks going in and out. Research told me it was a vast container terminal and shipping port, the result of a €450 million investment by a French group in 2012. It was a considerable business venture and placed the country in a strong position as a major export centre, although I suspect a larger share was imported.

The roads to the suggested camp were all sand – beach sand – and there was no way I was getting there. After several attempts and finding the blasted stuff everywhere, I headed to my alternative camping option, Chez Antoine, also known as Coco Beach.[62] Yet despite having been so careful to avoid sand, I was deceived by a camouflaged patch and found myself stuck – yes, again!

I climbed down and started to dig myself out, only to be joined by an old woman.[63] She muttered at me and I agreed; I had no idea what she said, but if it had been me it would have been something like, "How the **** did you do that?!" Obviously not encouraged by my feeble efforts, after a while she wandered off and came back with two young men, one of whom spoke some English. Some digging ensued and then more guys were called to push, so I climbed back in.

Now the situation was thus: BlueBelle is a rear-wheel-drive vehicle, the sand patch was at least five metres long and my rear wheels were just about a metre in. My opinion was that if they pushed from the front and I reversed, it would only need a metre to get me out of the sand enough for my rear wheels to find grip and the engine to do the rest. A 'disagreement' ensued as they decided it was better to push forward, so I tried to explain by gesticulating that if we went that way they would have to push me through at least four metres, whereas going back meant a much shorter push. Nope, my logic was either lost in translation or (more likely) 'a woman wouldn't know these things'. In an attempt to prove me wrong they did give a feeble attempt to push

---

[62] www.facebook.com/kokou2019
[63] That means she was older than me!!

her back, but then all shook their heads in disagreement and gave up.

I also gave up to the 'manitude'.[64] I was stuck in the sand but I wasn't getting out on my own and they weren't listening to me, so I waited to see how they got on.

I won't go into the excruciating details of the next hour (!), but it was a debacle requiring a large degree of patience on my behalf as they debated and argued and made little progress until eventually there were about fifteen men able to push me through by sheer force. But now came the tricky part: the more people who drifted over to 'assist' me, the more I realised that they were all expecting a payday. I called the man who spoke English to me and gave him some money, which I clearly stated would have to suffice for everyone. He put the money in his pocket and another guy came to my window. "No, that was for everyone," I said firmly, berating the first man, whereupon there ensued much muttering and debating until I thought I might have a riot on my hands.

What I had handed over was fair for any emergency situation, and quite honestly they had made far more work of it than was necessary. I stopped the van but stayed inside: my campsite was no more than fifty metres ahead and I didn't want someone coming after me with a grudge! I repeated that it was all I had to give them and thanked them again for their help – but sorry, I just didn't have any more. Soon they all relaxed and the man who took the money said it was fine, he would sort it out. Relieved, I took him at his word, thanked everyone once more and drove on to my stop. ARA 5 : DB 3

Chez Antoine was situated on a gorgeous beach of fine white sand lined with palm trees. The cabins were rustic huts constructed mainly of sticks tied together, with a few of them built of brick. There was a building that served as the office and kitchen with a paved terrace outside and a few tables and chairs, and this was also the spot where I could get a WiFi signal. The beach was deep sand so parking on it was impossible for me; I'd only just escaped the stuff! I was directed to a closed hard-standing parking area that had some view of the beach. It was in full sun but had a

---

[64] My new word for men's attitude when they ignore women and think they know best

tap nearby and I would be able to use the squat latrines and the open-air showers. It would do nicely and the price was very agreeable.

I parked up in a front corner to get the best view and set up my awning, tying it to a nearby post to give me at least some shade. The heat and humidity continued to be intense, but the view of the ocean gave a sensation of coolness. I was sweaty and filthy from my sand encounter so my first stop was a shower. The showers were next to the rustic cabins, each around a metre and a half square with sticks lashed together for a wall, the floor being the beach with some flat stones to stand on directly under the showerhead. A small wooden shelf hung on the wall for soap and a piece of wire had been strung across a corner for one's clothes and towel. Rustic indeed, but when I looked up I could see palm trees towering overhead and the blue, blue sky, or when I showered at night the fully starlit expanse of space. I loved it!

I would sometimes shower twice a day, once to wash and again in the evening to cool down (as much as that was possible) before bedtime. The showers were cold; hot water would rarely have been welcome, so I had come to ignore most hot water taps (although they were seldom found at the places I stopped). The run-off from the shower drained into the sand and inevitably the ocean, so I used as little soap as I could. The worst part of showering was the struggle to put clothes on: no amount of drying would suffice, as the moment the towel was hung up the humidity made my skin once again clammy to the touch. After so many months of this, I had begun to wonder if I would ever be dry again!

During my break times I also took the opportunity to give myself some maintenance. This included trimming my hair, giving my dust-encrusted feet a good pedicure in my bucket with a scrubbing brush, and cutting and painting my toenails. Just because I was hot and sweaty most of the time didn't mean I had to be completely untended!

Included in my personal care was the matter that I was not always able to access a decent shower or find enough water to have a proper wash. As such, I was extra careful always to clean the private parts to ensure that there was no build-up of bacteria, which I knew would create a whole set of new problems. I had also heard of many people who started with a small spot or a scratch and had ended up needing hospitalisation, so I made sure to prioritise these areas and used my aloe vera gel and colloidal silver copiously on any small abrasions – especially the mosquito bites, of which I had many!

I spent a couple of days doing my washing, sitting on the terrace with the WiFi, catching up with emails and staring at the gorgeous daytime view of ocean and palm trees; while at night the sea was sprinkled with the lights of the many ships waiting to enter the port. It was a strange sight in the morning to see the little old wooden boats and the men with their long poles heading out to fish against the backdrop of the huge modern container ships in the distance. This was the epitome of the continent today: the modern western mixed with the traditional African; and I wondered if we can ever find a way to mix these successfully to the benefit of everyone without losing what is quintessentially African.

One afternoon Kanfitine Yaffah,[65] a young man who was frequently doing work around the camp, approached me and told me he was an artist with a studio just down the road that he wanted to show me. Knowing that he would want me to buy something, I told him it was too hot for an old woman like me to be wandering around in the heat and maybe some other day… But I should have known better: the next morning he was there again, asking me to come. I knew this would never end, so I walked with him about a hundred metres up the sandy street and he showed me the room where he lived, with a mattress on the floor and his artwork all over the walls and standing about the place. It was interesting art and some of his pieces were rather good.

Now came the task of telling him how nice they were but that I lived in a van and couldn't buy any. He looked disappointed, so I told him that instead I would take a photograph of us together with his art and I would post it on my Facebook page with his link. He seemed pleased with this option and I was happy I had managed to do at least something for him. African men are difficult to understand from a western perspective. He invited me several times to join him for drinks, a party or a night out on the town, all of which I regularly declined (to his great

---

[65] www.yaffah.blogspot.com

disappointment). I could never be certain if he was simply being friendly or wanted something more and, nice as he was, I had neither the interest in struggling to speak French nor the energy at the end of the day to go anywhere other than my own bed. I'd become quite an old fart!

Anatole and Marion arrived a day or so into my stop and parked on the beach in front. We chatted about our mutual issue regarding Nigerian visas and how we thought we might go about getting them. This was the big challenge that had been on my mind since Morocco, this and the road crossing from Nigeria to Cameroon... But first the visa.

Firm in my belief that I would somehow be able to get through Nigeria, I set out to get my Gabon visa; and rather than take down my awning and pack my van, I decided to walk to the main road and hail a taxi. The staff at Chez Antoine had advised how much I should pay and I squeezed into a crowded cab – four of us in the back, two plus the driver in the front – and explained where I wanted to go. I was grateful for the lovely young woman seated in front of me who spoke English and helped me. There seemed to be some consternation as the taxi was not heading in my intended direction, but he said he would hook me up with another taxi in the city.

We stopped at a busy market and I was taken to another taxi where some negotiation took place as well as an exchange of money. I understood that my fare was being sold on and I was given the nod to get in. This driver spoke English[66] and when we arrived at the Gabon Embassy he offered to wait. I thought this a good option to prevent the nuisance of having to find a return taxi.

Inside the embassy I was given a form to complete. I had been warned that they would insist on all sorts of information such as a contact address in Gabon (which I didn't have) or a hotel booking (which of course I didn't have either), so I filled in what I could and explained to the woman that this was the best I could do. I had to wait while she went to find someone to talk to me in English and when she returned with a male official I explained about my journey, answering the usual questions. He stared hard

---

[66] I found a number of Togolese who spoke English, probably from the influence of living near the two Anglophone countries of Ghana and Nigeria.

at me as if to assess whether I would be a grave danger to his country – judging by past questions women my age seemed to present a high level of risk – but I managed to pass and was given an appointment to come back a few days later to pick up the visa.

My taxi took me back in the direction of Chez Antoine. I had spotted a supermarket about a kilometre away from the camp and decided to be dropped off there, do some shopping and walk the rest of the way back. The driver told me the fare and I was shocked as it was several times higher than I'd expected. There were several factors at play here: I had foolishly taken a taxi on my own (being alone makes for a more expensive ride), the embassy was further than I had expected, and the driver had waited twenty minutes for me. However, even taking all of those factors into consideration it was still considerably more than I was prepared to pay. I suspected he was trying to take advantage of me, so I informed him that I didn't have more than the amount I was prepared to pay – still more than I should have paid – and he could take it or leave it. I also gave him a strict dressing down for how costly it was and of course he acquiesced by taking my money, an indication of his overcharge. Taxis are the same all over the world!

Outside the supermarket there was a young woman selling fruit and vegetables and I made a mental note to support her rather than get them inside. I did my other shopping and came out to buy what I needed from her. The produce was fresh and at a good price and again she spoke English very well, so we exchanged a pleasant chat. My shopping was now unfortunately heavier than I had planned and the walk in the mid-morning heat had been further than I had anticipated, but I trudged on thinking of the lovely cold shower at the end of my walk.

A description of Togo would not be complete without a description of the men. A great many of them were dressed in tight-fitting pipe-legged pants and matching short-sleeved tunics coming just to the top of their thighs. These were in African prints, always bright and colourful, in slightly different patterns from those of the women's dresses but no less appealing. They call it their 'traditional dress', but it seemed to me more of an adopted and adapted fashion. Anyway I thought it looked perfect on them… except for the fat-bellied guys whose tightly stretched tunics lost them some of their charm.

Anatole and Marion left after a few days, but soon after that Michiel arrived in his 4x4 and also parked on the beach. Michiel is Dutch and I'd been in touch with him for a while, again via the West Africa Traveller's group. I was keen to meet him, but must confess I had an ulterior motive: I was looking for someone to accompany me on the Nigeria-Cameroon border route, as by all accounts it was not so much a road as a track with GPS co-ordinates, and I believed I would benefit from travelling with someone in a 4x4 to push or pull me if necessary. The route was legendary amongst overlanders and it was critical that I got through it before the rainy season started in a month or two, otherwise I wouldn't get through it at all for another six months at least.

Michiel and I fell into easy conversation; his being Dutch meant we could speak either language. When I broached the topic of travelling together he was willing to have me along, but he had to be in Gabon in a few weeks to meet friends who were flying out to spend some time with him; and he didn't have to solve the Nigerian visa issue as he already had one. This was too tight a schedule for me: it was only the end of March and Ursula had by now confirmed she would join me mid-May for the journey from Libreville in Gabon to Luanda in Angola, so I still had several more weeks to kill before I needed to be in Gabon. Michiel wasn't a match, but I believed the Universe would still come up with someone.

Meanwhile another French couple in a large 4x4 truck arrived in the camp and parked in the far corner diagonally across from me. Language being the biggest barrier, we exchanged cursory greetings but not much more.

Michiel only stayed a few days and then he was off to race through to Gabon. I still had to pick up my Gabon visa and this time I decided not to bother with the taxi option but instead packed up and paid my bill, figuring that if I got my visa early enough I would head into Benin. My appointment was in the early afternoon so I decided in the meantime to run an errand.

After leaving Guinea I'd realised I no longer had my Visitor Book for BlueBelle, in which all the people we had met along the way, including in Europe, had written kind notes and words of encouragement for me. (I also referred to it as my "Oh shit" book.) I had recognised when I started this whole adventure that there would likely be days when nothing was going right (hence the name) and I might seek some comfort from the kind thoughts. I had not noticed precisely *when* it had gone missing, but my search had determined that missing it surely was. However, whilst in Lomé I was contacted by Ismael of Les Palmiers in Conakry to tell me he had heard from Felix (my Ghana visa helper with whom I was still in touch) that I was in Togo. Ismael had found my book, and by chance he had a guest who worked for the Red Cross in Togo who was returning in a few days: was I interested in getting my book back? Yes, of course I was! I stopped by the Red Cross office in the city and was reunited with my book... and Africa suddenly became a wonderfully small place.

By the time I got my Gabon visa I was hot and sweaty and not particularly interested in tackling the border, so I returned to the campsite, carefully avoiding the sand traps. I noted that the French couple had taken my premium spot, so I was left with their vacated spot and reversed in with my side door facing the ocean. I had thought that the ground was hard; and indeed it had a hard crust... but underneath it was pure sand. I tried to get out but realised I was stuck – again! &#%!@? SAND!! When would I learn to stay out of it?!

I was done. This was a problem to tackle tomorrow.

In the morning I called one of the groundsmen with whom I'd had some friendly exchanges and asked if he could assist me getting out of the sand. Three men appeared and started to dig and then pushed BlueBelle while I tried to drive. Mr French from the overlanding vehicle came out and kindly helped by coordinating everyone. Speaking French helped direct the activity and soon some planks appeared, but BlueBelle spat them out and remained firmly entrenched; then some stones appeared and she spat those out too. The digging, pushing and manipulating continued, but still BlueBelle was having none of it. Everyone was sweating profusely and the heat was on in more ways than one. Eventually Mr French had enough. I watched him walk off to his van and start pulling down his awning, putting aside chairs and tables and closing doors, seemingly much to the displeasure of Mrs French.

Then he reversed the van in front of BlueBelle, unwound his winch and within minutes had managed to extract her.

I bought all the guys a big bottle of beer each, and for the disruption and inconvenience I later that day bought some small bottles of French wine to show my gratitude to Mr and Mrs French. Finally I gave BlueBelle and myself a strict talking-to: we had to stop doing this sand thing as it was becoming ridiculous – and far too expensive! ARA 6 : DB 3

Going to Benin was now out of the question. I was too exhausted and stressed by the whole thing and slowly, without realising it, Overlander's Disease[67] crept in.

I fell into a routine of getting up early, catching the cool mornings to do my washing, hang it out and hope that it would dry by the end of the day; getting clothes completely dry in a humid climate was a major challenge. I also tidied BlueBelle up. Hard to believe, but in such a small space stuff quickly got out of hand. My clothes cupboard, for example, had drawers that now wouldn't close, so folding and reorganising was on the to-do list. For the rest of the day I would research my ongoing journey and potential routes. I watched all the comings and goings, sat on the terrace and chatted to the staff or the owner Antoine, who although he spoke little English was a real charmer.

The weekend brought many day visitors to the camp and the hotel next door held some very loud parties, which disturbed the usual tranquillity of the beach and only subsided a little before sunrise. I was eternally grateful for my earplugs which were always to hand, but the bass music could still be felt through the tyres and into my bed.

The rainy season also seemed to be coming and a couple of nights before I left a real African storm was brewing. I could smell it in the air long before the darkest clouds rolled in, and as night fell the thunder and lightning displays were close and vivid. The rain came down like a torrent. It felt like the rain to end all rains and it lasted most of the night, and my thoughts drifted to Noah. The air became suddenly cold and I must have caught a draught on my back from the open roof vent, which led to a scratchy throat and feeling a bit off the next day. Apart from my knack for

---

[67] The effect of staying in a place longer than intended without any real reason

attracting mosquitoes I also have one for the catching of colds, and this was something I truly did not need now. I doubled up on my vitamin C intake.

I decided that I had to stop procrastinating about my Nigerian visa since Benin would be my last opportunity and I had to cure myself of the Overlander's Disease. I had unintentionally been at Chez Antoine for almost two weeks, so that was it: I was leaving the next day.

As usual I was all packed and paid up, ready to leave at first light. I had said farewell to my new friends at the camp and had settled into bed to get enough sleep before who-knew-what kind of road and border crossing… and then I heard it. I'd heard that noise before: I was *sure* I knew that engine… And sure enough, it was Livingstone rolling into camp. I had known from their Facebook posts that Laurie and Bruce were heading my way, but we hadn't been in touch for a while.

I excitedly stepped out into the dark and stood waiting while they parked up and got themselves levelled off with blocks. I'd been too lazy to do such and had become accustomed to sleeping at an angle when I couldn't get level. Livingstone, however, being much larger than BlueBelle, needed some *serious* levelling. It's also really a two-person job, one driving and the other directing and shifting in the blocks; doing it solo would have taken five times the effort, so another good excuse for me not to do it.

Laurie had seen me in the dim light and greeted me, though I knew she hadn't recognised me yet. Eventually, when they were sorted and parked, she looked over to me with an expression that read, You're still watching us, why? But when I said, "Hey Laurie, of all the campsites in all of Africa…" it suddenly dawned on her and she rushed over to give me a big bear hug. We started to chat but I recognised that they were tired and in need of food, so I bade them goodnight and agreed to catch up with them in the morning.

The next day, having spent more time than I'd expected happily catching up with Laurie and Bruce over breakfast on the terrace, I was late setting out… but I really had to go. I had to stop procrastinating and get that darn Nigerian Visa sorted out. It was now the beginning of April.

The coast road out of Lomé had an amazingly tropical feel, with sandy side tracks leading to the sea and plenty of tall palm trees. I wanted to explore the area, but to be honest I was terrified of sand by now, so BlueBelle and I agreed to be satisfied that the beaches were the same as the one we had just left. One section of the road passed close enough to the sea to afford a good view, and to my surprise the waters were a wonderful azure blue against the white sand and the tall green palms.

The Togo exit border post was small but relatively well organised. I approached an open building and presented my passport and the officer behind the counter informed me:

Officer: It is Sunday. You know we have a tradition on Sunday? You must buy us beer. (*I hadn't heard that one yet.*)

Me: Really, you get to drink on the job?

Officer: No, we drink it later. (*Yeah, right!*)

Me: Sorry guys, I don't carry beers around with me.

Officer: We will take anything you have. (*These guys were relentless.*)

Me: Well you're really out of luck as I don't have any booze with me – and besides, I don't condone drinking on a Sunday. (*I hoped that some religious reprimand would make them retract, but I was mistaken.*)

Officer: Oh, but it is a way for you to show your appreciation... but we will also take the money and buy the beers ourselves.

That was entirely the wrong thing to say to me. I went into a long tirade about how that was *exactly* what the problem was in Africa – corruption! And here I was being told that I had to buy them beers, and I was an old woman on my own and they were intimidating me to pay them, and they should be there doing the job they were being paid for and not asking people who have spent time and money visiting their country for money, drinks or favours..! I ended with: "You are the reason Africa is in such trouble, because everyone thinks it's acceptable to ask for things for nothing! It is disgraceful!" Seeing he had bitten off more than he was inclined to chew, the officer swiftly stamped my passport and handed it back to me. I thanked him and asked where I would need to go next, and he said the fellow standing behind me would show me. So I followed him…

We went to a room but there was no one there, so he took me to another room, where the officer told us to go to the vacant room we had just come from! My escort explained that there had been no one there and so the officer sorted out my van papers himself. As I walked back to my van, I realised I was being followed by my escort. I thought I was done, but evidently he had designated himself my fixer. He was obviously hoping for money, but when I was safely in my van he got his own reprimand. I told him that if he wanted to offer me a service he should have agreed a fee with me in advance and not just make me think he was being a kind and helpful person, only to find out that instead I was somehow employing him. I added that I also didn't think five minutes of help was something I wanted to pay for! I had some loose bills on my dash that didn't amount to much so I gave him that: I believe it was enough of an insult to clarify my point. All in all I was getting a handle on this border stuff, and 'crazy old woman' definitely seemed to be the best approach.

Chapter Nine – Benin Republic

31 March 2019

The Benin border post was relatively swift and painless, albeit a little chaotic. I had to ask around a bit to find where to get my passport stamped, and then I was directed to the other side of the road to get my TIP. Of course it took a while for all the necessary big black ledgers to be filled out before I was done.

Benin (officially The Republic of Benin) is famed as the birthplace of voodoo and for the former Kingdom of Dahomey, an important European trading region which historically boasted an all-female military unit known as the Dahomey Amazons. These women warriors are amongst my heroes as they were renowned for their courage and stamina in combat. Several times they bravely defended against the French colonisers until they were beaten by French bayonets and the Maxim machine gun, a powerful weapon often used by European colonialists to suppress uprisings.

The capital of Benin is Porto-Novo, where the national legislature sits, however the largest city and the country's main port is Cotonou. Driving into Cotonou on a Sunday was easy. There was little traffic and the streets of the city were wide and well-paved, a relief for both BlueBelle and me after some of the tougher roads we'd encountered. The only issue was that there was again little in the way of camping other than on the beaches outside the city, and the reviews of those had made notable mention of the dreaded S-word.[68] I had to find something in the city so I took a drive about to see if I could spot somewhere to park up safely… but nothing seemed worth taking the risk.

I finally identified another Catholic accommodation set-up, but this one seemed quite fancy and was being run like a hotel. I did a bit of begging to be allowed to sleep in their parking area and not have to pay for a room. The man at reception was obviously doing me a favour so I was most grateful, and he only asked that I 'look after' the guard when I left. No problem.

---

[68] Sand

I parked up under a nice shady tree and relaxed. By now it was late afternoon so I just chilled and made some early dinner. It was pointless waiting for the day to cool down sufficiently to cook – it was always hot! – but I made an effort to cook healthy meals at least three times a week to ensure that I was eating a balanced diet. These were my 'one-pot wonders': I would usually start with sautéed onions, then whatever vegetables I had (courgettes, aubergines, potatoes or butternut) and I would either add a tin of beans or make a Spanish tortilla as my friend Ana had taught me in Solsona. I tend to eat 'conveniently', usually junk, so looking after my health and strength in the heat, as well as maintaining a diversity of food, was extremely important.

The next day was Monday so I set out to tackle the Nigerian Embassy. With many papers in hand and having checked the map thoroughly, I decided to walk and buy a local SIM card on the way. (Such was the ever-persistent need for data which enabled me to stay in touch with the world at large, and find local information and view updates from the various overlanding groups.)

I'm often asked how safe I felt out and about. To be honest, I rarely had any issues, although there were some specific things I did to ensure my safety.[69]

I hadn't gone far and was already sweating liberally when I came upon a public garden that looked like it was being restored. There weren't many people about so I walked in to admire what was being done, but out of nowhere someone popped up to tell me that I wasn't allowed to be there. I returned to the pavement and walked a bit further down the street and past a wall of mosaics bordering a building. They obviously had some traditional significance and were absolutely beautiful, so I took some photos and continued ambling along. About fifty metres ahead of me I noticed a soldier on guard by a gate at the end of the wall. By now I was so accustomed to seeing men with weapons that I just smiled at him as I passed; however, I was surprised to have him stop me in quite a firm manner.

---

[69] See my blog on Street Safety www.goinghometoafrica.com/index.php/blog-travelog/blog/personal-safety-tips

It seemed I was not allowed to take photos of the mosaics, and apparently I should not even have been walking down that road as it was next to a secure facility. This may have accounted for the lack of people, but I was surprised that there were no signs and asked him, as a tourist, how was I supposed to know this? After some conversation about my 'illegal' activity, I simply apologised. Sometimes it was the only thing that would make the nonsense stop. He smiled, satisfied at my apparent contrition, and told me I could go. The paranoia of the armed forces in some of these countries was bizarre – but then again most of the feedback I'd so far received seemed to indicate that old women posed a considerable threat to national security!

The main coastal avenue was a prominent thoroughfare, with well-maintained green verges and central islands full of shrubbery, all very elegant and sophisticated, and with embassies and bold corporate offices lining both sides of the dual carriageway. It was all very impressive... until I noticed the signs warning people not to defecate in the central bushes!

Thanks to Ursula's contacts, I arrived at the Nigerian Embassy with a letter of invitation from a reputable accounting firm in the country. I was also armed with copies of every potentially useful document, including a list of entry and exit dates for all the previously visited countries, and a letter from my non-profit to explain why I was travelling to Zimbabwe. My folder of papers was thick, I felt confident that I was adequately prepared. Certainly I had been stressing about it long enough.

It started with the security check. I was admitted through the gate and told I had to leave my phone and bag. No, that wasn't going to happen. They could hold my phone (it had a pattern lock on it, so I was sure it couldn't be abused), but my bag? Under no circumstances! We compromised at a search. It was just a tiny over-shoulder bag with my wallet, passport and IDs, and I was keeping it with me.

I was directed to a side building where several people were seated waiting. I greeted everyone, and soon after an official entered and summoned me to his desk. I proceeded with my request, presenting all my documentation, and midway he halted me with the question, "Did you apply for your visa in your home country?" Well, how could I explain that I hadn't had a 'home' country for a while because I'd been travelling around for the better part of a year, without sounding like I was a high-risk individual? So instead I told him that I had not done this because I had driven a very long way and had no idea when I would reach the area. I once again thrust my invitation letter from a Very Important Business in front of him, but his response was firm: "No matter, we do not issue visas here for anyone other than Benin residents."

At this point I did get a tad upset, and then made the mistake of thinking that I could get him to change his mind if I just gave him all the rationale around my situation; but he was not even remotely interested and merely got up and dismissed me. I'm afraid I disgraced myself at this point by telling him how ridiculous it all was, upon which he asked me if I knew how hard it was for any Nigerian to get a visa to the UK. Now that was a sobering thought: why should I, just because I was there on a UK passport, expect any preferential treatment? If a Nigerian had tried to attempt the same in a neighbouring country, the UK Embassy would surely have told them to take a hike too!

This was an outcome I had feared since I'd been turned down so many months ago in Morocco. I knew of several overlanders who had stopped at every Nigerian embassy they came across on their way through West Africa, only to be turned away at each one. However, the advice Mr Visa eventually proffered was to apply for a VOA,[70] which could be done online. It was the only avenue open to me. He left me in a complete state, trying to hold it together and focus on what I needed to do next.

I wouldn't be able to do this online thing without data and fortunately I had located a mobile provider on Google Maps the night before, so off I went to get a SIM card. A short way down the other side of the road was the local head office, but they did not sell SIM cards and I would have to walk a considerable distance further to get to a shop. This did little to improve my mood. However, when I reached the shop the staff were incredibly friendly and helpful, setting everything up for me and giving me instructions on the *# numbers to dial for services. I was at least set up and still had some data left to investigate further, so I

---

[70] Visa on Arrival

decided to see if the small shopping centre opposite might have something cold for me to drink and a place to sit down to let my thoughts settle.

After finding a welcome air-conditioned oasis inside the mall, I noticed a well-stocked but expensive supermarket. It would be a good place to stock up on tinned goods later. I needed to get back to BlueBelle and start working on the visa solution, but I was now a lot further away from her than I had anticipated. I started walking back with the motorbikes beeping behind me, constantly offering a taxi ride. Me on a motorbike? That wasn't going to happen! I continued to weave my way through the streets with my phone navigation on. I was enjoying looking at the mix of residential properties, shops and the usual informal street traders; I was constantly amazed to see what they would sell on the side of the road. Eventually, in the intense heat and with my feet becoming uncomfortably sore I decided that I had to take a taxi, even though it was quite a short distance. I just couldn't manage any further and for the first time I had a blister forming. Blisters can be a dangerous thing in the heat and humidity: if they are not carefully tended to can turn into horrid sores and even, in some instances I'd heard of, cellulitis.

It was coming up to midday. I waved down a taxi car and told him where I wanted to go, but even though I knew from my navigation the route he should have taken, he opted for a longer route. I challenged him and said I knew he wasn't taking me directly where I had asked, but he defended himself with some nonsense. On our arrival at the hotel he told me the fare, whereupon I exclaimed that it was an outrageous sum but showed him a note in payment. I got out of the car and was waiting for my change when he pulled the 'I don't have any change' stunt. As you can see, my morning had not turned out as well as I had hoped... and now this. I scolded him loudly: "You've had how many customers today and you tell me that you don't have any change?! First you drive me further than is necessary and then you try to rob me by saying you don't have any change! Who comes on taxi duty without change?!" I further used some supplementary words to call him a thief, but eventually hurled the note at him and told him to keep the change and be damned.

I hadn't realised that I had an audience. At the end of my rant I saw one of the 'hotel' staff stalk past me, thoroughly unimpressed by my attitude. I didn't care... but I should have. Not much later, the parking guard came to tell me that I must go to the office. Oh, my day was just getting better! Mr Offended was there and told me that I could not park in the car park and had to take a room. I advised him that I had an arrangement with yesterday's receptionist, but he responded that he didn't know about this but if I didn't take a room I had to go. To his error I believe he thought this might pressure me into a room... I left.

My plan B option was a hostel just down the road, Haie Vive.[71] I had read that they didn't have much in the way of space for parking but there were no other options around. I drove there to ask and the staff were lovely and said I could park for slightly less than the cost of a room (cheaper than at the other hotel) and I could use one of the shared bathrooms and the shared kitchen. The parking was in their driveway within the compound and perfectly adequate. Additionally they had WiFi and a terrace with tables and chairs where I could sit and work from. To my delight there was also a small supermarket nearby which sold fresh bread, croissants, cold water and juice, with fruit and vegetables always available from the street vendors. I was perfectly located here and could at least relax while I applied for that elusive visa.

THE MAGIC OF SONGHAÏ

I researched and researched and finally applied online for the visa, after also checking the overlanding community networks for any updates. The challenge here was that everyone's experience was different and consistency, as with many African experiences, was distinctly lacking. However, having made the application, the advice was that it would take only a few days to get a response.

Optimistically, I also took the opportunity to get my Democratic Republic of Congo (DRC) visa a couple of blocks away. At the DRC Embassy I met the security guard, Theodore, the male version of my name reversed.[72] Recognising the reversal and surprisingly knowing the meaning, Theo and I struck up a

---

[71] www.guesthousebenin.com
[72] My full name is Dorothea and like Theodore it means 'gift from God'

conversation; like many Beninese he spoke reasonable English. When he asked I gave him my card and he stays in touch with me still today.

My DRC visa required biometrics, a photo and the completion of a comprehensive form; certainly the authorities weren't taking any chances with their visas. They said it would be ready the next day, but I received a call early in the morning from Theo who advised that the electricity was out, causing delays, and so it was Friday when I collected it.

I had not heard further about the Nigerian visa and most certainly would hear nothing over the weekend. I wanted to get out of the city. The beaches were out of the question – 'sand' was all I needed to say on that topic – and I hadn't seen any places inland that were interesting enough to spend the money driving up to. But then I found something that looked intriguing on the outskirts of Porto Novo, which lay in the direction of Nigeria.

One person had listed the Songhaï Centre on the iOverlander app, but there wasn't much detail and I was hoping that I would be able to park there. In the meantime Laurie and Bruce had been in touch and they were driving into Cotonou to attempt the Nigerian Embassy themselves for Bruce's visa. They had both applied for long-term Nigerian visas from their home in the USA, because although it cost more it would ensure that they could enter Nigeria whenever they got there. Their visas and passports had arrived in the UK, where they were at the time (they had used a second passport for the visas so they were not held up for their travels), but their predicament was that while Laurie's visa was long-term, Bruce's was not: they had only issued him one for three months and it had long expired by the time they were ready to enter Nigeria. Of course they were no longer in their country of origin and had been told by the Nigerian Embassy in Washington that he would have to return to the USA for any change to be made! So bottom line, Bruce and I shared the same visa issue.

I had told them I was getting out of the city and described where I was going. They were interested in joining me, but since I wasn't sure about the parking there I said I would update them on arrival. After picking up my DRC visa, I decided that it was also a good opportunity to apply for my Congo (Republic of

Congo) visa – two Congos in one shot![73] (I was still channelling *Absolute Certainty* that I would get through Nigeria.) It took a while to get to the Congo Embassy. The dirt roads were a challenge as they had either too much sand, pools of water or low-hanging electrical wires, so it took a few turns back and forth before I found a suitable route.

When I entered there was none of the security I had seen at the previous embassies. I was handed a form to complete, and on doing so they kindly found someone who spoke English to help me as no one could comprehend my French. I was not offended! I had believed I could collect the visa there and then, but since they closed early on a Friday it seemed impossible. I did what I hoped would work by putting on my distressed face and begging. They took pity on me and told me to wait, and twenty minutes later I had the visa. You gotta love Africa!

It was a long and traffic-filled highway to Porto-Novo and I should have known better than to attempt it on a Friday. It was always busy and a crazy time to be on the road, but no matter how often I told myself not to travel on this day, I consistently seemed to forget my own good advice.

After some interesting and poorly sign-posted diversions, I found the Songhaï Centre on the other side of the city. On my arrival I was directed to talk to the person in charge, who thankfully spoke excellent English. The Prince[74] listened carefully to my request to park up and use a shower (although I got the feeling he had never been presented with such an entreaty). He took me to a very nice office building where a young woman again heard my story, and after some consideration and assurances of my limited requirements and that I would pay a fee, she agreed that I would be able to stay. I was instructed to go to the hotels ('hotels'?) and notify the supervisor on duty of our agreement.

---

[73] It's slightly confusing but there are two similarly-named countries which border the Congo River: the Democratic Republic of the Congo is the larger country to the southeast, formerly known as Zaire and now sometimes referred to as "Congo-Kinshasa"; and the Republic of the Congo, the smaller country to the northwest, sometimes referred to as "Congo-Brazzaville".

[74] One of the first things Gerard told me was that he was a Dahomey Prince, so I shall of course convey him this honour.

The result was a parking spot near two well-appointed hotels at the end of a lane under a large shady tree which would offer respite for some of the day, plus the use of communal showers and toilets in the neighbouring dormitory. I updated Laurie and Bruce, who had also been turned away by the Nigerian Embassy and were coming to join me but were delayed by the traffic. They arrived as the sun was setting and parked up next to me.

The following morning we all went on a tour of the centre, which I had organised the previous afternoon with the Prince. The facility was exceptional and I had not seen anything like it before – certainly not in Africa. It was an entire eco-village for the teams of people who lived and worked on the estate and other day-workers, along with a team of trainers and facilities for the interns who came to learn about the various processes.

Some of their activities include bio-production using traditional farming methods to protect natural resources and the environment, and they sell their produce in their on-site shop and use it in their restaurant. Animal manure and plant waste are mulched to produce bio-energy for use in generating electricity and cooking gas; and bio-pressing foodstuffs such as palm oil into cooking oil and fruit into juices adds value to produce grown locally, rather than sending it overseas and then reimporting it, thereby supporting their bio-consumption programme. They also have a leadership academy where they teach young people the framework of their success.

I could go on and on about the place, it was so fascinating, but I have kept it brief and would encourage those who are interested to visit their website and take a moment to learn more about what this wonderful organisation does: www.songhai.org

One of the hotels had guests from Belgium and France; it seemed they frequently had international visitors staying at the centre. Amongst the guests, we also found out, were some of the Kings of Nigeria. Nigeria retains many of its traditional rulers, with their titles gained from the independent regions that existed before the formation of modern Nigeria. Most do not have any formal political power but they continue to command the respect of their people and can exert considerable influence. Their roles are more like nobility than monarchy, to make a western comparison.

These particular Kings were in Benin to meet with their counterparts from the area. For those who are not aware, when the Europeans colonised Africa they introduced borders where there were previously none and this split many tribes and families. Despite all the years that had passed, I often heard people refer to members of their tribe separated by borders.

Most of my time was spent sitting outside with Laurie and Bruce trying to glean any hint of coolness (not to be found inside our vans), and so I had the opportunity to acquaint myself with the Kings' entourage, which consisted of police security, drivers, a doctor and other aides. I of course greeted them all and a few struck up conversations. They were fascinated by what we were doing, driving across Africa, and wanted to see the vans. Mostly they were interested in Livingstone, the big American truck (men: the same all over the world, thinking bigger is better!), but I consoled BlueBelle that she was far more beautiful.

I thought that since some of the Kings' entourage were in the police there might be a chance to find a contact for that elusive Nigerian visa. I shared our plight with all who would listen and one of them said I should absolutely ask 'his' King, and he would introduce me. That seemed like good news indeed.

Early the next morning I saw that the Kings and their entourage were out and about, so I quickly pulled on a dress (imagine, me in a dress!) and tried to rouse Laurie and Bruce. I knew that Bruce was usually up early, although Laurie liked to sleep in, but after several attempts knocking on the door there was no response. I figured they were still sleeping and so, not wanting to miss any opportunity, I headed off to try to progress the business of the day: Nigerian visas.

In front of the hotel buildings were a whole lot of men dressed in layers of the most colourful robes. (I wondered if they were sweating to death underneath them.) I hung about in the background while a variety of photographs were taken, and I took a few with my phone too. Someone noticed me and asked if I also wanted to be in the photographs, so I excitedly said, "Yes!" – although I was looking decidedly un-regal! So it was that I came to have a photograph with the Nigerian Kings and the founder of Songhaï, Father Godfrey. They were all whisked off before I had a chance to ask anything, but I was assured that there would be a further opportunity later that evening.

As I was standing watching the dignitaries leave in their vehicles, I picked up a conversation with a very nice man standing next to me whose name was Lai. He was the Vice Principal of the Methodist Boys' High School in Lagos[75] and was accompanying a group of his pupils on a tour of Songhaï. He was joined by two other adults, including Michael the driver. I discovered that Nigerians are very friendly and love to chat, and on hearing of our overlanding adventures they too were keen to see our vans, again mostly Livingstone (sigh).

That evening Bruce and I went back to the hotel for another attempt to meet the King, and as promised we were finally introduced. We had a brief chat about who we were and what we were doing, and then I asked if there was any help he could provide in getting our visas since we were stuck in Benin. He was amazed – as are all people who never have to do things that others take care of – and said that we should speak to the ambassador, who had just left but would be back later that evening.

After dinner I took up residence in the hotel foyer, determined not to miss out on meeting the ambassador. He eventually arrived and, reminding myself that this might be my only opportunity, I boldly introduced myself and briefly outlined the situation. He said I should talk with John, whom he called to his side and instructed, "Meet with these people and see what you can do." We set up a meeting at the Nigerian Embassy for 11.00am the following Tuesday and I thanked the ambassador most kindly. Result! My wait was at an end and there would surely be a visa coming out of this…

We remained at the centre as there was no point heading back to Cotonou until Tuesday morning. On Monday morning the Kings' entourage was preparing the vehicles to return to Nigeria, and I saw one of the drivers walking to another vehicle with a car battery. I asked him what the problem was and he responded that it was flat. I had no idea how he thought he was going to get it charged by taking it to another vehicle, however I told him to reinstall it into his car and I would start it for him. I think he

---

[75] https://mbhslagos.com.ng/

believed that I was going to bring BlueBelle and jump-start him, but I returned with a small black pouch and they all gathered around to see what was going to happen.

One of my 'must have' items for my journey[76] was a compact portable battery charger. I had considered that if I was ever on my own and stuck it would save me – and it had. I fitted the clamps to the battery: the light went green and I told him to start the car, and on the first turn it started. Everyone was in awe and I felt like I had performed a magic trick! ARA 6 : DB 4

What followed was that everyone naturally wanted to have photographs – or 'snaps'[77] – of me and the charger with each of them individually and in groups. The photography took longer than the starting of the car!

Lai and Michael walked past and we struck up a conversation. My research had shown that there was little suitable parking for us in Lagos, so as they were from the city I asked them if they knew of any suitable secure places for a couple of nights. Lai immediately said it might well be possible to park at his school and he would ask the Principal on his return. That gave me distinct hope: having someone local to help was invaluable when one was a stranger in a strange land.

WATCHING AND WAITING

Anatole and Marion had been in touch. They were in Cotonou with another French overlanding couple and had also lucked out on the Nigerian visa, so they asked how I was getting on. I briefed them on the appointment and told them that while I had no idea what the result would be, they were welcome to meet us at the embassy. If we did get lucky, perhaps I could get assistance for them too.

We all met outside the embassy before the scheduled meeting on Tuesday and Laurie, Bruce and I went in. By this time we had all submitted our VOA applications but none of us had had any response whatsoever. It was frustrating as it was now over a week and we should have heard within seventy-two hours.

---

[76] See my blog for my list of overlanding essentials –
www.goinghometoafrica.com/index.php/blog-travelog/blog/overlanding-essentials
[77] Selfies are commonly called snaps in Nigeria

As we entered we asked for John and were told to come back some time later, so I replied that I had an appointment. I was then told that we should see the man in charge of visas – Mr Visa, the same guy I had seen before. I made it clear that there was no point seeing him as he was not able to help and that the ambassador himself had recommended that we speak to John, and repeated that we had an appointment. The story then changed to 'John had asked that we speak to Mr Visa'. This was starting to smell funny and I told them so. We were instructed to wait, and as we did so a security guard mentioned that John was only the ambassador's driver. It was then that I realised we had been fobbed off and there was little hope we would achieve any kind of result.

Mr Visa suddenly appeared and reiterated that there was nothing he could do, we had to follow the VOA process, so we told him that we had done this but not had any response. He did offer to take our names and email addresses and said that he would check up on our applications. I asked if he would also follow up for the others waiting outside and he said he would, so I dashed out and got their details too. He took these, made a phone call and then informed us that they would look into the matter. Somehow I had my doubts....

We gave the update to the others and then, mightily disappointed, we all decided to head off. Anatole and Marion suggested I wild camp with them near the beach, telling me it would be fine as there was not too much sand, so I acquiesced but said I first needed to do some shopping. Laurie and Bruce went looking for a hotel with air-conditioning as Bruce had caught a cold; and as we know man, flu is a dreadful thing to endure, especially in the heat. We all agreed to stay in touch.

I got lost trying to find my way to the beach camp. The last of my three phones wouldn't charge and had died what seemed a permanent death, and I had no idea where I was going with no access to my navigation. (I hadn't used my other phone since I'd dropped it in Ghana and cracked the screen so badly that it was more trouble than use.) However, I did remember how to get back to the hostel I had previously stayed at, so I decided to return there.

To my great surprise, Livingstone was parked outside the hostel and Laurie and Bruce were looking to see if they could get a room. They had not succeeded at their intended hotel, so it seemed fate had brought us back together again. Livingstone ended up squeezed into the other driveway because he just couldn't fit into the side where I had resumed my position.

One of the other guests at the hostel was Gautier, a tall, slim and very good-looking[78] young Frenchman who was overlanding on a motorbike. He had been waiting thirteen days for his VOA approval, but not without multiple visits to the embassy, emails and phone calls. However, within a couple of days of meeting him it came through and he was on his way, so I asked him to update me what the roads were like in Nigeria when he got there. He promised to do so and we exchanged WhatsApp numbers.

Luckily I managed to resuscitate one of my phones into working order so there followed days of sitting on the terrace, researching ways to get the visa and messaging any leads. There was still no response on the VOA application. We needed an email saying that we were 'approved' to go to the border, and from there we would be escorted to the airport in Lagos to get our actual visa. We waited and waited... and waited... After a few days, Anatole and Marion messaged us to say that they had met Mr Visa again and within a day their VOA had arrived and they were heading to Nigeria. Great! But why hadn't ours arrived?

In the interim, my Favourite Niece had been working her connections again and come up with a contact who could get us the VOA approval within twenty-four hours... but it would cost us $100 each. I really couldn't afford the expense, but neither could I afford to wait any longer. My concerns about the approaching rainy season were stressing me out, so it was time to go. Bruce agreed and we reluctantly paid the fee and proceeded with the application.[79] Finally, with our VOA approvals in hand, we spent a day getting ourselves organised for the road. I had now been in Benin for almost two weeks.

During our time together Laurie, Bruce and I had decided that it would be in all our interests to cross Nigeria together: I might need their help to cross into Cameroon on the legendary dreaded

---

[78] I promised him I would include this, but it's true!
[79] As fate would have it, Bruce's original VOA approval came through just after he'd paid for the $100 one... although mine never did arrive

road, and they liked my approach with the local people and also felt more comfortable with the backup (such as I was). We further agreed to cook meals in rotation, although I must admit they very kindly covered for me a few times when I was too exhausted after the day's drive.

Laurie was a nurse – a bonus, as she had already assisted me with tablets in Morocco for my shoulder pain and something to help with my sinuses. Then one evening, while I was cooking in my van, I had a freak accident and Laurie again came to my rescue.

I was chopping and peeling vegetables, but with my cooking space being restricted I had left a very sharp knife lying on a small metal dish on my pull-down shelf under the counter. I accidentally dropped what I was peeling on the dish and watched the knife take flight up into the air, turn tip down and plunge straight into my foot near the big toe. The blood began to spurt instantly; it all happened in slow motion and remains a movie in my head that I can never forget. I grabbed my small, dark blue hand towel that hung on the edge of the kitchen cupboard and applied pressure. (Thank goodness for all those medical TV series!) But now I was stuck, collapsed on my sofa trying to figure out how to keep the pressure on my foot and get it bandaged.

One of the staff members passed by my open door so I called out for her to please fetch Laurie. Laurie was there in an instant. She assessed the situation and dashed back to fetch her big medicine bag, telling me all the while to keep pressure on the wound. Gloves on, she got things prepared and we estimated that it had been about ten minutes since I had started applying the pressure. This was the magic figure, she proclaimed. The theory she shared with me was that in ten minutes your body has the time to respond to the pressure on the bleed and start to clot. I lifted the towel… and indeed it was no longer spurting. Cleaned and expertly bandaged, I finished making dinner – despite Laurie's best efforts to take over.

Chapter Ten – Nigeria

14 April 2019

We decided to follow the 'travel on Sunday' convention because we figured the border would be less busy. Clearing the Benin side was swift and uneventful; however, at the Nigerian border we hadn't counted on the fact that the person who *should* have been on duty was at church: it was Palm Sunday and he didn't appear until mid-morning. Eventually several forms were filled in and we were introduced to the Chief, who gave us a pleasant chat about how we had to look after the escort and pay him so he could take a taxi back to the border; and we should also give him food and drink. Reading between the lines, the taxi back would have been nowhere near the cost of the 'fee' and the balance would assuredly be going into his pocket, but as always there was no way to prove it.

Laurie and Bruce had a *carnet* for their vehicle but I still needed a TIP, so while we were waiting for of the immigration papers to be completed I set off to get one. The woman officer was at first very bolshie with me, so I warmed her up with some jokes and my story. With all the visa drama I had forgotten to check how much the TIP would cost, and when I asked her she in turn asked me how much I had paid in Benin. I hesitated. I thought it an odd question but considered that she was simply curious, so I stupidly told her it hadn't been much, about €15... and she replied it was the same here. Alarm bells were ringing somewhere in my head, but I just wanted the TIP and to get on my way so I soundly ignored them.

She put three different stamps on the form and we then visited another office where I got a further four stamps. (Seriously, seven stamps? It was an all-time African record!) She handed me the form and I offered to pay her in CFA, which she said she would accept – and another alarm bell rang. The money changer at the border had offered stupid rates so I had only changed the smallest amount of Nigerian naira I felt I might need on the road. I dashed off in the hope that my passport was now ready, but it was not yet. While I was waiting I looked through the form and remembered that I should have asked for a receipt, so I decided to return to the office to get one.

When I asked, the woman told me that the TIP wasn't something they gave a receipt for (that bell was now clanging wildly), so I said I didn't understand... although by now what I *did* understand was that she had taken the money for herself, hence there would be no receipt. I can play dumb when I need to, so I asked her if the charge was for the TIP, why was there no receipt? She gave me various dubious answers while I kept prying until eventually she offered to refund me. I was now confronted with the dilemma that if I angered her about this, what repercussions might there be for me later on? She likely had police connections (although I was probably overthinking it!) My decision was whether to reclaim my money to my own satisfaction or leave it with her to hers. I opted for the latter and took the hit as a sound lesson in checking my facts first!

Laurie and Bruce had cleared a space in the back of their double cab for Fredrik, our escort. They had air-conditioning and I did not, so he was much better off in Livingstone. They drove in front and I would follow, and I was told to stay close to them so that Fred could be sure to keep an eye on me... because you never knew what these old women were capable of, dashing into the Nigerian hinterland without the proper visa!!

The roads leading to the borders since CDI/Ghana had been good, but now it was back to poor conditions. In some distant past, the road we found ourselves on now had been a two-lane highway from the border to Lagos. Now it was a tattered and torn excuse with more earth than tarmac, and 'pothole' was insufficient to describe some of the gaping pits we were forced to circumnavigate. It was raining and obviously had been doing so for a while so the potholes were now pools. This meant it was impossible to assess their depth or condition, and therefore if you drove through one whether you might submerge and disappear forever. They had to be avoided at all costs. It was the most surreal experience: traffic would swerve to the other side of the road when their side became too challenging, and we wove our way over the barrier islands on to the opposite carriageway and back again with regularity. It eventually became a totally natural state of affairs and I witnessed not one accident, just the unnaturally natural flow of Africa.

Not only did the road slow us down but there were also innumerable police checkpoints. Fred managed to get us through most of them without too much time wasted, but occasionally I would be enthusiastically stopped and Fred would have to jump out of Livingstone and run back, shouting at the police to let me through. It took just over four hours of the most arduous driving and crazy traffic to cover the ninety kilometres into Lagos... and then we still needed to get our full visas from the airport, which lay north-west of the city.

On arriving at the airport (having navigated through more horrific traffic since it was now the afternoon rush hour), we parked on the verge in front of the staff parking lot and walked to the main terminal. Laurie stayed with the vehicles and the rest of us went in search of the visas. We wove our way through the large building, dodging travellers and their luggage taking their flights to far-flung destinations – or returning from them. By now I was regretting not having had a good breakfast.

Eventually we were brought into an office, papers were handed back and forth, a man came to shake our hands and we had to follow Fred again. On our way to the final stop, Fred asked if we could pay him before we entered since it would take him some time to find a taxi and get back to the border. The mere fact that he didn't want anyone else witnessing our 'transaction' gave more credence to my suspicion that the bulk of the money would be going to the Chief.

We found a waiting area with at least thirty people filling in forms or waiting to be attended. There we were directed to the man in charge, who viewed our papers and gave us a hard time for not having paid online. I apologised profusely because I truly had not seen the option to pay, and he softened somewhat. Bruce also took the opportunity to see if the payment for his defunct visa would suffice, but of course that was just wishful thinking. Our credit cards were processed, and after much writing and typing into a terminal we received a tiny stamp in our passports which belied the trouble it had caused and we were finally the proud owners of Nigerian visas!

Feeling enormously relieved at having overcome this ridiculous hurdle, we both tackled the next task, buying data. We needed to purchase SIM cards so we found a mobile provider (I forget which one: they all seemed to merge into one big inconvenience) and the process took a stunning forty-five minutes. It required biometrics, photograph (taken by them) and a long form to complete and sign, which was then all transcribed into a computer. I could not believe that this was all required for a SIM card, not even a gold-plated one! Task accomplished, we realised that we were starving. Laurie probably would be too, so we bought something at the airport; but the food was as usual expensive and not at all delicious. We trudged back to the vehicles, completely drained.

Poor Laurie had been harassed herself a few times by passing police telling her that we couldn't park there, and she had bravely countered that the customs officer had suggested that it would be OK. Well, at least the vehicles were still there and hadn't been towed, and I was again grateful not to have been on my own.

The light was fading fast and we were all exhausted. We had heard that the staff parking lot might allow us to park overnight, but I think Livingstone's size made them think that we were very rich because they asked a ridiculous fee for each of us. I said that it was extortionate and walked out, but Bruce continued to negotiate the deal and finally achieved a slight discount. By now we were so shattered that we just wanted to stop and be done for the day so we all succumbed. Only when we were parking did they bother to tell us that we would have to leave well before 6.00am when the next shift arrived. Yep, that money was going right into their pockets!

Before going to sleep I messaged Lai, whom we had met at Songhaï in Benin, updating him on our successful entry and asking if he'd had any luck getting the principal to agree to our stopping over at his school. Certainly the airport was no place to spend another night, what with the expense as well as the smell and noise of the place. I set my alarm for an early morning wake-up and fell into the sleep of the dead.

LAGOS AND THE BOYS' HIGH SCHOOL

Morning came and I hadn't yet heard back from Lai, so we decided we would do some of the necessary chores. Acquiring some local currency and then our Cameroon visas were the first order of business. That would keep us busy for the better part of the morning, and hopefully by then we would know if we had parking for the night.

We had seen several banks and ATMs on our way to the airport and therefore didn't think it would be too much trouble to draw cash… but could we have been any more wrong! We tried lots of different ATMs and they either would not accept our foreign cards or were empty. We continued into the city to apply for our Cameroon visas, hoping that we would also have better luck drawing money. The traffic was horrific and I had plenty of time to ponder life as we drove through areas of luxuriously rich and devastatingly poor.

The sprawling ethnic smorgasbord that is Lagos, Nigeria's largest city is built on a system of sandbars, islands and lagoons. Its population is currently estimated at twenty-four million[80] and still expanding rapidly, but unfortunately the meteoric growth of both the country and the city itself means that resources and housing continue to be spread extremely thin, and most of the inhabitants struggle with poverty. Lagos is also Africa's most populous city, marginally larger than Cairo and equivalent to the greater New York metropolitan area.

I was quick to notice that the increase in population had not been matched by the same in infrastructure. Most of the large city buildings – offices, shops and apartment blocks – had their own huge generators because the electricity was so frequently not working; and the roads continued to be variable, from pretty darn good to shockingly bad. The lagoon on which the main city lies with its various islands and waterways was littered with trash and flotsam and shacks built in haphazard style on the water's edge with ablutions not to be imagined. The poverty was oozing.

We arrived at the Cameroon Embassy and after I'd parked up I realised that I could not find my credit card. I'd had it when I

---

[80] Latter part of 2020

was getting in and out of the van trying various ATMs, but now I could not find it anywhere: it wasn't under the car, under the seat, under the mats… it was nowhere. I still needed to draw money, so I secured my funds by moving them into a different account and using another credit card, which I fortunately had with me. I didn't want to report the main credit card lost or stolen in case it was hiding somewhere, but this way if it was stolen there would be nothing to take.[81] In the meantime, Laurie and Bruce advanced me the visa fee.

I was armed with a letter of invitation to Cameroon which had been provided by an ex-Zimbabwean called Eric. I had put out a message some months before on a Zimbabwe Facebook group with a list of the countries that I was passing through, and suggested that if any Zimbabweans were on my route it would be good to meet them; and if they had a place for me to park, that would be even better! Eric had kindly responded from Cameroon and we agreed to stay in touch until I was closer, so while I was stuck in Benin I had advised him of my hopefully imminent arrival. He had offered a letter of invitation which might expedite the visa, and it was only upon reading the letter that I realised he was quite a bigwig in a major company in Cameroon.

Beyond the driving there was the constant visa planning: which one to get where, what papers would be needed, how much it would cost, which currency you had to pay in (often US$), what arrival date to put on the visa… Visas in West and Central Africa are valid from a specified date and usually only for thirty days, so if you arrive too late then no entry. So far I'd been lucky, but this preparation all took time, effort and energy.

The Cameroon visa duly applied for, we were advised that we could collect it later that afternoon. This meant it would be sensible not to roam too far away, and so the nearby shopping mall offered a good place to wait. Besides, I still needed a tow rope, which I hoped I could find at one of the big branded shops there.

The mall was modern and filled with goods all shiny and new, and the sheer contrast from what I had experienced for the previous several months was greater than my little brain could

---

[81] I never did find the card

grasp. I could have been in any mall anywhere in the world, but I just happened to be in Lagos, where once again the old and the new coexisted in the same space. Whist I made every effort on my travels to buy from local traders, there were times when only a supermarket or retail store had what I needed, but then my purchases in them were small: modern shops were expensive in comparison to what could be bought on the side of the road. I did find two tow straps with metal hooks though – and, as it happened, just in time.

While we were shopping Lai responded with positive news, confirming we would be able to stay overnight at the school. Bruce had been anxious to get some special oil he needed for Livingstone, so it was decided that he would pursue this whilst Laurie and I would return to the Cameroon Embassy to collect the passports, and we would meet up later at the school.

From the bliss of Livingstone's air-conditioning, Laurie was thrust into my 'African air-conditioning': windows wound down with the added boost of my dashboard dual-fan blowing all the hot air around. She also got the full Going Home to Africa experience of my world in a van. Through my open window I would chat to the drivers beside me (of course they were right next to me in their LHD vehicles), trade conversation and jokes with lane hawkers and wave at passers-by; and in the chaotic traffic she could witness the swearing – a lot of swearing and hooting. She was interested in my interaction with locals, and I realised that in fact *not* having air-conditioning was in a way a blessing because with my window open I let in more of Africa than I would with it closed. The amazing insight we picked up was that the Nigerians, far from all you might have heard, are incredibly friendly people: quick to smile, ready to laugh and can certainly crack a joke.

At the Cameroon Embassy we were solemnly asked to wait in the boardroom for the ambassador. When we were admitted to his office he asked us a few questions about what we were doing, and when we explained our overlanding journeys he was rather impressed, probably more so as he had two women in front of him. But he then proceeded to caution us NOT to attempt to pass through the border at Ekok or Ekang because there was a war on the Cameroon side and those borders were closed to foreigners.

We had heard mixed reports about this and had discussed whether it was worth taking the risk on that tarmac road – which would save us several hundred kilometres and provide a far smoother drive – instead of the uncertain road further north; but his stern warning now put that notion out of our heads.

After meeting Bruce as planned at the school, we made ourselves known and Lai introduced us to The Very Rev. Paul, the school's principal. They were so incredibly gracious and hospitable and let us park in the quad of the staff quarters, which was both secure and out of the public eye. The staff were lovely and excited to have us staying with them, and there was a steady stream of people coming by to greet us – "You are welcome" – all curious to see our vehicles. Once again Livingstone won the popularity stakes, but we were only a little jealous.

Each morning, as was my habit, I would wake early and be treated to the delightful voice of Comfort, the housekeeper, singing gospel songs as she worked. She was very much like her name and her voice: the sweetest woman who curtsied each time she greeted us. I had no way of stopping her from doing so, and even getting her to use our first names was a challenge. This is the African culture of respect that one encounters, but when you insist you can sense that they are delighted to be treated as an equal.

Michael, whom I had met in Benin as the driver, was very helpful. He organised a guy to change the engine oil and install the last of my oil filters. (As you may recall, this service had failed in Ghana.) The mechanic needed to remove the sump bolt but he was struggling. It turned out it was stripped and would be impossible to get off.

I sighed in despair... but TIA: all things are possible when you think outside the box. They decided to get a welder to weld a piece of metal to the bolt like a crossbar so it would be possible to lever it off. Bruce was very concerned: if the bolt ended up welded to the sump itself it would be a major job to remove; he wouldn't do it to his truck. I gave serious consideration to his concerns, but weighing up the information along with their assurances, and threatening to do terrible things to them if they screwed it up, I gave them the go-ahead.

They found a welder, but no sooner had he arrived with his assistant than the power went out so there was no electricity for the welding machine. This was not going well! Again TIA, and they went to ask the principal for his permission to switch on the generator, to which he magnanimously agreed. Generator on, they pulled up a power box on a long lead and stuffed the two wires from the welding machine into the plug holes. Yep, there was no plug on the welding machine, just the wires. I couldn't help but think of my father, who was an electrician, giving them a mouthful about the dangers of such a move. He always hated to see sloppy jobs like this! Nevertheless after ensuring that they were not likely to blow up my van, me or themselves, I watched as they proceeded; and indeed, within seconds the metal was welded on to the bolt, which then just needed a few minutes to cool down before it could be removed.

Once the oil filter and oil were changed, all was well with BlueBelle again. In the meantime I'd noticed that my passenger side mirror was loose and knew that if it came off I'd be in trouble, so I got out the Sikaflex and stuck it back on. Another task completed. The last was to get some dirty laundry washed, not knowing when the next opportunity would be, and which I did as usual in my trusty collapsible bucket sitting on my step.

The heat in Nigeria was even more extreme than in any other country I had been through: it was as if the humidity was so intense that it sucked the oxygen out of the atmosphere. I was truly struggling with it, and after my chores Laurie and I took shelter in a shady spot and watched Bruce wash Livingstone. It was such a monster job that neither of us could believe that anyone could summon such determination in the heat. However, when it comes to their vehicles being clean, men seem to find the kind of enthusiastic energy which is seldom found for washing dishes or clothes. Bruce had berated me once or twice about the 'state' of BlueBelle, but I retorted that I was quite happy for her to be grubby-looking on the outside because she looked less valuable and therefore less of a target for thieves. (To be completely honest, after doing everything else that was needed, washing BlueBelle – who would be dirty again the next day – felt like a 'tomorrow' task.)

BENIN CITY

The couple of days that we spent in Lagos allowed us to start planning the journey to the border as we checked, double-checked and triple-checked with all sources that we could find. There was something unique about Africa, in that each overlander seemed to experience roads differently: some would say that a particular road was great, another would say that it was unremarkable and still another that it was the most shocking route ever. There really seemed to be no consensus, and consequently referencing and cross-referencing were vital.

With our route determined, taking into account the Cameroon Ambassador's stern warning, it was time to leave Lagos and head ever eastwards and slightly north. Bruce and Laurie were late starters whereas I was always keen to leave early, so we set a meeting point in Benin City[82] later that day and I left to draw more cash and fill up with fuel. The ATMs only doled out 20,000 naira (about $50) per withdrawal, with a limit of three withdrawals at a time, so this was tedious: first to find an ATM that accepted international cards and then one that actually worked or had cash in it, since they had frequently run out.

I had made a change to my navigation system. Laurie had recommended Google Maps but I had not used it since it had failed me in Morocco, so I felt this was a good time to try it against my usual good-but-not-perfect navigation app. I had foolishly not considered that in leaving early I would hit peak hour traffic, but the navigation indicated that the hold-up would only be for a short distance. Now the thing about navigating and driving in manic traffic is that it is impossible to keep your attention on everything, so Google Maps had the navigating while I was watching the traffic. It indicated I should be turning up ahead, but I hadn't heard how far ahead and was now entering the highway *into* the city when I needed to get on to the one that intersected it to take me *out* of the city. Google had shown me three route options and I had gone for the shortest.

Then the inevitable happened. I knew I had to make a turn, but I wasn't certain where it was and didn't realise that Google

---

[82] Benin City is the capital of Edo State in southern Nigeria and not to be confused with the country, the Republic of Benin

was lagging, so I passed the turn before Google caught up and was suddenly heading directly into the city centre. At that time of the morning, in addition to the usual peak hour traffic all manner of taxis were on the road, stopping where they wanted, picking up and dropping off passengers; it was general chaos. After struggling through the traffic for a while I eventually got on to the highway, but in my heightened state of stress and lagging Google, I did it again: I took the wrong turn.

Now I usually have a great sense of direction, but I was completely and utterly out of my depth here with no idea where I was going. I pulled off the highway again and cut through another part of the city to get back on the highway in the opposite direction. Another round of swearing and cursing the taxis and their erratic driving, and I found myself on the highway that I hoped was right and was relieved to see less traffic. Google was now telling me that I needed to turn left.

My thinking was to stick to the left lane and be absolutely sure I didn't miss that turn; I wasn't sure I could survive another round of rush-hour Lagos! As I pulled into what I thought was a dedicated turning lane, some guys started shouting at me. I was by now well accustomed to being shouted at for whatever reason and paid no heed, but found I was in the lane with an island on each side. Within seconds of pulling up to the traffic lights and finding myself behind a bus and another car, suddenly five policemen jumped out of a car and came running toward me. I had no idea what was going on as they swarmed around BlueBelle, shouting and pulling at the doors on both sides. I was shocked and on high alert: what the hell was going on?

As the shouting continued I came to realise that I was in a priority lane for buses and taxis and was therefore breaking the law. Well, blow me down, if I hadn't found the only darn priority lane in the whole of Africa so far! Once I knew that I had made the mistake, I needed to figure out how I was going to get out of this. These guys were taking it so seriously that I felt they might actually throw me in jail. Safely locked in BlueBelle, I asked several times that they stop shouting at me, but they kept tugging at my door and telling me to get out. So I told them that if they stopped pulling at the door I would get out and in the meantime handed them my papers, which once again had the result of them letting go of the handle.

I reluctantly got out of my van – I always felt more secure when I was inside her – and, to my horror, within seconds they'd snatched the keys out of the ignition! That was the last straw. I had been driving around Lagos for almost an hour now, lost and in hideous traffic; it was already boiling and I had been shouted at; and yes, I had made an error but no one had died… It was all much too much: I burst into tears. Yes, hard to believe but I was completely overwhelmed. The tears were stress-induced and completely involuntary, but the men were now looking at me as I babbled my apologies: "I made a mistake, I'm sorry, I was lost! I need to get to Benin City and I am so sorry…!" The policemen then behaved like men everywhere when confronted with a woman crying, but with the added look of Oh no, we've broken her!

My papers had in the meantime been handed to a young man in his mid-thirties, the only one in plain clothes and seemingly in charge. He looked through them whilst standing directly in front of BlueBelle, only occasionally looking up at me, still snivelling. I can't say how long it took but eventually he walked over and handed the papers back to me and instructed the one officer to return my keys. I was now standing in my shorts and t-shirt looking bedraggled, tear-stained and sweating like a pig, and I looked at him with utter incredulity. "You may go," he said courteously, and the officers who had been shouting at me looked as shocked as I clearly was. It took a few moments to sink in: I wasn't going to jail, I was able to go free and clear, and not even a fine! I thanked everyone more profusely than I have ever done in my life. *Truly* I was grateful beyond measure to the Universe for getting me out of this one! I scrambled back into BlueBelle, waited for them to pile back into their car… and off we all went.

Lagos, as I said, is made up of several islands and lies to the west of the Lagos Lagoon. After the stress of nearly being arrested, the drive out of the city was gorgeous, taking me past waterways strewn with wooden canoes and fishermen doing what fishermen have done for thousands of years. But I was some distance along before I realised that the route I had set shouldn't have taken me past the lagoon at all. Google in its wisdom[83] had rerouted me to what it deemed a faster route, and since it *really* didn't seem worth heading back to the city for more drama, I decided to relax and enjoy the drive.

What I can tell you with certainty is that it wasn't long before my relaxed state of mind was challenged by the longest traffic jam I'd ever seen in the middle of nowhere: it took me five hours to drive just ten kilometres and, a little later, another two hours in spurts to cover three kilometres. There were roadworks upon roadworks and most of the journey was off-road on one diversion or another, and it was all made worse by taxis jostling and jockeying for position, elbowing their way in, driving down the verges and pushing in front. It was a nightmare of grand proportions. Add to this the heat and being in a confined space, and I couldn't begin to fathom how the people in the crammed-full taxis were coping. After an hour of music, I took to reading my book when I was stationary. I had fruit, water and snacks, so I would survive.

By the time I got to Benin City it was dark and I was more than a little stressed. I had chosen to keep driving rather than stop and message Laurie and Bruce, but eventually I'd had to and then my phone died again. It died the death of a phone that has been sitting in the heat and navigating all day and I just could not revive it. I had no idea where I was. I recalled the map in my mind and figured I needed to head towards the city centre, hoping that I could figure out the rest en route. I also knew the name of the hotel and remembered that it was on one of the roads coming off a really large roundabout. It was about 8.30 when I saw a young couple walking along the side of the road and decided to stop and ask them for help to make sure I was going in the right direction. They were, like most of the Nigerians I met, incredibly kind and helpful, and took out their phone to check their map and guide me. But it was about 9.00 before I found the hotel and parked up, tired, dirty, dusty, hungry and pretty fed up.

Laurie had generously organised a takeout dinner for me and left me to eat in peace, and we agreed to meet the next morning to

---

[83] It was also Google that told me it would only take nine and a half days to drive from Morocco to Zimbabwe along my predetermined route!!

visit the museum and King's Palace together. Needless to say, after I had eaten and washed in a bucket of water, I dropped into bed completely and utterly devoid of energy for having done mostly nothing all day.

In the morning I woke early, freshened up and set out to discover if there was anything interesting about the museum or the palace. I chose to walk as neither seemed far away. The museum was right in the middle of the enormous three-lane roundabout I had encountered the night before, but what I hadn't taken into account was that this was now busy with vehicles travelling at some speed, and there was no pedestrian crossing (although I doubted that one would have been respected) and no traffic lights to break the flow. So while I'm quite competent at jaywalking, here I would have to dodge the traffic like a gazelle – and I'm no gazelle! Nonetheless, I managed to cross without losing life or limb and walked over to the museum, noting the broken fence and untended grounds. Benin City is a major cultural centre in Nigeria and one of historical importance, so it was disappointing that those in charge were not giving priority to maintaining what was left of their heritage, especially for the tourism it could bring.

The museum was a small building with a lovely mural and I found the staff sitting in front of it giving no heed to the fact that I wanted to take a photograph. I asked what time it would open (it was listed as opening at 8.00 and it was now 8.15), and was informed, with an attitude, that it would open "soon". I further enquired where I could wait and from the bench *they* were sitting on I was directed to wait anywhere I liked. Right... I went and sat on the stump of a tree for a while, but seeing that nothing was happening at the museum I decided instead to find the palace, hoping for a better welcome.

Once again crossing the three crazy lanes of the roundabout, it was a short walk in the already steaming heat until I arrived at an impressive gate. It was made of metal, silver in colour and reflective so possibly stainless steel, with a huge eagle and several other symbols of historic and ritual importance. The gate was within a portico and made quite an impact at the end of a potholed and dusty street. I had obviously found the palace.

The Royal Palace of the Oba of Benin is a UNESCO listed heritage site and was once at the heart of a kingdom of great note and sophistication. The Oba is the traditional ruler of the local people, the Edo, and was the head of state of the old Benin Kingdom. Although he has no political role the Oba is considered a man of great influence and is still respected as the 'King of Kings' amongst the people of Nigeria. The original vast palace complex was unfortunately razed to the ground during the 1897 war with the British, and a new palace was built by Oba Eweka II during his reign of 1914–1933.

I enquired whether there was any possibility to have a tour of the palace and was informed that I should return mid-morning, when there would be a guide available. I decided to go back and find Laurie and Bruce, which of course meant another crossing of the enormous ring of hell, but this time I walked around the outer edge so I only needed to cross the smaller feeder roads. It took longer but gave me the chance to examine all the statues depicting a variety of scenes from the city's history. On my return I found that Laurie and Bruce were up, so I shared my experiences with them and they were keen to see the sights too.

Crossing the fearsome roundabout (I was by now something of a pro at this), we started at the museum. The woman at the reception was still surly although they had finally opened. We were given a price which was much higher than the one I had seen reported, although to be fair it is common practice in African countries to charge foreigners more for local attractions. The currency conversion rates are high and it is important to keep the costs low enough to encourage locals to enter. However, there was no electricity when we were there, so coupled with the sour taste left by my earlier encounter and the continued rudeness, I decided that I would give it a miss and left Laurie and Bruce to explore by themselves.

They did enjoy the tour, albeit brief and lit by a torch. By the time they finished it was mid-morning so we thought we'd visit the palace next, and here we were made to feel at ease with the usual "You are welcome" greetings. Most of the people at the gate were military, and as the guide was not yet available we were escorted to a room to wait and got chatting with one of the officers. We enquired what the tour would cost and, to our great surprise, were assured that there would be no charge at all. A good half hour later we were led to an old building near the gate and walked up some stairs to continue our wait on some wooden benches. The walls were decorated with ancient paintings and photographs of the Obas in days gone by.

Our guide eventually arrived and recounted some history of the palace and the current Oba. The palace was a large, middle-class-looking home and, by European standards at least, did not look in the least bit regal. We were not permitted inside the building, although I doubted that it would present much of Interest. Sadly, I would have found greater historical information online and more relics in the British Museum.[84]

We were shown the sacred grounds where ceremonies were held on a grass patch. None but the Oba or those he invited would be permitted in this area, and certainly no women. One end of the grounds was bordered by a nondescript single-storey mud building with a thatched roof but no windows. Our guide proudly told us that this was an ancient and most sacred building and insisted that we should take photographs, so we duly complied.

We were at some point joined by a friend of the guide who came bearing books. It always excites me to see books, especially those about Africa because in my opinion there are far too few. We talked, and I was interested to learn that he held the belief that the people of the Bini or Edo had always inhabited the area, and fervently disputed my understanding that most of the people in West, Central and Southern Africa (excluding the San) had migrated from Lower Egypt and Sudan. The history of Africa remains fraught with unresolvable differences because it has a tradition of verbal rather than written history.

All in all the tour was disappointing – not because the palace didn't look regal enough, but because there was no hint of the great kingdom that had preceded it; and the historical information was scant and without substance. Colonialism did much to destroy or diminish the true history of Africa and sadly this legacy lives on. There was a pride in their culture and past, but no visible

---

[84] At the time of writing I read that Benin City had secured the return of many of their artefacts which had been looted by the British in 1897, and that a new Royal Museum was being built to house them

evidence to substantiate it. True, part of this may be because culture in Africa was handed down in the verbal tradition, but as populations grow and more of them urbanise, this great heritage stands to be lost. It is for this reason that I constantly encourage people to turn their historical and cultural knowledge into books, so that future generations may revel in their stories.

Before returning to our vans, Laurie and I decided to wander down the street where there was an arts and crafts market to see what we could find of interest. When you live in a van and are travelling there really isn't much space for ornaments and artwork, so browsing was our main activity. The artwork was plentiful, much of it in metal and brass and stunningly beautiful. Regrettably what could have been another interesting tourist location was not much more than a grubby street with broken pavements, trash and dust.

Laurie, Bruce and I decided that we had time to make it to the city of Onitsha, a river port and economic hub about one hundred and fifty kilometres from Benin City and also host to the largest market in Africa. This time I decided to follow Livingstone and just hope that we arrived without delay – and together!

The landscape was becoming much hillier on the road to Onitsha and there were still the never-ending police checks. We eventually found that Bruce had more success in getting us through the checkpoints when he went first: they would chat to him and he would say that I was with them and they would usually just wave me through with a big smile. This all took much less time than when I was in front, when I had the usual interrogation of 'Why are you alone? I can come with you and be your driver/friend/husband…'

Laurie had been struggling with a cold and wasn't too well. I'd been keeping one at bay for some weeks now, but I wasn't sure I was winning. We needed to rest. Bruce did a grand job of getting us into the car park at one hotel. They weren't going to let us stay but eventually succumbed to his charm offensive. Our next stop was to get a cold beer or soda and we found a dark indoor bar with too much furniture, freezing air-conditioning and a blaring TV. We decided that outside on the terrace, although hotter, was a more bearable option.

Once seated we drew the usual stares, to which I used my award-winning smile and enthusiastic greeting; and they, in turn, responded with broad smiles and a bit of banter ensued. While we were relaxing I mentioned to Bruce that BlueBelle had not been performing very well that day and I was struggling to get power out of her, especially on the uphill sections. We contemplated all the possible reasons why this could be happening. Perhaps there was water in the fuel? The fuel in Nigeria was not the best quality. Perhaps it was an accumulation of water in the fuel filter? Perhaps (worse) it was the clutch? None of these sounded good, but we all agreed we were bushed and would tackle it in the morning.

As I was about to depart for the night a young man approached us and asked if he could take a 'snap' with us. Bruce immediately said, "Sure," but I, being a little more security-conscious and suspicious, asked why he would want one. He was a bit shy to respond but then admitted he had never seen white people in the flesh before, he had only seen them on TV. We were all utterly shocked. I guess living in a mainly white world it was a reminder that there are places where we are not present. With that, we thanked him for wanting to take a photo with us, but as we got up his tall friend bounded over to be included in the 'snaps' too. It was a humbling moment.

No Clutch and Radio Nigeria

Morning came after a stressful night fighting my cold, and I decided to see if I could find a garage to check my clutch since Bruce had determined it wasn't the fuel filter. My research showed that there was a garage nearby so I would try them first. I updated Laurie and Bruce and they said they would join me there when they were ready. BlueBelle was certainly not performing any better after her overnight stop as we stuttered across to the garage.

No one seemed to be about when I arrived. It was a Saturday and still early, but eventually I found a guy who suggested I drive into the bay so he could take a look. I did so just as Livingstone pulled in and Bruce came to give me some man support. The mechanic came out from under BlueBelle with a piece of plastic from the clutch: it wasn't a good sign. Bruce went down to check and confirmed that the clutch was in bad shape.

The mechanic said he would call a guy to call a guy who knew a guy who could help me out... which all sounded too dubious for our liking. Bruce and I agreed that we should head to Enugu, where there was a Ford dealership, and hope that they would be better placed to assist us. Laurie had given me a walkie-talkie when we left Benin City, and although its range wasn't far it was good enough, so this way we could update each other on police checkpoints and anything else of interest along the way and exchange the odd bit of banter.

The road became ever hillier and mostly it was up. BlueBelle was struggling, and although I did my best to rev up to change gear, the rises were killing us. It wasn't going at all well... and then it happened: we came to a grinding halt. I couldn't find a gear in the box that would move me and only gravity to take me back down the hill. While I was struggling with the gear lever, Livingstone was moving further away – and the walkie-talkie was out of range! I flashed my lights and hooted but watched despondently as he disappeared around the next bend. Fortunately, after a few minutes they returned. Meanwhile I'd put on my reflective jacket and was rummaging in the back for my reflector triangles and tow ropes as I had a feeling they were going to be useful. I was devastated.

The uncertainty of what was wrong was stressful beyond words: was this the end of the line for BlueBelle? Could I afford to get her fixed? Could I even *get* her fixed, here in the middle of who knows where..?! I hadn't noticed that something was wrong until the day before and then suddenly it was gone; and we were still some distance from the Ford dealership. I was ever so grateful that I had the Heimbigners and Livingstone around at the time. I'm pretty sure I would have made a plan, but this was better than I could have hoped. That guardian angel had worked her magic again and made sure that I had company *and* tow ropes!

After a test we decided to hook the two tow ropes together to increase the distance between us. This was in fact my first time ever being towed. I cannot begin to describe how dreadful it felt having no control, none at all – and no gear changing. All I had to do was make sure I didn't end up in Livingstone's rear garage, but the desire to change gears was overwhelming. I also had to make sure that when I braked for the police checkpoints, I didn't break the tow ropes by putting too much pressure on them; and then not fling myself forward when we pulled away. Bruce argued with one checkpoint when they told him he wasn't allowed to tow me because he wasn't a 'certified tow truck'. However, the tow trucks I had on occasion seen on the side of the road were no match for Livingstone, and Bruce eventually talked him down.

"You know that Livingstone can't even feel you back there," boasted Bruce over the walkie-talkie. "Show-off!" was my reply, but still I was inordinately grateful for BlueBelle's younger big brother and the everlasting kindness of his owners.

We had to cross over a central reservation to take the turnoff we needed for the Ford garage and then were faced with some roadworks ahead. We were on the outskirts of Enugu when the speed humps started, every fifty metres or so. They seriously felt much closer together than that because each time we sped up we then had to slow down again, and I had real trouble trying not to jolt to a stop and then bolt forward. The walkie-talkies helped tremendously: as I cleared each hump I would tell Bruce and he would speed up again. If he'd sped up too soon I would have been bouncing dangerously over the humps.

The humps lasted for several kilometres, sometimes with a greater distance between them, but always to return with several in quick succession. We struggled bravely on, but then… disaster.

I saw it first and radioed ahead. There was a huge barrier over the road that looked like a pipe painted in yellow and black stripes – and neither of us would be able to get underneath it. We were on a narrow, single-lane road and would have to somehow turn around and go back over the many humps to the main road some thirty kilometres away to try an alternative route.

Of course it wasn't long before people were piled up behind us, angrily hooting, and I was waving them by and stopping traffic while Bruce worked hard to turn Livingstone around. He managed to line up behind me to tow me out of the way and on to a dirt track which led up the hill. We began discussing our options and looked at the time: it was early afternoon and the alternative route into Enugu was some distance away. As we were talking, a modern 4x4 pulled up to get on the dirt track (which we had only partially blocked). They hooted us and, being hot and frazzled, my temper was not great as I shouted back at them, "I've broken down! My van won't move, but you can still pass a bus beside me if you don't care to help!"

Suitably berated, the two occupants got out of the car and came to assess the situation, and agreed that being towed into the city would be a long, arduous haul and the garage would likely be closed on a Saturday afternoon anyway. Great! However, they suggested we follow them up the hill. They needed to get there urgently as they were carrying essential fuel for the radio tower generator since their electricity was out. So Bruce hooked me up and dragged us up the steep dirt track and into the Radio Nigeria compound.

We were 'You are welcomed' by everyone and they were all highly intrigued by our journey and our vehicles. Then they organised a mechanic who would arrive later to fix my clutch. You've got to love Africa for its sheer tenacity. No one was put off that there wasn't a pit, or that my vehicle wasn't driveable, or that we were utter strangers: they simply set out to solve our problems. We were there, we could stay and someone would come. ARA 7 : DB 4

By now the stress of the entire situation was starting to take its toll. The cold that I had been keeping at bay for some weeks announced that it was coming and there was no stopping it, so I took the opportunity to give myself some maintenance too. I was grateful that I'd had the presence of mind to bring some decongestant medications with me and I made good use of them. However, I wasn't able to tell if I was just hotter than usual or if I genuinely had a fever: sweating and being super-hot had become standard operating mode.

I made the acquaintance of the compound guard, Anthony, a young but very intelligent man. We had some fascinating discussions about Africa, colonialism and Nigerian culture, and these were conversations I relished as they gave me real insights into the local mind-set and philosophy. I also learnt through him that the part of Nigeria I was now in was Biafra.[85] He also assisted

---

[85] Some of you may recall the photos from bygone days of starving children, but fortunately those I saw all looked quite healthy.

me in translating with the mechanic, who only understood a little English.

BlueBelle was jacked up and the gearbox removed, and the clutch plate clearly showed the poor state that it was in. The mechanic said he needed to take away the worn parts to buy the replacements, although I had my concerns about this; and I also had to give him the money upfront to buy them. I was assured he would go to the market and return the next day, even though it was Sunday. BlueBelle was let down, the mechanic left, and with the doors and windows open but the curtains drawn, I fell on to the sofa and into a sniffly sleep, too exhausted to think any more.

The problem with going to *sleep* early was that I tended to *wake* early. I found that if I got in six good hours then I was awake and ready to go, and there was little point lying in bed worrying about getting back to sleep because it was only 4.00am. I let my body tell me it had rested enough and then I would sit up in bed, read the messages and comments from my faithful followers and write update posts about my journey – always dependent on the reception of course; although being next to a radio tower that night, the signal was excellent! Radio Nigeria at Enugu is the country's oldest radio service and part of the largest network in Africa, and the team were very proud of this.

The following afternoon, despite my misgivings, the mechanic duly arrived with his assistant and the new clutch assembly. I summoned Bruce to inspect the parts with me because I couldn't believe that they had managed to find them in the middle of Nigeria. However, on close inspection, while it didn't all look exactly the same it surely was a match. Within a few hours they had installed the new clutch and I was testing it, and after some adjustments to the clutch pedal and a short test drive, the results were good.

At this stage I had run out of money and had to borrow from the Heimbigners to be sure I could pay for all the repairs. There wasn't an ATM anywhere nearby and again I was very grateful to have them with me. So far they had towed, nursed, supported and fed me, and now they'd been my bank. It dawned upon me that I was fast becoming a high maintenance friend!

The relief of having BlueBelle back in a drivable state, however, was enormous.

After a brief discussion, Laurie, Bruce and I decided that we would all take the rest of the day to get ourselves sorted out (which gave me some more time to recover from the cold) and we would leave the day after. Before setting off we all agreed to give Anthony a handsome tip for his immense support, but he absolutely refused to take anything for helping us.

AN ALMOST INTERNATIONAL INCIDENT

Feeling much better, I was happy to be back on the road safe and sound. Our next overnight stop would be Katsina-Ala, where we were recommended to check in with the police to assess the situation on a particular section of road renowned for kidnappings. We travelled in tandem again with me mostly taking up the rear, except on the odd occasion when I could pass them as I was now faster over the potholes.

Katsina-Ala was a small town with poor roads, but we found our way to the police station on a back street which ran parallel to the main drag. There were the usual shack-like stalls that alerted me to the possibility that there was a market, but there didn't seem to be much more to the town. At the police station, Bruce went to do the 'meet and greet' to assess the situation and ask permission to park overnight. Little did we know that we would be spending two nights there.

We were informed that we would not be able to proceed further because there had been a tribal family shooting and the fugitive was in hiding. Police were everywhere and for our safety we would be permitted to park on the side between the station and the staff quarters under a large tree (of which Livingstone took up the greater part). I thought this seemed a lot of fuss about nothing: one lone shooter in a family feud was highly unlikely to find us of interest. Nonetheless, we would stay the night and see what awaited us the next morning.

What I hadn't realised was that, after taking our passports, the Police Chief had reported our presence at his station to his superior who had then apparently alerted our respective embassies. Laurie and Bruce had already been in touch with their representative authorities about the Cameroon border crossing and were woken that night with a call from the embassy advising the Heimbigners to abandon their van and fly home!

The next morning I awoke to find the station chief in a tizz because we had been placed under his protection. The chief seemed a bit put out that he had been landed with the responsibility of looking after a bunch of tourists, who I'm sure he felt had no business driving aimlessly around Nigeria (an opinion mirrored by one of the staff at the US Embassy). It hadn't even occurred to me to consider contacting the British Embassy, as I was quite certain they would pay no heed at all.[86]

The chief informed us that an escort would be arranged – this was not negotiable – just as soon as he had vehicles available. We sat around watching, waiting and asking, but eventually it became evident that it wasn't going to happen that day. I spent my time chatting to the policemen, answering their questions and getting to know a bit more about them. It wouldn't hurt to have friendly relations with our 'captors' and get some inside information. One of them, Abel, found me most interesting and insisted on introducing me to his brother: he felt that I would be a good match as his brother was not married either. (Would this ever end?!) He instructed his brother to come and meet me, and an exceptionally large man stood up and shyly ambled over at Abel's bidding. As usual I thanked them both for the consideration, but explained that I was driving to Zimbabwe and wasn't particularly looking for a husband – upon which he proffered that we didn't have to get married if I didn't want to...!

On the second day I was again concerned that I needed cash, food and fuel to continue, so I let Laurie and Bruce know that I was going to organise these. Laurie decided to join me so she too could acquire some supplies. Living in a van, it wasn't possible to carry too much. For me, bread and eggs were the staples that lasted the longest and were usually the easiest to obtain.

We decide to go in BlueBelle so we clambered in and were about to drive off when we heard a commotion. The station chief was shouting at us: "Where are you going? You cannot leave!" He approached and told us in no uncertain terms that we

---

[86] I didn't hear from them in this instance and my opinion would be confirmed later in my journey!

absolutely could not leave the station on our own, and what were we thinking?! I replied in all innocence that we were just going down the road to do some shopping, but he continued to rant, asking if we wanted to start an international incident. I felt it was a bit of an over-reaction and added that it was just down the road and we would be fine, but "No!" was his insistent retort. I clarified that I needed food, so unless he could come up with an alternative I had to go. He took a moment, then called Abel, gave him some instructions and told us to go with him. Abel gravely warned us that he had been commanded by the Chief of Police to keep us safe, and should anything happen to us he would be held responsible for an International Incident.

Although I was entirely certain that we *would* be safe I didn't want him to lose his job, so Laurie and I got out of BlueBelle and followed Abel who, armed with an automatic rifle as well as an armed driver and another similarly armed officer, escorted us to a twin cab 4x4 in which they would drive us to the market. I was mortified: here were two white women being escorted by three armed men through the market, with people being chased out of the way simply because we wanted a few groceries. It was the epitome of white privilege and I was certain that if we had been local we would have been given no such attention. I mentioned my acute embarrassment to Abel, but he saw it from a different perspective: "If something happened to you, we would all get into severe trouble and be fired," he explained. Whilst I understood his point of view, to appease my conscience and discomfort I took to shaking hands and thanking everyone for allowing us to push in, and apologising profusely for the inconvenience.

In the first shop we bought sodas, eggs and a couple of other items. I had my reusable shopping bag for my goodies but the eggs came in a plastic bag knotted at the top. We returned to the 4x4 to drop off our goods so that we could go to another stall to buy bread... but I had this plastic bag of eggs. I was concerned about breaking them and I didn't want to carry them around, but if I left them on the seat I might sit on them. It was a dilemma of minute proportions. I looked at the guard quietly seated in the back with his machine gun in one hand. It seemed like a logical option to me, so with a big smile I asked if he would please hold my eggs. He looked at me with shock and horror, so I returned a bigger smile and stretched out the bag towards him. He now looked like a lost soul with no alternative but to suffer the indignity of having to take the eggs, which he then did without a word. I thanked him and went off with Laurie and our armed escort to buy bread, greeting all in the area. It was probably the most unusual sight that this small town has ever witnessed, and I wondered whether with such an escort they considered we were dignitaries... or criminals!

On returning to the vehicle I took back my eggs (with more thanks) and we headed back to the police station. I still needed cash and realised that this might be my best chance to get it before our early departure the next morning, so I politely asked if it would be possible to find an ATM. Yes it would, there was one not far from the station. We got out of the car but I still had my eggs to deal with... So with a coy smile, a questioning look and my eggs outstretched toward the guard, I thanked him as he again gravely accepted his important duty, this time with a slight smile – only very slight though.

I had to confront another dilemma of white privilege when we were escorted to the front of the queue at the ATM. With cash safely extracted, I shook hands with everyone in the queue and thanked them for their indulgence and went back to the car to retrieve my eggs. Laurie and I were returned to the police station, having successfully averted a Major International Incident – as only two elderly women doing their shopping with an armed escort in rural Nigeria are able to do.

While Laurie and I had been doing our bit for international diplomacy, Bruce was following up with the US Embassy and had received instructions to abandon his vehicle and take the first flight out of the country. That was *never* going to happen: it merely demonstrated the ignorance of the embassy staff in giving such instructions because the nearest airport was probably Lagos, several days' drive away! The Heimbigners' resolve that leaving was not an option seemed to push the diplomat concerned beyond his limits and he responded by berating them for being attention-seekers, purposefully looking for trouble to attract media attention so they could write a book. This was the furthest thing from their minds, and if they were upset, I was outraged. The guy was a pen-pushing diplomat and had probably never set foot outside the US compound in Lagos without an escort, so he had no real clue. In other words, he was being a total jerk!

It was an eventful and entertaining day at the police station. We had witnessed more men and weapons arriving from other stations to add their efforts to whatever was going on, and there was much coming and going with reports in the local language on what was happening where. In the afternoon while we were relaxing in the shade, two men from another station arrived, one out-of-his-head drunk. He started to shout at the chief and then threw a punch, whereupon there was much running around the cars as he drunkenly tried to avoid being captured. After a while he was caught and taken inside and certainly suffered a beating for his disrespect. As I said, a day filled with entertainment. It was a real live Nigerian soap opera!

The next morning, two 4x4s with extra seats in the rear loading area and eight men in each were assembled to escort us to the town of Takum. We had been told that the only way we could reach the town was with an escort, and the only way to get an escort was to fill their fuel tanks so that they could get there and back. Bruce and I agreed that we would each take responsibility for filling a vehicle, and since I also needed to top up my tank, the fuel station was our first stop. Once this was done we were on our way in their designated formation: one 4x4 in front followed by BlueBelle, then Livingstone, and the other 4x4 taking up the rear.

I didn't at the time ask what my American friends thought of the size and nature of the escort: to a foreigner it may well have validated the concern that we were in unsafe territory, but as an African, I thought it was total overkill. And unsurprisingly, the road was as deserted as an early morning of a holiday. At Takum we were deposited at the police station where we were expected to give the officers money for food and drink, so Bruce and I handed out cash to the respective vehicles and I said goodbye to my new-found friends.

It was good to be on the road again. The additional break had given me further time to recover from the cold and I was now feeling well, although filled with trepidation about the section of our journey that was looming ahead.

After a short drive out of Takum, a 'rest break' was needed and Bruce pulled over at the edge of a village – a risk, I felt, as stopping always drew a crowd; and we had just passed through many of what I assumed were illegal roadblocks, where they extorted money from locals. These usually comprised a few logs across the road and several young men stopping vehicles, and we had passed through a great number in the rural areas. The good thing was that they had obviously found out that stopping foreign-plated vehicles would provide more trouble than it was worth, so we had passed freely through any we had encountered. Local vehicles were not as fortunate.

The young men from the nearby roadblock and others in the village all migrated towards the mighty Livingstone, so I decided that I would get out and walk over. I took up position between Livingstone and the increasing number of people and started greeting them, in order to give Bruce and Laurie the freedom to exit the rear of the truck (where the toilet was) and get quickly back into the front, should anything go awry.

One youngster greeted me with, "Hi Baby!" and that set me off. I walked closer to him and said, "Young man, you need to take a closer look because I am absolutely *not* a baby. Perhaps you need glasses because I'm more of a cranky old woman!" Well, this immediately broke any tension and everyone started laughing – except the young man, who was clearly embarrassed. He then called me "Mama", which is a term of respect often used in Africa to older women, so I told him that was a lot better but I still wasn't his Mama! A bit more banter ensued and they asked for a gift, to which I told them that *I* was the gift there, entertaining them. They chortled at that. The Nigerians really are chancers, but always up for a laugh too.

We said goodbye and continued on to Serti, where we were allowed to camp overnight in the parking area of the National Park. During the night the dreaded rains came.

THE TRACK ON THE PLATEAU

The next morning saw us climbing a steep and winding road to the plateau region of Nigeria. It was to be one of the longest and most arduous sections of my entire journey back to Zimbabwe, but one where the views went from amazing to spectacular.

Seemingly the entire country lay spread out below us as we climbed toward the border with Cameroon.

In a small town called Guroji we turned off the tarmac road on to a dirt track, and from there we would follow GPS coordinates to the border. I was doubly blessed that Laurie was our navigator because she had at her disposal not just GPS but also a tablet and phone, so she could double-check the route as we crisscrossed our way along tracks barely visible on the maps. These GPS coordinates had kindly been set out by other intrepid travellers on the marvellous iOverlander app.

Armed with our walkie-talkies all charged up and with me holding my breath, we proceeded with Livingstone leading and me taking up the rear: this was going to be the ultimate challenge to see whether my 2WD could match a 4x4 on these tracks...

As we started out, Laurie informed me via walkie-talkie that Bruce had decided to leave Livingstone in 2WD mode to share my driving experience. But as the terrain got rougher – and with respect, he was a whole lot heavier than I was – it wasn't long before Bruce said he was switching to 4WD. I had to snigger, although I envied him having that option. BlueBelle would have to do the best with what she had.

As I went through the first rough patch, the anxiety I had been experiencing for so many months got the better of me and I almost lost my nerve, so I took a few drops of my Bach Flower Rescue Remedy®. I knew I needed to be calm and completely in control or I was going to make a stupid mistake. After struggling through some difficult rocky parts, Bruce stopped and helped me drop my tyre pressure to lower than I would have thought possible, but it proved very quickly to be the best thing. I could not have imagined the difference it made in control on both the rocky and sandy areas and I was thoroughly impressed. If only I had known this before when I was stuck in the sand!

This challenge was a defining moment of my journey for me. I had hit panic and I had to make a quick 'situation assessment' and then give myself a stern talking-to. Turning back was not an option: where would I turn to? Back to Europe after all that I had been through? No way! Stay where I was? Bit of a silly option really. Or continue to my destination – the *only* option.

I dug deeper. What was the worst thing that could happen? Well, 1) I could have a bad accident and die, or (probably worse) be majorly injured; but I was blessed with Laurie, who was a nurse and would be able to help. Or 2) I could damage or destroy BlueBelle; but while I loved her dearly it would simply be what it was: not the end of the world, just the end of my few meagre possessions; and at least Laurie and Bruce were there to rescue me. After thinking this all through, my rational brain took over.

"Dot, that means doing this section of the road as clearly and presently as you can to avert disaster!" I confirmed to myself. All the worry in the world wasn't going to get it done, but *I* could do it, and I was darn sure that BlueBelle could too! My confidence returned, and in doing so it also invoked a heightened appreciation of my travelling companions. I was *not* alone!

What made this particular *piste* so difficult were the parts of the track that were washed away, leaving only bare rocks that didn't offer much grip. Two-wheel drive BlueBelle really wasn't meant for that, but my brave little van undertook each challenge with the greatest courage. I took to walking the most difficult sections before attempting to drive them so that I could assess the ground and determine the route that would best offer something for her to hold on to. There were also several 'bridges' along the route consisting of logs or planks laid in a criss-cross fashion, and with no bearing struts or support they bounced like a demon as you crossed them. Some of them had significant gaps where parts had broken off, so it was critical to check them first.

Bruce and I walked out to assess one very uneven rocky section, which consisted of a steep incline and sharp turn to the left. A young man was moving rocks about, and I realised he was placing them to make it easier for us to manage this hill. I watched Livingstone struggle up the section with some guidance from the young man as he deftly positioned rocks under the tyres, and Livingstone made it to the top. Now it was up to BlueBelle and me. My tyres being much smaller and my engine nowhere near as powerful, I got about halfway up and found myself stuck. Bruce and the young man tried pushing me but to no avail.

I rolled back down the slope and reassessed the situation. The young man joined me and suggested I try the motorcycle track to the right, which would take me up over a grassy rise and down the other side and back on to the track. Bruce and I agreed that it looked viable, but it would mean filling in a deep channel that the rains had cut into the side of the track – and this the young man did with more gusto than I could muster. I backed up, revved and for the first time in a while employed the Dot Effect: the strategy of Velocity + Determination = Result.

I needed a push to get from the track on to the ridge as the grass made it quite slippery. I passed between bemused cattle who had been quietly grazing and were now wondering what this blue thing was, disturbing their peace. The young man was loping along beside me as I reached the top and turned back down toward the track, only to find a large rock and another in the way. The rock on the right was set into the side of the hill so there was no way around that; the rock on the left was on the edge of the track, and to the left of it there was just more rock and some impassable bushes. I estimated that I should be able to squeeze between them… just. I'd *so* had enough of all this!

I backed up a little to adjust my angle and then gently inched forward. I was right about the squeezing part: BlueBelle didn't do 'squeeze' and I scraped the bodywork above the front right tyre, but I got through and back on the track again. I gave the young man some of the little cash I had remaining, along with my very grateful thanks. He followed us for a way and it was only when we passed two young women sitting on the edge of the road that I realised who he was.

Several kilometres before the rocky slope, a motorcycle had passed us with a young man driving and two girls covered in the local traditional long headdress sitting behind him. I had waved at them and they had excitedly waved back at me with big smiles. The young man had obviously dropped them some distance further on and returned to help us because he knew that we would struggle over that slope. I was moved beyond words. This was the warm heart of Africa that I so loved. He took the time to consider us and yes, he may have hoped for some reward – of which there was no guarantee, and for which he never asked – but it was another wonderful example of Africa Roadside Assistance. The girls again waved enthusiastically as we passed them, content to have been waiting in the middle of nowhere while their friend helped us. Our final wave came as they re-passed us a short while later, disappearing into the distance as only a motorcycle could do on that road. ARA 8 : DB 4

By late afternoon we were completely exhausted, and as we entered a village Livingstone pulled up ahead of me and Laurie and Bruce came over to discuss options. We caused a bit of a stir as children peeped out of small homes and shawled women eyed us suspiciously, so Bruce sensibly suggested that we seek permission from the chief to park up for the night. We had been steadily climbing all day and were now high up on the plateau. The weather had changed significantly too. The temperature had cooled right down, the sky was a brooding grey and in the distance it looked like rain. I agreed that an overnight stop here was a great idea. This was the first village we had come across for a while, and who knew how long it would take before we found another.

Some men came over to assess the situation and were very friendly. Bruce told them that we were looking for a place to stay for the night and would like to ask permission from the local chief, and he was escorted off, leaving Laurie and me under the watchful eye of the women and children. I guessed that they didn't know what to make of us, both in long pants and without any head cover and me driving my own van. These were Muslim women in a remote area, and we were as foreign to them as online shopping would have been.

After some time Bruce returned: the chief couldn't be found but his second-in-command had permitted us to stay. We engaged with some of the men about our journey and experiences. Bruce had taken a shine to one particular man who reminded him of his dad. We had seen him walking into the village as we entered, wearing a thin windcheater and a hat and carrying an old portable transistor radio in the crook of his arm. After a few minutes the man told us that they had a sapphire mine near the village, but they needed help from their government or an investor.

This was where, as a professional business coach, I felt I had to give them some bad news. "Unfortunately your government doesn't even know you exist up here," I told them sadly. "They have bigger issues to deal with and you can be assured they are not coming to help you. Investors are not coming either because they have easier-to-access, more profitable opportunities that they can pursue closer to home. So if you want to get the mine to work for you, it is going to be up to you to make it happen." I gave them some ideas to consider and what practical steps they could take, as well as information they vitally needed to make intelligent business decisions, and I was rewarded when one of the younger men lit up with understanding. He told me that what they wanted most was to use the sapphires to fund the building of a school and to employ a teacher for their children. I was humbled. Anywhere else in the world, people would be thinking of expensive cars, rings, watches; but here, in the middle of the plateau, the thing they wanted most in their modest world was to educate their children so that they would have greater opportunities. Most parents want to see a better world for their children and here it was no different... but the opportunities were slim and very far away.

With our stopping place for the night arranged and the light disappearing fast, we decided to eat something simple in our respective vans rather than cook, and get a good night's sleep in preparation for what the next day might hold. As night closed in, thunder and lightning surrounded us and the menacing sky finally delivered the most dreaded of punishments out here on this road for BlueBelle and me – rain. It also got so cold that I had to pull down my sleeping bag from the overhead shelf, something I hadn't used in a very long time.

After a troubled night I was still up early and made myself a coffee and my usual fried eggs on a slice of bread. While I rarely wake up hungry, the lack of a decent dinner the night before and knowing the day might bring little chance to stop and enjoy a meal meant eating in the morning for sustenance alone. As I waited for my travel companions to wake up, I sat in the driver's seat with my coffee reviewing the offline maps (there had been no internet signal at all since we came off the tarmac road) and hoped that the rain hadn't exacerbated my difficulties.

We said goodbye to the locals after having some 'snaps' taken and were on our way. The road out of the village gave a slight rise and again the rain had washed most of the soil away, leaving ominous-looking rocks. After watching Livingstone conquer the terrain without issue, I checked my path and revved up to urge BlueBelle up the rise. A couple of slips made me catch my breath – actually, I believe I was holding my breath the entire time – but with a deep sigh of relief, I cleared the section.

For almost three whole days I was constantly switching between first and second gear and barely reached third at all. And remember that inconvenient clutch breakdown? I was eternally grateful that it had happened when it did, because had it happened on the plateau... Well, that would have been the end of that for some considerable time.

We continued to climb even higher and the views were incredible. Some parts looked just like the rolling green hills of England's heartland, but vaster and with no sign of habitation, quite pristine. Our ascent took us into what seemed like mist, but with our altitude it was actually low clouds, dense and moist, drifting about the mountains and affording us only occasional glimpses of the green landscape below. At one point it became so dense that it was hard to see Livingstone just metres ahead of me, which also meant that it was hard to see the road. It was dangerous driving indeed.

We cleared the worst of the clouds, but as we did so there appeared a huge pool in our way surrounded by several smaller ones. The challenge with water on the road is not so much what you can see but what you cannot see: was it mud at the bottom? Or rock? How deep was it? Bruce and I decided to investigate, but no sooner had we got out than it started to pour again and we were forced to return to our vehicles and wait it out. Fortunately the shower lasted no more than twenty minutes, at which point we reassessed the water and each chose a path that best suited our respective vehicles. Luckily we made it through without incident.

With the pools cleared we continued at the same snail's pace, but soon we were heading down out of the clouds and into a much warmer and drier clime. Within just a few kilometres conditions started looking better – at least as far as the weather was concerned – and it seemed we had cleared the highest point. The landscape continued to be very beautiful and I wished I had more time to take it in instead of having to watch the road. I often like to imagine what places must have looked like before humans arrived, and here was a vivid picture of untainted nature. This was Gashaka-Gumti National Park.

By mid-morning I asked Laurie and Bruce to stop so that I could take some photographs. The magnificence of the scenery demanded it, so we all decided to stop for coffee and appreciate the splendour around us. To my disappointment there was little visible sign of wildlife, but the birdsong and calls of the eagles indicated it was there in abundance.

We continued, crossing several rickety bridges. Despite their hair-raising appearance these were passable, and I was grateful that they were there or I would have made little progress. Several other rocky sections amidst the uneven track were conquered, and so, little by little, the hours passed and BlueBelle and I ate this huge elephant that had been the focus of my nightmares since arriving in Africa. It wasn't easy, but with each challenge overcome I felt a little more assured that I would make it.

Eventually the settlements became more frequent and we reached Mayo Ndaga. I had not been looking at the map but entrusting Laurie to get us where we needed to be, leaving me to focus on the challenge of driving. The town was a warren of roads that needed careful zig-zagging, and as we slowed down a group of children came running up beside us. I had my window open and waved at them to their shrieking delight, and they put out their hands and I put out mine and we did the equivalent of a sideways high-five. One boy ran next to us the whole way and guided us through the narrow roads between houses and shops and vehicles until we came to the other side. I had some Nigerian naira, which I gave him, and Laurie gave him a book and some pencils, and he couldn't have been more delighted with his rewards.

On the other side of town was an illegal tollgate. The surly man manning it approached Livingstone (who was leading) and I waited. He wasn't letting Bruce and Laurie through and there seemed to be some altercation, but then he approached me so I smiled and asked if he was having a bad day. He looked dumbfounded, but I figured this usually worked and so might break the ice. This guy though was *really* in a bad mood and not even the slightest impact did it have. I asked what the problem was and he said we had to pay to continue, but my general lack of cash always came in handy and I told him that we were on our way to the border and that there would be no more cash until we got there, so what did he want us to do? He seemed very displeased. The conversation went back and forth for a bit until an opportunity presented itself, when in response to my question, "What do you want from me?" he countered, "What do *you* want from *me*?" I turned to him, put my hand out of the window, gave him my sunniest smile and said, "Nothing but your friendship, thank you!" After all this debating I think he was genuinely shocked, and he shook my hand in a dazed fashion and walked back to let down the rope blocking our way. Sometimes the simplest respect goes a long way in Africa.

We weren't done though, as not much further along there was a bridge and another illegal tollgate. We were stopped and I could see that there was some argument happening by Livingstone, so I decided to get out, stretch my legs and see what was going on. Yes, of course, they wanted money. There was a wooden bridge that this gang were 'maintaining' and they believed that we should pay to cross it. Again I didn't have what they were demanding and wasn't prepared to be held hostage here, and I could tell that Bruce felt the same way. I informed the ringleader that we were making a one-time crossing and were not regulars on this road, and as such we didn't think we should have to pay for the general wear and tear on this bridge. Bruce and I agreed loudly that we would stop right where we were and spend the night if necessary. The road was narrow and Livingstone was taking up much of it, blocking all other traffic and therefore potential fees.

Our apparent seriousness about our intent presented a dilemma for the gang and eventually the man in charge said we could send the toll to him later; he had allowed some other overlanders to pass and they were going to send money back from Cameroon. I couldn't quite believe what I was hearing, but I took advantage of the situation and replied that we too could look into doing this (I made no assurances that we actually would). Oddly, this satisfied him – or at least allowed him to save face in front of his numerous lackeys – and he let us go with no indication of how we were to send the money or to whom. It wouldn't have hurt too much to give him a little cash, but if we had done so at every request it would have cost us a fortune. I do not believe in encouraging illegal tolls, of which there were plenty in Nigeria.

The road was still appalling and there was now a bit more traffic about, mostly motorcycles being used as taxis. In one village I noticed someone waving frantically out of the corner of my eye as I passed. I hadn't seen a checkpoint, but there was something about the shout and wave that made me think we should have stopped. I mentioned this on the walkie-talkie to Laurie, but we carried on anyway. Within minutes though (we were still within the village) a motorcycle sped past toward Livingstone, on the back of which sat a semi-uniformed man holding a machine gun and looking furious. Livingstone came to a halt on the left of the small track and I pulled up a little further ahead to the right. This way I could see what was happening in my side mirror.

Mr Machine Gun was shouting and clearly mad, so I decided I should head over. I sauntered casually across the road and, with a big smile, greeted him and his motorbike friend loudly as I approached and asked what the problem was. He turned toward me and proceeded to tell me that we had passed through a checkpoint (as I had already suspected) but had failed to stop: why had we not stopped? Did we really think we could continue?! Blah, blah, blah... The man plainly felt aggrieved and disrespected, and because he was still brandishing his machine gun, I didn't think it wise to argue the toss. I did my best Scarlett O'Hara gasp of surprise and confessed that I had not seen a checkpoint, apologising sincerely and confirming that had we seen it we would *surely* have stopped – as we *always* did; and also as there had been nothing in the road blocking our way, we really couldn't have known.

My apology was genuine and profuse, if a little over-acted. His eyes bored into me as he continued to insist that he had waved and shouted but we had ignored him, upon which I again apologised, adding that in our time in Nigeria the people had been so wonderful and friendly, and we had enjoyed our visit here so much, and this beautiful countryside... and I admitted that I had seen him waving and perhaps he had seen me waving back, but I thought he was just being friendly, like so many of his countrymen, and I hadn't realised precisely *why* he was waving... and I ended with another apology. He looked at me sternly and as my words sank in I thought I could see just the hint of a smile. Had I won..? He berated me again for good measure, told us to be more careful, got on the bike and went back to his post.

Another one down... And so back to the task in hand. We were nearing the border and I was hoping there would be no further incidents!

The border post at Kan-lyaka was a small, simple building to the right of the road with a flag pole and flag in front, and I had never seen such a welcome sight. We were swiftly attended to by two young men, not in uniform, who diligently stamped our passports and wrote everything down in several large black folio books. I sometimes wondered whose name one might come across and how far back these books went, as certainly most of them would be historical pieces.

Before leaving I had a Very Important Snap to take, one of me standing at the exit border sign. It was Very Important because at the earliest opportunity I would be sending it to Graeme Bell. In Morocco, on that first night so long ago, he had said to me, "People will notice when you get out the other side of Nigeria." And when I posted the photo, my message on his Facebook page merely reminded him of his comment, followed by the single word: "Notice." I was certain that he had never meant the comment to be of any major significance, but to me it had been a burr that was now, with immense pride, firmly removed.

Laurie and Bruce Heimbigner had been a huge comfort to me, not just by simply being there but also in their admiration and applause at my overcoming some incredible challenges – all of which certainly boosted my confidence. Their generosity at taking me on was so much greater than I had realised at the time. Honestly, they would have been looking at a woman with no experience on this type of terrain, in a vehicle that was totally unsuitable for it, not knowing how much they might need to be of assistance to me or how much I might slow them down. While there was only one occasion when I did need a push and some digging, they had no idea in advance how much of a challenge I was going to present, yet they still showed every enthusiasm for being my travel companions on this stretch.

I remain grateful to them beyond measure.

Chapter Eleven – Cameroon

25 April 2019

Entering Cameroon felt ever so sweet, but it was getting late and we would certainly not make it to Banyo that evening. The border post seemed to be in the middle of a village; or perhaps a village had grown around it. We were once again in French territory although the people there spoke some English – essential, I guessed, for being on the border with English-speaking Nigeria. Once the obligatory black book entries and my TIP were completed, we asked if we would be able to park anywhere nearby for the night. We were directed to a side track not far from the police station where we had to report anyway to get our passports stamped, and were assured that we would be entirely safe there.

Laurie kindly delivered some dinner for me: after a day of stressful driving, cooking was out of the question; and soon after that I fell into bed. Finally able to relax for the first time in days, I looked at the maps again. As I mentioned, I had been completely relying on Laurie to navigate for most of our trek across Nigeria, but we would be parting ways in Cameroon so it was time to get back into the habit. As I was reviewing the route for the next day, it dawned on me that the road to Banyo would be mostly dirt. Somehow in my mind I had anticipated that the section of road through the Nigerian plateau would be the worst and Cameroon would be just easy-peasy. I wasn't worried though: it had to be better than what we had been through. How bad could a mere forty kilometres of dirt road be..?

In the morning Bruce decided to test his drone, which meant we were not making an early departure, so I took a walk to our first river crossing that I'd only caught a glimpse of the previous evening. The bridge was in fair shape; however, the few metres of 'track' leading up to it were a horrifying mess of thirty-odd centimetre deep muddy ruts. I walked along the edges deciding what route would best allow me to stay out of that mess, and as I was walking back to the van, out of the corner of my eye I saw a huge… bug? – No, wait, it was a vehicle, but the like of which I had never seen before. It looked like a landmine vehicle, set high off the ground with six wheels on an inverted v-shaped axle – truly the oddest looking vehicle I had ever seen.[87] I should have been nervous when I saw it: it was a portent of forty exceptionally challenging kilometres, and the only other vehicles on this stretch of road would be these beasts and the odd motorbike.

We set off, and with my tyres still deflated I was able to cross the ten metres of mud with minimal slipping and sliding, taking advantage of the less rutted outer edges where possible. I found that keeping at least two wheels on the more solid ground gave me an advantage as I developed the new skill of mud-managing. There were three more river crossings on this section but we didn't have to worry about rickety bridges... because there weren't any: no bridges, just water – although to be honest one crossing was over a weir that was just under water (at least I could see the edge of the concrete posts on the side!)

The biggest challenge was the sections of road either side of these fords,[88] which were a muddy mess from other vehicles picking up water in their tyres with every crossing. The routes that were possible for Livingstone were not possible for me, and on one occasion I erroneously took the same track which rose steeply up from the river through deep mud. The wheels started spinning and I knew I wasn't going anywhere from there, so I decided that before I dug myself further in I would roll back on to the ford, reverse up the slope and start again. I looked up at the road ahead to see Laurie filming me and Bruce cheering me on, so I calculated an alternative route and pointed BlueBelle firmly in that direction. It would mean having just two wheels on the grassy bank and hoping this would give us enough traction up the steep slippery slope while the other two were in the thick mud.

Holding my breath and employing the Dot Effect, I gathered momentum on the downward slope, crossed the ford and coaxed her up the other side. It was a nail-biting ride as I really wasn't sure we could make it. As I cleared the worst of it I threw my arms up in victory. Bruce came bounding over to congratulate me, exclaiming, "I've seen 4x4s driving on two wheels, but never a

---

[87] I found out some time later from another overlander that it was actually a 6WD or 6x6. Unlike 4WD, this configuration is mostly found in heavy-duty off-road and military vehicles
[88] A location on a road where a river is shallow enough to cross with no bridge by driving through the water

2WD van!" It was too much, and I immediately told him not to give me any more information: the thought that I had done *any* part of it on two wheels simply didn't bear thinking about! All I knew was that BlueBelle had done it and we were both still in one piece.

The last river was a lot wider and the mud again intimidating. Bruce decided to walk it to determine the depth of the water and what was underfoot, and fortunately he deemed it passable for us because of BlueBelle's slightly higher clearance. As we were assessing the crossing, a crowd from the field and nearby village started to gather on the opposite bank. This must have been like match night: who would win and who would lose?! Livingstone took some strain going up the steep slope on the other side but he made it, and I could barely watch for thinking what it would take for us to cross.

It was our turn. I was already quite close to the water's edge, but as BlueBelle doesn't do well up a slope I decided that I needed a bit more speed. The water would slow me down and if I went in too slow she would struggle to get up the other side. I reversed back up the track, took a very deep breath (I don't think I breathed again until I was on the other side) and hit the accelerator. I can't recall actually crossing the river because I was totally focused on the mud and the slope ahead, and once I'd cleared the mud I couldn't stop as the slope was steep: I had to keep her going or we might not make it. Poor BlueBelle strained in first gear as I coaxed her up, but eventually we made it on to the brow and I came to a relieved halt near Livingstone.

That day we truly experienced as much intensity as I could ever have imagined over a mere forty kilometres.

BANYO

In due course we arrived in Banyo and gloriously potholed tarmac roads. Clearly this meant that the worst of the ordeal was over and BlueBelle had the scars, mud and dirt to prove it! Now it was the business of getting organised for this next country, which meant changing cash (again there was no money changer at the border), buying a new SIM card and refuelling.[89]

Once the chores were done, Laurie wanted to top up on some vegetables, so we walked through the small market and I bought a few goodies too. As I was strolling along I immediately noticed that the people were nowhere near as friendly as those we had met in Nigeria, and for the first time in my entire journey I felt uncomfortable. Cameroon is a country at war: in the north with Boko Haram having spread from Nigeria, and in the south-west fighting a civil war between the Anglophones and Francophones – literally a war based on language. Perhaps this made them mistrustful of us, as we were indeed Anglophones in a predominantly Francophone country.

It was afternoon by now and we needed sustenance. Laurie and Bruce felt that we deserved a celebration and insisted on treating me to lunch (how did I manage to get so lucky?!) so we found a reasonable restaurant and ordered the coldest sodas they had and a basic but quite delicious meal. Armed with cash, SIM cards, fuel and food, we finally felt ready to tackle the country. However, it was now late afternoon and I was quite frankly not up to more driving. We decided it would be best to find the local hotel and see if we could park up for the night, as it would be our only option in the Banyo area.

The hotel was an uninspiring building standing on a rise in the middle of rain-worn and rutted grounds with nothing around it but dust. There were steps up to a terrace where we found the reception and an unfriendly woman who told us she couldn't help with parking. After pressing her, she reluctantly said she would have to call the owner and we should wait. Bruce and I had a beer and Laurie a soft drink, and after some thirty minutes another woman arrived. We had no idea who she was: she didn't introduce herself or speak to us. Guessing she was the owner we offered a fee which was generous, given what there was – or rather was not – yet she still insisted on haggling. Bruce and I agreed that we would leave and take our chances elsewhere, after which she

---

[89] In changing money I discovered that whilst the currency was still known as the CFA franc it was in fact the Central African Franc, which was separate from the West African Franc but effectively interchangeable as they have the same value.

sourly accepted our offer. It was just a parking spot and the grounds were not even secured.

As we were finishing our drinks a hawker came by with some power banks, mobile phones and phone cables. I was interested in a power bank as they were very useful and two of mine had succumbed to either the heat or over-use. As I bargained with the vendor, Ms Surly the receptionist came over and took a seat with us, entirely uninvited, and started looking at the mobile phones. Suddenly she shoved one at me and announced that I should buy it for her. I almost choked on my drink and told her in the nicest but firmest possible way that she was out of her tiny mind!

We parked up for the night and decided to take advantage of the evening show: the sun was setting amid a glorious technicolour of violets and reds, orange-pinks and golds, so Laurie and Bruce pulled out their folding chairs and an extra one for me. While they were inside the van organising themselves, Ms Surly came over – again uninvited – to inform me that she wanted me to give her one of the (expensive) folding chairs that were waiting for Laurie and Bruce. The woman's audacity seemed to know no bounds! Incredulous, I told her that they were not for sale and she couldn't have them. She then wanted to see the inside of my van, which of course I also declined, telling her it was private. She was now getting on my nerves and her attitude also indicated 'sticky fingers', but I was much too tired to be hassled by her.

Since there was something I didn't trust about Ms Surly, I made sure that Laurie and Bruce packed and secured everything before nightfall. Then I too locked up and set my window alarms... but I was still quite uncomfortable: I had this eerie feeling that someone was looking inside. I pulled the curtain over the small window by the bed which I kept open to allow in some air and fell into a fitful sleep.

The following morning I made an early departure. I had already said goodbye to Laurie and Bruce, knowing that they would be leaving later than I would. They were likely to try for Yaoundé that day, whereas I was heading for Douala and had decided to stop for a couple of days at an interesting-looking monastery I had identified en route.

My research indicated that the first half of the road on my drive that day would be a dirt track, and there was also a report of a bad bridge to cross. However, after what I'd been through on the plateau, it couldn't be that bad... right? Well, I was less than ten kilometres out of town when I came upon it, and I really couldn't believe what I saw. It looked like an old colonial bridge, except all that remained was the metal framework which included the arched sides and two metal beams for the base. Over those beams had been laid planks of wood, although some were broken and there were visible gaps so probably several missing too. It was no more than fifty metres in length.

I decided it would be wise to walk the bridge to assess it, and as I approached a truck belted over it and the planks bounced alarmingly in all directions. When I got on to it it was even worse than it looked from afar: all that lay between me and the river underneath were two metal bars and a bunch of uneven wooden boards that were not even bound together. I looked down through the planks at the water, stepping carefully to avoid falling through the not-insignificant gaps. With my tyres being smaller than the usual 4x4 or truck I would need to reduce the gaps as much as possible, so I started moving several of the planks to even things out; but they were long and heavy and I struggled. A man on a motorbike stopped and came over to help me, and by now a small group of people had gathered to watch.

When I believed we had done the best we could, I went to get BlueBelle. Aiming for the metal beams to be directly under the tyres to get the best support while also trying to avoid the gaps, I set forth with the Dot Effect: if I maintained a moderate speed I would be able to keep the momentum going. The kindly man who had helped me with the planks now decided he would guide me over, but when I was three-quarters of the way across he realised that there was no space for him to stand to one side, so he had to scamper off it to avoid being run over! The uneven planks made it difficult for him to get off in time and I had no option but to slow down... and then I was stuck.

The five other men who had gathered to watch now came over to help and tried without success to push me free. I decided I would have to reverse instead, and in doing so managed to get the rear wheel out... but then the front wheel jammed! You can just imagine the swearing, cursing and sweating – and it wasn't even 8.00 yet!! With some more manoeuvring, plank moving, pushing and shoving, BlueBelle eventually shifted and we made it off.

I got out to express my eternal thanks to the men. Only one of them spoke English and he asked about the stickers he had noticed on my side window, so I briefed him on my journey and he translated to the other men. They were listening intently when one of them asked why Cameroon was missing, so I snapped around and indeed it was gone. I couldn't believe it and recalled my feelings of disquiet the previous evening, as I realised with a shudder that the stickers were located next to that small window at the rear of the van. I had to explain that the sticker had clearly been stolen and they shook their heads sadly. Before I left, those who had phones insisted on taking photographs with me, and once these were done I again thanked them with all my heart and gave them some of my TIA cards, which they took eagerly. ARA 9 : DB 4

For the next sixty or so kilometres there was a continuous nasty red dirt road littered with potholes and ruts, but at least there were no further dodgy bridges or rocky challenges. Simple things became blessings on this journey, and while I hated the dust I felt grateful to be on it in comparison with the previous days. As I approached a steep mountain pass, the dirt became tarmac, and I was really happy that this was in a good condition because there were a myriad twists and turns. The views were spectacular and I could see Mount Cameroon in the distance with a vast valley lying between us. Known locally as Mongo ma Ndemi ('Mountain of Greatness'), at 4,095m it is the highest point in sub-Saharan Western and Central Africa and the fourth most prominent peak on the whole continent. It is also an active volcano, part of a range known as the Cameroon Volcanic Line.

I wished I'd been able to stop to take photographs from the road, but there were simply no places to pull over. With the road being so winding, I didn't want someone belting around the corner and taking me out, so I did what I did best which was just appreciate the moment and the spectacular view. Meanwhile I had noticed a dusty red line at the bottom of the mountain and, as I feared, the nice tarmac road disappeared.

I regularly tried my 'people-friendly' test, waving at locals and smiling as I passed, and the results impacted me deeply. Apart from the Mauritanians, most people had thus far responded with their wide smiles and waves; Nigeria had given the most charming reactions, with people gleefully shouting to attract my attention and waving with both hands raised in the air, and children chasing after the van, cheering and laughing... yet here there was nothing. Only a couple of people had bothered to return my wave, none had smiled and even my "Bonjours" had lacked a response. I was confused: how could the people in one country be so cheerful, but over a border so utterly unfriendly?

Approaching Mayo Darle, I came to a most impressive new bridge and stretch of tarmac, although I was unable to use it and was instead diverted through the dust for a distance, bypassing the bridge; but then I was rewarded with a good road surface, something I had not seen for days. The town had wide streets with the usual vendors along both sides, and my priority now that I was back on tarmac was to get my tyres pumped up. I was too hot to bother using my compressor or foot pump, but then I saw a man with a compressor at a 'shop' on the side of the road, so that would do. While I was waiting for the tyres to be slowly inflated (because the valve was broken), I chatted to a fellow customer. He was an Anglophone, a refugee of the civil war who had fled to safety in this area. It was my first encounter with the turmoil of the country.

Once pumped up there was no stopping me, especially as the conditions continued to be good. I was feeling very pleased with myself: I'd conquered the worst of the roads and was making good headway. However, my elation subsided when I faced a police check, my second at that point. I immediately handed the officer my papers (which usually prevented delays), but he started at me in an aggressive tone saying it was illegal to drive a RHD vehicle in Cameroon. I politely explained that I had a TIP, pointing to the folder in his hands, which meant that I was allowed to drive my vehicle through his country. This did not satisfy him and he persisted in his claim that I was driving illegally. I tried again to show him the document, but he continued to repeat the same thing until I got quite annoyed, so I told him he should look at the paper before he made that decision. At this, he announced that my tone was disrespectful, to which I replied, anger ripe in my voice, "*You* are the one disrespecting your government and the document issued by it!" Undeterred, he advised me that the police had nothing to do with customs and this vehicle was still illegal, so I launched into a lecture about how all government employees should respect the same laws and not come up with different ones to suit each department.

Things were not going well and I wasn't sure where this was going to end. I informed him that as a tourist to his country I was deeply offended by his manner and the trouble he was causing and that he could be certain that I would be taking this up with my embassy (not that this was ever going to happen). He seemed to reassess his position, although he still clearly felt the need to assert himself. After some more blah, blah, blah and my unrepentant responses, he eventually told me curtly that I could go. It was the most unfriendly interchange with any checkpoint officers I'd had and it put me in a bad mood. I was muttering about it to BlueBelle, in outrage, for some miles.

MEDITATING WITH MONKS

My destination was Koutaba and I was certain that I would make it for the evening, but not too far away in Foumban I made a wrong turn in a crazy roundabout system and it took a while to find my way back. I decided that I needed to reward myself with an ice-cold drink to refresh my brain and body, so I stopped at a garage with a shop – almost always a good place for cold things. The cashier asked where I was from, thinking I was German (Cameroon was once a German colony). "Zimbabwe," I replied, and he looked surprised and impressed at the same time but did actually smile. A man standing drinking coffee at a tall table near the tills muttered something in French, but I missed it as I was concentrating on the money to make sure I got it right. The cashier then said to me in simplified French, "He doesn't believe you come from Zimbabwe." I turned to the man and asked why not, and with a smart-ass smirk on his face the man rubbed his forearm with his index finger, indicating that I was the wrong colour. I had encountered this before and asked him if no black people were ever born in Europe, at which his eyes widened in surprise and the man behind the till began to laugh heartily. I gave the coffee man a raised eyebrow, thanked the server with a wink and bade him goodbye. Some conversations are just not worth having.

By the time I reached the edge of Koutaba it was 5.00, and with the navigation and heat once again my phone battery died. I too was suffering from the heat, and while I had a vague recollection that I should be turning left somewhere up ahead, I had no idea precisely where and there were several dirt tracks presenting options. Praying for a sign (of any sort), I drove back down the road and there it was: a worn and barely recognisable board for the Cistercian Monastery. The track was rough and bumpy but I eventually came across a long brick wall, and around the corner I saw a 1970s-style octagonal church with its doors open. I found the guard and asked about stopping overnight and he advised me to talk to one of the monks, who was on his way. Meanwhile another 4x4 vehicle turned up with people sitting in the rear. They were obviously French because when I greeted them they blatantly ignored me and continued chatting loudly and laughing amongst themselves.

When the monk appeared the French people rushed over to him, obviously devoid of manners, and after a brief chat they were directed further down the road. Then I approached him with respect and, delighted to find me speaking English, he said I would need to find the brother responsible for the accommodations, but it was vespers and he would not be free until later. I was invited to join them, which I politely declined, and instead went to find out where I could park, safe in the knowledge that with the day winding down I wouldn't need to drive any further.

Once my phone was recharged I tried to contact Laurie and Bruce but the signal was non-existent. I had to walk up the road a bit to connect, which I found odd in light of the fact that there was a huge mobile tower a few hundred metres away! They had not only left later but had also taken longer over the dirt road and would likely be stopping at the monastery for the night too since they wouldn't be able to make it to Yaoundé before nightfall. I said I would look out for them.

After vespers I managed to find the monk in charge of accommodations, who was very surprised that all I wanted was a shower and to park in their small grove of trees. He agreed and told me I could pay whatever I felt I could afford. My parking spot was away from the former monks' rooms, which were now being rented out to visitors, and I found myself amid a tiny forest right next to a plantation of immaculately pruned coffee bushes. It seemed the monks made their own coffee.

It was getting dark as I walked to the gate, and fortunately I managed to catch the guard before he locked it and asked him to wait for my friends to arrive, to which he warmly agreed. The sun had set and the short dusk revealed headlights in the distance, and indeed it was Laurie and Bruce. I guided them into the little forest where there was plenty of space to park and Bruce and I went to find the monk to inform him of their arrival. By the time we came back it was pitch black, the way it is in rural Africa, with no light except that from the stars. We could easily make out Livingstone but Bruce had to ask where BlueBelle was as he could not see her among the trees. I guided his line of sight to her and he was mightily surprised at how she disappeared into the night. I just proudly smiled.

The next morning it was time to say a final farewell to the Heimbigners. They were continuing to Yaoundé while I had decided that, after the last few hectic days, I needed to rest and reorganise. We each felt sad at the parting, but oddly also liberated to return to our own routines. Overlanders love company, but no matter how great our shared journey, we equally love independence.

My shoulder was relieved at the respite from driving, but the thing on my elbow that had been bugging me since Ghana was becoming irritating and more painful. Nothing I had done had as yet been able to get rid of it and sometimes it felt like it was gnawing through my skin. I determined to get it attended to in Douala.

With Ursula joining me in a few weeks, I decided to take the time not only to clean the dust out but also to move things around to make a bit more space for her. I was extremely happy in the coolness of the little forest, but there was still the intense humidity to deal with. I got into the habit of starting early and worked at a leisurely pace until about noon, then relaxed for the rest of the day; I even managed to read a book! Stopping to restore my energy was essential: the intense demands of getting the Nigerian visa, my clutch breakdown, having that cold, the stop with the police at Katsina-Ala, the days on the border crossing (not to mention the worry beforehand)… and of course the incessant heat. It was absolutely necessary to take some downtime. I also took to attending the evening vespers to listen to the sung mass and the playing of the local drums and kora. I found it meditative and peaceful to sit and enjoy these moments.

The monastery and grounds were enchanting. There were very few people about but I was kept company with the birds singing all day and the crickets and frogs all night. During my evening walks back from the chapel I was treated to stunning sunset spectacles as the last light rapidly fell from the sky, only to be replaced by the Milky Way in all its star-bright glory, until I reached the canopy of trees that kept BlueBelle and me cooler both day and night. It was the perfect place to regain my energy and focus. The only downside was the dreaded mosquitoes, and I had to refit my rear mosquito curtain again since my best attempts at keeping the little biters out had failed yet again and they kept sneaking in.

Before I left I managed to buy some eggs to top up my supplies at the monastery's small shop, as well as a couple of jars of locally made preserves and some bags of their delicious coffee. I thought these might make good gifts along the way.

THE KINGDOM OF BAMOUN

Before continuing south I opted to drive the few kilometres back to the ancient city of Foumban, the one-time capital of the Kingdom of Bamoun, to visit the museum which is housed inside the royal palace. The Bamoun dynasty thrived for nearly five centuries from 1394 until the advent of colonialism. It was founded by the Mbum, an ethnic group from north-east Cameroon, and the walled city of Foumban was its epicentre. It is known for its political significance in the formation of Cameroon's history, which is rich in art and culture and filled with tales of tribes conquering and being conquered. My fascination with pre-colonial Africa is pervasive and I made an effort on my travels to see any vestiges of that time that still remained.

When I arrived at the large gates I was permitted entrance to visit the old museum, housed in a side wing of the palace, and an impressive structure stood before me. After paying my entrance fee I was advised that many of the artefacts had been moved to the new museum, which had been built next door but was not yet open. I was then taken upstairs and saw through a window a structure that I can only describe as quite extraordinary.

Before me stood a unique arrangement of essentially two buildings, one inside the other, the outer of which was in the form of a double-headed snake and the inner a giant spider consisting of four levels. At the entrance was an archway in the shape of two bells. According to the museum's architect, master builder Issofou Mbouombouo, the two-headed serpent symbolises the strength of the Bamoun people to fight and conquer on several fronts, while the spider characterises wisdom and the bells signify the celebration of victory.

The contents of the old museum were sparse but my guide, who spoke some English, led me into a fascinating glimpse of the lives of Bamoun royalty and the traditions of the area. The most significant figure in Foumban's history was King Njoya, who ruled from 1883 to 1931 and then voluntarily placed his kingdom under the protection of the German colonisers. In 1897 he converted himself and his court to Islam, a move which would impact local culture to this day. He was also responsible for modernising many elements of the society and he invented the Bamoun script, a written language formed so that the people could record their culture and history. It was purported to be sub-Saharan Africa's first written language, but was very complex and fell out of use after the king died.

There were several books in French for sale, which I would never in a life-time learn to read, but I eyed them enviously for the information they might hold. Instead I purchased some replicas of local masks or 'passports', with a use similar to those I'd found in Côte d'Ivoire. As my tour ended I was taken outside on to the balcony to meet some local musicians, who wanted me to buy all manner of treasures from CDs to musical instruments. To try to persuade me, they insisted I sat in a chair while they played an interesting assortment of music for me. After several minutes I excused myself, feeling bad that they were entertaining me when I would not be able to purchase everything they offered. I bought a CD of their recordings and said my farewells.

Included in my entrance ticket was also a visit to the 'Big Drum', and while I had no idea what this was I am always up for something interesting so I went to look. A large man was called over from the market, handed a big bunch of keys and instructed to escort me. My guide was called Moïse, and although he spoke no English he intimated he was happy to take me if I would stop at his craft shop on my return. We walked through the market and I couldn't help but be attracted to the vibrant pieces of printed cloth that were hanging on a variety of stalls, mixed in with the usual mobile accessories, plastic kettles, buckets and second-hand clothing rejects from Europe. I wished I had unlimited space and money to buy pieces of the bright beautiful fabric, particularly when I found out that there was a blue and white pattern which was only permitted to be worn by royalty – a pity, as blue and white are my colours.

We eventually came to a building surrounded by a fence in a state of disrepair with a large metal gate secured by a huge chain and padlock; I wasn't sure why it was there as the fence looked quite easy to climb over! The grounds were full of weeds and strewn about with plastic seats and wooden benches in various states, as well as trash that had blown in from the market. The building looked like it had seen better days too. It was constructed of narrow wooden slats or bamboo tied together to make the walls and the wide double doors, with thick wooden corner posts and a thatched roof. Around the doorway and along the top of the door there were small statues of spooky-looking black men with white eyes, about thirty centimetres in height, standing on top of each other. I guessed they were to ward off evil spirits but Moïse didn't know.

When the unevenly slatted front doors were opened, I entered a room where the only light came from little side windows, and as my eyes adjusted to the interior I could see a massive circular section of a huge tree trunk. This was the drum. It must have been three metres long and at least a metre in width, and it had the carved emblems of the snake, spider and bells on each side. Behind it stood a very tall carved wooden statue of a man with a spear pointing forward, and there was another, slightly smaller (my height) statue standing at the rear of the room. The back wall was covered in a mural, which looked like it could be fascinating were it not for the dim lighting, but it was obviously not wearing well partially exposed to the elements. There were also some beautifully carved tablets along one wall between a stack of dusty plastic seats.

I understood that the drum was used to bear the king through the town during processions. It looked ridiculously heavy and I wondered how many men would have been necessary to carry both it and him. It would be beaten as it went out on to the streets, and I'm certain that being so large it must have made an incredible sound.

As promised, I stopped on our way back at Moïse's shop and also to look at the work of the other artisans, a long row of people selling local art, sculptures and jewellery. The pieces were beautiful and all extremely well crafted, but I had no money to spare and no space to carry anything unnecessary. Instead I chatted, admired their work and made jokes with them to the best of my French ability.

I returned exhausted to the peace of the monastery, but it would be my last night there: after five days I had to continue on my way. I needed to do some shopping and I had been without an internet signal during my stay, so my last update was a short video informing people I had survived the crossing into Cameroon before falling out of contact. It was important that I kept my loyal followers apprised of my progress and I was concerned they might be worried about me.

Before departing the next morning I met Benson. He was a new guard at the mission and an Anglophone, so I asked him about the civil war in Cameroon, which I learnt was based around language and sometimes referred to as the 'war of words'. In his view, simplified and summarised, the war centred on the fact that Anglophone education was not as good as the Francophone: there was no university for English-speaking students and far fewer work opportunities – basic minority rights. This bias had resulted in protests by the Anglophone community, to which the Francophone government had retaliated with force; and this had escalated, with many of the locals fleeing to safer areas. According to Benson, when the African states were granted their independence the people of the area could elect to join either Nigeria or Cameroon. They'd opted for Cameroon, but I believe some might now regret not joining English-speaking Nigeria.

DOUALA AND SOUTHERN HOSPITALITY

I continued south toward Douala and on my way I once again encountered a checkpoint where the officer insisted that my RHD van was illegal. I had a slightly less antagonistic and unpleasant interchange with this one than the previous, but I still received a thorough quizzing and was only reluctantly permitted to proceed. The road was in reasonable condition until reaching the regular toll points, where the surface became obscenely worse than in any other section. Each toll was 500 francs (about ninety cents) – a tiny amount, but it was still eating into my available cash. There was never any booth, simply a man in the middle of the road with a small ticket book, taking cash and handing out tickets. In each instance the way to the toll point was littered with hawkers selling plantains or bananas,[90] water and assorted other items in the usual metal bowls on women's heads, all accompanied by the trash I had come to consider as standard.

Of course I was a difficult customer. I was on the 'wrong' side of the vehicle, so they would tell me to wind down my passenger window, which was impossible as my table was firmly planted in the foot-well next to the door, thus blocking the winder. I would smile and wave them over to my driver's side, and most were surly and seemed quite aggrieved at having to do this… but that was the only way they were going to get paid!

I had been in touch with Eric, who had helped with the Cameroon visa and offered me hospitality in Douala. He was in the UK and expected to return the following evening, but he assured me that his second-in-command at work, Casey, would do whatever was necessary to assist me. I had contacted Casey before I went to the monastery and had not received a reply, but on my way to the city a message came through from him. Since I had already planned to enquire about parking at the German Seaman's Mission, I told Casey that I would let him know what

---

[90] I still can't tell the difference between those two!

happened when I got there. In the meantime the road conditions had improved and my drive into Douala gave me some excellent views of Mount Cameroon.

Douala is the largest city in Cameroon and the country's economic centre, mostly due to offshore gas and oil drilling and production. It is also an impressive port from where most of the country's exports are shipped, including cocoa, oil, coffee, fruit, timber and metals. It sits in what was considered the Anglophone area of Cameroon, close to the centre of the civil war, and it was apparent that the prosperity of the region would assuredly prevent independence.

I was impressed with what I saw as I arrived in Douala. It seemed to have a well-retained economic structure and was a better mix of old and new than I had seen for a while. My first stop was to find an ATM so that I could then top up with fuel and food, and I soon found a small mall which ticked all the boxes – apart from the fact that the modern supermarkets, while being well stocked, were expensive and lacked that personal roadside experience I had become so fond of.

Living in a van meant I got to take shopping home immediately. It was quite literally one-stop shopping and storing: from the shop straight into BlueBelle and packed away. After the mall I continued to the German Seaman's Mission. I was disappointed when I got there as the parking area was tiny, busy and offered no shade: certainly not a comfortable space to park up, although it would possibly do just for one night. I decided to ask anyway, but after being fobbed off by several staff members and then a long wait, the manager advised that the only way I could park there was if I took a room.

While the rooms were not very expensive, it was still way beyond my budget and I said I would think about it. The problem of the lack of camping or parking opportunities in and around cities remained, and I realised that if Casey couldn't recommend a parking spot I might be forced to take a room for the night. It was the beginning of May and I still had some two weeks to go before I was due to pick up Ursula in Libreville. I wanted to kill time and spread out my travel until then – but not at that kind of room rate.

I updated Casey and he said he would get back to me with a plan. In the meantime, my friend Ana back in Solsona (Spain) had put me in touch with a Spanish friend, Sergio, who works as a tour guide in Cameroon and Central Africa.[91] He happened to be in Douala that day and came to meet me for a drink. The Mission was a nice location and popular eating place and they allowed me to use their WiFi – a good exchange for the cost of their drinks.

Sergio and I had just begun chatting when Casey and a colleague appeared. He had found a secure place for me to park but I had to leave right away. I dejectedly said goodbye to Sergio, who courteously agreed that the opportunity to park up could not be missed, so I paid for the drinks and we were off.

My parking was at a restaurant called Le Lili Marleen,[92] run by German-born Yves. It was in a compound with a grassy yard and a couple of goats that kept everything trimmed. However, to get into the compound I had to drive over a very nasty and uneven ridge. It was either that or park in the street and the compound seemed a whole lot better. I pushed BlueBelle over with a cringe-making scraping sound, but I was in. The downside was that there was no shade, so Casey insisted that I stay with him and his wife at their apartment a few blocks from the restaurant.

On my first evening Eric arrived, and it was a great pleasure to finally meet him and thank him for his kindness. He and a group of expats working in Cameroon became my drinking buddies over the next week and earned themselves the moniker 'the troublemakers'. While I was chatting with Eric I mentioned that my fuel filter needed changing after the poor quality fuel in Nigeria, and a slow leak in my front right tyre needed attention. Eric immediately made arrangements and told me that his mechanic would drop by the next day to help me with both of these. I had one additional requirement: I absolutely needed to see a doctor as the painful thing in my elbow had become very problematic, so Gerda, Casey's wife, was tasked by Eric to sort me out an urgent appointment with their local doctor. It meant so much to have local support and I was very relieved not to have to

---

[91] www.sergiomestre.com
[92] www.facebook.com/LiliMarleenDouala

go hunting about for these things. But Eric did even better than that: he generously covered all the costs for me too!

I also fell into the *best* hospitality. Gerda is South African and an amazing cook, and for the few days I was there I ate like a queen. After my simple all-in-one-pot meals, I was truly spoilt! She also escorted me to the doctor, where the verdict was something rather unpleasant called filariasis[93] which had come from a mosquito bite (bastards!) "Time to be away with it!" I said, and was given a script for three tiny tablets which I was told would kill the worm within a few days. After six months or so I would need to get another blood test done to ensure that it was dead, and in the unlikely event that it was still alive I would need another single treatment or further regular treatments to manage it. I wasn't sure if I was more horrified by the prognosis or delighted to be treated for it! Happily though, within a few days it was indeed gone.

I got a taste of the life of an expat in an African country, which was quite new to me. There was a driver to take me wherever I needed to go, whether for drinks, shopping or work. Shopping was done mostly in the mall or western-type shops and gated apartments or houses were provided. For me, who had been walking and socialising in the streets for months, it felt very strange. The flipside of this was the fact that expats, being paid good salaries and usually working for wealthy organisations, often found themselves targets for local criminals, so it was obviously in the interests of the company to keep their staff and families safe.

I enjoyed socialising with the 'troublemakers' although the drinking was fierce, considering that alcohol was something I rarely had on my journey since it was both expensive and greatly dehydrating; I had enough trouble drinking the many litres of water I needed each day to stay properly hydrated. One of the first symptoms of dehydration was that my finger joints pounded like they were on fire and the soles of my feet were tender in the morning. Being launched into expat drinking was something I

---

[93] This is a parasitic disease whereby the filarial worm is transmitted in a mosquito bite, spreading its tiny infectious larvae throughout the body and potentially wreaking havoc over time, especially if they enter the lymph system

tried to avoid, but my weak-willed arm was always being twisted and I would just find another drink in front of me... and heavens, I couldn't be rude and not drink it!

One evening – I confess I was a few gin and tonics in – I had been standing for a while and decided to sit on one of the high bar stools behind me, even though everyone had been complaining about how uncomfortable those stools were. They had metal legs and the floor was tiled (this is all forming part of the excuse I'm going to be sticking to) and as I climbed on, the stool just slid right away from me and I landed on my back on the floor, my right big toe throbbing like a demon as I caught it on the foot bar. In a way it was fortunate that I'd had too much to drink because I didn't feel a thing other than my toe – and trust me, I fell hard! Well, that was the end of the drinking for me and a good indication that I needed to get away from these troublemakers: it was clear that the consequences of staying were going to be extremely bad for my health... and besides, I might *never* leave their generous hospitality..!

So a few days later I bade a fond farewell to the troublemakers and the wonderful Eric, to whom I remain inordinately indebted for such kindness. I was also immensely sad to say goodbye to Gerda, who had become a real friend, but I was sure we would catch up again south of the equator. It was time to continue to Yaoundé and prepare for my crossing into Gabon.

YAOUNDÉ

The drive from Douala to Yaoundé was a pleasant one through green and slightly undulating countryside. The road conditions were fair, although there were many diversions due to Chinese-led construction where they were building proper water channels under the roads. In the rainy season the downpours are intense, and on my journey I had seen too many roads destroyed by poor channelling, leaving the heavy runoff to erode both the base and the surface. The Chinese were everywhere it seemed – which one might consider a noble thing, except that their investment in infrastructure was tiny in comparison with the value of the minerals, timber, and crops that they were transporting out of these countries. The road improvements were an investment in facilitating their extraction of the natural wealth of Africa.

As I approached a checkpoint I noted that the officer was oddly on his own; usually there were at least two or sometimes more. I stopped and employed my usual friendly greeting, handing over my papers through the open window. He spoke little English but I understood him perfectly when he started with my number one topic: that I was illegally driving a RHD vehicle. It was a case of déjà vu from the second checkpoint and I again pointed out that I had a TIP but no, I was still illegal, at which point I became irritated. I was fed up with this nonsense, so I took my papers out of his hands and waggled my TIP under his nose to verify my status. At this, he also advised me that I was being disrespectful: he was a police officer and I should respect him; to which I tried the same tack and advised *him* that *he* was being disrespectful to his government and the document issued to me by *his* government. He did not shut up either, merely continued to blah, blah, blah at me in French, and by now not only did I no longer understand him but I also wasn't really interested. It was clear that he was going to keep me there – although at no time did it occur to me that a bribe might get me through (not that I would have been prepared to give him one!) So I simply sat back in my seat, eyes forward, arms crossed, and tried to calm myself while he blathered on. I had hoped that my obvious indifference to him might shut him up, but regrettably it did not. My mind raced for a new tactic (and don't ask me where I got my idea from, it was pure instinct): I clasped my hands together, thrust my wrists forward through the open window as if ready to be handcuffed and said to him: "Arrest me!"

The officer looked at me with utter shock and disbelief – but at least it did have the required effect of shutting him up. Somewhere in my brain I had taken in the facts that (a) he was alone, (b) I was a foreigner and he'd best have a darn good excuse for arresting me, and (c) we were in the middle of nowhere, so where was he going to take me? I had called his bluff, and without another word but throwing me a look of disdain, he shoved my folder of papers back at me and waved me on. I double-checked that I was free to go (he was armed: I wasn't taking any chances!)

and he nodded with disappointment; while I, with a wide smile, thanked him and drove off.

The traffic into Yaoundé that Saturday afternoon was hectic but didn't rival some of the other capital cities I had negotiated. I made my way to an orphanage where the people were reportedly hospitable and the parking safe. It took a couple of passes around some odd intersections and roundabouts before I eventually found it. The map was not very accurate, and once I'd left the tarmac road it was the usual potholed dirt.

The two hundred and forty kilometre drive had taken longer than anticipated with the multiple diversions and checkpoints, so it was mid-afternoon when I arrived at the orphanage. I knocked at the large metal gate and a young man opened it and told me I could come in, so as usual I asked the rate and was told I could pay anything I liked. As I entered I noticed, in their very large overlanding truck, the French couple who had been with Marion and Anatole at the Nigerian Embassy in Benin. We greeted each other and made a bit of small talk – limited since neither of us spoke the other's language well – but I did ascertain that they were leaving the next day to head into Gabon.

The yard was paved but small so I had to park nose-to-nose with the French couple, but at least my door opened on to a nice green lawn. The buildings were very smart and the whole area clean and pleasant. I noticed that the French woman went to shower in a newer building which seemed to offer accommodation and house the staff, and I figured that was where I would be showering too. When I had asked the young man about the ablutions he'd fobbed me off and I didn't press it. I was going to relax and fine-tune my route.

The next day I decided to top up my shopping and look for a place to get photocopies, which I thought I might need for my entry into Gabon. I headed into Yaoundé and again got lost on the roundabouts, driving up wrong streets and getting stuck in a lane up to the main road, having arguments with chaotic drivers who insisted on paying no attention and blocking all the traffic. By the time I was done I was well acquainted with the city! I eventually found the supermarket, did my shopping and chatted with the guys in the street. Then finding myself as usual hot and dusty, I decided to return to the orphanage.

I was in serious need of a wash by the time I got back. I asked around and was eventually led to the shower for the children's dormitory, having been told that there was no other bathroom. The door barely closed, one window didn't close at all (and there were people constantly walking by), there was nowhere to put anything except on the basin, and someone's washing was hanging to one side. The shower consisted of a simple nozzle in the corner of the room and the water was unfeasibly cold. Cold water wasn't usually a problem for me, but this was truly freezing and must have come from some deep underground source.

I wasn't very comfortable in the orphanage. Apart from not speaking French myself, no one seemed keen to converse with me either, so I decided I would leave the next day. However, when I was organising myself for travel, I realised that after getting lost in the city the previous day I had forgotten to get the photocopies I needed. I would have to do it on my way out.

That evening I was again parked at the edge of the lawn. It was after dark and there was a bit of a commotion outside, but I paid little heed. I was in bed relaxing, checking facts about routes and stops. I would spend much time checking, double-checking and sometimes triple-checking, because once on the road I preferred to reduce the surprise elements as much as possible. There were enough challenges that presented themselves and I felt my route should not be one of them! The noise outside continued and it sounded like they were unloading furniture, but suddenly I felt myself being jostled about in my van as people bumped into it, and I even heard the occasional clank of metal on the side. That was enough!

I got up and upon opening my door found that most of the lawn was covered in old school desks and chairs which the children had just unloaded from a large container by the gate. I was clearly in the way, so why had no one just asked me to move? I turned BlueBelle around and re-parked her facing the gate, putting a couple of metres between me and the lawn. For the first time I noticed the priest who ran the place, who gave me a dirty look. I just ignored him. Yep, it was definitely time to be leaving.

In the morning I asked for the young man who had first met me so I could settle up. I gave him a 'whatever you want' sum and he looked at me in surprise and told me I was short. I knew from the app that other overlanders had paid this amount for *two* people, so I reminded him that he had said it was up to me what I chose to pay. I also reminded him that I was alone, had used their shower only once, had never used their toilet and had basically done nothing more than park, and therefore felt any additional charge unwarranted... but he seemed intransigent; so highly annoyed and against my better judgement, I paid up simply to be done and leave.

I admit that I was now in a grumpy mood, not improved when I got my photocopies and was charged an unreasonable rate, followed by taking the wrong turn on the way out of the city on one of the no-sign roundabouts. But no sooner was I on the right track than I hit one of the dreaded police checkpoints... and this one had several officers, several barriers and nothing unofficial-looking about it.

The officer in charge looked at my papers and then advised that he wanted to inspect the inside of my vehicle. I asked why he would want to do that as it was my home and there was nothing to see. But he insisted, and when I disagreed he told me to pull over just ahead. That meant parking half off the tarmac on an uncomfortably downward slope and with BlueBelle's height I wasn't happy, so I told him I wasn't going to do it by indicating the angle of the incline. He then directed me to the opposite side of the road near a building slightly up a hill, but level and where there was more space. As I continued to protest, he berated me and shouted to some other officers.

Disgruntled, I moved across and sat there and waited. A new officer approached to say that he too wanted to inspect BlueBelle, and I again protested that this was my home and he could see anything he needed from where he was, simply by looking behind me. As you know by now I was always reluctant to let any strangers into the back of my van. I had no control over what they might lay their hands on, plus so far the police in this country had instilled little confidence in me. As a woman travelling on my own, BlueBelle was my shell, my protection, and letting in someone unknown with unknown motives felt not only like an invasion of my privacy but also like losing a bit of control. At this point several other officers approached. One spoke more English and came to tell me that I was being disrespectful (I think I'd heard that before), so I asked for a third time why they needed to see inside my vehicle. No explanation other than because they were the police.

At this I lost my temper, grabbed my keys, stomped around protesting vociferously to the sliding door and opened it... and to my utter surprise they only peered around the edge of the cupboard but did not get inside. A win for me certainly... But then they *all* wanted a look – and that was it, I'd had enough! I shut the door, locked it and got back into the driver's seat. I asked if I could go but they were still on about something or other, so I told them this was a fine way to treat tourists and I would be glad to get out of their country! One of the policemen took out his mobile phone and started overtly taking photos of me and my registration plate. I in turn took a photo of him and his pals and drove off.

I was thoroughly shaken since I had no idea if he would report me to other checkpoints and I would be further harassed. As I slowly simmered down, I realised that I had likely contributed to the situation with my grumpy attitude. All the other incidents I had experienced thus far had influenced my mood and my negative emotions were escalating. I needed to change the dynamic.

Throughout my journey I had taken each day and each checkpoint for what it was and done my best to find humour in most instances; but I wasn't feeling that now. The general disdain and unfriendliness I had encountered since coming to Cameroon had impacted how I was approaching everything, and I was allowing this to influence my attitude such that these small things were clouding the bigger picture. I could *not* let it affect me and my journey. I did an attitude check on myself and vowed to do better, focusing on the now and letting go of the irritations.

BLUEBELLE THE AMBULANCE

The next few checkpoints were unsurprisingly much better, and while I was still concerned that the officer had notified them of my insolence, my fears again surpassed reality. One fat chap did overtly try to get a bribe, but I just treated it like a joke and laughed it off and he eventually gave up and let me pass... but not without my first proposal in Cameroon!

The roads were relatively good, albeit narrower than comfortable, and in some cases the equatorial forest looked intent on taking back this barren strip of foreign tarmac as bushes endowed with bright orange flowers took the lead. The usual traditional villages lay in close proximity to each other on either side of the road, demonstrating a bemusing mixture of old and new. Prosperity showed where homes were made with blocks instead of sticks, mud rather than thatched roofs, and in some instances a modern new-build sat foursquare alongside the rest of the tribal village... and so the traditional moved into the contemporary.

I was trundling along at my usual seventy to eighty kilometres per hour, but the large trucks in the opposite direction were a problem on the narrow road as they never seemed to hesitate or break their high speed. Then there was the added problem of motorbikes, and it was one such doomed combination that I faced that morning. The oncoming motorbike was to one side of the road going at a slow but steady speed and there was a truck coming up behind him. It looked likely that we would all pass each other at the same time and there was little room for me to move off the road at the speed I was doing. As I approached it, the truck did not change either its path or its speed, and its proximity to the motorbike was such that it nudged the bike, flipping it into the air. I helplessly witnessed the collision in my side mirror as I passed, whereupon I immediately stopped and switched on my hazard lights.

Motorbikes hold an unpleasant space in my psyche: I lost my first husband in a motorbike accident and witnessing this one gave me a sick feeling in the pit of my stomach. I knew I wasn't that good with first aid – or blood for that matter – but I just couldn't leave the man on the side of the road and continue. I got out shakily and walked back toward him, along with a couple of local villagers who had also seen the incident. I suddenly realised that if they had not witnessed it I might have been blamed: the reckless truck had continued on its way without stopping.

The fellow had lost his helmet, probably because he hadn't fastened it. His face was banged up with one eye already swelling and half-closed, and he had abrasions on his hands and feet; but it looked like it wasn't as bad as I had first thought – and thankfully, he wasn't dead. However, he clearly needed medical attention and we were some distance from the nearest town. Everyone spoke French and I did my best to enquire, with my limited vocabulary, if someone would take him to the hospital, but it seemed that no one had a vehicle and there was no phone signal to call an ambulance. The nearest hospital was some forty kilometres away, so there was only one thing to do. I indicated that I would turn BlueBelle around so they could put him in my van, but one of them had to come with me.

While they took the motorbike to safety, I made room for them to lay the injured rider in the middle on the floor; lifting him on to the sofa would have been a challenge, and anyway it wasn't long enough. Meanwhile my escort and guide, Mr Helpful, sat on the sofa to keep an eye on him.

With my hazard lights on I hit the accelerator. BlueBelle did her part, and having been an ambulance in a previous life, probably felt quite at home as we sped as fast as we could to the hospital. At one of the bigger checkpoints, Mr Helpful got out to report the accident to the police. I could see that they were asking if I had been the one to cause it, but fortunately he cleared that up. We continued at a pace without further interruption until we got to the city, when we had no option but to slow down a bit for the potholed, gouged and uneven dirt roads. But not even an old single-lane bridge with crumbling concrete edges could deter us. The fellow in the back was moaning, obviously in pain, and this made me even more eager to get him help.

The hospital was a single-storey nest of buildings with a security guard at the gate who was at first reluctant to let me in. With a man bleeding on my floor I wasn't sure what the issue was, but Mr Helpful cleared the way. I parked up (no fancy emergency entrance or doctors rushing out to help as they do in the TV series) while Mr Helpful went to summon aid. I had the side door open by now and noticed that there was a reasonable amount of blood on my floor and floor mat: I would have to be careful. At that thought, two people in white coats came out to assess the situation, looking closely at him but not touching.

I was informed that they could not take him out of the van without payment for protective gloves. "Listen," I replied, "I got him here but he's your problem now, so please just get him some attention." But nope, not until someone paid for gloves. "How much are the gloves?" I asked them. It was the grand sum of about fifty cents – darn, what was the fuss about?! But this is the reality in Africa: that pitiful amount of money is not something that they have to spare; added to which hospitals and clinics are woefully poorly stocked. I found a small note on my dashboard and handed it over and asked that they *please* help the man.

Gloves purchased, they came back with my change (which I insisted I didn't need so Mr Helpful eagerly pocketed it; I figured he deserved it) and the patient was awkwardly removed from BlueBelle and placed on a stretcher. I was looking at the mess on the floor and wondering how best to tackle it when Mr Helpful, who had donned gloves himself – a bit like closing the stable after the horse had bolted because he had already handled the injured man at the accident site! – came back with some paper towels and scooped up the bits and pieces and most of the blood.[94] I asked if he knew if the patient was OK and it seemed he was just very battered and bruised; anyway his family had been called. Job done, it was time to get back on the road. It was only 9.30 am, and so far it had proved to be an eventful day!

I asked Mr Helpful if he wanted a lift back and he did, so with him this time in the passenger seat we headed off. I was relying on him to direct us back to the main road, however it seemed that Mr Helpful felt that this was a great opportunity to take advantage of being chauffeured and he directed me into the town. He motioned me to pull over, got out and entered a small shop, returning only after several minutes. I had been trying to adopt my Reviewed Attitude, though I must confess I did start to get a bit irritated. But with language being a problem it was obvious that I wouldn't be able to understand him if he had just said, 'Hey, could you do me a favour and just stop for a minute while I get something?' After another stop to say hi to his girlfriend, we eventually got back on the main road and drove in silence until he indicated that I could drop him off. ARA 9:DB 5

As I set off on my way again, I soon realised that all that adrenalin was running out, so I found a spot to stop and make coffee before continuing to Gabon. I rested for a while and

---

[94] I cleaned everything properly with disinfectant when I stopped for the night

restored myself with the hot drink and the surrounding equatorial forest, which thickened into a dense variety of foliage in all the imaginable colours of green, contrasted by the gorgeously ever-present orange flowering bushes edging the road.

I had noticed on the map that there were two possible routes into Gabon and one looked more direct, but just before the turnoff to the alternative route there was a checkpoint. As I came to a halt behind the few vehicles in front of me, I sat back and attempted to refine my patience while bracing myself for another challenging exchange. I noticed a variety of structures to my left which indicated that it was a Serious Checkpoint. An apparent altercation ahead meant the queue was not moving, and eventually a uniformed officer approached from the buildings. His assured manner and the epaulettes on his well-pressed shirt alerted me to the fact that this was no ordinary policeman. He spoke fair English and we chatted.

We did the usual where I was from and what I was doing, but after a few minutes he asked me if I would like to have a drink with him. I was speechless: surely I had misheard? Was it a trick question or was there an ulterior motive? However, I was intrigued, because not once had I been offered anything at a checkpoint. In fact I had become more accustomed to being asked if *I* would buy *them* a drink, especially in Cameroon where the officers had been less than helpful. I decided to take up his offer, with some caution, so I moved off the road and we walked over to one of the structures which served as a shop-cum-social-drinking/eating-spot.

His name was Armand and he offered me a drink, insisting I take a beer, but I politely declined and took a soda – not only because I was driving but because I still wasn't certain if he was trying to catch me out. Many African countries have a zero drinking and driving policy, so I wasn't taking any risks.

We chatted for nearly an hour: we discussed my travels, Mugabe, dictators, colonialism... it was all very interesting. Eventually I realised I had to leave if I was to make it into Gabon that day, so I excused myself and we took the usual selfie by BlueBelle and traded cards so that I could send him the photo. I was delighted to have had the chance to exchange ideas and found it a thoroughly pleasant checkpoint experience. My Attitude Adjustment Exercise had delivered an interesting turnaround.

As I continued to the border, I became aware of some exceptionally long and wide trucks carrying huge logs which looked like mahogany. There were so many that I began counting them. Each truck had at least eight logs on the back, all stacked on top of each other, and the weight must have been enormous; if you've ever picked up something made of solid mahogany, you'll understand. Yet these trucks hurtled by at a great speed. By the time I reached Gabon I guessed I must have passed at least fifty of these trucks over the two days, and I wondered how many this meant over the course of a year, and whether there would be any mahogany trees left by the end of the 2020s...

I arrived at the border at about lunchtime. The border post consisted of a small office with a huge parking area which looked like it might usually hold a lot of traffic, but fortunately there was absolutely none when I arrived. I had my documents cleared without incident and after the obligatory black ledger entries I was out within ten minutes. It felt almost a let-down! With the frantic morning I'd had, I hadn't stopped for my usual mid-morning breakfast, so I thought it best to do so before I made the border crossing. Certainly parking was no issue. As I munched on some fruit, I pondered my journey over the past almost six months.

At this point I had driven more than eleven thousand kilometres and was well over halfway home – not without my fair share of problems, but I had made it nonetheless. I finished my lunch, started BlueBelle up and drove quietly away, breathing a heartfelt Thank You to the Universe and all my supporters for helping me get this far.

Chapter Twelve – Gabon

13 May 2019

As you may recall, I had concerns about crossing into Gabon. When I was getting my visa they had wanted a lot of information, and the overlanding groups and apps confirmed that they were pedantic about providing the correct documentation, particularly when it came to proving that accommodation had been booked for the stay. The authorities had cottoned on to the fact that people were making a booking, printing the information off and then immediately cancelling it; consequently the border officers had taken to phoning the accommodation to confirm the booking. I had decided that this was nonsense. I had not booked any lodging and I wasn't going to. The problem with making a booking was that if I didn't cancel it in time I would end up having to pay for it, and this all became more complicated once I entered Gabon as I would have to get a local SIM card to either call or cancel online. It was a nasty catch-22 and I wasn't taking the risk.

Instead I had copies of all the papers that I thought they might ask for, a list of where I had been and the dates I had entered and exited; so along with my business card and my award-winning charm, I believed I was fully equipped to handle the border officials. How far I had come in a relatively short time when it came to handling border posts! Taking a deep breath, I crossed into Gabon on a long, low bridge with a wide and beautiful river running below me.

At the end of the bridge, on a slight rise to my left, there was an odd-looking structure which served as the border post. It was square and had low walls about half a metre high, with pillars on each corner and a roof. I entered through an opening and there was an ancient wooden desk to the right where sat a uniformed officer who was close to bursting out of his shirt, a tall uniformed man with sunglasses and two other men of unknown function. I rolled out my most enthusiastic "Bonjour!" and my biggest smile and took off my sunglasses so that they could look me in the eyes.

In return they greeted me enthusiastically and we started chatting, conversing in my typically poor French and their equally poor or non-existent English. I was immediately invited to sit on the built-in concrete bench that ran around the edge of the wall and Mr Sunglasses started asking me the usual questions. There was a breeze coming up from the river and I was in the shade, so I relaxed and gave them my full attention. I thought I would need all my wits about me to ensure I got through on my scant paperwork. I regaled them with the story of my journey and they were all astonished that I had come so far on my own. In between the chatting, my papers and passport were handed to Mr Burstingbuttons and Mr Sunglasses decided he wanted to have a look at my van, which I openly invited him to do in the hopes that he would then overlook my lack of booked accommodation.

The others eagerly followed to inspect this 'amazing vehicle', which they admired with impressed nods and congratulations, and then we returned to the business of my passport. Shortly after this Mr Burstingbuttons enquired about my accommodations, and I explained that I *always* slept in my van and usually stayed at missions, adding that my stop that night would be at the cathedral in Oyem. Mr Sunglasses nodded his approval and Mr Burstingbuttons continued scribbling in big black ledgers. My sociable demeanour had paid off because I was eventually handed back my passport without further enquiry, so I wished everyone a cheery "Bonne journée" and was off on my way again with friendly waves and good wishes. My only other stop was a bit further down the road to have my passport checked, which passed without incident after the usual black book entry. Now all I needed to do was continue to the town of Bitam to obtain my TIP.

Bitam was some distance from the border and the iOverlander app had everything well marked, thanks as usual to the efforts of previous intrepid adventurers in whose debt I constantly remain. The TIP office was situated exactly on a roundabout that I wasn't expecting, so I missed it, and when I realised I would have to turn around I decided instead to first buy a SIM card which I had seen advertised at a nearby shop. The necessary purchase made (although I was horrified at the cost of the data and the top limit of 700Mb), I felt better placed with a connection and returned to get my TIP.

The office was in a single-storey colonial building that stood at the edge of the roundabout, so I parked in front of the low wall surrounding it and greeted the staff seated outside on the veranda. I was informed that I had missed the chief and would have to come back, so I said that I could not do that but I would wait. Some grumbling ensued, a phone call was made and then yes, I could wait. The chief returned after thirty minutes and entries into black ledgers were made plus a form completed, and without further ado I was the holder of a Gabonese TIP. Onward to Oyem!

It was now getting quite late and I was worried if I would make it before nightfall, my diversions of the day having eaten into much of my travel time. The equatorial rainforest was now the densest I had seen and I tried to work out all the varieties of plants that made up this greenery. It seemed to start with small weeds and grasses followed by taller plants, then small shrubs leading to taller shrubs, then trees and taller trees, and towering above all of these the majestic mahogany. The foliage was a kaleidoscope of colour, size and form.

I came to understand why so little of the countryside was under cultivation: clearing jungle like this would take some serious work and upkeep, as I noted that the rainforest always seemed keen to take back what belonged to it. The beautiful orange flowering shrubs continued to be prolific along the sides of the road, sometimes encroaching so much as to leave only a single lane in the middle. Clearly there was not as much traffic here.

I was about twenty kilometres from Oyem when I had to stop for a moment to take in a sight that was utterly out of context: there was a huge, modern concrete sports stadium and parking lot, complete with flood-lighting, in a space hewn out of the jungle. It looked like it would be able to hold thousands of people, but although it was brand new it seemed virtually unused. Who would possibly use this? Was there even enough of the regional population to fill it? And how many locals would realistically be able to afford any event in such a place? It was probably the biggest white elephant I had ever seen and I felt an inevitable oriental hand and a local politician at play.

The fading light convinced me to drive on and I arrived at Oyem just as the sun was about to set. Turning off the main road (which I must mention was in really good condition), it was back on to familiar uneven, potholed dirt track up to the cathedral, with its distinctively tall tower. As I neared it I realised that there was no compound as such, just some residential buildings to the left; but no matter, a church was usually a safe location. When I asked for someone in charge, a priest came to me, and he was quite the oddest man I'd seen for some time. Using my best French mixed with my most deferential English I told him I required a place to park for the night, and in return he began with a story about two French women who had come about an hour before to ask the same thing but he had sent them away... and for a moment my heart sank. But then he continued that as I was Anglophone I would be able to stay, and indicated a place behind one block of buildings. I thanked him profusely and he waved me away nervously, saying I must park immediately.

I had no idea why the French women were less desirable than I was, but I was grateful to have a place to park. It had been an eventful day and I was happy to have a quick bucket wash, disinfect the van floor, shove the mat into the laundry bag and lock up. I decided to set my window alarms as there was no security to be seen, and quickly fell asleep knowing that I would wake early to depart in the cool of the day.

Just before midnight I woke with a stomach cramp and felt I needed to use my convenient toilet. I didn't switch on the main lights as the glow from my switch panel was sufficient, but as the cramp subsided I heard someone try my rear door handles. Just to explain, the connections inside both doors had broken in Barcelona and since then the handles turned freely on the outside without having any effect, such that the doors would only open from the inside. So sitting on the loo, my reflex was to shout out; but when I couldn't hear anything I quietly stood up, made myself decent and listened. I peered through the side windows to try to see the culprit... but nothing. So I climbed back on to the bed and there, through the rear window, I saw a man in a hoodie standing some metres away from me, just looking at the van.

I immediately decided that opening any doors was unwise, so instead I went to the driver's seat and wound down the window, stuck my head out and loudly asked him who he was and what he wanted. But he said nothing, just slowly turned and walked away, seemingly not at all concerned or threatened... but at least he was leaving. After a few minutes I checked through all the windows again and, not seeing anything out of the ordinary, returned to bed and eventually to sleep.

KILLING TIME TO LIBREVILLE

There were three more nights until I picked up my niece, Ursula, in Libreville. I didn't have far to go and I preferred to spend time outside the city, but the options were limited. The only thing that looked appealing was a jaunt into a reserve, but the roads were reportedly bad and given the time frame it was probably optimistic. The last thing I wanted was to get stuck or be late. I decided to see what I could find to occupy myself locally and set out to look for wild camping spots, since most of the hotels[95] involved spending money and I had very little left. However, the dense jungle afforded few suitable options other than villages where there were clearings.

I continued at a slow pace, savouring the lush, dense greenery surrounding me and trying to understand this totally foreign environment. I was interested to note that instead of the huts being built with a timber frame and roof struts and packed with mud walls, the homes here were totally built from wood. It seemed logical, given the limited access to mud without having to clear the thick jungle: trees were a naturally easier option. Doubtless with Gabon being on the equator the rainfall would be consistent, and wood probably provided a better, more stable structure. One house I passed was obviously built by a master carpenter, with planks of various colours combined into a wonderful pattern that was so impressive I was compelled to reverse to take a photo.

By now I had been on the road by myself for nearly six months and had fallen into my own way of doing things. I can't say 'routine' because I'm not much of a routine person, often forgetting to strap something down and discovering it while driving along when it went bang or fell out. No matter how many times I told myself to check this or secure that, I'd be distracted by something and forget; and I can't tell you how often my

---

[95] I use the term loosely: they were often quite insalubrious places!

kitchen drawers had fallen out! But I had come to relish doing whatever I wanted whenever I wanted, without consultation, negotiation, consideration or compromise; and I liked it – *a lot*! Ursula would be joining me in BlueBelle for two whole weeks, and while we normally get on really well, there is a difference when you're living with someone in a very confined space. I was hoping that our time together would not be too taxing on either of us and had to admit to being a little nervous.

I had gone to considerable trouble to clear out a drawer for her things and make space in the rear for her bags. Only overlanders or people living in genuinely tiny spaces can understand that every corner is precious and everything has a place and a purpose. I had instructed Ursula to bring a soft bag as a hard case would have been difficult to fit in. I had also taken out some spare sheets; blankets were unlikely to be needed and I had plenty of pillows. It would be necessary to move things from the front seat to the back during the day and vice versa at night, using the front for storage so that we could move more freely around the living area.

My niece is an avid adventurer herself and had travelled to many more places than I had, but she had never taken on West Africa as I was doing. It was one thing undertaking the journey myself and being prepared for the risks, but to take on a family member too..? Only time would tell if we were up to it…

At around mid-morning it was time to have coffee and breakfast, so I found a space to pull off the main road. My stop gave me an ideal vantage point of the huge logging convoy I had seen earlier, with at least five trucks travelling together and a 4x4 leading them. Most of the drivers were Chinese. This was how the rainforests were disappearing, one truckload at a time – or in this case several dozen per day. Even if the trees were replanted immediately, it would take more than twenty-five years for future generations to see these majestic giants again. Remember this when you want that mahogany floor or original piece of furniture. Instead come and see them in nature, where they belong!

I made my breakfast and sat in my captain's seat[96] with my window open, enjoying the view and entranced by the diversity of vegetation within such a small area. However, within ten minutes I was inundated by tiny flies that stung like mosquitoes, so I shooed as many of them out as I could and shut the window again, preferring to sit in the heat than bear the attacks. Darn it, if there was some biting insect within my vicinity it always seemed to find me! These were nasty and I was told later that they were probably tsetse flies, the ones that can give you sleeping sickness. Fortunately I managed to dodge that bullet, as well as malaria.

I trundled on at a very leisurely pace. The roads were good and for part of the way I followed a crisp clear stream tumbling over some large, very smooth grey stones alongside the road, only partially obscured by the dense jungle bamboo that again formed a stunning green vaulted cathedral roof overhead. Despite being in a man-made van on a man-made road, I felt intensely liberated and so in love with this rainforest and wild nature that I was fully in the moment and relishing every bit of it. The sounds of the wind in the leaves, the water rushing past, the buzzing of insects, the smell of life…

I had identified an old quarry that looked like a promising spot for an overnight stay, but I was too early so I passed it to see if anything more promising lay ahead. After a few kilometres with nothing apparent, I turned back and decided that I would wait nearby: I didn't want to park up until it was close to dark, keeping my location as unseen as possible. I had passed two men on my way and again on my return, and as usual I waved at them in both directions. A while later they startled the life out of me as they walked past again, having approached my window from the rear. I had been fully occupied on my phone, checking my maps.

They only spoke French and were very friendly, so we shook hands but I stayed in my vehicle. From what I could make out, they were talking about 'the house on the hill' and I just wasn't getting it, so after some five minutes of trying to communicate with me, they smiled and left. I thanked them and took to Google to try to translate some of the words they'd kept repeating, and

---

[96] Without a doubt my best buy as I'd been able to drive so many kilometres a day without backache!

finally I realised they were telling me *not* to stop there as the man on the hill was a bandit and I would be at risk. They would have no reason to warn me if it wasn't true and I had felt their friendly intent. Well, there went my plan for a park-up and now it was getting a bit late to find somewhere else, but I decided it would be wise to heed their caution.

I recalled that I had seen a hotel/motel in the previous town, so I returned there to see if I could park for the night. As usual they tried to sell me a room, which I declined, but fortunately the owner agreed to a reduced sum and I had safe parking next to the building. It was just off the road and although there was no fence or compound there was a guard for the night and I felt sure it would be safe. I had a cold soda on the small terrace and chatted to the locals until night fell and the biting things came out to suck my blood, whereupon I fled back to BlueBelle and locked myself inside with all the fans on.

There was no reason to leave early the next day, but I did because I so enjoyed the cool mornings. I had no idea where my next stop would be but hoped to spend another night in the countryside before getting into Libreville. I had covered – at the slowest pace I could manage with stops for coffee, breakfast and lunch *chez* BlueBelle – about two hundred kilometres, when I passed a nice-looking building with well-tended grounds carved out of the jungle. It was a typically colonial-style single-storey building with central steps up to the door, a flag-pole in the middle of the front lawn and a wide parking area. It looked quite alien there. Two men standing on the steps looked at me as I passed and I smiled and waved at them, and they returned the courtesy with a smile. I drove on, but my mind was busy thinking what an ideal place that was to park up. I had nothing to lose so I turned around.

The men were naturally surprised to see me pull into their parking area and came over to speak to me. I had read the sign on entering the grounds and it turned out that this was the local courthouse and prefecture building. I tried my best to explain that I just wanted to park on their grounds for the night – obviously an unusual request – but they were unable to give me permission and said I needed to ask the prefect, who was currently out. I figured that they were quite friendly and so I would take my chances and wait for the prefect to arrive, which eventually he did. (He lived in a very nice house at the rear of the building.) I showed the proper respect for his position, told my story and made my request, and he agreed to let me park there. He did ask if he and his family might view BlueBelle inside and of course I was happy to let them do so. They were suitably impressed as we discussed my travels with my limited French. Thankfully they left me to my own devices for the night, which I spent peacefully parked up next to the jungle. I departed early in the morning before anyone was up.

I decided to head into Libreville, withdraw cash, fill up the tank, top up on supplies and make my final preparations for Ursula. Thus far the roads in Gabon had been amazing, mostly single lane but well tarmacked, and I wasn't expecting anything different for the main road into the capital city. I was in for a shock though. About eighty kilometres before the city the road fell apart – and I mean that in every sense of the word! This stretch was just as bad, if not worse in places, as the road from Benin to Lagos: potholed tarmac that was more pothole than tarmac, rutted dirt, pools of water, ravines of mud... It was a horrid, awful, *terrible* road. How could the main access to a capital city be left to deteriorate into such a state, and yet not far away in the middle of the jungle sat an unused sports stadium?! I was incredulous. But while I was pondering this dichotomy I made a rookie mistake: I thought that one water-filled pothole probably wasn't very deep, but realised my error when the front bumper smacked the tarmac as I went through it; and then the back bumper hit equally hard as I came out.

On such roads it was common practice, and one that I had adopted, to weave about the road trying to find the best route options. Whilst I was engrossed in the art of dodging water-filled potholes and muddy slides, I didn't see the convoy of logging trucks come up behind me. I became aware of it when the 4x4 advance vehicle undertook me at speed and splashed muddy water all over me through my half-open window. I was hopping mad. I noted the vehicle and hoped I would catch up with him at some point to give him a piece of my mind. The trucks sped by too, but at least by then I had closed my window.

I did indeed catch up to them at the next checkpoint a few kilometres ahead, where I pulled up next to the 4x4 and politely asked the man standing outside it if he was the driver of the vehicle. When he replied that he was, I launched into a tirade of what an inconsiderate driver he was and displayed my mud-splashed t-shirt and face, ranting that not everyone was privileged enough to drive an air-conditioned vehicle and accusing him of helping the rape of Africa's resources. (When I get mad, everything comes out!) The man, most bemused, obviously understood English and apologised profusely. I left him with a strong warning to be more considerate and drove off feeling much better, but I could imagine him wondering where on earth this crazy woman and her blue van had dropped from.

One of the main checkpoints into the city was in the centre of a market and was also some sort of stopping point for the many trucks that ravaged the already decimated road still further. An officer came over and I handed him my papers as usual, but it seemed that he'd never encountered a foreign vehicle and I was told to wait while he went off to discuss things with a portly middle-aged colleague. The latter sauntered over to me and started to give me a hard time, firstly about the illegality of my RHD van (I directed his attention to the TIP), then about the fact that I was an Anglophone and didn't speak enough French. I explained that I was from Zimbabwe and that the language there was English, but obviously still unimpressed he walked around BlueBelle and then instructed me to get out.

Of course my annoyance levels rose at having to leave the safety of my van, plus my guard was instantly up. The officer escorted me to the rear of BlueBelle and showed me my broken right light cluster. This had happened somewhere in Nigeria, when someone had damaged about a third of it across the three different colours (orange, white and red) so that the bulbs were now partly exposed. To be honest I had forgotten about it, mostly because I didn't think I would be lucky enough to find a replacement, so I told him that I was going to sort it in Libreville. The officer clucked, shook his head and then pointed to the other light cluster, which had the tiniest corner of the plastic missing and was not noticeable unless you looked for it; neither did it impact the effectiveness of the light. I clucked back at him and raised an eyebrow with a look that said, Really!? But his look in response was, Yes, really! Non-verbal communication is sometimes *so* much more effective than verbal! He continued in French about something or the other, but my brain was trying to work out what I should do and I wasn't fully paying attention. (In hindsight I think his tactic was to get me to pay him something but, dumb blonde that I am, this didn't even occur to me at the time.)

He was still blabbing on when my fight-or-flight response automatically went into action – and you would know by now that I don't tend to do flight. I shouted at him, "Well here I am in the middle of nowhere: do you have the spare part here? Show me where! Show me and I will go get it and replace it right now. If not then my best hope of fixing it is in Libreville, so you can keep me here arguing about this and tutting about the fact that it is broken or you can let me get on and I can go find someone to fix it!" My getting mad means that I can only find English words (which I can fire off at great speed), so of course he probably didn't understand me; but I also believe that he had seldom – if ever – met an old woman who would stand up for herself in quite the way I did. The officer looked at me, trying to assess whether to pursue this or not. He seemed to fully comprehend my intent and decided to berate me again, then changed his mind, shook his head and told me I must get it fixed in Libreville... but I could go.

On my arrival in Libreville I sought out my parking place for that night. The indicator light would, of necessity, be the next thing to attend to as I now had less than a day to resolve it. I had some trouble finding the seminary where I knew overlanders were allowed to park, probably because there was quite a large yard just in front of the entrance filled with old cars seemingly under repair. Believing that someone had got the description wrong or that the place was no longer there, I asked a tall man if I could park and he nodded. I then tried to ask him about getting someone to repair my indicator light, but I wasn't having much luck. He didn't understand me much and I certainly didn't understand him.

As I was desperately considering my next move, a man approached me and asked in English if he could help. Pleasantly surprised and excited, I introduced myself and asked where he was from. He was Maxwell and was from Ghana (hence English-speaking) but had lived for many years in Gabon and spoke fluent French too. He was a courier and taxi driver, and when he had seen me enter the grounds had noticed that I had a Ghanaian flag on the side of my van along with all my other country flags, so his curiosity had been aroused. I gave him a brief rundown of my journey, including my travels through Ghana, and eventually brought him to my current problem.

He looked at the light and told me he would bring someone in an hour to have a look at it, so we exchanged numbers. I discovered the seminary further along and entered, but no one there spoke English and they seemed unaccustomed to being asked for parking. Eventually the secretary told me it would be fine, so I found some trees and waited for Maxwell.

When he arrived he was with Alexander, who assessed the light and said he would try to find a replacement, but since this was highly unlikely he could fix it instead. I was uncertain what 'fix it' meant, but Maxwell assured me it was in good hands. We agreed a price, the equivalent of about €30 – more than I had hoped, but if it solved the problem it would be cheaper than any fine or more incidents with checkpoints. They said they would return at around 5.30 and took the entire light cluster with them.

I now set about getting cash. Naturally I couldn't drive BlueBelle without her rear right lights, so I started to walk to the location of the nearest ATM, apparently a couple of kilometres away. You know the saying, 'Only mad dogs and Englishmen go out in the midday sun'? Well that was me. It was hot, humid and intense, however the streets were clean, the traffic orderly(ish) and the buildings I passed impressive, most of them embellished with extensive mosaics or statues on their facades.

I tried three cash machines with my only remaining card and received an error message on all of them. I was furious, but bought the most expensive bottle of cold water I had yet found (it was either that or die of dehydration) and walked back to the seminary with an empty wallet. By the time I reached my van I was totally done in. I had walked about five kilometres, the furthest I'd done in months, and I was seriously stressed about BlueBelle and now money. I contacted the card company and it seemed there was an error on their system, so I gave them hell about being stuck in the middle of Africa without funds. They assured me the problem had been resolved.

By 7.00pm neither the men nor my light cluster had reappeared and the gate was being locked at 8.00, so I sent a message to Maxwell. It suddenly occurred to me that I was in a strange country and had given strangers a piece of my precious BlueBelle, and if they disappeared with it I would have a much bigger problem! Mild panic ensued. But then I got a grip and remembered that the incentive to return was that they would be paid – and immediately Maxwell responded, apologising that the repair had taken longer than expected but they would come in the morning. I told him that it had to be before 10.00 because I needed to be at the airport by 11.00.

In the morning I sent a reminder message to Maxwell and headed off in a different direction to find an ATM. The people seemed unperturbed to have me walking in their midst, but I set about warmly greeting anyone who made eye contact with me, making sure to look them directly in the eyes. I finally had success with an ATM and, funds in hand, immediately felt more assured. My bank account was now empty but I knew Ursula was bringing some cash.

Shortly after I returned, Maxwell and Alexander arrived and replaced my light unit. They had been unable to find the spare part, so Alexander had carefully removed the jagged edges of the plastic, cut matching strips and pieces from another unit, and fitted and glued them all together. Only if you looked closely could you see the joining lines and that some of the plastic patterning was different. To me it looked like a work of art and I was deeply impressed. Once again African ingenuity and practicality had found a workable solution.

By now Ursula had messaged me to say that her flight was delayed with an unexpected stop. I had to kill some more time, so I decided to go to the airport anyway and see if I could find a place to park. Surely it couldn't be difficult. When I drove in, I noticed that not only was their parking area quite small but also the costs were quite hefty, so I decided to find somewhere nearby and wait for the flight arrival to be confirmed online before parking in the car park.

At the roundabout immediately before the airport turnoff, I noticed a car parked in a lay-by. This looked like the perfect option, so I pulled in and sat there in my van checking the landing times and catching up on messages. I looked up and noticed two officers walking toward me with a couple, clearly the owners of the other vehicle. As the couple got into the car and drove off, the officers approached me and I noticed one had a car clamp in his hands. They proceeded to advise me that there was a sign stating that I could not park there, and when I replied that I had not noticed one they said they didn't care. I retorted that I wasn't *parked* as much as *paused*: I was checking my phone for the landing time of my flight and assumed it was a parking area due to the other car being there. However they still didn't care and threatened to clamp my vehicle. Well, that set me off!

While I was tackling them on how it was possible that the others had been allowed to park there but I was not – "Besides, I was not technically *parking, really, truly Officer, I was about to go to the airport!*" – it slowly dawned on me that they were angling for a bribe; I could tell by their delaying tactics. So I told them I was not paying any fine (nor would I wait for them to clamp me), said a hasty goodbye and made my getaway. I headed straight for the airport car park, deciding that hefty fee or not it was a safe bet. Heaven only knew what the clamping or fines might have cost.

Inside the airport I was surprised to see a Paul restaurant,[97] and knowing they would have delicious croissants I bought some for the next morning. The cost was high (it seemed it was true that Gabon was an expensive place), but I felt it would be a nice and highly civilised surprise for Ursula's first breakfast in BlueBelle.

AND THEN THERE WERE TWO!

With a flourish, My Favourite Niece eventually appeared some considerable time after the plane's arrival, and after a fond greeting, we loaded the bags into the back and headed off. I offered Ursula two options: either we could return to the seminary (although it was pretty boring, I told her) or we could go on an adventure. Ursula, unsurprisingly, opted for adventure. In an earlier chat with Michiel (my Dutch friend from Togo), he had

---

[97] This is a well-known French bakery and patisserie chain: www.paul-bakeries.com/en/

suggested a restaurant near the beach out of the city, and though the directions were vague I didn't think we could get too lost. We were looking for La Maison Bleue.[98] I confess there was some spontaneous 'sight-seeing' of one suburb when I doubted the road, but eventually we came around a bend on the dirt track and immediately knew we were in the right place.

It was certainly blue, and that shade of shabby I'd grown accustomed to in West Africa where the food was usually excellent. Most appealing though was that I had identified it as a good overnight parking spot. On the terrace the drink options were few, so we decided on a refreshing beer and lemonade shandy, or *panaché*, as it was called locally. Ursula and I caught up over a few drinks and the staff seemed keen that we order food, so I took this opportunity to enquire whether, if we stayed for a meal and more drinks, they would allow us to park overnight. This was met with their enthusiastic agreement, so with that decided we ordered another panaché and fish with plantain. The waiter trotted off, obviously to the local fishermen we had seen nearby, because a while later we saw him return carrying a bag with our fresh dinner.

We had been told that the beach was just twenty metres around the corner and decided that before dinner it would be a good idea to stretch our legs and have a look. We clambered over fallen palms on to a gorgeous little strand lined with palms and littered with driftwood and I couldn't help but think of my nephew Gary, Ursula's brother, who makes the most amazing art, lights and furniture from driftwood and reclaimed wood.[99] He would have been in his element here and I wanted to take some of it with me (though of course I hadn't the room). We even came across a large log of mahogany that had escaped and found its way on to the shore! The water was warm and we paddled our feet and strolled along the soft cream-coloured sand as we watched the sun dip below the horizon. Then we returned to the restaurant in the warm dusk and wolfed down the most delicious meal.

When we had finished eating it was totally dark outside, and since our hosts seemed anxious to close and we were driven to

[98] www.facebook.com/CapEsterias
[99] www.instagram.com/infinitelightsdesign

move by the ever-unpleasant mosquitoes coming out to bite, I settled the bill and we went to sort out our lodgings for the night. Ursula unpacked a load of goodies that I had ordered online in Europe, all of which had been successfully delivered to Gary in Barcelona, and Ursula had picked them up on a visit to Spain before coming to Gabon. This had involved some careful planning from my end and my lovely family had all played their part, innovative Africans that we are! The parcel contained essential items such as new screens and replacement batteries for my phones and one for my tablet (which had also died some months before), a new lock for my back door (the previous one was lying somewhere on the road from Nouakchott to Diama), several other small but helpful items and finally some new underwear and vests that my cousin Dineke in Belgium had kindly donated to my cause.

It took a bit of arranging and then briefing Ursula on where everything was in the van and how it all worked, but eventually we were able to get settled for the night. My Favourite Niece was safely with me and all was well with the world.

LAMBARÉNÉ – ALBERT SCHWEITZER MUSEUM

In the morning we enjoyed delicious hot coffee and croissants. Ursula went for a swim in the ocean at the little bay around the corner, while I opted for a bucket wash and set about moving things around for the 'daytime' formation. It was then time to head back to Libreville and on to our route south, and as we passed through the city I did a little tour around to show her the buildings and statues that I'd seen a few days before.

I had warned Ursula about the condition of the road we would have to take on our way out, yet it seemed my warning had not sufficiently expressed how bad it was and she was totally aghast: phase one of bad road encounters! Little did we know what still lay ahead.

There was already one benefit of having an additional pair of eyes on board: Ursula could see things that I missed while I was so focused on the road and she spotted an incredible art display and several other local delights as we drove along. One thing that I insisted she look out for was a sign identifying the equator. I had crossed it not just once but *twice* in Gabon but not seen it, and as this would be my final chance on this journey I felt I had to record the moment! With much delight we found the huge board, and the moment was suitably chronicled in the annals of my expedition before we continued south.

The road fortunately improved and it was mid-afternoon when we reached Lambaréné. I felt it necessary to have a mechanic check BlueBelle over as there was an odd sound when turning the steering wheel sharply plus another unusual noise (technical terms, these), so I knew something was wrong; I just didn't know what. But how to find a garage and then describe the issue in French? I tried at a fuel station but they couldn't assist me, so I jumped back into BlueBelle... But just across a bridge over a huge river flowing westwards, we were flagged down by two policemen and I was thoroughly rebuked for not having my seatbelt on. I *always* drove with it on! (Except on the horrid dirt roads where I was bouncing and swaying with the movement of the van and the belt just became annoying.) I was horrified to be caught and repentantly explained that I was trying to find a garage for BlueBelle. They discussed something privately and then quite surprisingly turned to me and said something about an Anglophone mechanic, and I should follow them.

About a kilometre down the road they turned off, and there was the usual messy mechanic's yard with an assortment of vehicles in various states of repair (or disrepair). The policemen spoke to the staff who in turn called for the boss, so we profusely thanked the policemen who were obviously prepared to forego the fine. An English-speaking mechanic appeared, my guardian angel delivering again. He was Emmanuel, a Nigerian who had lived in Gabon for many years and thus also spoke fluent French.

Whilst Emmanuel set a man to investigate my van, we girls became the centre of attention for the men in the yard – specifically Ursula, with two young men in their early twenties taking a real shine to her. With BlueBelle being sorted, I realised that here I was in a workshop with tools at hand and the opportunity to refit one of my rear side bumper pieces, which had come off some time ago and was taking up precious space in the rear storage area. However, the mechanics were not going to let *me* do anything, so one of the guys fitted it quickly for me and secured the other side too. I also needed to fix the bolts that held the side step in place when it was open – I suspected that the super bump in Douala had squashed it – and with a few hefty whacks of a heavy hammer, this too was fixed.

Back to Emmanuel, and it seemed there was an issue with some rubber on something to do with the steering (more technical terms) and he also found that the suspension spring on the driver's side was broken. I wondered if my drive through that pothole on the road to Libreville had been the cause. He emerged from under the van with a loose piece of it and advised that I should drive very carefully and avoid any more bumpy roads. (How on earth was I going to do that in Africa?!!) He was certain that I wouldn't be able to find replacement parts in Gabon, but on seeing my concern he assured me that everything was fine. He then looked me in the eyes and brought tears to them when he said with the utmost sincerity, "You are such a brave, good woman. I know that God will see you safely home as he has plans for you." I sighed and decided I'd have to trust the Universe on this one again as I pondered the broken spring piece in my hands.

I asked what the charge was for his time and assistance and he responded that it would be up to me to pay him what I felt was appropriate. They had all been so kind and helpful, so I summoned up some cash and hoped it would be enough. This was always so difficult to assess, as the 'value' of service varied from one country to another. At any rate they seemed happy as we waved goodbye.

We drove off to find the convent school where we hoped to park up for a couple of days. It was now Saturday and we planned to stay until Monday morning since the place would be empty all weekend apart from the odd nun. When we found it the convent turned out to be a charming old bare red-brick building with a distinctive colonial feel and a large tree in the courtyard where we would be allowed to leave BlueBelle. We were also given the use of the school ablutions, which included toilets, basins and showers of cold water – basic but adequate. The humidity was exceptional because the convent was built on an island in the middle of a wide, fast-flowing river.

We had a good opportunity to reorganise Ursula's things to make ourselves more comfortable and also to catch up on washing. I hadn't done any for about a week so it was taking up valuable space. I had a special tin box with a length of cord and some clothes pegs, essential for the instant washing line I always strung up. Ursula helped out and got better acquainted with the living space and where things were to be found. In the mornings she also took to doing yoga on the decking under the tree. Little did we realise how important these two days of peace would be.

We left early on Monday morning. The children started to arrive at about 7.30 and we needed to get out of the way, but by their looks it was easy to see that they found the sight of two women in a van quite bizarre. Before leaving Lambaréné we decided to visit the Albert Schweitzer Museum which was situated on the banks of the Ogooué River. He was one of the people Ursula and I had both learnt about at school as a paragon of missionary work in Africa. I remembered he had worked with lepers in Central Africa in the early twentieth century, however the museum revealed so much more.

Dr Albert Schweitzer was an accomplished musician, a theologian, doctor and humanist, and I was fascinated by all the photographs and the new information that I learnt about him there. He was truly a giant among men and his legacy was obviously greatly respected locally, so it seemed appropriate that he and his wife and daughter were all buried in a small graveyard next to the hospital.

We were escorted through his clinic which was furnished with a dentist chair, and there was also an apothecary, a library and some other consulting rooms; and whilst it all looked a little worn, it was still a surprisingly extensive museum. On our walk to the building we passed a large bell in a stand with a rope attached to it. Ursula looked at it twice and decided it was there to be rung and proceeded to do so, at which our guide almost had an apoplectic fit. It seemed that the bell was only rung on special occasions – and this was not one of them! We were suitably admonished.

Tour over, we continued toward the Republic of Congo border with the plan to stop in Ndendé for the night. It was still some forty kilometres to the border from there, but we had to check out at immigration in the local police station. Having spent more than I'd anticipated with the repairs I found myself low on local cash again and needing to top up with fuel, so on arriving in the town I set about looking for a bank. There were two, but the recommendation from both was that to change currency I needed to go back to Libreville. I was crushed. Images of the road flashed back to me, along with the knowledge that Libreville was over five hundred kilometres away! I set out to find a kind soul who might be willing to change cash: there was always someone... but not in Ndendé. It really was a one-road town. Defeated, we went to find the church to park for the night.

The priest agreed that we could park wherever we wanted and make ourselves comfortable, which we duly did by having a picnic on the grass under a shady tree. The church had a house for the four attending priests – a seemingly large number for such a small town – and there was also a block for storage with a small pharmacy. On one side of the yard there were outbuildings which housed tools and a tractor and all this looked quite neat and tidy, but behind the main buildings there were some very dilapidated and dirty staff quarters. I asked if there was a shower we might use and was shown to two outbuildings, one a toilet pit (which I didn't brave looking into!) and the other a most disgusting shower, with mould hanging off the walls and surrounded by mud. I thanked them but opted to use the broken outside tap for a bucket wash, and my inside toilet would do just fine. While Ursula and I were both accustomed to 'rough', 'repugnant' was something at which we drew the line.

EQUATORIAL RAINFOREST AND BEACH

While we were discussing our next move and checking the maps, we came up with the notion of taking a detour to the coast. This seemed like a fine idea. I had enough fuel and we surely should be able to get some cash at Tchibanga, a larger town en route. Thus the next morning saw us depart to find the beach at Mayumba. The route south of Libreville had not demonstrated the same dense jungle that I had seen in the north and I was hoping that leaving the main road would improve matters as I wanted to share the sights of nature with Ursula.

Our heading was directly west with about one hundred and sixty kilometres to the coast, and as anticipated the rainforest appeared in all its splendour, showing off its swathes of bamboo and glorious cathedral arches. The road was good and I let Ursula take over the wheel – a rare honour as thus far I hadn't let anyone else drive BlueBelle![100] It wasn't far before we came across some large piles of gravel on the side of the road, several metres high, and as we turned the bend we not only left the tarmac road for a dirt track but saw ahead of us three enormous muddy pools of water. We stopped and I got out to assess the situation.

We had not long before passed and waved at three men with machetes, and they now approached us while I was sizing up the pools and stopped to greet us again. They assured me that it would be no problem to pass through, but that I must drive straight through the middle and not try any other approach. I decided to trust local knowledge but first released some air out of the tyres for better traction. I then took the wheel, held my breath, kept my focus and set off at a slow but steady speed. I managed to traverse each muddy pond in turn, and thankfully only one of them presented some terrifying slipping and sliding action. Relieved, we shouted our thanks to the men and waved enthusiastically as we continued on our way.

The uneven red dirt road continued until we reached Tchibanga. This was indeed a larger town than Ndendé and my hopes were high that I might find a bank or someone on the black market. I traipsed in the unpleasant humidity to four different banks, each of whom referred me to the next, but without success. I then tried the money transfer stops but they couldn't help me either. Finally one suggested I look for a guy called Mohammed by the betting shop a few streets away.

I found the betting shop as directed and asked around for Mohammed. Two dapper young men who had been hanging about outside decided to make it their mission to assist me in finding the elusive man. No one there seemed to know him, so we started with the shop next door. No, they couldn't help, but perhaps at the back of the shop on the corner? I decided to keep following the leads, hoping that where there was smoke there was cash; and besides, the young men were proving to be fun company. At the

---

[100] Except when Rob tried to get her out of the sand in Senegal and reversed her into a tree… but that doesn't count!

back of the corner shop there was a small yard with chickens running about and some junk, followed by a warren of dark rooms. Mr Dapper One knocked on a door and was told to wait outside, so we waited.

Eventually the door opened to reveal a white man. I was very surprised as I hadn't seen one since Libreville. I presented in my best French that I needed to change money and was looking for someone to help me, and he replied in English (far better than my French) that yes, perhaps he could help. I was both surprised and relieved that he spoke English and berated him in jest for letting me carry on in my shocking French. He gave me a wry smile and introduced himself. His name was Jacques and the rate he offered wasn't great, but I guessed the odds of finding a better one were unlikely; consequently I decided to go on the modest side and only change a small amount. He opened a drawer stuffed full with notes, and I'm certain my eyes widened like saucers as he counted out a small pile and handed it to me. With the transaction complete, I gave him my sincere thanks and bade him a "Bonne journée". Mightily relieved to have topped up with cash, we carried on to the coast. I was grateful that the road conditions had improved: there was almost no traffic and the scenery was quite beautiful.

Mayumba was separated from the mainland by large lagoons and sat on a spit of land which could only be reached by crossing a bridge. On the other side of the bridge we were almost immediately stopped at a checkpoint. I handed the officer the papers and he went off to a table under a large tree and spoke to another man, obviously his superior from his hat and uniform. He returned and asked for our passports, which I showed him but would not let him take. I said if he needed to confirm our identities there they were... but no, he insisted on taking them. I was not happy about this and as a result Officer Superior came along and started berating me in French for being an Anglophone and not speaking French. My response was *I was trying*!! He insisted on taking the passports and it seemed that there was no way out of this, so I reluctantly handed them over and he stalked off.

Some ten minutes and no passports later I got out of the van and walked over to the table, where our details were being written up in a big black ledger by the junior and Officer Superior was scribbling in a notebook. The details are not important, but what ensued was an argument about the return of the passports and him being really rude about Anglophones, adding a hefty dose of officious for good measure. Ursula joined me with a pen and notebook and immediately wrote down his badge number, which was fortunately well displayed on his shirt. This inflamed him and he snatched at the book, but my niece, being swifter, turned and walked determinedly back to my open van door and, with a flourish, tore the page out of the book and placed it with deliberation in the door pocket in full view. Something about this struck me as odd but I returned my attention to Officer Superior. I told him that he could keep the passports for as long as he liked and then I went back to the van too, loudly suggesting to Ursula that we were late for our lunch and now was an ideal opportunity. I made coffee and something to eat and we sat in full view of our captors, dining, laughing and acting as though we didn't have a care in the world.

Once again in hindsight a bribe may well have smoothed the way, but of course it hadn't occurred to me; and by now you know I wasn't going to give the nasty officer a cent. He eventually approached us with our passports and indicated that he would return them in exchange for the page from the notebook, and the reason for my clever niece's actions suddenly became evident. He was facing us with the passports raised in his left hand and I reached down to get the paper from the van door pocket. As I slowly handed it to him, Ursula snatched the passports from his grasp and, with a confident stride, walked to the other side of the van and climbed into the passenger seat. Now that I felt safe I gave him a parting piece of my mind in English, to which he responded with a smirk, clearly believing he had won. But as I drove off Ursula said softly, "There's a copy of his number still in the book" and we both burst out laughing.

It was now nearing 4.00 and the sky was worryingly dark with rain clouds hanging low. There were no campsites. We had planned to look for a place to wild camp, but it would have to be well out of the way in case Officer Superior came trying to find us. We came to a junction and I turned left, and as we drove further it became obvious that while this was a beautiful wilderness, it had almost zero tourism, which was endorsed by the burnt-out buildings at a disused airstrip. We had driven a few kilometres when I spotted a track that turned in the direction of the beach. It was a perfect place to park, with stones on the track for better grip and an uninterrupted view of the ocean and approaching storm. However, there were houses nearby so I decided it was best to check the area before parking up.

As I was looking around a man came out of one of the houses, so I greeted him and asked if it was possible to park overnight. To my surprise he replied in English (that's how bad my French was!) His name was Robert and he was from Ghana, he told me as he happily walked with me towards BlueBelle, and then he said that we could park anywhere we liked as no one would disturb us. I specifically had my eye on that beach view. He informed me that the entire property belonged to a local minister but it was not in use, hence its rather dilapidated state. Robert was employed to keep the place secure but obviously didn't see us as a threat, so I reversed up the lane until the side door was facing the beach. I was very pleased with our spot.

Robert returned a little while later to introduce us to his family: his wife Charlotte, a buxom woman with a sweet personality, and their four children. They were all charming and we had a wonderfully long conversation with them, discussing all manner of things. Charlotte loved baking and was very good at it. She told us she sometimes sold her bread and cakes and her dream was to open a bakery one day. Eventually we were interrupted by the large drops of rain which foretold of the deluge to follow, so we took some quick selfies and agreed to meet up again in the morning.

My fears about the weather proved well-founded. What started as big drops developed into a steady soaking downpour, showing me that the rainy season had not yet fully left the south. My concern was based on the fact that I had heard a couple of weeks earlier from Laurie and Bruce, who were at that time travelling with Michiel, that they had been stuck in deep water and mud for a day on the Gabon-Republic of Congo border crossing. I had hoped that by the time I crossed with Ursula the rain would have moved north of the equator... but for now we were cosy and dry in BlueBelle and fell asleep to the rhythm of the rain drumming on the roof.

In the morning Robert passed by whilst we were having breakfast, so we had a chat and I told him we would be going for a drive into town to get some supplies. This time I had badly underestimated the amount of drinking water we needed, so that was top of the shopping list. Mayumba was considered a tourist town so Ursula and I also wanted to see the sights, but when we arrived we found the whole place consisted of just a bad dirt road and a ragged assortment of small shops. Since one little emporium offered a variety of goods, I added some tinned beans to the necessary water and loaded BlueBelle up, causing some intrigue amongst the locals. As usual we responded with smiles, waves and "Bonjours", to which we received a mixed response.

Hoping to find a beach on the lagoon side of the peninsula, we headed down the main road with thoughts of a café to enjoy a coffee with the spectacular view. I was driving slowly, heeding my broken spring on the uneven dirt road, and we noticed that the area was sparsely littered with simple single-storey homes in a variety of conditions. Our not-very-exciting sightseeing was interrupted abruptly when a 4x4 came racing along and pulled up beside us, its occupant hooting and waving. I stopped, wondering what on earth the problem was.

The man clambered out of his vehicle and rushed over to Ursula's passenger window, babbling something about we should have stopped further back. I am always suspicious of people who are not in uniform[101] telling me what I should or should not be doing, so I advised him curtly that I had observed nothing informing me to stop. He became indignant, insisting that we must turn around and go back to a building some way behind us. He told us that he was with Immigration, so I responded that we had already legally entered the country and had stamps and visas as evidence and I saw no reason for a check there, in the middle of nowhere. (Added to this I had just driven most of the way down this awful road and I was not going back until I saw what was at the end of it.) I informed him that we would pass on our way back, but no, that was not good enough; so then I told him simply that it *was* what I was doing – and besides the only way back was along this road, so what on earth was he worried about?! It seemed

---

[101] ...and sometimes in uniform too!

he finally received the message that I had no reason to evade whatever it was he so desperately needed me to do, and eventually he acquiesced.

We drove on for about another kilometre and were met with a dead end. Now I felt incredibly stupid for insisting on driving down a road that lead to nowhere, and Ursula and I had a good laugh! I turned around, disappointed not to have found either the lagoon or that coffee, and as we drove back we passed the 4x4 that had stopped us. It was parked outside a slightly larger building than the little houses and some men were sitting outside. So this was the Very Important Immigration Office, out there in the middle of nowhere on a dead-end road. Being a Very Important Immigration Officer must be a *very* important job! However, the Very Important Officer checked our passports, smiled and simply let us proceed. We were astounded at the whole incident and couldn't work out why this was such a paranoid place. No wonder there were no tourists here if this was how they treated them!

Ursula and I were now on a serious quest to find something to eat and drink after our unsuccessful mission along the lagoon. We scoured Google Maps and identified a spot that served our purpose and I was about to turn in when a vehicle cut me off. I breathed deeply, remembering that I wasn't in the kind of rush these guys were in. (Actually it was the most activity we had seen in the town thus far!) It seemed we were all going to the same place as I followed them down the muddy and twisted lane until we arrived at a steep slope. I looked at it and reckoned it was OK to go down, however as soon as I was at the bottom I realised that it had not been such a good idea: the slope was muddy and I was concerned that I may not make it back up. I decided to tackle the problem immediately or else I would have spent any potentially enjoyable food and drink time worrying, added to the fact that later there might not be any people around to help, should I need it. I let Ursula out and attacked the track, and all was well until very near the top when the tyres started slipping on the grass and I had to apply the handbrake to prevent BlueBelle from rolling back down.

The men, having watched me, decided to come and provide their 'expert advice', and they decided to push while I coaxed her up. Fortunately, within a few minutes of touch and go she got enough of a shove to make it to safety, so I parked her on the side of the road and joined everyone back at the bottom. The bar was there but in a dilapidated condition, and there was no food and only one type of beer, but I bought the guys some large beers and Ursula and I shared one with lemonade as a panaché. ARA 10 : DB 5

Disappointed that our watering-hole lacked any of the things we had been looking for, we took the time to reassess our situation. Our general location was nice enough overall – apart from the official harassment – but it didn't have much to offer. I shared with Ursula my concern about the rain and the road and we decided to return to Ndendé and continue to the border the next day. Whilst the sun had returned and it was now baking hot again, the clouds in the distance suggested that more rain was imminent so it seemed sensible. However, we could not leave without saying goodbye to our new friends.

When we returned Robert and Charlotte were delighted to see us. They didn't know our whereabouts of course and thought we had already left. We updated them of our plans to leave and gave them some money for our parking the night before. They were both adamant that they would not accept our money, but I pressed the notes firmly into Charlotte's hand, telling her that it was our investment in her bakery and she could not return it. With a teary smile she accepted it, admitting that no one believed in her like we did, and it brought tears to my own eyes that this wonderful woman had never felt the confidence of another. We said our goodbyes then, but Robert and Charlotte remain in regular contact via WhatsApp, and one day I hope to be able to tell you all about her bakery...

When we passed the checkpoint at the bridge we were not stopped again and heaved a great sigh of relief. We'd had enough of the officials there! What with the shopping and the financial gift to Charlotte, I was once again almost out of cash. I was constantly in that struggle of not having enough liquidity and yet not wanting to repeat my Guinea experience. I still needed to refuel prior to crossing the border so I decided to visit Jacques again for some more cash out of his drawer, which he obliged with the same wry smile as before.

It was late afternoon by the time we reached Ndendé. We tried to get our passports stamped out at the police station so that we could make an early start, but we were out of luck: they were closed and would only reopen at 8.00 the next day. We fuelled up – one thing less we needed to do in the morning – and as the 'hotel' in the town refused us parking, we returned to the mission for our final night.

ACCOMPANIED BY AN ANGEL

We were bright and early at the police station and an officer indicated for us to take a seat at one of two old wooden desks in the room. There was the obligatory writing into the regulation big black ledgers, followed by the search for a working stamp pad. Whilst this was all happening I enquired about the condition of the road to the border. The officer had no idea but suggested I ask the man in the blue t-shirt who was sitting at the other desk, also having his papers seen to. I did so in my simple French and the man said little but intimated that the road was not good. I asked how much water there was and would I get through in my van, but he shook his head and mentioned something about towing.

I heard him, but I ignored him – after all, what was I going to do, go back?! Nope, the only way was forward, and much like the rest of my challenges, this one would have a solution too. I translated what I had understood to Ursula and we agreed that we would see what we would see... and set off. They probably thought that we would be back again later that day; at the very least they must have considered us insane!

The tarmac ended abruptly as we left the town and it was unclear whether we were on the right track or not. It was a familiar mix of uneven potholed dirt and mud, but according to the locals we asked we were indeed heading for the border. I was driving again since by now I was well acquainted with BlueBelle's preferences on dirt roads, although I had no idea how I would handle the mud; I'd not had enough experience to feel confident. However, as with everything, practice makes perfect and I was sure I'd get the hang of it soon enough.

In writing this I must take a moment to reflect on how much I had come to trust that there would be a solution for every problem this journey threw at me; indeed it had been proven time and again. I had gained a level of confidence and acceptance – an assurance even – that I believe I'd always had deep down, but which had come out in full force. In hindsight I do believe that there was something insane and yet magical about my journey. I also often wonder (especially whilst writing my stories down) whether I would be able to exactly replicate the experience, even with all the insight and knowledge I gained along the way.

Ursula had come fully equipped with a homeopathic kit[102] comprising several small brown bottles filled with tiny pills for the treatment of all sorts of ailments and conditions. The dust has set off my sinuses and my shoulder was again taking strain, the combination giving me a headache on top of my stress. She plied me with a variety of remedies at regular intervals whilst I was driving, and I was most impressed as they all seemed to work rather well. She also took on the duty of feeding me from the jar of mixed dried fruit and nuts that she had brought with her, making sure that I was regularly nourished and my blood sugar levels were good. It was nice to be taken care of for a while.

The road was dusty in some parts and muddy in others. The rain evaporated off the higher sections very quickly, but there were sections of pure mud interspersed with often murky pools of unknown depths and hidden mysteries. My deflated tyres were helping me navigate, and having successfully traversed a few challenging sections I was feeling quite proud of myself. It was only forty kilometres: this would be fine.

The elation didn't last long. After several kilometres of slow driving, still nursing the spring (which made an awful noise when I wasn't careful), I was gaining confidence and at one point I moved aside to allow a very large aggregate-type truck to pass. Unusually he didn't pull ahead at great speed but instead remained at a close pace in front of me. I didn't particularly notice at first because I was watching the road, but after a few muddy pools I realised his indicator lights were flashing alternately, and it was always the same side as the side of the puddle that afforded me the easiest crossing. I thought it coincidence at first until we had

---

102 This, along with colloidal silver and aloe vera, has become part of my essential health care supply: www.pegasuskits.com/the-bluebox-kit

been through a few more, whereupon I turned to Ursula and exclaimed, "This guy is indicating which side of the puddle to pass!" She looked at me sceptically and then made a noise in disbelief. "No really, watch!" I told her, and as we did so my guess was confirmed.

This excellent system worked for several kilometres until the truck passed through a particularly nasty muddy pool, and when I saw the height of the water against his much larger tyres I knew that it wasn't going to be possible for BlueBelle. I pulled over and the truck stopped on the far side. I jumped out to assess the situation and look for options and simultaneously a man in a blue t-shirt got down from the cab. We stood on either side of the pool, looking at each other. He motioned that I should go, but I shook my head that it wasn't going to be possible, so he told me to wait while he checked if there was another way across. He climbed back into his cab, reversed through the muddy morass and aligned himself for an alternative route, but as he drove through he slipped like a kid on a waterslide. He deftly adjusted course and, once back on the other side, he again got out and shook his head in agreement with me.

Most of the conversation had taken place in sign language, because he was French-speaking with zero English while I was doing the best I could with my pidgin French. I asked if he would tow me across but he shrugged that he didn't have a tow rope. I *knew* that purchase would come in handy again! I nodded excitedly that I had one and set off to dig it out of the back of the van. For safety's sake I also took out the air filter and put a bag over the box, hoping that this would prevent water from getting into the engine. Then I lined up behind his truck and he hooked us together and motioned for me to turn slightly left before moving carefully off.

The tow rope tightened but, still unaccustomed to being towed, I had overturned the steering wheel and got seriously stuck in the mud at the edge of the road – and one of the straps snapped. The truck was now in the middle of the water and the driver climbed out and walked along the side of the truck toward me to reassess what to do. By now another truck was held up behind us and the occupants also came to help. They tied the remaining strap into a convoluted knot and, with an extra push from the rear, the big truck pulled us through the water. I was convinced that Ursula and I were both holding our breath during the entire procedure, but rather the video evidence (taken by Ursula) gives me away: I was not so much holding my breath as I was swearing and praying at the same time! Throughout the towing I could feel BlueBelle sliding freely in the mud and knew I could never have made it to the other side without all the help.

Once through this pool – which was a good few metres wide – the truck did not stop, and I had no option but to continue being towed. My primary job was to pay close attention to my saviour to ensure that I didn't end up in the back of his truck, and I was once again reminded of how helpless and out of control I felt and how much I disliked it. We continued through another two slightly smaller, but still as intimidating, pools before he stopped and unhooked me, but indicated that he would keep the strap on his truck until we were certain it wasn't needed again.

I could not begin to express the relief I felt at this man's assistance, or that of the men in the truck behind us who chose not to pass but escorted us from the rear. Ursula and I were laughing, huge guffaws that only come with the release from stress, at the fact that we now had front and rear escorts. We must have looked a sight: two huge, mud-splattered trucks with little BlueBelle in the middle. We were also bursting with sheer gratitude for them being there to help us.

The road continued to be challenging but without any more large muddy ponds, so although the going was slow we made progress. But then more problems: a truck was stuck on the side of the track next to an impassable morass of mud that had clearly been churned up by bigger trucks. We all stopped and got out to see how we could proceed and it seemed the only way to get past the truck and avoid the mud was to make a tricky left-right manoeuvre between them. It was impossible to be towed through this, so I had to do my best to drive it solo and stay 'on track'.

Our front escort went first and once he was clear I followed, keeping a steady pace. If I faltered I would certainly get stuck. The manoeuvre meant a slight right turn just past the truck's front bumper and then immediately left. I thought I was doing OK, but then I felt BlueBelle slip and hit the truck. The only thing in my mind was that I needed to keep going, because if I stopped that would be that! I pushed her forward to the sound of scraping metal... and then I came free and guided her up the slight rise to be clear of the mud.

I got out and assessed the damage. It was nasty: I had 'can-opened' the side of my beloved van from the passenger door right into the sliding door, the metal torn away leaving jagged edges and no way to open either of the doors. I was devastated, mad at myself and generally pissed off. However, there was no way to fix it there and we were not done yet.

The men used my crowbar to get the front wing off the tyre and I managed to push some of the most jagged edges back, but it was still a mess. From inside the footwell you could see the road, which meant that once conditions were dry then red dust would be pouring into the van. It was at this juncture that our front escort told us the road would be manageable from then on and unhooked the tow rope. I asked his name and I think he mumbled "Salvo" when I gave him a wad of money (although he didn't seem to be expecting anything). Ursula had looked up the French words for 'saviour' and 'hero' on Google Translate and we enthusiastically expressed our gratitude so that he would understand us because he truly was both. He merely nodded stoically.

The men in our rear guard said that they would stay behind us for a while longer, which was exceptionally kind of them and thoroughly reassuring. Off we trundled. The mud had somewhat subsided, but we were still not going very fast.

It was only as my mind started to relax a bit more and I was replaying the morning's events and wondering at such immense kindness from a stranger that it suddenly came to me: Salvo, our 'Saviour', was the man sitting next to us at the police station that morning. I had been so focused on the task at hand that I hadn't thought about anything else – until now! I excitedly told Ursula, but she hadn't had a good look at him because she had been too busy watching the policeman with our documents. She agreed it was an incredible stroke of luck that he had taken pity on us, and we could only imagine him impassively telling his friends over a beer that he had come to the rescue of two silly middle-aged women trying to drive that road in a 2WD van. Honestly, tourists!!

Eventually just before lunch we came to the border post that was another building on its own in the middle of nowhere. We all entered: the three men from our rear-guard went into the office on the right and Ursula and I the one on the left.

At that moment, I did wonder what would have happened if we hadn't checked iOverlander and found out about the mandatory stop at the police station in Ndendé. If we had missed it, would they have turned us back now? I quickly moved on from that thought: it would have broken me to have done that road three times!

The immigration officer thankfully spoke some English and we had a pleasant chat whilst enduring the usual black book entries. When I noticed the men from the truck waving outside the window, I excused myself to shake their hands and again thank them from the bottom of my heart for their assistance. Waving goodbye, I realised I'd met more angels in one day than I could ever have imagined. ARA 11 : DB 5

Chapter Thirteen – Republic of the Congo

23 May 2019

Stamps and paperwork thankfully done, we pulled up under a nearby tree to catch our breath and have something to eat before facing our next foray into ROC, the Republic of the Congo. I was sitting in the driver's seat with my arm resting out of the window, but no sooner had I started to relax than some biting thing found me and proceed to eat my forearm. It hurt like a demon and a large red swelling quickly emerged. I didn't see what it was; I just know that it was a… biting thing… And boy, do they love me!

We drove the mostly dry, dusty road to the next country – my thirteenth in Africa and one that also used CFA, so fortunately changing money was not required. It was again some distance to the Congo border post, and just as we were questioning whether we were on the right track a few tired buildings appeared. There were some men sitting outside the ones to the left amongst some empty stalls, indicating that a market was held there sometimes, but we stopped at the building on the right: it looked more 'official'. A man came out and motioned us to the other side of the road, and on closer inspection the motley array of single-storey buildings behind the stalls did appear to be offices, although they were old and grubby with paint peeling off the walls and ceilings from years of neglect. As we walked past the group of men and greeted them, a tall man addressed us and directed us to follow him into a small room dominated by an old colonial desk, where we were asked to take a seat on some decidedly dodgy ancient chairs. Having handed over our passports, we watched as he set to seriously inspecting them and our visas, followed by logging several entries into the ubiquitous big black books.

My passport duly recorded in the annals of time, he attended to Ursula's, but he was really taking his sweet time so I enquired about the TIP, hoping to achieve that while I was waiting. I was directed to a different building to the side, but there was no one there. I looked at the men sitting on wooden benches in the shade of a large mango tree, and seeing me they shouted out to someone (I assumed the person who should have been in the office). After a few minutes, a man with a large wooden spoon and a dirty white apron appeared from behind the buildings. Apparently he was the local cook… but surely he couldn't be in charge of sorting out my TIP?! However, on seeing me he put down the spoon, took off his apron and walked into the office, taking a seat behind another ancient desk and directing me to sit too. I confess to feeling mightily uncertain about the local cook dealing with my papers, especially when he informed me that I should pay him for the TIP.

There had been mixed reports about whether the TIP was free or not, but if there *was* to be a payment it was due in the next town, Nyanga; this border post should merely have needed me to sign in. I expressed my misgivings about the fee, which clearly surprised Mr Chef, as did the fact that I knew about the Nyanga office. He assured me that it definitely *wasn't* free and I would have to complete and pay at the border and not in Nyanga because apparently the Chief there was at a funeral. So here I was, with a man who not five minutes before had been in a food-spattered apron telling me that I must give him cash to get my documents here. 'Dubious' was an understatement! I asked him how I was to know that he was actually a customs officer and authorised to provide me such documents, so he made a phone call – allegedly to the Chief – to confirm. I was still suspicious because he could have called anyone… But at that point I was recalled to the passport office.

I returned with my passport a few moments later to find Mr Chef gone. I waited for a bit and then went back to the van with Ursula to fetch some money, but after ten minutes Mr Chef was still nowhere to be found, so I figured I would just take my chances in Nyanga. As I turned towards BlueBelle I saw him coming out of an ablution block with a towel around his waist and looking all clean and shiny, and wondered about that. I waited impatiently for a few more minutes, and then just as I had again had enough, he came walking towards me, this time in full uniform.

"Merci," I said, for want of anything better to say. I could now confirm that he *was* an officer, but this did not prevent me from giving him a lecture about how I would be returning to get my money back and beat him up if I found out he was stealing from me! He smiled and assured me that everything was as it should be, but because I still felt a bit unsure, I wrote down his name.

Ursula had the privilege of putting the Congo sticker on the window before we trundled off down the dirt road with the music from our broken doors and spring gaily accompanying us. I had by now become accustomed to the variety of ramshackle border posts, but it was Ursula's comment on this, her first border crossing on this journey, that made me think how little a government can respect its employees to have them working in such conditions. Indeed it was an indictment to *all* such governments who did not give their employees proper working conditions, leaving the door wide open for the corruption I had previously seen.

Having left behind the rich, lush rainforests of Gabon, the countryside remained green but less dense and eventually turned into a mix of shrubbery and grassland. The landscape was again transformed as we passed through an extensive area of low hills covered with long tufty grass which looked a bit like burial mounds, but there were too many and the area was too vast for that. The lack of villages and just the long, light green grass that swayed elegantly in the breeze suggested a reserve of some sort and, sure enough, one map verified that it was the *Domaine de Chasse de Mont Marvoumbou*, a Congolese National Park. Several other maps showed a tarmacked road a short distance to the left of our little blue dot (which seemed to be in the middle of nowhere), but no matter which map we looked at, there was just no way to get from where we were to this mystical thoroughfare.

We continued along the dry dust until it eventually became muddy again. It had obviously been raining in the area and I must have become weary because I misjudged one particular section and we ended up stuck in mud again on the edge of the road. It was precisely what I *didn't* need after an already trying day! I got out to judge how bad the situation was and saw I was in trouble on the left rear wheel, but felt that some digging would get us free. As I was preparing myself some young kids came along, one probably no more than nine and the other, a sharp operator, about fourteen. Young Sharp told me he could fetch a shovel from the nearby village but the man would ask a fee, so I agreed to the small cost. Little Lacky was sent off with the money to fetch the shovel and upon his return Young Sharp negotiated a fee to get me out. It was more than the shovel would have cost but would save me some unpleasant mud-work, so I agreed. The lad set about his job, but after a good attempt it seemed that the front wheel also needed digging out. They were almost done when two older men came along and enquired after the situation, but when they found out that I was paying Young Sharp, they were outraged and gave him a severe talking-to and told him that he should accompany us further down the road. Evidently they knew something I did not.

Having cleared the mud I still had to traverse a large muddy pool. I had walked through it while the guys were digging to assess its depth and what I might find under the wheels, and Young Sharp indicated that going through the middle was the best option. I trusted that he knew best, after all he would be digging me out himself if he was wrong – and I *wouldn't* be paying extra for it! Having passed through relatively easily, we loaded Young Sharp into BlueBelle under the watchful eye of the men and drove down the road a few more kilometres. Here we came to a hideously muddy mess, which I most certainly would not have been able to negotiate alone. Young Sharp, however, had already made a plan. To the left of the road he had cut out of the brush a track that was both dry and passable and set booms on either side. Although my French was limited I clearly understood, as he proudly showed me the way, that it was *his* track and he would move the booms to let us pass. Clever young man was also charging a toll to people who wished to pass this way, and the men further back had negotiated the inclusion of this toll within my already paid fee. This little guy was going to be a *very* rich entrepreneur in the future, I was certain of it! ARA 12 : DB 5

Thankfully the track became dry and dusty once again, but with all the hassles of the day we had only covered about sixty kilometres and it would soon be dark. I had already established that the only place we could park up was at the prefecture in Nyanga, so I drove as fast as I could on the uneven dirt road with the sun setting rapidly beside me, and we made it into town just as the last rays of light were disappearing. I asked at the office if we could park up in front of the building for the night and yes, it was possible, so we did... next to a large truck.

In the glow of the light outside the prefecture, I took a good look at BlueBelle's injuries. I was quite frankly depressed about her state and wondered how on earth I would be able to get her fixed out here. Meanwhile Ursula had fallen in love with the dozens of pygmy goats that were settling down for the night in little clumps around the large grounds. I had already seen enough of those goats to last a lifetime.

As I returned to the driver's side I noticed something extraordinary: the truck I was parked next to was Salvo's! I shouted out to Ursula, and she replied that it couldn't possibly be, but I was certain of it. I'd been staring at the rear of it for long enough! She found a photo of the truck when it was towing us and indeed, it was Salvo's.

Although we tried to find him, we gave up after a while and went back to eat. Dinner was a simple affair; I wasn't up to much after the trying day. We ate outside on the steps of the prefecture because the van was hot inside and we were unable to open anything other than the driver's door. We sat in silence, both of us exhausted and neither looking forward to a hot and sticky night in the dusty van, but the Universe smiled on us when we finally saw Salvo back at his truck with a few other men. We greeted him enthusiastically and again thanked him profusely for his aid, and in the same manner as before, he stoically nodded his head and left.

OUT ON THE TOWN IN DOLISIE

The next morning we knew that we had to check in at the police station for the signing of the black ledgers before continuing. We had another day of driving on dirt road to our next stop, Dolisie, and I was praying for it to be dry. We set off from Nyanga and not far out we passed a man I had seen the previous evening as we arrived in town. He had stepped to the side of the road as we passed, turned and given us a thumbs-up, and at the time I had noted his very kind face and a huge backpack. That morning he had done the same again, stopped, turned and given us another thumbs-up. I cannot account for why, but I felt I needed to stop and speak to him.

I reversed to pull up alongside him and Ursula wound down her window. I asked him where he was going and he replied to the next village, so I looked at Ursula and said, "Let's give him a lift." She agreed eagerly and went to sit on the sofa at the back as I helped him and his enormous backpack get in via the driver's door. He was quietly spoken and knew only a few words of English, and my few words of French were limited to police checkpoints and border crossings or asking about parking, so not really suited to general conversation.

However, as I like to say: a willingness to communicate was all that was needed. I gleaned that he was from Pointe-Noire on the coast of ROC, at least three hundred kilometres from where we were, and his backpack was filled with medications – painkillers, generic over-the-counter medications, bandages and so on. This may seem strange to most readers, but imagine a world where the nearest pharmacy or doctor's clinic is hundreds of kilometres away – if you can afford it, that is. This Samaritan was fulfilling the role of travelling pharmacy, and he was on foot because the cost of a taxi would erode the small sums of money he made to support his family in Pointe-Noire. I can tell you, it was no small feat to be walking along these dusty roads in the heat and humidity each day carrying that heavy backpack, and I was filled with admiration for him.

As we passed through the villages I waved and the children constantly shouted back at us as we drove by. They shouted one of two things, and the first we deciphered was they were asking for a ball. This was such a simple plaything but something that was evidently dreamt about by children throughout Africa. A ball was an absolute treasure to them and provided endless hours of entertainment. The other cry, we came to realise, was "Gimme!" with outstretched hands opening and closing. There was no way I could ever conceive of enough money to support all of these children, but the least I could do was offer a smile and wave, as paltry as they were. However, my guest could not believe what he was hearing and was appalled at their behaviour. The cultural differences between us were obvious, as I'm certain he was never greeted in this way.

When he told me about his work I asked if he had something for the bite on my arm, which was now a big red angry-looking blob which both hurt and itched. I had tried not to scratch it, knowing that this would simply make it worse. He dug in his bag on the floor in front of him and brought out a small tube of white ointment, which he assured me would work. I immediately applied some on to the bite and, lo and behold, within ten minutes I had relief!

It was not at the next village but a fair number later that we dropped our new friend off. We weren't at all bothered by this. It wasn't out of our way and we felt that it would be of substantial help to him, saving him at least a day of walking. When he did eventually ask us to stop, thanking me humbly for the ride, I offered to pay him for the tube of miracle medicine, but he steadfastly refused to take my money. Ursula took a photo of us and with a wave goodbye we left him to his work, as the local villagers came up to greet him enthusiastically.[103]

We got into Dolisie as night was falling to find ourselves in the midst of hectic traffic, and tried to navigate our way to a small hotel that sometimes allowed parking since there were again no campsites in the city. When we arrived I couldn't immediately find any staff, but a man eventually approached and haughtily advised us that we could park up for the exorbitant equivalent of $8 per person – and that would *not* include any shower option. By now we were covered in red dust and had not had a decent wash since Lambaréné, so that was, by any standards, an outrageous price for nothing. Nevertheless I thanked him politely, got back in the van and drove off. No matter how tired or late we were, I was not going to pay up for that!

We headed to the next hotel which had no parking, but they would let us have a room for $40 per person. So nope, off to another place around the corner, where this time they said we could make use of the small parking area within the walls of their compound plus a room with a shower, all for just $15. That sounded more like it! As BlueBelle could not be properly secured at that time, I decided that I would sleep in the van and Ursula in

[103] While I was writing this book, his son sent a message to tell me that his father often spoke of me and had proudly kept my business card.

the room. I blessed the Universe that we had finally stumbled across this hotel. The dust in the van was thick, especially around the sofa where Ursula had been sleeping.

First on the agenda was a shower, cold and invigorating, and then some clean clothes. The shower floor was positively red as the water washed out days of dust, again returning me from strawberry blonde to my natural colour. Feeling totally refreshed, we decided that cooking was out of the question. However, we were on a main road and had spotted some restaurants, so we went out to see what we could find. The streets were as busy as during the day, with garish neon lights lighting up the bars and clubs and hawkers still selling their wares and cooking on the side of the street. We were soaking up the atmosphere and I was, as usual, greeting everyone I walked past, friendliness being the best form of defence.

We identified a nice-looking place, its tables and chairs set outside with a long buffet table where you could select the food you wanted; and best of all a meal would only cost us a dollar each! We selected our food and drinks, and as the only two blondes in the place, took our seats – to the highly interested looks of the locals – just as the music started. Congolese music has a very specific rhythm and sound to it and I found this great listening, albeit a little loud for my tinnitus-affected ears. We chatted and laughed and ate and drank, with the blessed relief that followed days of mud, dust and tension.

After our meal, we returned exhausted to the hotel to grab enough sleep to tackle the next day. Our plan was to reach Pointe-Noire and get BlueBelle repaired.

TENDING TO BLUEBELLE

Before leaving Dolisie, after days of driving on deflated tyres it was important to have them inflated and also fill up with fuel. Ursula topped up too with take-away croissants and coffee from the local shop, and I then handed over the keys for her to drive. The road would be tarmac and I'd had my fill of driving for now! The conditions to Pointe-Noire were indeed good with little traffic, and I enjoyed the view from the passenger seat as we wound our way through the magnificent mountains.

The night before we left, Ursula had contacted her friend Peggy, who had recently been in Pointe-Noire, to ask for any local information that might help us. Peggy had organised a contact to be our fixer in the city, a guy by the name of Patrick who thankfully spoke English and would sort out whatever we needed to get BlueBelle repaired. This was incredibly helpful to us as it would otherwise take a lot of time to locate the right people and places, especially with my limited French. We needed to keep moving as we had just over a week left to get Ursula to Luanda, from where she was flying back home.

Pointe-Noire is the second-largest city in the Republic of the Congo (the capital is Brazzaville) and the main commercial centre of the country. This was announced as we arrived by an informal market stretching for miles. There were traders along every inch of the trash-littered road, some with rickety wooden frames from which hung any manner of strange things, and those less wealthy simply sitting or standing with their wares in the dust. All types of goods were available: clothes, pots, plastic goods, motor spares, electrical parts, mobile phones... As with all African markets, you can find pretty much anything you need if you are diligent enough.

We were looking out for Patrick and he was on this street, somewhere, looking out for us. He finally told us via WhatsApp that we had already passed him, so we stopped and waited for him to reach us. Once we had located, greeted and loaded him into BlueBelle, our first task was to find accommodation for the night. I took over the wheel, being more experienced with chaotic African city driving, and Patrick directed us to a hotel he could recommend, not in the tourist sector but in a residential area some distance from the city centre.

I usually have a good sense of people and something about Patrick made me uncomfortable. He was cocky and somehow mistook us for the expats he usually looked after, believing that he could dictate our actions – big mistake! However, I realised that I was in a situation where he presented our easiest option, so I figured I just had to keep an eye on him and not let on that I actually knew a bit more French than he thought.

In my research I had noticed that hotels in Pointe-Noire were expensive, but we would need to spend a couple of nights at least while BlueBelle was being fixed. We reached the place Patrick had recommended and I remained in the van (which was blocking most of the narrow alleyway) while he went with Ursula to ask about a room. While I was waiting I chatted with the locals hanging about in the street, and one even tried to sell me his wares. Ursula and Patrick returned to advise me that the hotel was full.

Patrick had earlier called some panel beaters to come and take a look at the van, and they found us in the alley at the hotel discussing options. They were two young fellows who told us that they would take the doors away for two to three days, repair them and return them to us for 30,000 francs (about $55). I told them that there was no way they were doing that: I knew that 'two to three days' could turn into a week or more and we simply didn't have that kind of time – not to mention the security issues I would have with BlueBelle full of my 'valuables' and no doors! "No," was my answer, so they shrugged and left.

We moved on to Plan B – in more ways than one because that was the name of the next hotel. We had been referred there by the first hotel as it seemed to be their overflow option. Must do good business, I thought. Ursula went in to enquire but came out shortly afterwards, saying their only availability was a dark and dingy room at the end of a passage. She also expressed concern that the room rates listed at reception showed that they were available by the hour, and she'd seen some elegant women seated on sofas and 'dressed for the occasion'. We opted to try a place listed on iOverlander in the city, and Patrick came along with us to check it out.

On our way there we passed the usual traders and businesses on the sides of the wide dusty road, and Patrick spotted a panel beater with a shack for an office and several cars parked outside in various stages of repair. Patrick called him over to the window and did some negotiating in French and informed me that the sum was similarly 30,000 francs, so I agreed but on the conditions that (a) he finished it in a day, (b) we stayed with the van and (c) they had to be ready to start at 9.00 the following morning – even though it was a Sunday. The man eagerly nodded.

The next hotel option didn't look like much from the outside and again Ursula and Patrick went in to check it out. Ursula returned with a look of horror on her face and told me it was more hostel than a hotel and a poor one at that: the rooms were dirty and in dreadful condition, with doors not closing properly and filthy shared bathrooms; apparently it looked more like a squatter hold-out than a hotel! We decided to grit our teeth and return to Plan B... but first I had to find a Western Union for cash, which I would need to cover the mounting costs of repairs and accommodation.

The centre of Pointe-Noire was like that of any modern-day city, with supermarkets, car dealerships, banks and boutiques... and hectic traffic. At the Western Union I got my cash, and now I was ready to get things done. I asked Patrick if he needed to return to the hotel or if we could leave him in the city, but he was adamant that he should stay with us as we would need him. Ursula and I looked at each other: obviously he had underestimated us! We firmly told him that we would have no problems finding our way back to the hotel, but he continued to insist that he should stay with us until I managed to divert his attention by telling him to find me a mechanic and meet us at 9.00 the next morning at the panel beater's. Finally getting the message, he agreed and we went on our way.

Plan B[104] was not a very big hotel, but it did have space for us to park securely between the two buildings – and that was most important. When we returned they showed us to a better room near reception, and while I was planning to sleep in the van for security, I did really want to take advantage of the bathroom after a day of dashing about. Things always looked better after a cold shower. Nothing would improve the décor of the room though: while it was clean, the green walls and thick red velveteen curtains were quite garish! It was still light outside and Ursula took responsibility for the Very Important Tradition of setting up our sundowner drinks while I, preferring air over air-conditioning, opened the curtains and windows which looked out on to the driveway between the two buildings. It was barely seconds though before there was a knock at the door and we were told that we could not have either our windows or our curtains open, to which we simultaneously launched into a tirade of, "What the heck?!" – but of course we were forced to comply in order to keep our room.

---

[104] www.facebook.com/PlanBPNR

It was obvious that the hourly clientele were concerned about their privacy – as if we knew or cared!

About ten minutes later they came to tell us that they had made an error in the booking and would we mind going to another room? (Funny, that.) I said we would consider it but they should show us the room first, so they led us to a large suite across the driveway, right next to where BlueBelle was parked. I couldn't believe our luck! Two disgruntled 'ladies' came out as we arrived, and on entering we found a bedroom with an en-suite shower, a lounge area and a small kitchen. I saw the advantage of this suite immediately but naturally didn't want to appear too keen, so I told them that we would consider it but I wasn't able to pay any more. Of course they said that there would be no extra charge, so I tried not to smile too widely and agreed to move. In hindsight they probably considered that we posed too much of a disturbance for their 'regular business' and it was better to keep us out of the way.

There was an immediate change of plan now that we had space and it made sense to take most of our things out of the van and lock them in the room. With the work being done the next day on BlueBelle I wanted there to be as few 'nickables' as possible. Inside she was shrouded with red dust, so thick you could write your name on just about everything. It all had to be washed down and cleaned before setting it aside, so the kitchen was coming in very handy. Once again the Universe did a splendid job of over-delivering on what we needed. Our bedding, cushions and clothes were all infused with the same red dust too, so we set down a huge pile of washing on the floor to attend to later. Exhausted by the end of that, we resumed our drinks and relaxed for a while. I was even looking forward to being able to sleep comfortably on the sofa in the room that night and keep an eye on BlueBelle through the window, since she was of course unlocked.

The plan was to divide and conquer: I would attend to BlueBelle and Ursula would sort out the washing. But when I saw the manager and asked about a laundromat, he immediately offered a member of the staff to do the washing for a nominal fee. Ursula looked delighted – there really was a lot of it – and I also noted that the aversion to household chores ran in the family. At any rate, this left her free to help me.

The next morning, after a sound night's sleep in our 'suite', we were surprised but delighted to find the panel beater and his team ready and waiting for us when we arrived. They set about banging and reshaping the doors and adjusting them so that they were in just the right place to open and close, and while they were doing this Ursula and I began to undertake cleaning the inside of the van. I had several bottles of tap water, a bucket and plenty of cleaning cloths, and the water was deep red within seconds. Patrick sauntered in around 11.00 and I punished him for his tardiness by sending him on an errand to buy cold drinks for everyone, which he seemed none too pleased about.

Shortly after returning, Patrick took on his translator role and advised that we needed to go somewhere a few kilometres away where they could use an oxyacetylene torch to weld the pieces of the doors together. Everyone piled into BlueBelle – I was pleased we had taken out a lot of the things to make room – and we set off. We drove to a large empty space in the middle of a housing area – or at least it would have been empty had it not been full of taxis in various states of disrepair. I pulled up in the only vacant spot, trying not to block the thoroughfare.

No sooner had I switched off the engine than the sound of caterwauling hit us. It was a Sunday, and diagonally opposite the open lot was a small building obviously being used as a church. I usually thoroughly enjoy the sound of African singing, but this was the worst sound I had *ever* heard – worse even than the howling of the early morning preaching in Ghana. And if that wasn't bad enough, to add to the agony it was being blasted out to the entire neighbourhood via the loudest speakers known to humankind! I don't know how long it went on for but suffice to say it felt like an eternity, and Ursula kept laughing every time I said, "FFS are they not done yet?!" And it was not only out of tune but amplified to boot!! I was in hell.

The sound of the panel beating continued to fight the noise of the wailing (sorry, *singing*) and Ursula and I continued cleaning away the layers of red dust that had found every nook and cranny in BlueBelle. Due to the heat, the remaining doors were open to facilitate some ventilation, and in true African fashion, passers-by often stopped to peer curiously inside. I was informed that the sight of two women 'like us' doing any kind of cleaning was particularly intriguing. I answered lots of the typical kinds of questions about where I was from: "Zimbabwe, and yes there are white people there!" and "No, there is no man!" I very much enjoyed the chit-chat and had a lot of fun with them. Eventually I was advised that the doors were fixed, so I made certain that they could do what doors do and, after a few minor adjustments, BlueBelle had survived her fifty-dollar African Panel Beating Job. It wasn't pretty – we didn't have time for pretty – but the doors worked and the dust invasion should be alleviated.

Everyone clambered into the van and we returned to the panel beating 'shop', where I gave Patrick the cash to pay the guys and also something extra to them without him seeing (the reason for which will become evident later). Then we went back to the hotel, where I enquired of Patrick where the mechanic was. He mumbled some excuse but assured me we would see him the next day. It would be necessary for us to stay an additional night.

The hotel driveway was occupied, so I waited outside the gate while Ursula went in to see if we would be able to keep the room for another night. Fortunately they let us use the same suite at the same price, which was a relief because we had stuff literally everywhere; and since our washing had apparently been done by hand, with all the humidity it was still wet.

Whilst I was waiting in my van in front of the gate, a very dapper man in his late fifties wearing a smart African print shirt came out and greeted me. I assumed that he had been using the hotel for an hour's entertainment as I'd not seen him around earlier. He obviously spoke some English because he came up to the open passenger window and said to me, "Madam, where is your chauffeur?" and I replied, "I *am* the chauffeur," and he laughed and chatted to me a bit. When I commented that I liked his shirt, he made a suggestion that I might like to entertain him – erm, thanks but, well, no thanks! I deflected him with humour and he asked again where my driver was, to which I reiterated that I *was* the driver and slapped the steering wheel, and he suddenly realised that I was in a RHD vehicle.

He looked utterly shocked. I explained that I was waiting for the other vehicle in the driveway to move, and he said that it was his and he would now be leaving. He expressed some concern that I would have to reverse down the road, so I told him that I would pull forward so that he could pass me and then reverse into the driveway. I would *reverse* into the driveway? he enquired incredulously. My response: "Yes indeed, a woman *can* reverse!"

I continued cleaning BlueBelle the following day, this time attending to the other end because so much dust had been sucked into the rear storage too. I was out of data and had asked Ursula to go down the road to buy some credit. (I still had a little money on the phone and just needed the top-up ticket so that I could buy the data, which was only sold in small bundles.) Meanwhile Patrick appeared with the mechanic, who started to check the steering and broken spring. I was busy with boxes and dust when Ursula returned, but without my realising it Patrick had also taken it on himself to sort out my data top-up, and I came around the corner to find him with my phone. When I asked what the *heck* he thought he was doing, he guiltily blurted out that he was helping me. I was hopping mad. I snatched back my phone to check what he'd done, only to find that he had purchased a package that gave me *less* data for the price; and on top of that my balance was gone – all of it! I asked him what he was playing at and he denied any knowledge of my balance, but there were missing confirmation messages which should have come when he purchased the package and I strongly suspected he had done something – either to buy himself a package or to move the funds. I was beyond furious by now. I could not prove it without the confirmation messages, but something was very wrong.

Despite my rage I left the phone alone – there was nothing I could do about it now – and turned my attention to my van. The spring had been removed and the mechanic was saying that part of the steering needed to be replaced as it was not looking at all good; and he recommended doing both sides. I had no idea what this was but it looked as worn as the mechanic had intimated. Most astonishing though was to find that two of the bolts on the left part had completely sheared through. This was probably the noise that Ursula and I kept hearing on the way from Gabon. It was sheer luck that we hadn't had something go wrong on the road and I was elated it had been identified then, because heaven only knew what could have gone wrong further down the line!

The mechanic was confident he could find parts, but I was dubious and gave him direct and clear instructions: "Do *not* bring me anything that is not *exactly* the same as these parts. Don't bring me *similar* or *almost*, bring me *precisely* what is here or don't bother – and bring back the original parts!" Patrick estimated what the cost should be and, although I was rather taken aback at the amount, I reckoned that this was an essential fix to save us even greater problems further on.

Three hours later they returned. Firstly, I was presented with a bill that was considerably higher than estimated, and secondly, I had to pay on top of that the taxi fares to and from. My expenses were mounting horribly. I checked the replacement parts. The steering parts, under my unprofessional inspection, looked exactly the same but the spring... well it was *nothing* like the original spring: it was longer and narrower and the coils were thinner and it was clear that they had completely ignored me! They then started to mansplain me with, "This spring will do the job as well as the other spring," at which point I completely flipped. (*DON'T* MESS WITH MY VAN!!)

With as much sarcasm as I could muster I asked if they had not heard me when I said I wanted an *EXACT* replacement (because I had no doubt that anything else was going to cause untold other issues down the road). However, they were not getting the message and interjected, "This spring is new and the other one is old and worn." It was the final straw of 'treating the little woman as ignorant' and I went ballistic, just flat out crazy. I shouted at them to stop talking to me like I was stupid – in fact to stop talking altogether. "Take that spring, get my money back and put the old spring back!" I yelled and I stalked off. They went away and an hour later returned with the right replacement spring. Hmmm... amazing!

The repairs were all made within a few hours, during which time I finished my cleaning and repacking of the van. When the mechanic was finished I told him that I would do a test drive before he got his money, so off we went and I set about rigorously testing the steering and springs through the deeply rutted and uneven dirt roads around the hotel. All felt good so I curtly paid the man as agreed. He thanked me and got out, but said he would wait for Patrick.

The final order of business was to settle with Patrick myself. I won't bore you with all the details of what came to light over the time I spent with Patrick, but suffice to say he had negotiated a daily rate with me of about $15, which I was told was fair for the country. Firstly, however, he wasn't always with us for those two and a half days. Secondly, I knew he was getting kickbacks on the hotel room. Thirdly, he had separately negotiated a deal with the panel beater but had told him to give me a higher price (I knew that much French). Fourthly, the spare parts were excessively expensive and it was clear that the mechanic, while already having been paid by me, was waiting for Patrick to give him his cut. But the missing credit on my phone was the thing that really topped it for me.

I decided that I would only pay him for two days, generous even so considering the 'extras' he had scored. I wanted to be fair: he had certainly helped and expedited matters that would have taken me much longer alone. However, I was not letting this go without making him aware of my insights. I confronted him with the facts as I had understood them and I could tell that he was mortified to have been discovered. He literally had nothing to say. The only thing he offered in his defence was the claim that he hadn't taken the money off my phone. He was adamant that he was not a thief. I gave him my hardest stare, paid him his cash and told him I hoped he would think twice before ripping off the next visitor.

I took newly-refreshed BlueBelle back to the hotel. After all the excessive payments I would need to top up with cash again (always the toss-up between the risks of carrying too much or too little), so I decided to walk the few blocks to where I had seen an ATM and on my way back picked up some cold drinks. This was tricky as the woman wouldn't let me take the glass-bottled drinks I had selected because I didn't have any empty bottles to give her, and we debated this for a few moments: if I had never bought bottled drinks there, how could I bring her any back?! My logic won the day, and after promising to return the bottles I was buying she finally succumbed. Then at the street trader's outside I bought some bags of deep-fried yam snacks, a bit like potato crisps, very yummy and great to have with drinks or as an 'on the road' snack.

When I got back we finished the job of neatly packing everything back into the van, and for our final night had to relinquish our suite for a single room which Ursula took. I missed my bed so I slept in BlueBelle, all clean and beautiful again.

ON THE BEACH

In the morning Ursula returned with her things and immediately told me, "I'm not sleeping away from you again!" Awww, so sweet that she'd missed me. But no: what had actually transpired was that, without me there to be the usual mosquito magnet, *she* had been plagued by the little buggers all night long!

We headed out after the expected morning rush-hour, with Ursula jumping out to return the glass bottles as promised back at the store. Then before continuing further, I took BlueBelle to the car wash for a much deserved and long overdue clean on the outside. The last few days had been filled with things to do and problems to overcome, so we decided that this would be a 'relax' day. There was a beach restaurant that allowed overlanders to park overnight, and since we needed a change of scenery we agreed that this should do the trick.

The restaurant was in a poor suburban area but situated right on the beach, and we treated ourselves to a mixed seafood platter and fries as well as ice-cold panachés. I had been in touch with Michiel (from Togo) who was also in Pointe-Noire, and he met us at the restaurant later that afternoon. He too was giving himself a break from sleeping in his Land Rover for a few luxurious nights in a hotel.

The plan for the next day was that we would cross the border into Cabinda, Angola. Michiel was also planning to make the crossing the same day, and since we were both heading to the same parking at a Catholic church, we were sure that we would see each other again.

Chapter Fourteen – Cabinda, Angola

29 May 2019

The next morning I needed first to find a copy shop to make copies of my documents to present at the border, and then submit the application for my Angolan visa, which I could do online. I had completed an e-visa for Benin and it was easy, hence I hadn't stressed about this one... that was, until I looked at the Angolan application. They wanted all sorts of things: letters, contacts, accommodation confirmations, most of which I didn't have; and in addition I had to make sure that all the documents were in a specific format with the images resized. This was *not* going to be as easy as I had thought.

I eventually had all the necessary components in place. I had made some adjustments for the 'confirmation of accommodation' (I sent a photo of BlueBelle) and for the address in Angola (I sent a photo of BlueBelle). I had started just not to care. I pressed the 'Send' button and guessed I would have to wait a few hours for the approval... but no, it came back to me like an auto-responded email that my visa was approved. After all that painstaking information and a stress-filled morning, no one had even reviewed my efforts!

By mid-morning I had my online visa, but I needed to take copies of it with me to the border. I wasn't going back to the copy shop I'd found earlier as they had ripped me off, but I had read that there was someone doing copies at the border. I would take my chances there.

The distance between Pointe-Noire and the border was about forty kilometres and the road was pretty good. The border post going out was quick and in better order than the one we had coming in, but just a short distance into no man's land and we entered an entirely different world. There was neatness and cleanliness, with well-maintained booms and buildings: here was a government that set a different standard! There were no crowds of people offering to assist through a chaotic process because

399

there were signs, and no hawkers pushing SIM cards or wads of cash into our faces. The border area was secured by guards and only people doing business within the area were permitted entry. We parked up and entered the cool office building.

Ursula was travelling on her South African passport and Angola had recently removed the need for South Africans to have visas, so she was cleared quickly. Since Cabinda was formerly under Portuguese rule, I greeted everyone in Portuguese. My four years living in Portugal had given me some language skills, but I feared that, after attempting to speak French for about six months now, my old brain was having some trouble distinguishing which language I should be speaking. The difference in the people was immediately evident: they sincerely appreciated the few words of Portuguese I did recall and I wasn't reproached for being an Anglophone!

I was asked for a copy of my visa, so I in turn asked for the copy shop… but apparently none existed. Well, *that* posed a problem. However the man behind the glass screen evidently took a liking to me and invited me into his office to sit beside him while he completed the necessary forms online. I just had to answer his questions – name, address, and so on. Someone was sent off to make a copy of the papers and I had only to give him some money to cover it: no problem. It took ages because, like the Portuguese, the Cabindans loved chatting… and besides, you don't rush public officials, so I just sat and relaxed. Ursula, on the other hand, was patiently sitting on a bench on the public side of the window while I was having a great time with these guys who were doing all the work to sort out my visa.

With immigration completed it was still a while before I was able to leave. There was a lot of messing about with the TIP payment since their bank's lines were down, but eventually they sorted the problem using another bank. In between all this Michiel arrived with a fixer. All my payments were made in one office while the papers were issued at another, and then it meant returning to the first to get the police stamp. Despite the impressive facilities, the processes left something to be desired.

We caught up with Michiel at the exit boom, obtained our final stamp to enter Cabinda and agreed that we would go on at our own pace and meet up again at the church where we would be overnighting. The day was coming to a close and we still had over a hundred kilometres to cover.

Formerly known as Portuguese Congo, Cabinda (or Cabinda Province) is a small exclave of Angola which has been hotly disputed by several political factions in the territory since it was first colonised in the mid-fifteenth century. The people of Cabinda had been assured self-determination right up until the 1970s, but when it came to Portugal shedding its colonies they were packaged with Angola to the south, separated by the Democratic Republic of the Congo (DRC). This causes political and social unrest to this day and there were reports that Cabinda was a dangerous place, particularly inland (although we were lucky to witness no trouble at all). The reluctance of Angola to grant Cabinda its independence is likely influenced by some of the largest offshore oil fields in the world which lie just off its coast, and yet there were constant fuel shortages within the province.

The scenery compared with previous countries was relatively nondescript, but the road was good with only the occasional pothole. We saw a number of large hotels, seemingly still under construction, and a shopping centre that showed no sign of activity. Suddenly in the distance we spotted a large blob and just couldn't figure out what on earth it was. Ursula took a photo as we neared it, zoomed in and we saw to our disbelief another white elephant football stadium! I just couldn't understand: even if you are a Chinese corporation and have loads of money, you'd rather build giant football stadiums than give people proper homes? It makes me really mad!

It was dark when we arrived at the church just as the evening service was starting. Michiel was a little way ahead of us and we both pulled in behind some buildings and parked up. Ursula fulfilled her duties most effectively and got out drinks, while I started dinner and invited Michiel to join us. He would be attempting to cross the border in the morning and we were keen to see how he got on. After mass the priest came to chat, welcoming us and telling us that we could stay as long as we liked and he would not accept a cent in return. He sent someone to fetch a key to the bathrooms, which consisted of one semi-working shower and one working toilet; but as they say, beggars can't be choosers. The grounds behind the buildings were littered with cars and buses but benefited from some large shady trees.

NO ENTRY

For a couple of weeks I had been aware that there were problems with DRC visas that had been issued outside the country, especially those from Benin where I had got mine. It first came to my attention when Laurie and Bruce, who were now ahead of me by several weeks, had been turned away from the DRC border and been forced to return to Cabinda for several days before their embassy managed to get clearance for them.

The fact of the matter was that everyone who was overlanding through West Africa heading south – and I knew of around twenty vehicles at that time – was going to have a problem. It was the same as Nigeria: you needed to obtain the visa from your *home* country, the snag being that the visas were only valid for six months. No one travelling through Africa had the slightest clue when they might arrive in a country until they got within vague proximity, hence organising a visa from home presented a near-impossible challenge. So now everyone was contacting their embassy in advance and hitting every contact they had. Nelly, a Brit from one of the Facebook overlanding groups, was trying to get some traction with the British embassies, but I didn't hold much hope. Michiel and I were ahead of most of the others who were days and sometimes weeks behind us, waiting to see how we got on.

In the morning Michiel set off early from the church. We reached him via WhatsApp in the early afternoon to hear that he was still at the border and they were not letting him through. He returned that evening looking defeated, so Ursula and I hauled out the drinks, made dinner and got the details.

The next day he left again, this time deciding to attempt crossing at one of the smaller border posts, which meant going back into ROC, heading up around Cabinda and into DRC from ROC. A few other overlanders had gone through the smaller border posts on the ROC-DRC border north of Cabinda, but by all accounts these were strictly for 4x4s. While I knew I had developed some awesome driving skills, the conditions they described were challenges I was just not prepared to take. It took Michiel several days before he was in touch with us again, confirming that it was incredibly tough going and in some parts there was literally no road at all. Clearly that route would be out of the question for BlueBelle.

In the meantime, Ursula and I had decided that we would give the border a test ourselves. We had nothing to lose and the only alternative would have been to return to ROC, drive several hundred kilometres up to Brazzaville and then cross into DRC by ferry to Kinshasa. Reports on this route were that it was full of hustlers and I didn't like the odds, so early the next day we drove to the crossing some thirty kilometres away. I was feeling confident: I had managed to overcome so many hurdles thus far. Ursula had a valid visa from her country of residence and we were travelling together; and I too had a visa, paid to their representatives in Benin. They *must* let me through. There had to be *some* flexibility...

The Cabinda-Angola border post was surprisingly efficient, although they were aware that others had been turned back. Fortunately the Angolan visa allowed multiple entries, so I wasn't concerned about being let back in should things not go according to my high expectations.

We crossed through what couldn't have been more than twenty metres of no man's land before entering the Democratic Republic of the Congo (DRC)... but we could have gone to another planet, such was the difference! The boom was old and rusting, the driveway uneven dirt, and there was a motley array of scattered buildings that looked shoddy and dilapidated, clearly not having seen a coat of paint in decades. I parked under the shade of a tree near the largest building and Ursula and I walked over.

Laurie and Bruce had equipped me with a contact at the border, another Patrick, who looked after the 'foreigners' when they came through. As we entered we asked for immigration, and there was an open veranda with rickety wooden benches where a surly woman in uniform told us to take a seat. It was Patrick who came to meet us. He was a large, friendly-faced man who had lived in the USA for some time and as such spoke very good English. We talked with him for a bit and he asked a number of questions, and then left with our passports to speak with his boss.

I'll keep it brief, but for the better part of the morning I did everything I could: I smiled, I cried, I looked depressed, I cried some more, I asked questions, I listened to the biggest load of BS I'd ever heard… and after much toing and froing and calls to department heads and ministers, the answer was: Ursula could go through… but I could not.

Ursula was sitting in BlueBelle with the door open when I got the news and she was in close enough proximity to the veranda to hear my reaction. Her Favourite Aunt completely lost it! I went nuts and started shouting at them that this was the most ridiculous response *EVER* – did they expect my niece to *WALK* to Luanda?! I gave full vent to the crazy old woman in me as I screamed at them, "You're leaving me with no choice but to drive through Chad and South Sudan just to get around your country, and let me tell you if I die or I'm murdered or kidnapped it will be on YOUR conscience and an international enquiry will find you GUILTY!" Yep, full-on crazy! Throughout this exchange I was pointing my finger at both Patrick and the head of the local immigration department, and Ursula kept begging me to leave, realising that I was making a complete ass of myself. But when I get that mad, I just don't care!

I stormed off to BlueBelle and turned back whence we had come just hours before. We drove in grim silence through to the Cabinda border post, got our previous exit stamps cancelled and returned to the church. I was mad as a snake. It didn't make one bit of difference though. The question now was what were our options?

Ursula was running out of time; she had already delayed her flight while we tried to work things out. The first step was to figure out who could help, so I contacted everyone: my overlanding friends, the online overlanding groups, the British Embassy in DRC and the Home Office. I posted on social media on all my pages, groups and followers to see if *anyone* knew *anyone* who was able to assist…

Unbelievably, Laurie and Bruce had at that precise time while camping in Angola met both the American and British ambassadors to Angola and managed to secure their contact details, which they forwarded to me. I contacted the British ambassador and received a limp reply using the word 'try' (which to me always feels like an excuse in advance for doing nothing), and the British Foreign Office responded to my email and phone call with statements that they 'do not interfere in the policies of foreign governments'. Who asked them to interfere? All I was asking was that they request that the DRC honour the visas that British citizens had legally purchased!

What it came down to was either I got through or... well, there *was* no other option: I just *had* to get through. The rains had by now gone to the north and there was absolutely no way that I would be able to backtrack on roads I had barely managed to cross in the dry season. I had my destination and that was the only place I was going. I've always had a problem with the word No and find it terribly hard to accept. Well, so far everyone was saying, "No!" and apart from being a word I hated hearing, I just wasn't having it!

ON MY OWN AGAIN

Ursula and I sat down and talked about alternative solutions. The most obvious was for her to drive BlueBelle through DRC and I would fly from Cabinda to Soyo or Luanda (in Angola) and find a way to get back together with her. However, I was highly uncomfortable with this. While Ursula was very savvy and well-travelled, there were several issues. The documents for the van were in my name, for a start, and I was certain this would cause her problems, even with a letter of authority from me. She didn't know BlueBelle as well as I did either, increasing the risk of something going wrong. And it would require the kind of stamina that I had built up through the previous months for her to tackle DRC. More selfishly perhaps, I also didn't want to jeopardise my only niece – or BlueBelle – in any way: if something happened when I was there I could take the responsibility, but I wasn't sure I could live with any other consequences. Dramatic as that sounded, my gut was saying no... and I had learnt over the last year that it was generally right.

So we sadly decided the best option was for Ursula to fly from Cabinda to Luanda and then catch her flight back home.

While we had been waiting for the inevitable, we were entertained morning and evening by singing from different choirs practising in the church or its grounds. Unlike the singing we had heard in ROC, this was all very beautiful. Each group was dressed differently, with the singers wearing a similar dress or headdress to identify which group they belonged to; and they were all singing different pieces. Certainly it was the busiest congregation I had experienced in years.

The day arrived to drop Ursula off at the tiny airport in Cabinda, and I went in with her to ensure she got through. It was a sad farewell as we hugged goodbye and I watched as she followed her escort into the waiting area. I was used to being on my own, but I had enjoyed such intense highs and lows with Ursula by my side that it felt strange and lonely now without her.

The next few days I spent fully focused on messaging, posting and talking to as many people as I could about my situation and trying to find a solution. When I wasn't doing that I was reorganising BlueBelle: now that Ursula was gone things could return to 'normal'. I decided to investigate other options too, one of which was to ship BlueBelle to either Soyo or Luanda. I knew that I could fly to either of those destinations from Cabinda; and much as I didn't want to leave her, I decided I should at least find out. However, I had no idea where to try...

Once again Laurie and Bruce came up trumps. As I said, they were a few weeks ahead of me and already in Luanda whilst I was still in Cabinda. They were heading for a camping spot when they got lost in the centre of Luanda – easy enough to do when the roads were full of one-way streets. Seeing their dilemma, Luandan residents Sonia and Luis came to their rescue and led them where they needed to be, and then somehow I came up in their conversation.

As it happened Luis was in the shipping industry in Luanda, and when Laurie and Bruce mentioned my predicament Sonia contacted me on Messenger to offer any help she could. I outlined my need to assess shipping options and she duly arranged for someone to contact me. While everyone was truly very helpful, the bottom line was that I would need to spend around $2,000 to ship BlueBelle – and that didn't include my flight or accommodation – but there was no guarantee there wouldn't be delays or complications getting her out of customs. It was unfortunately a non-starter, but I thanked Sonia and Luis and promised them a gin and tonic when I got to Luanda in exchange for their kindness.

Still in the churchyard, I was disturbed one night by some noise outside the van. It was sufficiently far away for me to feel that it was no threat, but the next morning I woke early to find a tent put up a few metres from BlueBelle. I went off to buy some rolls and when I returned the occupants of the tent, two young men, were up and about. It turned out they were South African and planning to drive their motorcycles up the coast in the opposite direction to the way I had just come. They had many questions for me and I spent some time answering them and giving them tips that I thought might be helpful.

They had bypassed DRC and come by local fishing boat from Soyo (in Angola proper) to Cabinda, and had been on the ocean the day before for what they described as a 'treacherous eleven hours' in a large wooden dugout. Meanwhile their motorbikes were on another boat and due to arrive that evening. Personally I thought they had taken a great risk separating from their bikes, but they seemed confident. I offered to take them to the harbour later that afternoon to collect them.

The 'harbour' lay at the other end of a disused lot and we had to weave between buildings, shacks and trash to get to the small area where fishing boats seemed to assemble. The boys found their contact and established that their bikes had been delayed and could not be collected until the next day, so I was further concerned for them. But sure enough, the next morning they received confirmation that the bikes had arrived overnight.

Ursula's return to South Africa actually ended up being of great advantage. Once home she caught up with her friend Peggy (who had helped us in Pointe-Noire) and made her aware of my dilemma, and it so happened that Peggy collaborated with the French embassies in Africa – the reason for her being in Pointe-Noire just weeks before – and so she had many useful contacts. Peggy talked with someone in the French Embassy in South Africa, who in turn talked to someone in the DRC Embassy in South Africa, and hallelujah: they secured an agreement for me to be able to pass through!

It had been almost a week since my first attempt and when I heard the news I nearly fainted. It was the hottest part of the afternoon, so I decided to leave early the next morning as I would need the better part of the day to get to my overnight stop in Matadi. I'd also heard via the overlanding network that the DRC ambassador in Benin did not understand why there was a problem... but then frankly, neither did I!

I took the whole afternoon to find diesel and still I came up empty. It had been impossible either to draw cash or get fuel without long queues, but mostly there was zero diesel at any of the stations I stopped at. I managed to draw cash early the next morning though, without any queues, knowing that any I had left I could use in Angola.

Filled with hope, excitement and only a tiny drop of dread (because I *had* to be successful this time!) I braced myself and called on all the Universal energy, angels and guardians that had been overseeing me thus far, and told them that I needed this push.

I swept imperiously through the Fronteira do Yema, the Cabinda border post, and when someone suggested I might be turned back I assured them that I would absolutely *not*; in fact if necessary I would be spending the night – the whole week even – waiting stubbornly at the DRC border until they let me through. I was *not* taking No for an answer this time!

Chapter Fifteen – Democratic Republic of the Congo
6 June 2019

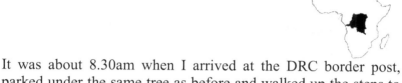

It was about 8.30am when I arrived at the DRC border post, parked under the same tree as before and walked up the steps to the veranda. I was greeted by everyone with a level of familiarity. By now they had either heard *about* me or had *actually* heard me! I acted like I had amnesia and just smiled at everyone.

It was not long before Patrick came to greet me. I offered no apology for my previous behaviour and continued as if I had memory loss. (Apologies imply defeat and I was *not* to be defeated today!) We discussed the matter at hand and I assured him that I had approval to go through, citing all the information I had. He said he hoped it would be enough for the Minister of Immigration.

It then dawned on me that I had a trump card I had not yet played: I had the phone number for the Minister of Immigration. Laurie and Bruce had sent me a photo of his business card which they had somehow acquired. Patrick said I had to wait for the Chief who was on his way from his home some distance away, so while I was waiting I messaged Peggy in South Africa to say I was being held up at the border and then put the details for the Minister into my phone contacts. I was very surprised to find he had WhatsApp, but I was also beyond blessed to find that the Angolan SIM card was still working here in DRC. Bonus! I promptly sent the honourable Minister a message – after all, what did I have to lose?

Me: Minister, my name is Dorothea Bekker. I am a British Citizen needing to pass through your country and I am again at your border trying to get through.

Some ten minutes passed. Then my phone beeped.

Minister: Do you have a valid visa?

(I considered this question carefully before replying. I genuinely believed I had a valid visa: I had bought and paid for it, I'd had my biometrics taken and got a stamp with my photo in my passport. However, he may have been asking if I had one from my home country. I needed to keep my answer short so as not to create more issues.)

Me: Yes.

No response, so after five more minutes I sent another message.

Me: Can I go through?

A further wait of ten minutes, then...

Minister: Yes.

WOOOOOOHOOOOOO!

I dashed around to find Patrick, confirmed that this was indeed the Minister's telephone number and showed him the messages. He grinned and said he would go and talk to the Chief, who had by this time arrived. I trotted after him, thinking that I had been burning enough time and needed to get going. I wasn't having the Chief putting a spanner in the works now.

Some chatting ensued and eventually I was directed to the desk where I would get my immigration stamp into the country. There my details were typed laboriously into a computer with two fingers, and because that couldn't possibly be enough they were also entered into the obligatory big black book.

From there Patrick escorted me to an ATM. I knew that I could get US dollars at this one, but since I only had a hundred available in the bank to withdraw, it would have to do. I used some of my remaining cash to pay for my TIP, then a further stamp for something or other, and finally showed them my Yellow Fever certificate, which was checked and entered into yet another big black book. I needed change from my TIP payment and Patrick was trying to find some, but I decided not to wait and instead tip him the change to thank him for his help. As I headed off, Patrick left me with a warning not to stop – and especially not in the middle of nowhere. If I had to stop anywhere, he told me, stop where there are people.

Patrick's warning did little to allay my heightened tension around DRC. It had such a terrible reputation as a country, and I was aware that only the year before a German overlander had been murdered getting out of his vehicle after being crowded by motorcyclists.[105] It was of course on my mind. I was nervous about all the horrid stories I had heard about DRC and I was on my own again now. There was also precious little information about good places to stop on my way to my destination, Matadi, so I knew I had to make the two hundred and fifty kilometres in a single day. More than half of that was a horrible dirt road, and it was already past 10.00 when I left the border.

However, 'Team BlueBelle' had crossed its biggest bureaucratic hurdle yet: we were through and on our way. I sighed a great big sigh and sent an equally great big wave of gratitude out to everyone who had helped and encouraged me so far. But I still had DRC to negotiate, and I had no idea what lay ahead...

The Democratic Republic of the Congo is a country with a brutal colonial history, and should you ever have the courage to read about it you will be horrified at the manner in which the Belgian King Leopold II and his successors treated their people. Vicious beatings and the chopping off of hands for not paying taxes were amongst the least offensive, and I believed this had left an entire country with a legacy of brutality that continued to the present day. I might be travelling through some of the less dangerous parts, but any foreigner could present as a target for kidnapping. Kidnapping had always been the least of my concerns on this journey though. I remained quite confident that after a few weeks with me they would probably be paying someone to get rid of me; beside the fact that no one I knew had the money to pay for my release.

A MARATHON DRIVE

It was back to an uneven, potholed road of red dust and then I had the phone navigating me to Muanda on dirt tracks. My first stop – or checkpoint, if it can be called that – was about ten kilometres out from the border. I knew it was coming because it was a 'toll' stop. They would charge me for passing through the roads *into* DRC and there would be another toll further along the route before *leaving* it. Stories about the toll varied: some overlanders had paid a fortune while others had paid nothing at all. I had

---

[105] Thankfully his wife escaped unscathed

decided I would try to negotiate them down, but my primary aim was to get through the toll and on my way as soon as possible.

They started with $50 and I had a dilemma: all I had was the single hundred dollar note from the ATM at the border or a few smaller notes that were nowhere enough to cover the toll. I certainly wasn't prepared to give them the hundred. Firstly, they might have thought I had even more money and secondly, they would inevitably try the 'We have no change' scenario. I offered them a few small notes which amounted to about $15, but this was unacceptable.

As I was negotiating with them, an officer in uniform came over and asked for my passport so I showed him a copy. He told me I had to pay 1,000CDF[106] (about fifty cents), and while this is a paltry amount, it sparked the realisation that this was not a fee I was officially required to pay; it was more likely going straight into his pocket. I told him I wasn't paying it, that I'd just come through the border and paid all the costs I needed to pay there, but he insisted. I told him firmly that he could do whatever he liked but he was not getting a cent from me, and I would gladly return to the border to clarify the matter with them. At this he shut up.

Back to the toll. I added the offer of some euros, which they were reluctant to take, but eventually they muttered their consent and I breathed a silent sigh of relief. I insisted on a receipt though, fully aware that I may be required to produce it further on to avoid being charged again.

I noticed that the uniformed officer, who had been standing on the periphery of the other men while they were trying to get their toll, had quietly disappeared while I was busy negotiating with them. Clearly my threat to go back to the border was the clincher.

So finally I was off...

There was a zigzag of dirt roads and the map had even less idea where I was than I had. It was all sandy, but I decided that sticking to the wider track would be best. As I drove I noticed my blue dot on the screen diverging ever further from the route set out, and I worried that I was not only getting lost but also burning both daylight and fuel. There were of course no signs, and a closer

---

[106] Congolese francs

look at the map told me this track would take me to the coast. I would then have to backtrack to Muanda, where I needed to stop to get fuel and a SIM card and find the road to Boma.

While driving along and considering my options, I noticed a man up ahead of me carrying several bags. I pulled up next to him and asked about the road to Muanda and he indicated I could get there on this track with no problem. I asked if he was going there himself and he nodded that he was and I was now confronted with a dilemma: he had been kind and given me reassurance, so did I offer him a lift or leave him in my dust? The chances of him getting a ride with anyone else seemed slim as I'd barely seen another vehicle, so there, in the midst of dangerous DRC, I decided to help this stranger. My gut told me it was OK because he hadn't asked for anything; on the contrary, I'd asked *him* if he would like a lift. The initial look on his face was one of utter astonishment. I'm certain that no lone woman of my persuasion had ever done that before!

We loaded his wares into the back of the van, he climbed into the passenger seat and off we went. It was in reality one of the best decisions my gut had made because I could well have missed the turnoff to Muanda; to boot he helped me find a place (that I wouldn't have found on my own) to change my dollars for Congolese francs and buy a SIM card. Once all of that was done, he showed me where to get diesel because I didn't want to stop again until I got to Matadi.

I would never have spotted the fuel station myself as it was set against the wall of an old building on the opposite side of the street. The pumps were positively ancient. They looked like they had been installed at the beginning of the last century, with mechanical dials that clicked the numbers over as the fuel went in. The numbers were very confusing and the wrong way round to normal pumps, and there was no way to tell what was litres and what was the cost. A crowd was growing around me. Most Europeans here were expats and it would be rare to see one in the street getting fuel without an escort. I started joking with the attendant that I would pay the smaller number because it didn't tell me what the amounts were for, and the crowd thought it was hysterical. There I was, in dangerous DRC, chatting with the local people in my paltry French... and I felt as safe as anywhere. I paid and said goodbye to all, including my travel companion who I am certain would later regale his friends with the unbelievable tale of the strange woman who picked him up in her blue van.

On my way out of Muanda I was smiling from ear to ear. I had an unshakable belief that everything would be fine, despite the already shocking condition of the road. Little did I know that I would soon be driving Hell's Highway's Nephew, another dreadful red dirt road with uneven surfaces that would turn out to be almost as bad as the two hundred kilometres I had suffered in Guinea en route to Boké. All it lacked was the deep gullies and any sign that there had ever been tarmac anywhere on it.

I tried to make the best speed I could but the road conditions were atrocious, so I trundled along taking in the landscape and the people. I started with my wave test and the locals, while surprised to see me, waved back – although most without huge enthusiasm. However, wave they did, and that told me they were more friendly than I had anticipated and allowed me to relax somewhat. The countryside could have been pretty much anywhere in Central Africa: a sort of savannah mixed with some hilly areas; and there were pockets of rainforest sprinkled with mud and thatch villages.

My progress was slow but steady and I finally reached Boma. On approaching the town I was on high alert to ensure I saw the turn on to the new road over the bridge. If I missed it, I'd read that I would find myself in the morass that was the daily market with its throng of traffic and people. My research had also revealed a place called Stanley's Baobab and I was intrigued. I didn't have much time to stop, but as it was only a short distance out of my way I certainly intended to see it. Walking in the footsteps of the intrepid explorer and writer Henry Morton Stanley (of "Doctor Livingstone, I presume?" fame) just felt like something I should do. My thoughts raced at what these historic adventurers must have seen and what the country must have looked like at that time. It had certainly given me something to think about while driving that tortuous road.

In Boma a sign clearly indicated the small but very busy bridge I needed to cross and I easily found my diversion through the narrow streets of the town. I was driving slowly and the odd person shouted out to me, but not knowing what it was about and believing it to be friendly I just waved and continued on my way.

I came to an almost deserted street near the river that was home to a gigantic baobab tree with a wall around it. Apparently it housed a small museum.

The story was that Mr Stanley landed on the riverbank late one night in 1877, and having travelled downriver some eighteen hundred kilometres from Lake Tanganyika to Boma, decided that the best place to spend the night was in the trunk of this nineteen metre round, approximately seven hundred-year-old tree. (There was no specific evidence to support this, but it is thoroughly enshrined in local legend.) Since I had already lost the better part of the day on the bad road, I stretched my legs, took a photograph of the infamous tree and then headed back to the road that would take me to Matadi.

On the outskirts of the town there was a police check which I cleared without too much hassle. They did ask me for money, booze, food and water, pretty much in that order, but I said I had none and they just let me pass. It seemed I was heading out of the province when I came to a stop with a great many officers in different uniforms and, as usual, I was immediately waved down. I offered a friendly greeting and instantly had five men all standing as close to my window as they could get, peering in over my shoulder. The first officer to speak was not too friendly a fellow, but I kept up my winning smile and handed over my TIP papers. Next I showed them the copy of my passport, and then another asked for my driver's licence so I showed him the copy of that too.

But then they asked to see my insurance... and I didn't have any. I hadn't planned to spend more than forty-eight hours in DRC and frankly I had been so excited to get over the border and get going to Matadi that I forgot. I admit it was a risk, but at the same time finding out where to get the insurance would itself probably have taken half a day and half my cash. I feigned ignorance, shrugged my shoulders and told them I had no idea what they were asking me for (bearing in mind they were speaking French and I had already told them I was English-speaking from Zimbabwe). I looked at them with an air of suitable confusion and took out all my other papers, handing over my van registration and just about anything else I could find. *"Pas d'assurance, pas d'assurance,"* they kept saying. Then one of them said, "Pas d'assurance, you must pay fifty dollars." Well, that woke me up! I scrabbled through my papers and found my *carte rose,*[107] the insurance that covered me up to ROC (but did not include DRC). It was still valid, so with a look that enquired, "Perhaps this?" I handed the paper over. It had *Assurance* written all over the top and the date was clear, the countries it was valid in being written on the back. I held my breath and he started to nod in confirmation that it was acceptable.

They now realised there was no payday and started looking at each other. I put my hand out to get my papers back and they gave them to me, but the one officer wouldn't return my driver's licence. I watched him as he watched me, then I smiled and put out my hand further for the licence. An officer in the background, who obviously outranked this one, barked something at him and he reluctantly returned it.

I asked if I could go and they responded with a request for whisky. I replied with a disgusted look that I didn't drink whisky, so they changed it to gin. Here, I confess, I lied: "I don't drink," I replied. That had them stumped. Then we went down the list – money, food, water – and I also said I had none. After this game of chess the ranking officer in the background, who clearly had sway over the others, finally gave the word and they all stepped back. I thanked them enthusiastically and waved goodbye as I drove off. Phew, that was a close shave!

MATADI AND AFRICA'S LARGEST RIVER

After the dreadful dust road leading to Boma, the next stretch to Matadi was tarmac, warped in some sections but all in all in pretty good shape. I still had a fair distance to cover and it was now afternoon. The landscape became greener and more undulating hills appeared, as well as an increase in traffic and people, indicating that I was getting closer to the city.

Matadi, which was founded by the aforementioned Mr Stanley, is located on the Congo River close to the border with Angola. Its nickname is the Stone City because *matadi* means stone in the local Kikongo language and the town is built on steep

---

[107] Literally 'pink card' which I had originally bought in Senegal and renewed in Cameroon

hills. Although it is situated over 150 kilometres upriver from the coast, Matadi is a major maritime port and handles around ninety percent of the country's shipping. Chief exports are coffee and timber but also include copper, palm oil kernels, sugar and cotton. The mighty Congo, Africa's second-longest river (after the Nile) and second to the Amazon in water outflow, is very much a lifeline in a land with few roads or railways.

I was now driving in the twilight and going as fast as I could to reach the town before dark, but I already knew that it would not be possible. The sky was lilac and gold and heralding the swift arrival of night when I reached a toll booth before the bridge. Before I crossed I found I had a signal so I sent a message to my host for the night, Philippe. I waited for a response, but by the time he got back to me with instructions to a rendezvous point, it was dark. It was again Chloe of the West Africa Traveller's group who had put me in contact with Philippe, a French expat who with his wife Anne had generously offered to host me for the night in Matadi.

The toll turned out to be for the Matadi Bridge which crosses the Congo River just south of the town, and I was horrified to find that the cost was the equivalent of almost $15. How on earth did the locals afford such prices?! At the toll booth I had to perform the usual operation to extract myself from the seat (the booth being on the opposite side of my RHD position) and walk around to pay and get the receipt, and then reinstall myself. This all took time, usually to the annoyance of those behind me.

I was sorry that I'd missed the amazing view in daylight, but the city lights twinkled on the steep slopes of the river and reflected in the wide expanse of water below. The bridge was a huge surprise: after crossing so many broken or dilapidated ones on my journey, this was a work of real engineering. Crossing the Congo River at its narrowest point, this was an impressive suspension bridge with a main span of five hundred and twenty metres, and had been completed by a Japanese consortium in 1983.

I drove slowly over, trying to take in as much of the view as I possibly could, and after passing through another toll booth on the other side (to prove my having bought a ticket; I did wonder how people got on to the bridge without one!) I proceeded into the town.

As soon as I was off the bridge and into Matadi proper, the traffic became chaotic. I was inching along and it felt like forever before I saw the garage where I had arranged to meet Philippe. The forecourt was full and several vehicles were parked half on the curb, so seeing a free spot I decided to do the same. I switched off my engine to wait and listened to the noises of the traffic, the music and the people talking (or shouting) that filled the air. I looked over to my right and noticed a tanker a few metres away on the forecourt and, leaning against it, a group of five young men who were looking at me, very cool with their arms and ankles crossed.

I had seconds to decide whether they might be a threat, but chose my usual self-defence tactic: I looked directly at them, smiled widely, waved and said loudly, "Bonsoir!" (Good evening). This threw them off guard and they immediately unfolded their arms, uncrossed their feet and responded in like with wide white smiles, waves and greetings.

They then coolly approached my half-open window and started talking to me, and I had a fleeting thought that no one would believe me if I told them I was here in DRC chatting with a group of young black Congolese guys at night! I had to tell them to slow down, explaining that I spoke only a little French. They got very excited to hear I was from Zimbabwe, and when I informed them that I had driven through Africa and told them to look at my flags, they each popped around to the other side and then ran back, excitedly asking questions which I tried to answer as best I could. They were so incredibly cute!

Philippe arrived not long after and indicated that I should follow him. I quickly said goodbye to my new-found friends – all of them insisting on shaking my hand – and headed into the evening traffic. It was pretty terrible so it was slow going. We were stuck in a jam and the road seemed to be constantly winding up the steep slopes of the city. The incline was steady and with the constant stop/start BlueBelle wasn't doing so well hauling her heavy backside up. I knew we were in trouble when I could smell the clutch burning – which of course put me in a panic – so I remained focused and said some prayers.

At the top of a steep driveway I saw a beautiful home and breathed a sigh of relief that we had made it in one piece. I got out to greet Philippe properly and meet his wife Anne, who spoke about as much English as I did French, but she was delightful and the perfect hostess. Philippe spoke more English and although he wasn't fluent we managed well. They showed me a lovely room with my own bathroom, and while I had been intending to sleep in BlueBelle, she was parked at an impossible angle which would have made it quite awkward, so I gratefully accepted their hospitality.

After spending a pleasant evening getting to know my hosts, answering their questions and discovering that they were also looking forward to overlanding themselves in a year or two, I was quite exhausted from the drive and excused myself. Lying in crisp, fresh sheets after a wonderful shower in a clean and modern bathroom (I had not had that pleasure for some time!) I considered how exhausted I really was, and the thought of pushing through to the border the next morning just felt like too much. Furthermore, it would be a Friday and I believed it might be exceptionally busy. I decided to ask Philippe and Anne if I might remain for another day and depart on Saturday.

As expected, my kind hosts were not at all fazed by my request and I spent the next morning getting BlueBelle in order and doing some washing. By mid-morning it was sweltering and I sat on the terrace by the pool overlooking the valley and the river. Sadly the pollution, along with the heat haze, reduced the visibility, but it truly was a beautiful city location. If I hadn't been so concerned about the crazy traffic and getting back up the hill I might have gone for a drive to discover more of the place, but I felt that relaxing was my wisest choice. I didn't know what the next day would hold and I'd learnt that border crossings generally required me to have my wits about me.

On Saturday morning, all ready and organised, I drove out early after thanking my generous hosts. Philippe had recommended that I cross the border at Lufu because the crossing closer to Matadi led to a bad road on the Angola side. I'd had enough of bad roads so I took his advice. Despite my being early the traffic was already chaotic, the primary reason being that the main road out of the city was narrow with only one lane in each direction; not to mention the vehicles that parked randomly on the side of the road, or the stopping taxis. I ended up stuck in a long queue of traffic behind several snail-pace trucks which were finding it a challenge going up the slopes. I empathised.

I left the city behind and found a garage to fuel up. I still had some CDF and I wanted to use up as much of it as possible.[108] The day before I had pulled out my two jerry cans that I had stashed in the rear storage: with the fuel issues I'd had in Cabinda, on top of updates of shortages in parts of North Angola, I thought it wise to have reserves. I only expected to drive about a hundred and sixty kilometres that day, but I felt more comfortable with a backup plan.

The fuel was expensive at about $1.30 per litre, which meant my cash permitted me just to fill the jerry cans and add a few litres into my half-full tank; it wasn't worth changing any more money. With a full tank doing on average about five hundred miles (my vehicle being British), I was sure that I would comfortably reach my destination.

The road to Lufu was much like it had been on the way to Matadi: tarmac with sections that had melted and warped under the weight of overloaded trucks. I was trundling along nicely and the scenery was largely the same, but somehow a little different and still hilly. About midway to the border I encountered an unexpected sight: toll booths in the middle of the road. As normal, I pulled up to the window and did the usual handbrake-seat-cushion-seatbelt thing to get out and go to the booth.

At the window I was advised that I had to pay at the bank, which was located in a prefab building to the side. I moved the van in front of the bank, whereupon a man came up to me and told me that first I would need to go to another toll booth to *get* the ticket before I could go to the bank to *pay* for it. You really couldn't make this stuff up! I asked if the payment I had made after passing through the border would suffice, but it seemed that this was a different toll. (Of course it was!)

I traipsed back to the toll booth to get the ticket, with the man who had taken it upon himself to 'escort' me getting a bit pushy and telling me that the toll had to be paid in US dollars. Seriously?

---

[108] Angola's currency is the kwanza

How did local people pay?! I had to pay five dollars – an outrageous sum for DRC – and to add insult to injury it took about ten minutes to get the ticket as there was a queue waiting for the most inept man to perform a simple task.

I realised that I had some one-dollar bills that I had forgotten about, so it seemed like a good opportunity to get rid of them rather than breaking a bigger note from what remained of my US currency. I picked them up from my van and joined the queue at the bank, and when it came to my turn I put down the five dollars in single notes. There was a shaking of heads and the notes were shoved back at me, so I shoved them back with an, "It's this or nothing, guys!" The counter clerk from the next booth was called over, a woman with five words of English who told me, "No." So I stared hard at her and retorted, "Yes!" She turned the dollars over and then held them up curiously and asked, "US dollars?" It seemed they had never seen a one-dollar bill! The supervisor was called and, as luck would have it, when I had pulled up to the bank he was driving in and I had been courteous enough to give him the right of way. Now he looked at me and I smiled broadly: surely he would recognise me? He returned a slight smile, nodded to the staff and I got my receipt. I thanked everyone and wished them a good day: "Merci, bonne journée!"

I wasn't going to get in and out of BlueBelle again so I walked to the toll booth with my ticket and receipt. The little man took the ticket and I continued on my way, marvelling at the most complicated toll system I had ever encountered. The simple fact was that to prevent corruption they had created a crazy, convoluted system of chaos. Happily it was the only one I encountered.

I approached my turnoff from the tarmac road and ahead of me lay a wide, red dirt track that looked like it had recently been graded. Some distance along I thought I had come to a checkpoint, but I discovered it was the mirror toll of the one just after the border. I parked behind the other vehicles and walked confidently to a table with some seated men checking the receipts, where I presented my receipt from Yema. I had my fingers metaphorically crossed because I had heard of overlanders whose receipt had not been accepted and who had been pressed to pay again, so I took my usual defensive position. "Bonjour, ça va?" (Hello, how's it going?) with an amiable smile. It seemed to do the trick as they looked surprised to see me, but checked my receipt and with friendly greetings sent me on my way.

I was happy with my lot until I reached the kind of chaos I hadn't seen for a while: the grand melee. It was a morass of market shacks cobbled together with bits of wood and anything else that lay about, people milling around everywhere, some running back and forth, and motorcycles laden with goods. As I got closer to the border the going got more difficult, with the road becoming deeply potholed and uneven.

I eventually arrived at an assortment of old buildings which indicated it was the *douane* (customs), so I guessed this was where I would be able to sort out my TIP. I had to ask several times before I found the right room, which was tiny and filled with two desks and lots of men. I squeezed in, smiled and greeted everyone, and when a man kindly insisted I sit in his place, it felt rude to decline.

They were mostly speaking their local patois but I could tell by the body language I seemed to be causing some consternation. A door opened to the back and a man negotiated his way through the people. There was some conversation and then he turned to me and motioned me to follow him. We went to two more offices until everyone was satisfied that I was cleared to leave, but then just as I got in my van a uniformed man near the exit barrier indicated that I now had to see *him*. He looked at my papers, stamped them and kept them, but when I objected he merely waved me on. I sighed and hoped like hell that I wouldn't need those papers again and took a good hard look at him, should I need to recognise him later.

The rope that was acting as a barrier was lowered and some two hundred metres in front of me stood a magnificent new building. I was mesmerised by the sight, but as I neared it I could see that it was barricaded shut and that everyone else was driving around it through some sort of wasteland, so I reversed and followed the other vehicles. I came around the other side to find a mass of people standing in groups around a small colonial building that had seriously seen better days. I parked as close as I could and some young men started shouting out at me. As probably the only person of my persuasion in the entire area I must have stood out, so not knowing what they were saying I just smiled, waved and purposefully walked toward the building. As a woman I feel that hesitancy and uncertainty make you an easier target, so I always made the effort when I was out of BlueBelle to look like I knew what I was doing and where I was going– even if I hadn't a clue!

It took a while to find the right room in which to get my passport stamped. I was directed to an office around the corner and again I came across two desks crammed into a tiny room with a large, elderly, rotund man behind one and behind the other a younger officer who was dealing with a guy who looked like he had a big problem. While I was being attended to by Mr Rotund, people kept coming in and stuffing folded bills of money in his hands. (Nothing suspicious about that of course.) These bills would find their way into his drawer where they were carefully placed under a book, and it was then that I realised again how chaos at borders provided ample opportunity for corruption. Inevitably this is why new buildings sit empty: because they would create order and process, which are the enemies of corruption.

Mr Rotund eventually took my passport along with several others, left the room and told me to wait outside. Instead I followed him and waited in the shade on the veranda. I watched as he walked in through the front, disappearing for some fifteen minutes, and when he reappeared I asked after my passport which he still had in his hands. He looked at it and then at me and informed me that I had to wait further. About the same amount of time later he passed me again, and again I asked him about my passport, but his response was a gruff snort and he continued on his way. I was getting more and more hot and agitated.

I occupied myself watching the turmoil that surrounded the building. I wondered what kind of control there was for the vast number of motorbikes crossing the border with cages on the back, which were being used as trolleys and filled to the brim with goods of all descriptions. They were usually pushed by a handful of men (possibly cheaper than fuel) and oddly I saw a good number had small, disabled guys at the front steering. There were people carrying bags of what I assumed was maize meal, most of them rushing back and forth as if their lives depended on it... and perhaps they did. It was chaos. Anything and anyone capable of carrying was doing so and the flow never stopped, most of it coming from the Angolan side into DRC.

On his next pass, I again stopped Mr Rotund. This time he looked at the passports in his hands, mine a different colour so standing out from the others. He made a point of looking at me and then at the passport photo again and, deciding it was a match, handed it back to me.

I thanked him without enthusiasm and returned to BlueBelle, who was now entirely surrounded by other vehicles. That intransigent grumpiness that comes with excess heat and frustration was seeping in, but fortunately I managed to find a way to squeeze myself out as none of the vehicles had parked in anything resembling an orderly fashion. With the absence of signage I decided that turning left should see me in the direction of the border post, and yes, this took me to another small building where I had my details once again written into the obligatory black books before being given the final nod to move on to cross the border.

Just beyond the next queue of traffic was a single guard box with a couple of men checking people through. What had been obscured by trucks in front of me, however, was that the bridge ahead was only single lane. It was spanning the not very impressive Lufu River and probably less than fifty metres in length, but I had already assessed that it would be near impossible to cross, such was the constant stream of traffic coming from the other side. I asked the guard how I was supposed to get across, whereupon he whistled to a man at the edge of the bridge and instructed me to follow his lead and go when he told me.

There was a narrow path to the side of the bridge where people were walking alongside the traffic, and I had to ensure I didn't hit them with my side mirrors, it was that narrow. I waited patiently and the guard eventually frantically waved at me to GO! Now I'm good at take-off, so I hit the accelerator and floored it. I got to about three metres from the end of the bridge when an oncoming truck, slightly bigger than BlueBelle but overloaded with goods precariously piled and strapped on at least a metre above the cab, decided that *he* was going on to the bridge.

Fool, but I was almost off it! He started waving and shouting that I should reverse – like hell I would: I was on the bridge first! – but there was no way for me to get off as he was blocking the way. It was a stalemate. I shook my head, gesticulating and shouting that he should reverse, but he indicated just as heatedly that he was going to tip over if he did. My response was, "Tough luck mate, that's your problem! You should have just waited thirty seconds!"

This went on for a bit, the guard from the Angolan side joining in the argument and telling me to reverse too. I was hoping that by now there was a pile of vehicles behind me making it impossible to do so, but even if I was clear I wasn't reversing all the way back off the bridge, just because this idiot was incapable of thinking. I was such a short distance away from the end of the bridge and it was such a comparatively long way for me to reverse, so it truly made sense that he should have waited until I was off. I switched off my engine and sat back in my seat with a firm and resolute look of, "FU if you think I'm moving in any direction other than forward!" I'd had enough of the mayhem. I can confidently add that after seven months of negotiating border posts, they no longer intimidated me.

When the guard came over to my window to convince me that *I* needed to reverse because the truck might topple under the load if *he* tried to, I raised my eyebrows and replied, "Well then either he shouldn't have loaded it so much or he's an incapable driver if he can't reverse as well as he can go forward!" (My response was in English, but I'm quite certain everyone got the gist of what I was saying.) Thankfully he returned to the truck and told the driver to reverse.

The guy was outraged. He grudgingly reversed all of two metres, which fortunately allowed me to get off the bridge, and as I passed he hurled an angry stream of abuse at me. With a beaming smile I thanked him with the universal sign language that is one finger and drove on into Angola.

Chapter Sixteen – Angola

8 June 2019

On the Angolan side, the border post consisted of clean respectable buildings, one of which even had air-conditioning. I was now in what all overlanders called 'easy Africa': from here on the borders are more orderly and the systems better, (although never forgetting TIA!) It didn't take long to get my visa stamped with a re-entry and my TIP documents reinstated – in fact, within an hour I was done and dusted. There was notably not one big black ledger, something I wouldn't come to miss. Instead there was a modern concept called 'computers' which managed the entire process. It was actually, dare I say, quite boring. The previous borders had at least kept me on my toes.

Angola is another former Portuguese colony and as such the local colonial language was Portuguese. This is a Romance language that is based on Latin and in many ways closely resembles French... but of course is entirely different! I used to do quite well speaking Portuguese when I lived in Portugal, but my need to speak French regularly had got it all jumbled in my brain and I was never quite sure what language was going to pop out. The border officials were professional and friendly, especially since I managed to speak at least a few words of Portuguese, which was always enthusiastically met.

Leaving the border, my direction was toward the nearest city which was still about sixty kilometres away. The road was good but I noticed that the navigation said I should have turned off some distance back, so I was again in the middle of nowhere according to the map. I doubled back to check that I had not missed the alleged turning but found nothing. These types of anomalies occurred regularly on African maps online and I could never totally rely on them; I often had to apply common sense as well. I took the opportunity to make a pit stop and refuel with coffee in a layby on the side of the road. I also put in my Angolan SIM card and noticed a message coming in. It was from Nina.

I had come into contact with Nina and her overlanding family via Facebook and we had been in touch from time to time along our similar respective journeys. I knew that Nina, Jon and their teenage daughter Bianca were somewhere in DRC, but they had crossed further north and were following a different route. Now the message said they were at the Angola border waiting for their vehicle documents and I couldn't believe it: I had left just twenty minutes before and missed them! They were still on a DRC network and would lose contact when they left the border, so we agreed to meet on the outskirts of the nearest city, M'banza Kongo, where they would need to get fuel.

I stopped at the first fuel station I found as I had less than half a tank, but was told that there was no diesel. I created a show of it being a disaster and not knowing what I would do – which was more or less true. I decided to fuel myself up instead with some cold water from their shop. I left to try to find some diesel in the city, but after trying several stations, none had any. This would be bad news for the others too. I considered that I had enough to get to the coast, which meant that I could give Nina and Jon at least one of my jerry cans to top them up, which would help.

I returned to the first fuel station as it was our meeting point. It was of course hot, and as none of the pumps were working I decided to stop under the shade of the roof rather than in the blazing sun. I casually parked next to a pump with my door open, playing music, checking the map for fuel stations ahead and considering where I wanted to park up for the night. I picked a wild camp about an hour out of the city.

After twenty minutes I noticed the pump attendant I had spoken to earlier coming out of the shop with another man who could have been his boss. They were looking in my direction and talking and I thought they were going to tell me that I couldn't park there, so when the attendant walked over I was ready for battle. Instead he said, "Come to the diesel pump." Err, um, what..? "Come to the other pump and you can get diesel." I couldn't believe my ears and stared at him in shock, but he was already walking to the pump. I didn't waste a moment longer and rushed over.

I filled BlueBelle up to the brim and was grateful for the extra kwanza I had managed to exchange in Cabinda. Now I was all set to go, and fuel was off my list of things to worry about; plus I would be able to give Nina and Jon all the fuel in my jerry cans if they couldn't find any themselves. I had just finished and paid when they pulled up. We greeted each other like old friends and I told Jon to quickly go and see if the man would allow him to fill up too, which indeed he did. I not only tipped the attendant very generously, but I also gave a word of thanks to my angels and guardians who always seemed to pull something out of the hat for me.

A MOUNTAIN AND A BEACH

Nina and Jon wanted to go to the city to get a SIM card and look for a campsite, so I told them about the wild camping spot I had identified. I needed to get going as there wasn't much sun left, and on hearing my plans they decided they wanted to join me. I showed them the location on the ever-helpful iOverlander app and they said they would come along as soon as they were done, so we headed off in opposite directions for the time being.

The road continued to be excellent and the scenery lush and tranquil, littered with the usual traditional villages. The spot that I had identified turned out to be next to a police training camp and adjacent to the lone mountain in the landscape, but away from the road by over a kilometre. I found the clearing at the end of a track: it would suit perfectly with nothing but nature around and under the watchful gaze of the rugged, interesting-looking mountain. By the time I had parked on some degree of level ground (essential for a night of good sleep), Nina and Jon had arrived and the sun was announcing its departure in a bold array of golden colours.

We were outside chatting and catching up on our travels and experiences as the darkness drew quickly in, but then the biting started and I found myself being massacred. It was so intense and severe that the insects were even biting through my jeans! I offered my apologies but they too were being affected, so we bade each other an early goodnight and agreed to catch up in the morning. Annoyingly there was no internet signal in the area, which gave a distinct disadvantage to my plan of staying a couple of days.

The next morning found me as usual up bright and early and I decided to take a walk in the cool dawn air. With the vicious mosquitoes and the lack of internet, I had already made up my mind to move to a beachside location I had found and perhaps spend a few days there. The stress of the days leading up to the border crossing into DRC, plus the manic drive across the country, meant that I needed a couple of days of downtime to restore my energy and plan my ongoing journey through Angola in greater detail.

I came to realise that Nina and Bianca were terrified of being out in the 'wilds' of Africa and of any animals they might encounter, so I assured them that there were no dangerous animals out there, just the dreaded mosquitoes or tsetse flies or whatever it was that was biting the heck out of me. I eventually convinced the family to take a walk with me, but we didn't get far before they all turned back and said that they would meet me at the vehicles. They too wanted to stop over at the beach, so they would wait for me to return.

I didn't walk far, probably only a few hundred metres, but I really needed to feel close to nature. The mountain looked amazing in the early morning light as the sun's rays crept down its face, illuminating a large cave about halfway up. I took in the scent of the bush, the sound of the birds and the total feeling of being in Southern Africa, sensing that my destination was truly within reach. After all these months I was starting to feel it becoming a reality. Until then I had been taking the countries one by one, making sure I managed each one individually as I passed through it: eating the elephant bite by bite. Now my biggest challenges – the corrupt Senegal border, the Nigerian visa, the Nigeria-Cameroon border, the Gabon-ROC border, getting through DRC and the many dreadful roads I had encountered – all those lay behind me, and BlueBelle and I had made it into *Southern Africa*. I don't tend to get too excited about things before they happen, but now I did feel like I was seeing the light at the end of the tunnel. But at the same time I was having so much fun that I wasn't sure I wanted it to end..!

Reinvigorated from my walk, I returned to meet the others and we set off toward the beach, agreeing that in N'zeto we would stop to try to find bread and basic groceries. I followed them, but while neither of us was going fast I was having some difficulty behind them. The road was good but undulating, meaning that on the downhill stretches I needed to go slightly faster to achieve enough momentum for the upward slopes. BlueBelle and I had developed our own pace of doing things.

In N'zeto we parked and went to look for a *padaria*[109] but the best we could do was a small grocery store, where we found ourselves at the usual counter with all the goods behind it. We kept getting in trouble asking for things in Portuguese, and although Jon and Nina spoke Spanish, the owner got frustrated and finally let us behind the counter where we rummaged for what we needed and put it all on the top. We bought some bread from a street trader around the corner and then we were all set. Our destination was a few kilometres away down a dirt road to the beach, so I was hoping that it would not involve too much sand. BlueBelle and I still had a phobia.

We turned off the dirt track heading west and just as the sea came into view we arrived at the Landmark restaurant. It was Sunday afternoon and the restaurant was busy. We stopped to ask the owner for permission to park up and he generously invited us to make ourselves at home a bit further along the track, where we would be disturbed less. He also permitted us to use his toilet and beach shower – incredible hospitality.

We noticed a large 4x4 parked at the end of the track next to a neat, open building with a concrete floor, corner pillars and a roof. It seemed they had commandeered the spot as there had been no one else around (I would have too if I could have got through the sand!) I went up to greet them, an elderly South African couple and their daughter who were on a fishing and exploratory trip. The husband had wanted to see the origin of the Zambezi River and the mouth of the Congo, which was where they were headed now with some breaks in between to fish. I spoke Afrikaans so we could chat at ease and they were thrilled to hear my story. They also generously offered me food, which of course was delicious. South Africans know how to cook on a camp braai,[110] and by now you know how much I appreciate someone else's cooking. (BlueBelle still refused to cook, or even make coffee.)

Our location was a small bay with a pristine white sandy beach and to one side some flat rocks which jutted from the land

---

[109] Bakery in Portuguese
[110] Afrikaans for barbecue

into the sea. The water was unexpectedly warm and clear and there was a cooling breeze – a good thing too as there was no shade; so I put out my makeshift awning to keep some of the afternoon sun off the side of the van. Best of all there were no mosquitoes to spoil this little slice of heaven! And for the first time since the plateau in Nigeria, the nights were cool – so much so that I needed a blanket in the early morning.

The following day we said goodbye to our new South African friends who were continuing north. Using the restaurant's tap, Nina, Jon and Bianca spent the morning washing while I, as usual, dusted out the inside of BlueBelle and spent the time relaxing and looking at ideas for my stay in Angola.

I also took the time to send a message to the British Ambassador to Angola, from whom I had not heard in almost a week, letting her know that it was with the help of the *French* that I had managed to get through the border. My implication was clear: there had been a distinct lack of support from the British. Her response was limp and echoed the same stance that the Foreign Office had taken: "We do not interfere in the foreign policy of other countries." By way of comparison, the US, French and Dutch governments had all managed to assist their citizens... but the British would not. Evidently travelling on a British passport no longer held the advantages it used to.

On Wednesday morning Jon and Nina decided to move on towards Luanda, whereas I opted to stay an extra day. I had no rush to get to Luanda myself. At the weekend I had planned to meet up with Sonia and Luis who had so kindly tried to help me whilst I was stuck in Cabinda, but other than that I had nothing pressing.

A couple of days before, the family had found a huge turtle on the beach. Jon had picked it up and I think this had frightened the rest of them away as I had not seen them on the beach at all since then. However, later in my stay I did notice the occasional turtle fin pop up and several heads bobbing up and down in the water between the rocks. They were keeping an eye on me, I was certain. I was thrilled to find myself in such a pristine place where these animals might still delight in their natural surroundings without interference from man. Facing the ocean, I would sit on my step with my side door open, watching them while the golden sun set directly in front of me, the colours and the clouds on the horizon painting vast pictures in an exhibition of luminous surrealism.

On my last evening, after I had watched this wondrous spectacle, I decided to treat myself to a movie. I had copied many of my DVD films and box sets on to a portable drive so that I could entertain myself from time to time. I chose an Italian series and settled down with my usual sundowner to concentrate on the subtitles, my side door open and a cool breeze blowing through. It was almost dark and I had nothing but the stars for company... and the security guard by the restaurant armed with an AK-47.[111]

My attention was firmly focused on the movie, so I literally jumped off my seat when I heard a loud thud on the front of BlueBelle. I couldn't see out of the window as I had my thick sunshade covering the windscreen, but my first thought was that it was a mango. I'd had a similar fright in Cabinda when one had dropped from the tree I was parked under. However it took me a moment to realise that here there were no trees within some considerable distance. I froze, listening intently and wondering what on earth it was, but I could hear nothing further. I couldn't just sit there speculating, so I grabbed the handy little torch that my nephew had given me – always within easy reach – and climbed cautiously out of the van. There was still a glimmer of light, and as I stepped a few feet away and turned back to look at the van, the cause of the noise immediately became evident. On the bonnet, grappling with the windscreen wipers, was a young pelican.

I don't know which of us got the bigger fright. The poor thing had obviously flown into the windscreen in the dusk and was holding on to the wipers and the edge of the bonnet for balance. It still had the mousey grey-brown feathers of a young bird, but it was big enough that it took up the whole windscreen with its enormous body and wings. I shrieked with fright and it started flapping vigorously and then managed to get some lift before flying off into the darkness.

---

[111] For some reason he insisted it was an AK-45!

I was sufficiently spooked now to pull in my step, close and lock my door and set all my alarms before finishing my drink and continuing with the movie.

I did see the youngster again the next morning. It had not flown far in the night and I was glad to see that it had suffered no injuries from its altercation with BlueBelle. It soared gracefully along the edge of the beach in front of me until I lost sight of it in the distance.

LOVELY LUANDA

I was leaving my beautiful beach with a refreshed body and replenished soul, ready to tackle whatever challenge came next. The morning was cool and I breathed in the fresh air deeply. Young Master Pelican had blessed me with a fly-by, and as I was leaving a stunning eagle had flown right next to BlueBelle and me for a few metres before veering off. I felt that all was right with the world.

The drive to Luanda was about three hundred kilometres. It was by now the beginning of June and therefore winter in the Southern Hemisphere, so many of the deciduous trees were bare of foliage. I found myself driving through a landscape that was as foreign to me as any I had ever passed through. Mile after mile of baobabs were intermingled with the other trees in a stunning forest. The baobab is the source of many myths and legends in Africa and is often called the 'tree of life' or the 'upside-down tree'. I cannot resist telling you one of my favourite stories:-

When God created nature in all its glory He made the animals and the birds, the insects and the flowers, but when He came to make the trees one tree asked that He make it the most beautiful tree on the earth. God agreed and made the majestic baobab. But the baobab looked at the next tree to be made and said, "This tree has shinier leaves," then at another tree and said, "This tree has nicer bark,", and to the next, "This tree has prettier flowers," and "This tree is taller." So it went on until God eventually became incensed and took the Baobab by the trunk, uprooted it and turned it over, putting the crown of the tree in the soil and leaving its roots above ground. "This is how you will remain, you ungrateful tree!" said the Lord. And this is why the tree looks as it does today, as if it has its roots in the air.

The fruit of the baobab is an olive-greenish colour, oval and furry on the outside, and it dangles from the branches by a long rope-like stem. I bought one in Angola and when I decided a few weeks later that I no longer had space for it in my van, I ate it. I can only say that it tasted disgusting, although in its defence I believe I may not have waited long enough for it to dry out. However, it is highly desired these days as a superfood because it contains a high content and variety of vitamins and minerals.

I think all Africans have a fondness for this odd-looking tree and I was bemused to see so many here. In my country they are sparse, although much larger. My day was indeed turning into one of many delights, but it was not done and the baobab trees eventually were replaced by date palms. They looked naturally growing, not like they were in a plantation, but there were a great many and I had not seen any like this since Morocco. They were also laden with fruit and I couldn't understand why such a valuable delicacy could be left untouched over such a large area.

As I continued the landscape changed again, and since I was driving closer to the coast from time to time I could see the ocean. I passed through a town where fishing was obviously the primary occupation and I saw large drying areas packed with salted fish being dried by the sun. This was probably a method adapted from the Portuguese, who have a love of salted fish which I've sadly never shared. I saw colourful fishing boats basking on the beach while more modern craft were sedately moored in the water.

I advanced ever closer to Luanda and, as with all city approaches, the buildings became larger and better constructed; the roads not necessarily so, although here they were in better condition than most I had encountered for quite some time. The traffic of course also became more intense, as to my annoyance did the taxis and taxi-buses with the same chaotic habits as elsewhere. The drive through the outer areas of the city seemed to take forever. Give me any kind of landscape rather than 'civilisation' to occupy my eyes!

I had been in touch with Sonia and Luis, and although I was coming early and heading for a campsite, they insisted that I meet with them after work and stay with them. I confess I hadn't been looking forward to the camp. It had a busy bar and a reputation for being very noisy, which I could do without. But I didn't want to inconvenience these kind strangers and was hoping that there might be somewhere I could park outside their apartment. They gave me their address in the city and my drive there took me past the docks which, once you got past the shantytown, had a pretty imposing infrastructure. In the city proper the buildings were modern, the roads wide and in good order and there were islands with well-tended plants and flowers: all very impressive.

Luanda had a reputation for being a very expensive city and there was an element of danger too, which I suppose one will always find when the 'haves' and the 'have-nots' are forced to share the same space. I found the apartment and their friend came and directed me to a parking space just outside the building and immediately in front of two banks, both of which happily had twenty-four-hour security.

Sonia and Luis arrived not too long after, and I can only say that meeting them was one of the highlights of my whole journey. I could not have found kinder, lovelier or more hospitable people if I had advertised for them – and all by chance! They insisted I stay in their spare room, and although being away from BlueBelle always made me anxious, I hoped the security would do the trick. While I was with them and their beautiful dog and cat, they did all the things that delight me: they welcomed me, fed me and informed me, and we became firm friends.

I only stayed a few days and they were both working. On Friday they went off to work and found it hard to believe that I was quite content to sit quietly in their home and catch up with my correspondence (free WiFi, another of my favourite things!) It was a perfect opportunity to do jobs I had not done in months, such as backing up my photos. I also needed to map my onward journey and make contact with the people ahead. Planning and organising took time.

During the preparations for the next part of my journey, a woman who had been in my class at high school, Jann, had seen my request for contacts and possible hosts in Namibia. Since she had previously lived there she had put me in touch with Georine, whom I had contacted, and Georine had seen that I was in Angola and tagged on Facebook a young woman she knew in Luanda called Neila. (Truly Facebook has been responsible for some wonderful connections!) Neila had messaged me and expressed great interest in meeting me, so I told her I only had one window of opportunity, Saturday morning. And so it came to pass that I met this amazing young woman.

She hailed from a small town in Southern Angola, but during the years of civil war it was bombed, forcing her and her family to walk for many weeks to Namibia as refugees. She and her sister managed to get scholarships and achieved a sound education, and Neila went on to get her pilot's licence. After many years working for a company as their pilot, she had recently been accepted to fly for the Angolan national airline. I have truncated things here but sincerely hope that Neila will one day write a book telling the whole story. It would certainly be worth reading as proof of sheer willpower and incredible determination against the odds. I was full of wonder and amazed at what she'd achieved, and she revealed that she in turn was in awe of my adventure and hoped to do something similar in the future, so with our mutual admiration we had a splendid meeting.

Neila took me on a tour of the city. I was quite impressed by the buildings with their very first-world look until we passed a large, ostentatious and expensive memorial to a late president (funded apparently by the Russians), a monstrosity of an edifice with a lot of concrete and marble but little else. Immediately opposite this were the shacks of the poorest people and I wondered what they thought about the millions that had been spent on honouring a dead politician, when they lived cheek by jowl with no running water or electricity and who knew what kind of ablutions. This was the sad reality of Africa.

Nonetheless I was very impressed by the city as a whole and by what was being achieved there. The current president had an active agenda to remove corruption from his government – no small task and certainly one that threatened his life daily. A leader of vision has a challenging task wherever in the world he might be, but in Africa the dangers are very real.

Over the weekend it happened to be Sonia's birthday and she graciously included Neila and me in her festivities. I met some wonderful people and relished the community and celebration of such a lovely lady. On Sunday I was treated to lunch and later a walk with the dog to see the Luanda skyline at night. It was such a strange and imposing sight that I almost felt I was on a foreign continent.

By Monday I knew I had to move on. I had delighted so much in the company of Sonia and Luis, their love for each other, their easy way of being with each other, that it left me slightly envious; but I had also come to know that they'd each had their share of sadness in their lives, making it even more precious that they had found such joy together. Their love warmed everyone around them too, as I had experienced on Sonia's birthday. I felt a great loss at leaving them, but knew I had made life-long friends – and that was a blessing in anyone's book, especially mine.

CALANDULA FALLS

I had often, during this journey, heard the second-largest waterfall in Africa described as extremely beautiful, and since Zimbabwe proudly boasts one of the seven natural wonders of the world, the UNESCO heritage site of Victoria Falls, I therefore felt it was my duty to scope out the competition. It was quite a distance inland at about three hundred and seventy kilometres east of Luanda, and I would have to return via almost the same route. That made a round trip of around seven hundred and forty kilometres, but the fact that diesel was the equivalent of only about thirty-five cents per litre meant I had no excuse.

On the drive out I once again passed through acres of baobab forests, but I could not tire of seeing them. The road was mostly good with little traffic, so apart from the ever-intensifying heat it was a pleasant trip as we wound upwards on to the African plateau. At one point a bus had broken down and, according to some unspoken African code of conduct, it simply stood where it was in the middle of the road. The issue for me though was that here the road narrowed, and the only way to pass this obstacle was to drive half off the edge.

The tarmac was somewhat higher than the verge, of which there was little, and apart from the fact that it sloped away it also merged almost immediately into thick bush. The bus was diagonally positioned and neither side of the road looked promising. I pondered what I was going to do and eventually decided to hold my breath, trust my angels and hope that BlueBelle didn't topple over on her side as I passed. It was a close call as I willed her not to give way to gravity, but I made it through and prayed that the bus would have been moved by the time I returned.

The turnoff to the falls led to a potholed but passable road which slowed me down a fair bit, and it was mid-afternoon by the time I arrived at the Pousada Calandula.[112] I had read there was a campsite but I seemed to have missed it, so I thought I would ask someone at the Pousada to direct me. There was some construction going on and as I got out a man came over to greet me. At this stage I still hadn't recovered my Portuguese, but I did my best to greet him and ask if he could direct me to the campsite, or if not whether there was somewhere else I could park for the night.

We shook hands and he told me to wait to speak to his wife, who spoke English. (I think he decided that I was probably more comprehensible in that language!) Someone was sent to find her and when she arrived she introduced herself as Lena and her husband, Francisco. Then she intriguingly said to me, "I know you, I'm glad you have come," and my first thought was that Laurie and Bruce, who had been there a few weeks previously, must have said something. I smiled and replied, "Yes, my friends from America were here last month, did they mention me?" She looked at me confused, "Americans? I do not remember. I have been following you on Facebook." Well, blow me over with a feather!

I honestly could not believe it. Only much later did I recall that she had indeed commented on one of my posts, telling me to come visit her at Calandula; but what with all the recent dramas I had entirely forgotten. It is a very strange thing to post my life – or at least part of it – on social media and then find that people recognise me from it. It sounds silly, but there are so many people in the world and the chances of someone actually knowing me seemed so small... Yet here I was: fame at last!

---

[112] www.facebook.com/Pousada-Calandula-124088828231253

I asked about camping but she would not hear of it and insisted that I be her guest. She told me she would give me a room and, as usual, I said that I was quite happy to stay in BlueBelle and all I needed was a space to park. But Lena is the kind of woman you just cannot say No to and I eventually succumbed. She took me up some steps into the Pousada, which was full of African artefacts and furniture, and we walked through the reception to the bar area that looked out on to the terrace... And there was the waterfall, in all its glory.

Calandula is about a hundred metres shorter than Victoria Falls and nowhere near as wide, but the open aspect gave one a far better view. While the water at Victoria Falls tumbles into a gorge, here it fell into a semi-circular open space, exposing the full magnificence of the cataract – especially from the raised terrace. There was no denying that it was truly beautiful in its own right and in some ways incomparable to the mighty Victoria Falls; but I was captivated. Below the terrace were laid out the most beautiful gardens.

Lena showed me upstairs to undoubtedly the most exquisite room in the hotel. It was immediately above the terrace and closest to the falls, so my view was quite breathtaking and I could hear the thundering water just a few hundred metres away. She insisted that I join her for drinks and dinner later and left me to settle in. I took another look around the room: with its comfy high bed, neatly made up with the plumpest pillows, the stunning walk-in shower and the large glass sliding doors that opened on to a small patio from which I had this amazing view, I had entered a paradise of the highest luxury. How did I get so darn lucky?!

While we were having drinks I learnt that Lena and Francisco owned a large golf estate outside Luanda with several houses and a hotel, and with their extensive involvement in hospitality they had been asked by the Minister of Tourism to revive the Pousada. Lena explained how the property had been unused and abandoned for a long time and they had spent the last few years bringing it back to life. They were adding three rooms to expand their capacity to thirteen, hence the construction, making it more a high-quality boutique hotel than a small guest house. Dinner was delicious, and on returning to my room I counted my blessings and fell asleep to the rumble of the waterfall.

It was Monday when I arrived, and while I'd only intended to stay one night I was feeling so spoilt that I stayed an additional night, spending my Tuesday finishing up the sorting of photos and consolidation of all my data cards on to my external disc drive. I didn't want to lose a single shot, so I sat relaxed in bed with my laptop and worked.

I had also finalised arrangements with Michiel, whom I had agreed to meet on Friday in Lubango. A terrible thing had happened to him the previous week that had shaken the whole overlanding community.

Michiel had been wild camping in a lovely spot outside Lubango when he was approached by two men and held at knifepoint, then tied up in the back of his 4x4 for several hours while they searched for valuables, stealing his camera, laptop and other personal items. At nightfall they had taken him into town, where they tried his credit cards for cash but somehow seemed to have failed, so fortunately they gave him back his phone and cards and left him in his vehicle. While this is everyone's nightmare, it was also an exceptional event. Even the locals who heard about it were shocked to the core because this type of crime just does not happen in Angola.

I knew that Michiel was travelling to Namibia and I had the feeling that I could not let him spend his first few days back on the road alone. He said that he was fine, but I knew if it had been me I would have been hesitant about 'getting back on the horse', so to speak. Having a degree of apprehension would only be natural and I thought that he might appreciate some company while he found his feet again. I had decided that it was within my capability to accompany him, and so that was what I would do. However, I now only had two days to make it across Angola – the seventh-largest country in Africa – to meet him.

On my departure Lena and Francisco came out to bid me farewell. I wished I could have stayed (Lena even offered me a job running the Pousada!) but I had to finish my journey. Now that I was so close, I had to complete what I had set out to do. I'd had an amazingly luxurious two nights, with great food and great company in the most beautiful surroundings, and I was very satisfied with my decision to drive all this way. It had been totally worth it for so many reasons.

I now had to drive back to Luanda and Lena generously offered me her yard at the golf estate: they would not be there but I could stay in the secure grounds. I was in a high mood and making excellent time when, an hour into my journey, my phone beeped. Lena had sent me a message with a photo of something she believed I had left behind in my room, and indeed it was one of my external hard drives. I was mad as a snake with myself. How had I managed to miss packing it?! There was no option but to go back and pick it up.

By the time I got back on the road to Luanda I had wasted a couple of hours, and my annoyance was increased when I found that the broken-down bus was still stuck in the middle of the road. This time there was more traffic, but I had passed it once so the second time was easier (although no less scary!) The day got progressively hotter and when I finally reached Luanda I was in peak-hour traffic on a narrow section of coastal road, so I wound down the window and took in the beautiful coastline while I inched toward my destination.

It seemed that I was forever driving late and getting to my destination just before nightfall, and this day was no different. The sun was about to set when I entered the golf resort and made my way to my park-up for the night. My spot was at the edge of a small lake set in superbly designed and manicured grounds, and I took the opportunity to have my side door facing the water and the setting sun so that I might relish nature's evening display of oranges and golds, pinks and reds, mauves and finally indigo. I counted my blessings and settled down for the night.

AMIGOS DE PICADAS

The thing that I marvelled about most on my journey was how generous people were to me, a complete stranger. There was always someone to help, someone to host me or direct me, and it was this that convinced me that there was something more than luck helping, guiding and protecting me: the Universe had my angels and guardians working overtime.

Lena had assisted me further by putting me in touch with Mario in Lobito, my next stop after Luanda. Mario didn't speak much English, nevertheless we managed to communicate somehow and agreed that I would contact him when I got to the city. The drive to Lobito started well but soon deteriorated into regular stretches of road construction, which meant the most appallingly long detours. Getting into Lobito was a further challenge with dirt tracks and tarmac roads criss-crossing and a distinct lack of any signage. I was thankful for my navigation.

Arriving in Lobito, I first went to find an ATM, followed by fuelling up ready to leave the next day, and then I contacted Mario. I was near the railway station so he easily found me there and had brought along his friend Dio, who fortunately spoke great English. I was looking my usual hot, sweaty, dusty, grimy self, but Mario insisted on taking photographs of me and BlueBelle before we headed off to a restaurant where I would be able to park. Most overlanders, the men said, parked on the beach, but the mere mention of sand made me shudder, and I could feel BlueBelle's wheels retracting at the thought too.

They also referred to some Spanish overlanders who were already parked there, as well as a French guy on a motorbike. On arrival at the Alfa Beach Bar,[113] I found that the Spanish people were Nina, Jon and Bianca who were already settled on the beach. It was a great surprise to catch up with them again, but no one seemed to recall the French guy's name, and anyway he wasn't there at the time. Mario, Dio, Nina, Jon and I sat down for a drink and a chat and I mentioned that I was looking for a secure park up in Lubango. As I related what had happened to Michiel, Mario and Dio were horrified and immediately set out to find a solution, inviting a friend to join us.

While waiting for the Lubango contact I found out who the French guy was: it was Gautier, whom I had met at the Benin hostel. I was surprised to see him. I had been getting something out of BlueBelle when he came along, and while we were not really friends in Benin, I think the miles and the challenges that we had both endured suddenly made us so and we hugged a big hello. His first words were (and in your brain please say this with a charming French accent): "I cannot believe zat you made it all ziz way in ziz piss of sheet car!" I had to laugh at the way he said it – and his utter honesty!

---

[113] www.facebook.com/Alfa.Beach.Bar

It was in that moment – and I mused on it while on the road the next day – that I realised something that had blindly escaped me before: very few people had believed I would be able to complete this journey; I guess it was a surprise to me too that I had come this far! I reflected on various comments people had made throughout, and I had simply laughed them off. The realisation made me even prouder of what I had managed to achieve.

Gautier joined us for a drink, filling me in on his travels since we'd last seen each other and apologising for not updating me on the road conditions as he had promised to do when leaving Benin. The day after reaching Nigeria he had come down with malaria and quite frankly forgotten all about it. No apology necessary, I told him. Malaria was a bullet I had thankfully dodged. While chatting we were joined by a lovely man who was in charge of a local motorbike crowd called the *Amigos de Picadas*. It seemed that there were several serious groups in Angola who frequently met up for long drives and trips to various places, and I was assured that with an *Amigo* (friend) sticker on my vehicle, no one would mess with me. I needed that sticker for sure!

The nice gentleman contacted someone in Lubango and arrangements were made. I was given a name and telephone number and told to call them when I arrived in town so that Michiel and I would be securely parked. I was more than relieved to have this organised. The *Amigos de Picadas* sticker is still on the back of BlueBelle and I remain ever so grateful for their help.

The restaurant was in a beautiful location on a pristine beach, and although I was not able to park on the sand, I was assured that being just outside the restaurant on the road would be perfectly secure. With an early start planned, a couple of full days driving behind me and a lot more still ahead, I certainly needed the rest, so I gave my thanks for the hospitality and said my goodbyes not too long after the sun had set. From Lobito it was still eight hundred and twenty kilometres of unknown road to the border with Namibia.

The morning air was beautiful and cool with the sound of the waves lapping on the beach. I took a short walk along the deserted sand and filled myself with the serenity of the start of the day and the sun rising in a glory of burnished copper. I returned to do my usual vehicle check[114] and then quickly departed, wanting to get out of town before the traffic and heat picked up. While the nights had cooled down substantially, the days remained hot. The road to Lubango was thankfully a reasonable one and took me up on to the inland plateau again. The surrounding landscape was becoming visibly drier, with much more savannah than the trees I had previously seen.

Michiel had been staying in Namibie[115] but we met in Lubango, where I called the contact I'd been given who in turn sent our host for the night, Joaõ, to meet us. Fortunately Joaõ spoke English and we followed him to his home in a cluster of buildings around an open parking space, all within a compound. There was an outside seating area and a basic toilet and shower too so we were all set up. Instead of cooking we found a small restaurant up the road and ate a typically satisfying Portuguese meal. Over an early dinner Michiel and I caught up on our travels since seeing each other in Togo and he told me of his ordeal. He seemed to be coping with it well, but I was still pleased to be able to accompany him. Our host Joaõ was in a band and had invited us to listen to him play, so while we were both tired we stopped by after the meal. We only stayed a short while, but it seemed there was a lively nightlife in Lubango.

As we drove out of the city in the cool of the following morning, our route took us through a pass, to the left of which we saw a huge statue of Christ – much like the one in Rio de Janeiro, but smaller – known as *Cristo Rei* (Christ the King). The statue was built in 1957 by the Catholic colonial settlers from Madeira and has been listed as an Angolan World Heritage Site, and standing thirty metres tall it was an impressive sight.

We were high – about 2,130m above sea level – but the climb continued ever upward. The road surface was again good and there were several long straight sections. Good roads and straight sections had not been encountered much on my journey and I confess, ungrateful person that I am, to feeling a bit bored! The day was also relatively uneventful and the scenery uninspiring and I was glad to reach our stop for the evening, a Catholic

---

114 Oil, water, steering fluid and brake fluid
115 An Angolan city, not to be confused with the country of Namibia

444

mission. While it was not in a compound it was quite safe enough, being some distance from the nearest town. We were given access to a bathroom that barely worked and we had to use water from a big barrel, but a wash of any kind was welcome after a hot day behind the steering wheel. I dug into my pantry and came up with one of my one-pot wonders for dinner, which Michiel ate heartily. I wondered what his cooking was like as he always seemed to devour everything I placed on his plate. I had given him the larger share of the food, and after sending him off with the pot to finish the rest I took out some pâté, a rare treat I had found in a supermarket, accompanied by crackers to finish off my meal.

We did not have too far to travel the next morning and we again left early, stopping only to top up with fuel (too cheap to pass up) and some bread rolls (the Portuguese rolls were too good to pass up too!)

The border was inspiring, boasting a relatively new building with orderly parking bays: the going would surely be easy. (It was interesting to notice how small things excited me!) The building was surrounded by a chain-link fence and we had to pass a guard to enter, so I greeted him enthusiastically and asked for directions on where to go first. With it still being early there were only a few people in the queue ahead of us and Michiel let me go first. Within minutes I was done and told Michiel I would meet him outside.

I chatted to the guard at the gate who spoke good English. I don't recall exactly what the conversation was about: it might have been about my journey, or about my love of Africa and its people. In Europe I was often chastised for being chatty, but in Africa no one minds so much. What did surprise me though, and it may be why I've forgotten most of the conversation, is that he asked me if I was a pastor. I asked him to repeat himself, believing I had misheard. (I probably had been 'sermonising' about the topic, but it was not religious, of that I was certain!) He responded again that he thought I was a pastor, and when I asked him why he thought that, he replied that I had a certain aura about me. Me? A holy aura? The man must have been standing in the sun too long!

Chapter Seventeen – Namibia

23 June 2019

The Namibian side of the border was as orderly as its Angolan counterpart, with clean, structured buildings and plenty of signs. Luckily there wasn't much of a queue because as I was standing and waiting I started to feel decidedly bad: physically ill and quite green around the gills. I barely made it out of the place and back to BlueBelle where I urgently needed my toilet. With the curtains drawn I was immensely grateful to have this on-board facility, as I'm not sure I would have had the time to find one elsewhere.

I washed my hands, splashed water on my face, and hoped I looked less pale when I bade farewell to Michiel. We each had a different destination in mind once we crossed the border. Overlanders love company but as you know by now we also love our freedom, so we said goodbye feeling sure we would see each other again somewhere down the road. I believed it was a good thing to make the final drive out of Angola with Michiel, and hoped to return there in future to discover more of this beautiful country.

I set off gingerly, having to remind myself that for the first time in many months I would be driving on the left. Whilst this was a much more natural position for my right-hand-drive BlueBelle, what had become automatic now needed to be unlearnt. I had a handy sticker in my windscreen which acted as a reminder of which side of the road I needed to drive on and which I now changed around. I did catch myself a couple of times on open roads when there was zero traffic, and once approaching a roundabout, wondering if I was in the right lane.

My first stop was the town just beyond the border to buy a SIM card so at least I had data. This done, I was still feeling very off-colour, so instead of heading to my intended destination in north-west Namibia, I decided to find somewhere closer to give me time to recover. As usual, iOverlander gave me a suitable option and fortunately it was only about ten kilometres away.

As I left the city I encountered the usual police checkpoint, and by then I felt decidedly not myself, so all I wanted was to find a shady spot and lie down. However, a middle-aged pot-bellied officer in a too-tight shirt had other ideas for me. He asked the usual questions but I was much less friendly and chatty than usual. Let's get this done so I can be on my way, was my objective. But he had other ideas and the questions intensified: "Why are you alone? Why do you not have a husband? Why not take me?" I fobbed these off curtly and several times informed him that I was not feeling well, and could I please go.

He wanted my telephone number so I told him I didn't have one for Namibia yet – a lie, but truly I didn't remember it and this guy was becoming more than creepy. He insisted then that I write *his* number down, and since there was no way I was getting out of there without it, I handed him my notepad in which I recorded my fuel and he proudly wrote his name and number. As I took back the notepad he offered his hand to shake, so I took it limply... And then it happened, something that I had not experienced since I was a teenager dating: he shook my hand and with his middle finger scratched my palm. I shudder at the thought of it, even now as I write.

For anyone who doesn't know, this gesture is an unspoken way of expressing sexual interest. I was shocked, withdrew my hand feeling utter revulsion and said to his smug, smiling face, "Can I go now?" I gave no sign that I understood what he had done or what it meant, but inside I was furious at this repulsive creature. He smiled and told me to call him... and as fast as a disgusted scalded cat, I drove off.

My campsite was down a dusty track, and after thinking I was lost I finally came to a gate. I hoped the place wasn't shut because it seemed deserted, but I opened the gate, drove in and closed it behind me. Closing gates is an important thing in Africa: if you leave a gate open animals, both domesticated and wild, can enter or escape and cause havoc.

It seemed to take forever to find someone but finally, feeling increasingly queasy, I was shown into a sandy space with some trees for shade and recommended to park in the camping area. This was empty and closer to the ablutions, which I thought in my delicate condition was a good idea. However, on driving in I found myself once again stuck in sand. I was now feverish and feeling both hot and cold (the latter being the indicator that I surely was not well), so I decided simply to leave it. I had some shade and would deal with the problem when I felt better.

For the rest of the morning the toilet and bucket were my best friends. I considered that it was probably the pâté that was responsible for my ill health. Although it had been sealed, the heat in the van may have been too much for it. Note to self: pâté not good option for van-living in Africa!

When I wasn't on the toilet I slept, and thankfully I awoke the next morning feeling considerably better and decided that I didn't want to stay. I cleaned out my chemical toilet (yes, the convenience of having a toilet meant the inconvenience of having to empty it, but the former by far outweighed the latter!), cleared up inside the van (I had dumped everything the day before), and started digging myself out. BlueBelle *really* didn't want to leave the sand and I had to enlist the help of a member of staff, but with a good push we eventually got her out. It was the fifth such episode on the journey and honestly, I was fed up with it! Namibia, however, was full of the stuff and I wasn't sure how well I would do at avoiding it…

THE HIMBA PEOPLE

It was the oddest thing, but by simply crossing the border I had entered a land drier than I had encountered since Mauritania. The soil was a pale almost-white, replacing the deep red-browns that I had become accustomed to for so many thousands of kilometres; and there was little in the way of grass, just sparse smatterings of small evergreen trees and shrubs; but it was hard to know if the other trees were dead or just dormant.

Most of Southern Africa, and especially Namibia, had been enduring a severe drought that had lasted between three and seven years, depending on the area. In Namibia I was told that at that time their usual rains had failed for the past seven years, and this was evident in the landscape. Many people think that Namibia, like Morocco, is entirely made up of desert, but the northern regions are a combination of savannah and scrub and these need rain to survive.

The roads were wonderful, one lane in each direction without much of a hard shoulder but in great condition, and there were lay-bys of a sort, areas where you could pull off and stop on hard ground. These were usually furnished with a concrete table and seats under a tree or some other form of shelter. I could have done with plenty of these on my previous thousands of kilometres: the small things that could have changed the journey. On the upside, the improved conditions permitted me to do more looking – not that there was an awful lot to look at.

I took up my original plan to drive west to visit a local tribe, the Himba, who are much admired for their cultural pride. An interesting organisation called *Living Culture Foundation Namibia*[116] supports tribal villages in Namibia to retain their lifestyle, their traditions and their values through tourism, and the village I was visiting was part of this programme. I must add that I *loathe* being this kind of 'cultural tourist', intruding on people's lives and having a poke around: I would hate anyone doing it to me. Nevertheless I had long been fascinated by how traditional tribesmen managed to retain their culture in today's ever-accelerating consumerist world, so I set out to go and investigate – but mindful to treat the people with respect and not like museum objects.

The thing about good long straight roads was that I got very bored, very quickly. So many months of watching every metre for potholes, goats, donkeys, tarmac, no tarmac, mud, sand, dirt, water… it demanded constant attention. And now I had nothing to do but drive. After seven months on the road that felt very strange. I hadn't often played music, except in heavy traffic, but I felt that with nothing to watch on the road and the landscape being less than interesting, I needed something to keep me awake. I slotted my music card into the stereo and the vast emptiness was suddenly and unequivocally abused by my loud road trip playlist, blaring out of my ever half-open window.[117]

I was driving at a steady 80kph/50mph on the main road and heeding the lowest speed limit sign I had seen, so I knew I was

---

[116] www.lcfn.info
[117] www.facebook.com/183690055374474/videos/455948024998982

doing fine.[118] I paid attention to the fact that when entering villages or passing schools, the signs indicated a reduced speed to 80kph, so I would slow down more to ensure I was well within that. I wasn't in a rush and I had plenty of time to get to my destination. Then, in the middle of nowhere – well, I had just passed a small village – I was waved down by a policeman. I thought it one of those 'for no reason whatsoever' police stops which I had become accustomed to on my journey, but it was not: I was being stopped for speeding!

I informed him that there was no way I was speeding because I never went above my set speed of 80kph, and he nodded his agreement: I was indeed doing 80kph. However, he advised that the speed limit here was 60kph. I told him this was not possible since I had not seen a sign denoting such a reduction in speed anywhere, but he assured me that there *was* a sign – three kilometres back down the road. Hindsight is a great thing: I should have told him that I would go back to check (although he probably wouldn't have let me). He asked me to get out of my vehicle and view the video and of course there I was, as we both knew, recorded at 80kph. I told him I had no money to pay a fine. He replied that he would present me with a ticket and I needed to go to the next town to pay it, so I promptly told him that if that was the case, I would be turning right around and heading straight for Zimbabwe since I would not be able to tour Namibia *and* pay the fine.

Now Namibia takes tourism very seriously. It is one of the country's major revenue streams and job generators, with approximately one million tourists annually contributing around $4million to the economy. I had heard that the police were specifically instructed to be helpful to tourists, hence I was using what I believed to be the most effective argument to get out of the ticket (apart from the fact that I still doubted the speed limit). I ranted on and eventually he sighed and said to me, "OK, you can go." Although this was most definitely the outcome I was hoping for, I hadn't thought I would win! I thanked him and skedaddled

---

[118]The speed limit was usually 120kph

to BlueBelle as fast as I could and headed off – at the prescribed speed.[119]

I arrived in Opuwo, from where I would drive another forty kilometres north to the Himba settlement. I stopped briefly for cash and some supplies and was astonished to find women in several types of local traditional dress, from the half-naked Himba to the fully over-dressed Herero, and a couple of others in bright colours that I was unable to identify. The people walked around without anyone leering (except the tourists like me). This was life here: everyone merely got on with their lives in whatever form of dress – or undress – they chose. It did strike me as entirely incongruous, however, to see the half-naked Himba with their traditional hair and colouring, many carrying babies, walking around carrying plastic shopping bags.

The village I was visiting had a campsite but it was forty kilometres of terribly rutted white dust road to get there. It had taken me months to find the speed at which I could traverse these corrugations without feeling like BlueBelle was going to fall apart; it took a specific strategy. On a 'reasonable' stretch I needed to get her up to about 45kph and then, while things still rattled about in the back, the going was smoother; just a few kph off that mark and the whole van shuddered unbearably. Needless to say those forty kilometres of track took their toll on my nerves, and in hindsight I believe killed my solar panel.

I arrived literally in the middle of the bush, where a neat signpost directed me to the campsite. Passing the tribal village on my way, I was then greeted warmly at the site by the camp caretaker who told me I could park anywhere since there was no one else there. He also very kindly said he would heat the donkey boiler[120] so that I could have a nice warm shower later. By now hot water was most welcome: winter made the groundwater icy cold. I arranged to have a full tour of the village the following

---

[119] I paid special attention to the speed limits for many kilometres after that, but never saw a sign lower than 80kph until I got to a large town. When I returned along that road, I paid careful attention to the signs and there was absolutely no 60kph sign anywhere, so I felt fully justified in getting off the fine!

[120] A donkey boiler is the easiest, cheapest way to create hot water in places where there is no electricity or solar power. A metal container, usually cylindrical, is securely mounted on legs, bricks or stones and a fire is stoked underneath to heat up a tank of water. It's a simple but effective solution applied in many African countries.

morning, which would enable me to see all aspects of village life. It would cost more money than I would usually spend but I wanted the full experience.

The next day I was up ready and eager as Robert (probably his 'Anglo' name) came to collect me at the camp. He was very tall and dressed like any young city kid, however he told me that one of his parents was Himba so he spoke the language (as well as several others) and he had relatives in the village.

The first thing I saw as I approached was a circular 'fence' of sticks and branches from the nearby thorny acacia trees to keep wild animals out of the village. Inside the enclosure, which was always cleanly swept, I saw the tiniest mud-packed homes I had ever seen. They were well-spaced and interspersed with tiny wood and straw 'huts' on stilts. This clever storage solution prevented dry goods from getting wet (if it ever rained), protecting it from any animals that might decide to take advantage and most importantly kept ants and termites out. Storing food like this also protected it from the heat of the earth and the thatched roof kept it cool.

There was a larger mud hut which served as the community house where meetings and other important village events were held. Outside this was a sacred fire which was kept burning day and night and considered to be the spirit of the village and was the source of all fires. There was also an inner enclosure or *kraal*, again constructed of sticks and thorny branches, where the livestock was kept, with the cattle, goats and chickens in specific 'homes' around the edges. The safe-keeping of the animals was very important as they were the wealth of the village and relied on for food and occasional trade, and as such their protection from theft or wildlife was essential.

The village was home to about twenty people, but on that day several had gone to a funeral in another village (funerals are a most important part of African culture and tradition). I was introduced to the remaining inhabitants, the most important of whom was the Headman, a tall thin man with a friendly face. This was quite an honour. In addition I met a metal-worker who made arrows and spearheads as well as the tiny metal beads that the women used to make jewellery to adorn themselves, and also a woman who made pots to hold butter for cooking and cosmetics.

The Himba are egalitarian but polygamous and the girls become brides at a very young age. All female members of the tribe are adorned with different beads and hairstyles for different periods of their lives, each style indicating their position: children, menstruating girls, mothers, women in menopause and so on; very interesting. The women also follow the traditional practice of covering themselves with a red paste called *otjize,* which is made from dry clay pulverised into a fine powder, then mixed with butter and rubbed all over their bodies and their strangely-braided hair. This is done to cleanse their skin because water is scarce in this part of Africa, and it also acts as a sunscreen and insect repellent. Only the women deodorise and they use bush herbs which they singe in a bowl and hold under their armpits.

My tour ended with some tribal dance and a demonstration of mock fighting, which the men practice to keep their skills honed. This was accompanied by singing and clapping, the dancing demonstrating the men's skills to the women and the women in turn showing off their musical abilities to the men. I loved watching this performance, and of course they moved as all African people do with that extraordinary fluidity that is unique to them. Many African people walk barefoot and are deeply connected to the earth, hence I always say that the earth moves in them; whereas we westerners have been wearing shoes for so long with concrete underfoot for much of the time that we have lost our connection with our world, which I believe may be reflected in how we treat it.

I had a wonderful morning amongst the Himba and greatly valued their making me so welcome. I do encourage people to support these kinds of places: while it may be described as 'touristic', this is their only real source of income apart from their precious cattle, especially with drought having impacted them for several years now and causing their crops to fail. This is the only way that they can buy staple foods and keep their culture alive.

Giving my sincerest thanks to everyone, I started wending my way back over the gruelling forty kilometres to Opuwo, but my slow progress meant that I did not have enough time to reach my planned destination. Instead I opted for a nearby lodge on the outskirts of town. It would probably be more expensive than usual but there were no other choices.

I followed the map and saw that the lodge was located on a hill, but on my way there I had to dodge roadworks and when I reached the gate it was shut. There was a sign directing me to another entrance and a number to call but I had no signal, so I remapped to where I believed the alternative entrance would be (a diagram on the first gate would have been useful, people!) and set the navigation. There were no tarmac roads out here, it was all dirt, and some of it pretty rocky and rough, especially as it was on the hillside. I checked with one of the workmen and he confirmed that I was heading in the right direction, but when I reached the indicated turn-off it was an uphill slope with lots of ruts and loose rocks and I wasn't at all confident to drive it. The map indicated an alternative route so I passed the turn-off and carried on.

But that route petered out into another impassable rocky track and I had to turn around. There was a slight bend in the road and as I was on a slope I decided to roll back to get a better angle to turn. However, what I hadn't noticed was the slight ridge behind me and as I went over it I realised I was in trouble. I immediately throttled forward, but with the loose rock and the angle of incline BlueBelle was not having any of it. With most of the weight being in her rear, she just couldn't get up over that little ridge.

I pulled on the handbrake, jumped out and put rocks behind the tyres to prevent any further backsliding. While I was assessing the situation a young boy walked by and I managed to commandeer him. He was a great help moving rocks out of the way and then removing the stone chocks when I wanted to accelerate forward, but I still couldn't get her over the ridge. I even unloaded all the rear storage boxes to shift her centre of gravity forward, but nothing helped. I struggled for the better part of an hour, having to stop several times because I was burning the clutch and overheating the engine. Eventually I realised I had to start thinking about other options. I decided once again to try to call the lodge to see if they could offer any assistance, and fortunately I now had a signal.

Their entrance was no further than a few hundred metres as the crow flew. They were immensely kind and sent out a vehicle with a tow bar to remove us from the ridge, which took all of ten minutes. Well, there was an experience I hadn't had before: getting stuck on a rocky slope. Let's add that to our list of Things

To Never Do Again, BlueBelle! The young man who had helped me had left while I was being towed up and I regretted not being able to reward him for his help. The men unhooked me from the bar, then escorted me on to the track I should have taken and up to the lodge. ARA 13 : DB 5

The lodge was situated on the top of a much larger ridge with wonderful views down the valley. It was a swanky place as the reception, lounge and dining area were magnificent, all of which told me I couldn't possibly afford to eat or drink there! I paid for my night's accommodation and found my designated parking spot. The camp was virtually full with all the best viewing spots taken by 4x4s, most of which displayed roof tents. The reception was universally icy as they all looked down at my beautiful BlueBelle when we drove in: she was looking particularly dusty after the rutted-road-and-slope incident. There was not one return smile or wave forthcoming as I passed by, nor a greeting when I was parked. Obviously not happy campers – and certainly not African.

OTJIWARONGO, SWAKOPMUND, AND WALVIS BAY

I was happy to leave the beautiful but unfriendly lodge early the next morning and head in the direction of Otjiwarongo. There I would be hosted for the night by Marica, a friend of Georine, for whom I would in turn be housesitting in Windhoek. The roads remained tediously good and the landscape, which had been dry as a bone, seemed to be getting even drier. The drought was severe. The main difference I noticed was that the pygmy goats, which had plagued the roads I'd been navigating throughout Western Africa, were now nowhere to be seen and had been replaced by wild warthogs. These could be found grazing down on their front knees and frequently there were also cute babies accompanying their moms. As I approached they would, quite literally, hightail it off in the other direction, their grey-brown tails with the tufty end poking straight up in the air as they ran in single file into the bush. The families had taken to feeding on the road verges where there was still some grass. I believe that the condensation of the cool night air on the hot tarmac allowed for some dampness away from the devastatingly dry bush.

Marica's address was easy to find and she warmly greeted me on arrival and showed me my secure parking for the night. I was astounded to find that she was the mother of ten children! However, all but two had left home and were living and working elsewhere. She was a deeply religious person, something that I often found disturbing, but I decided that I would be honest in my conversations with her. What happened was that, despite coming from opposite sides of the spectrum – me no children, she ten; me spiritual, her deeply religious – we managed to find a place where we could speak freely as women. It was a profound thing.

I spent two nights at her home. She proudly showed me around her town and we spoke about all manner of subjects. It was an unexpectedly rich encounter, and I promised that on my return back up through Namibia (which was my plan), I would take her out for a night in BlueBelle. As a mother, devoted to her remaining teenage children, she seldom spent time for herself, so she was very much looking forward to my suggestion and return.

I continued onward toward the coast, hoping to visit both Swakopmund and Walvis Bay before going to Windhoek. Again my network had found me a place to stay at a stable and riding school just outside Swakopmund. The drive was uneventful but the landscape was fascinating, not quite desert but certainly semi-desert, and it was easy to see the impact of the drought with trees blackened by death and barely any grass. I passed strange hills and ridges of a very different geographical structure from previous landmarks, and observing these changes alleviated my boredom of the good roads.

In Swakopmund I was greeted by Christine, who kindly showed me a spot to park up at her stables next to a very nice facility with toilet and hand basins. I was free to come and go as I pleased, which suited me perfectly. I had also been connected through my local network with a man who had expressed an interest in meeting me and had invited me to have coffee with him in the town. So the next morning I took the short drive into Swakopmund to meet Bernard, a man in his mid- to late-sixties who clearly took pride in his appearance and had a very pleasant manner. I didn't know much about him, but suffice to say we chatted easily – or rather I did most of the chatting as he asked question upon question about my travels, which seemed to fascinate him.

After coffee he told me that he was going to Walvis Bay, a short distance away, and if I would like I could accompany him and he would show me around. I jumped at the chance to be driven rather than do the driving and have the opportunity to see things I probably would not otherwise see, including being able to take photographs with both hands!

The trip to Walvis Bay was fascinating. It was here that the desert became beach as the vast Namib met the vaster Atlantic. I was intrigued at how that strip of road stayed clear, with dunes several metres high on one side and the wind constantly blowing offshore. The dunes were an interesting shade of ochre and we passed by the famous Dune 7, the highest dune in Namibia, and I saw people scrambling up the steep sand or riding quad bikes to reach the top. While it was an impressive sight, I was content not to have any more sand between my teeth. I'd had quite enough for my lifetime.

After completing his business in town Bernard took me on a tour of the wetlands, and the first thing I saw was flamingos – thousands of them in great flocks around the lagoon. There was something unnatural about these birds with their flaming shades of pink in contrast to the icy blue of the water and white bleached sands, with their unfeasibly long necks bent over and spindly legs holding aloft a comparatively buxom body. I had last seen flamingos in Mauritania on the Senegal River wetlands and it was good to see them again here, near the end of my trip. We parked to take in the view and I took a great many photographs, most of which failed to capture fully their beauty. My pleasure was only slightly spoiled by the wind, which was frigid and filled with... sand.

We drove further down the road to a giant salt-works, the largest production plant in sub-Saharan Africa. Salt is exported raw from Namibia, then processed in South Africa for industrial use (as opposed to that from Swakopmund, which is for human consumption). Surrounding the works were the salt beds, pools of seawater that evaporate in the heat leaving the salt behind to harvest. These beds were also varying shades of pink to a deep crimson, a pretty spectacular sight against the flamingos on the other side. Sadly, as the lure of money from salt extraction increases, there are fears that the entrance to the lagoon will close and the lagoon itself will one day dry up.

We drove back to Swakopmund and the wind had continued to increase to such a speed that the road was barely visible under the sand from the dunes being blown across to the ocean. This would be one place on earth I could not live! Bernard invited me to a late lunch, and since you know by now it is hard for me to say no to a meal cooked by someone else, I gratefully accepted.

After lunch and thanking Bernard for his hospitality, I took the time to walk around the town a bit on my own. It was a charming place with many small shops and galleries which retained the appeal of the area, rather than your typical crowded high street shops. It was also very clean and in good order, and certainly I could see why the tourists came in flocks almost as large as those gorgeous flamingos.

WINDHOEK

I spent the evening checking my route and finding my next campsite. I decided to stop a short distance before Windhoek, allowing me a leisurely drive so that I could tackle the city the morning after. The road took me east and the landscape fortunately remained fascinating, with plenty of mountains to gaze at on the long, otherwise uneventful route. My campsite for the night was just off the main road and had nice clean ablutions with a basin and counter on a concrete floor beside the parking spot, which meant I could avoid the dust when getting in and out of the van. I was sick of sweeping sand out of BlueBelle: it seemed ever-present, despite all the mats I used.

The next morning my destination was Windhoek, the capital city of Namibia and home to more than three hundred thousand people. Windhoek means 'windy corner' in Afrikaans, and despite the dryness was a small oasis amid an arid landscape already worsened by drought. The city stands at 1,700m above sea level but I was surprised to see that it was almost completely ringed by the distant mountains, making for a very pretty sight. It had some very European-style buildings hailing back to its days as a German colony. Many of the white people there are of

European descent, and even a few generations later German is still widely spoken along with Afrikaans.

I was met by Georine and Eckardt, whom I had been in touch with for some weeks thanks to my old classmate, Jann. They had mentioned that they would be away for ten days but I would be welcome to stay at their house anyway. (The generosity and trust people had in me always blew my mind!) We had arranged that I would arrive before their departure and then look after their three dogs, one cat and a parrot while they were away, which was a great deal for both parties: I loved animals and missed having them around, and they had the comfort of knowing that someone would be living there with them, relieving their neighbour of daily feeding duty. A win all round.

Georine and Eckardt were immensely nice people and I immediately felt at home. I loved it best when people didn't fuss over me and allowed me to find the balance between being with them and being on my own. In the few days before their departure I also made the acquaintance of their son, who made homemade fudge as a small side-line. He had named his brand Elgin[121] and he was making fudge and other delicacies which he then sold at markets. I offered to help him ~~eat~~, sorry *pack* his latest batch of fudge and was rewarded with the crumbs. Of course I needed to be careful with my dairy sensitivity, but fortunately it left no ill effects… except on my hips…

My stay coincided with a visit by my old classmate Jann and her husband, so we coordinated a meeting and Georine generously organised a dinner. It was odd to reminisce about old school days, but it was also so nice to have the opportunity to personally thank Jann for putting me in touch with her generous network of friends in Namibia.

When Georine and Eckardt left for their trip, the parrot and I had a falling out, nevertheless after a couple of days she figured out that we could be friends and would let me take her out of her cage and sit on my shoulder. I was not accustomed to birds so this was a new venture for me too, but soon we were best buddies. The dogs and the cat were no strain at all as they loved me from the start, and since I'm an animal person we all got on.

---

[121] He had chosen this because it was his grandmother's name and he was using her recipes

I had several things planned during my stay, one of which was to unpack BlueBelle and give her a good clean and reorganisation. I removed almost everything and washed all the curtains and covers to remove months of accumulated dust and grime. It took more time than I anticipated and my toe and especially my shoulder were still giving me problems, meaning there were only so many things I could viably do in a day without messing up my back too. Oh, the charm of getting old!

Another thing on my list was to find a mechanic who could give BlueBelle a thorough inspection and change the filters, and I needed to fit some new front tyres since the tread was down to the wire (although the sidewalls looked perfect). I couldn't complain though: they were on BlueBelle when I bought her and not new at that stage, and with me they had done at least twenty-five thousand kilometres already – and most of that on roads that they were quite ill-suited to!

I decided to first try the local Ford dealership for a check-over and a service. I was in for a surprise because I inconveniently arrived during their 'tea time' between 10.00 and 10.30 (a sign on the wall informed me). I was told to wait. I felt like I had gone back in time to the 1970s when I last had a 'tea time' at work! As I was standing outside waiting, I observed that the only vehicles in the yard were large shiny new Ford 4x4s, mostly white, and my old BlueBelle parked next to them looked decidedly shabby in comparison. Ronnie eventually arrived with a sort of 'Well, what do you want?' attitude, but when I gave him the van's specifications his immediate reply was, "We don't look at vehicles that are not registered in this country."

I was so shocked. I thought that the point of dealerships was to get support for a brand *wherever* in the world one was. But it appeared I was wrong because Ronnie went on to explain that foreign vehicles were too much trouble. I thought I might sway him by telling him about our journey, although from his response he seemed to think I was delusional; or perhaps he saw twenty-year-old Ford Transit vans from the UK driving through Africa every day of the week. Nevertheless while I was processing the information, he reluctantly offered to give her a quick inspection. But the man looked at BlueBelle like she was covered in poo, and I decided that there was nothing about this place that inspired confidence and hence there was no way I was leaving her there – even if they did deign to work on her. I needn't have worried because his final answer was no, but he offered a 'friend' who might help me. Thanks, but no thanks Ronnie! I realised then and there that I wouldn't choose one of those shiny new Fords over BlueBelle for all the tea in Tanzania.

Luckily, Eckardt had given me a contact, so I was enormously grateful to find L. Barnard Auto & Truck Repairs,[122] where Len and his wife ran the workshop. I was greeted with the utmost respect – and trust me, you have to be a woman to understand the difference this makes! Furthermore he immediately understood exactly what I wanted and told me it would only take a few hours to run the checks. Not only did I get a full report of all the things that needed attention, but he also fixed a couple of other things that had been nagging me with the clutch and the handbrake – without charging me.

The report highlighted several issues, but at the same time the news could have been worse. I would have to replace the same steering thingies from ROC (again), the shocks had gone (not surprising, and I might have noticed had I not become accustomed to the bumpy ride), and she would also need a complete set of new filters and a full service. I only had one oil filter left and Len had not been able to find any of the parts in either Namibia or South Africa, so this probably meant shipping them from the UK. Ouch.

I set to work checking with various online groups and forums about parts, and it appeared that for my particular model of vehicle there might be parts available in Zambia. However, at this stage Zambia was almost as difficult to drive to as the UK and getting parts shipped from there would be an even more complicated set of logistics, so I decided to concentrate on sourcing the parts from the UK.

I asked the Overlander Mules group on Facebook,[123] a community where people help each other out by offering to take spares or needed items to or from a destination, and was contacted by Mike from the UK. Mike had been driving down the east coast of Africa in his 2WD Mercedes van named Ludwig and had just

---

[122] www.facebook.com/l.barnardauto/
[123] www.facebook.com/groups/Overlander.Mules

crossed through to Namibia. I thought it would be very interesting to meet someone else undertaking Africa in a 2WD, although his challenges were different from mine. Ludwig was a 1992 Mercedes 310d T1 van which had been converted into a camper by someone who promptly decided he didn't like camping. Mike had bought it from him with incredibly low mileage some seven years previously, and since he had always fancied the idea of driving down to his other house in Gordon's Bay (South Africa) he was finally making the trip.

Mike was arriving in Windhoek within a few days. He planned to leave Ludwig there and fly back to the UK to buy Ludwig's spare parts, and then return with his girlfriend to continue the drive to South Africa. I was astonished at his generosity when he offered to fetch BlueBelle's parts too. Once again my angels and guardians had pulled one out of the hat and I couldn't believe my luck! He was going to get his contact for his own spare parts to find out the cost of mine, so we arranged to meet where I was staying and he could also park there for the night.

In the meantime I continued cleaning, washing, organising and repairing. I also checked out tyres but decided I wasn't buying them until all the repairs had been done; then the new tyres could be fitted and balanced. I wasn't prepared for the cost but BlueBelle needed them, so I chose some 'all terrains' that would do the job nicely.

As it happened Mike arrived on the same day that I got a message from Gautier, my French motorbike friend from Benin and Angola, to say that he too was in town getting his motorbike repaired and wanted to meet up. It seemed poor Gautier wasn't having much luck with company at the hostel and had found that everyone else 'on the road' was much older than him, so he was feeling a bit out of sorts.

Before I forget, Gautier has enlisted me as his dating consultant. In exchange for allowing me to mention him in this book, I am to forward the phone numbers and photographs of any hot young women reading this who are looking for a tall, lean, good-looking young Frenchman who speaks English with a cute French accent.[124]

I decided that lunch was a good idea so I did the easy thing: I bought a ready-roasted chicken from the nearby supermarket and made some salads. (I had a skill at getting out of cooking!) But while Mike and Gautier were great company individually, I'm not sure that English-French relations were at the same level. I could understand each of them perfectly, but there were some points where their widely differing sense of humour just wouldn't overlap. I did my best to distract them from each other.

Mike spent the night in his van and left early the next morning for secure parking closer to the airport. I would collect him and his girlfriend on their return in a week's time.

The cleaning continued, but I was also delighted to hear from the Bell family. They had finally caught up with me and were going to spend a couple of days in Windhoek so I invited them to overnight where I was and we spent the time happily swapping stories of our respective journeys.

I became more acquainted with the city and even found a nice little café in a garden centre to drink my coffee. (It felt a lot like being back in Europe, except I was sitting outdoors in winter.) I found a shop where they could replace both of the broken screens on my mobile phones with the spares Ursula had brought, and I also decided to buy a spare jerry can for diesel. While I already had two, I knew that there were fuel shortages in Zimbabwe and I was allowed to bring a hundred litres over the border (I couldn't afford more). The shopping was the best I had experienced for a while, so I stocked up on necessary items and replaced one of my plastic storage crates that was now more duct tape than plastic. It was the simple little things that just made life more liveable. I was starting to feel very pleased with my progress in reorganising my boxes and lightening the load by ditching some books and items that were not being used.

Georine and Eckardt returned and I stayed on for a few more very pleasant days, but I then had to fetch Mike and get the van repaired with the parts so I decided to camp out for a few nights. The airport was some way out of the city and I picked a campsite

---

124 Be warned though: he is a charmer!

quite close by. The camp proved to be a long distance from the main road down a dusty track and I found it expensive for what it offered. I consoled myself that it was only for one night.

The next morning I arrived at the airport amidst Zimbabwean flags flying on lampposts and banners with our inestimable leader's face all over them. It seemed that ED (as we 'fondly' call the president of Zimbabwe) was in town; in fact with all the radioed-up security guards in black suits, it seemed like he was coming to meet *me* at the airport... but we missed each other. It took a while to find parking as all the bays had height restrictions – a frequent and major annoyance. Eventually I was allowed to park with the buses.

I was early and spent my time looking around the tiny airport, which seemed to have a constant flow of visitors. Certainly I was surprised at how small it was considering how many tourists came through. After the flight had landed I thought Mike must have missed it as it took so long for them to clear customs, but eventually he and his lady emerged with several huge, heavy bags containing his spare parts and mine. Everyone and everything was loaded into BlueBelle and I drove back to Ludwig, where we said a fond farewell before they set off to tour Namibia and then head on to Cape Town. I owe Mike a huge debt for helping me out so selflessly and he has given his word to visit me in Zimbabwe.

I happily took my spares to the garage and within a morning BlueBelle was fixed with her new parts, all serviced and ready to take me on the last leg home. If you're ever in need of a fabulous garage in Windhoek, I highly recommend Len and his team: they are great at what they do and thoroughly nice people too. Once all the necessary repairs had been completed, my final expense was the addition of two new front tyres.

TROPIC OF CAPRICORN

I could not consider my journey complete without having crossed the Tropic of Capricorn. Although it was out of my way, I had decided that I wanted to complete the challenge of crossing the Tropic of Cancer, the Equator and the Tropic of Capricorn in a single journey, and to do that I had to go a bit further south than my anticipated route home required. The line lay just south of a town called Rehoboth.

The repairs to BlueBelle made her feel significantly better, especially the new front shock absorbers which made my ride much more comfortable than it had been for a great many kilometres. I'm not sure that I can adequately explain to you my relief and contentment at knowing that my 'girl' was well again. Feeling nostalgic, I took to reminiscing about how far we had come, recalling the incredible experiences and all the support I had received; and I was filled with an overwhelming sense of gratitude. What a privilege it had been to be able to make this journey!

As usual for Namibia, the road was sound and straight and the landscape dry and getting even drier and flatter. The drive was further south of Rehoboth than I had anticipated, and for some time I wondered if I had missed the line as I had with the Equator; but just when I was about to give up I came upon the signs. I took my photo on both sides of the road and made absolutely sure that I had crossed over the invisible line. Tick that box! Now I just had to make the long drive back.[125]

I had identified a camp on the edge of Lake Oanob and I was intrigued to see if there was actually water there. My expectations were not high. I had seen so many dry lake beds during my time in Namibia, but the searing drought had left the majority empty. Yet I was in for a surprise. The campsite was delightful and I was allocated a lovely spot right on the shores of the lake with a great view. Admittedly the water levels were low and the area around dry, but it was proving a haven for birds and bees which I'd not seen in Namibia thus far.

My first campsite outside Windhoek had alerted me to the fact that my solar wasn't working, and with the few remaining hours of sunlight I tried to see if I could fix it. I couldn't find the issue so resorted to plugging into the camp's power supply,[126] thankful that I had brought an extension cable with me. It was only some weeks later, after having the solar system tested, that I

---

[125] The Tropic is only about twenty kilometres south of Rehoboth, but in BlueBelle that feels longer!

[126] Fortunately many camps in Southern Africa include the use of electricity at their sites.

discovered my solar panel was dead. I believe that all those rutted roads were just too much for it. I missed it sorely, but it had served me very well and I would have struggled without it during the preceding months. The solar gave me the ability to charge my USB devices, operate my fan and LED lights and (with the converter) keep my laptop going.

My site had an open 'living area' under a roof with a sink, a counter and a bench to eat on. On my way through town earlier I had bought myself some hot takeaway chicken and rolls, so after my failed repairs I set up outside to enjoy the view and the food. It didn't take long before I was approached by a cat, who volubly informed me that the chicken smelt rather good. I finished what I wanted and made sure to leave her some scraps.

She made short work of her impromptu meal, and when the sun was setting and I climbed into BlueBelle to organise myself for the night, madam made her way inside too and inspected every corner, including the bed. She seemed to approve and finally made herself at home on the sofa, completely unfazed by my bumbling around. By the time it was dark, I had packed up the step but left the door open so that she might leave when she wanted. I got into bed and she came in for some cuddles. I did have a thought about taking her with me, but it wouldn't have been very practical; and being as friendly as she was, I guessed she had a home close by. Eventually she left and I locked up for the night.

In the morning I still had a small amount of chicken left and, without anything to keep it chilled, I decided to leave it for the cat, who was still around but seemed quite skittish. I wondered what was wrong with her until I saw another cat looking so similar that I could barely tell one from the other. Clearly she had family there, so I left both the chicken and the cat.

WATERBERG PLATEAU

I was on my way north to Etosha National Park, and from there east into the Caprivi Strip and then down into Botswana on the last leg of my journey. Etosha is a renowned game reserve situated around a large area of salt pans and I wanted to compare it with Zimbabwe's Hwange National Park, which I had frequented in earlier years. I would again be passing through Otjiwarongo and, true to my word, I was in contact with Marica for her promised weekend break.

She was very excited and had arranged for us to spend the night on a farm with some friends of hers, and the following day we would visit the Waterberg Plateau, another National Park. Her youngest daughters would stay with their father. I had moved things around to accommodate Marica, hoping that she wasn't going to have too bad a time of spending the night on my sofa. I'm fully aware that van life is not for everyone!

We drove a fair distance south again from Otjiwarongo toward Lake Omatako where Marica's friends, Mac and Lorraine, had their farm. As we passed the lake we saw no evidence of water and I had my doubts about what kind of farming could survive in such an arid area. There was no grass visible and certainly no crops or animals. The dryness of Namibia was something I found difficult to adapt to. Having grown up in a drought-prone area I was well accustomed to dry spells and the constant consideration of water, but here the earth was so parched I felt its pain. I was never happier than when I was driving through dense, lush rainforest, and I felt uncomfortable seeing nature struggle.

Some way along the rutted dirt road we came to a gate which someone came to unlock for us. As I drove up to the house there was still no evidence of farming, but there was a lovely lawned garden surrounding the homestead, evidence of underground water that was accessed by a borehole.

Mac and Lorraine came to greet us warmly and had a look over BlueBelle and my flag stickers before inviting us into their large farmhouse kitchen for tea. They had many questions about my journey and I about their lives. I learnt that they had been on that farm for some time and their son had an adjacent farm. They farmed cattle and some small crops, but with the severe drought they had reassessed their approach. Many farmers had been forced to sell all their livestock, but Mac was determined not to be one of them. He firmly believed that the rains would come and then everyone else would need to start their herds from scratch, while he would have the advantage.

Marica survived sleeping on the sofa and the next day we were happily treated to a delicious farm breakfast, after which

Mac took us out to see his farm. I was nothing short of astonished: there, in the parched landscape, suddenly were fields of lush green. They had thirteen boreholes which they used to irrigate the crops and his son had started planting onions and potatoes; and to feed the cattle they had planted oats. Namibia is well known for vast reserves of underground water, but I always worry how vast is vast: it cannot be limitless. Nonetheless these men were harvesting up to sixty tonnes of onions per hectare. It was impressive, considering the punishing conditions.

I don't know much about cattle but I could tell these were fine animals. Mac was concerned that they had all lost some weight but it wasn't noticeable to my eye as I watched them munching out of a trough. There being absolutely no grass on the land, they were totally reliant on being fed. Mac and his son harvested a highly nutritious local shrub which they shredded to supplement the cattle feed along with their B-grade potatoes, and soon they would be adding in the oats. In Afrikaans there is a popular saying: ''n Boer maak 'n plan' (a farmer makes a plan). It alludes to the harsh farming conditions to which Southern Africans find themselves constantly adapting, and I can affirm that this family had certainly adapted!

In addition to their farming activities they had struck on a profitable activity: pulling up invasive shrubs and burning them for charcoal, which they were then selling in container loads to the German markets. While I appreciated that these farmers were in difficult straits and had come up with an ingenious new commerce, conversely it was another way that Africa was sustaining consumption outside of itself. But there was a more worrying aspect.

The thing that I couldn't seem to get anyone to understand was that, whilst this particular shrub was an invasive species and it would be a good thing to remove it from the landscape, doing so during a drought meant that there was less vegetation to stabilise the soil, and this practice was unfortunately occurring throughout the country. The roots of this shrub would also contain grass seeds, and with the devastation there were already few enough seeds in the environment to sustain growth even if the rains did arrive. My concerns were realised in October when there were news reports of greater than normal erosion from offshore winds, with valuable topsoil being blown into the ocean and apparently across to fertilise the Amazon.

We said our grateful goodbyes mid-morning and Marica guided us to Waterberg Plateau, but I had foolishly not checked with her how far our drive would be before setting out the day before. I had forgotten that 'not far' in Africa had an entirely different meaning and I was now running low on fuel, having set aside my rule of keeping at least a half tankful as there had been so many fuel stations in Namibia. Now there were none to be found anywhere and we were off the beaten track, and I was anxious that we wouldn't make it. We had been showing empty for twenty miles and I had no idea how much further we would get on the fumes. I surrendered to the fact that I still had the jerry cans of fuel I had filled in DRC, and if absolutely necessary I would just have to brave the dust and heat to unpack the back to access them. We weren't going to be stranded.

The turnoff to Waterberg was another horrifically rutted road and I recall bitching about it to Marica for all of its twenty-kilometre length. At the end of it, to my extreme relief, I beheld what I most hoped for: a fuel station. The upside was that I now knew that I could go some forty miles on an apparently empty tank with the help of my angels and guardians – and BlueBelle herself of course, who always managed to pull a miracle out of the blue (forgive the pun).

After paying our park entry fees, we drove up a steep slope to get closer to the plateau itself. The Waterberg ('Water Mountain' in Afrikaans) is a prominent table-looking mountain that rises above the vast flat plains of the Kalahari, and I am certain that I do not have sufficient words myself to describe this extraordinary landscape. The first thing that I noticed, which was seemingly incongruous to me, was that the land close to the mountain was greener than I had seen for many hundreds of kilometres – obviously not bright rainforest green, but there was a distinct verdure. This clearly explained the ecological diversity of the area, which I learnt was host to over two hundred species of birds and several antelope. There were also some two hundred million-year-old dinosaur tracks, which regrettably I did not see as it would have required more hiking than I was capable of in the heat – and this was winter!

As we drove closer to the berg we could see that the rock face was a myriad different colours, and as we later climbed up the stony slopes it became apparent that this was from various lichens, yellow, orange, green and white, intermingled with black streaks from water staining the rock. We followed a trail up the steep slope to the sheer sides of the mountain, from where it was impossible to go further without climbing gear. Near the end of the trail Marica and I sat down on some rocks. (I was gasping for air, having been more accustomed to driving than climbing the last several months!) The view was quite breathtaking: not only could we observe the rock face close up, but we could see how high we were on the plateau in relation to the land below. As far as the eye could see there was nothing but flat plains, dry and desolate-looking.

At the end of our hike we went to visit the small museum below a restaurant, formerly the colonial police station, but sadly it was closed. I did find out later, however, that this area was the site of the Battle of Waterberg, where in 1904 the local Herero tribe lost somewhere between three and five thousand men in their last encounter against the German colonial forces who had been systematically subjugating them. This in turn prompted what is considered to have been an act of genocide, when the vast majority of the estimated eighty thousand Herero remaining were slaughtered or left to die from thirst and starvation.

With a full tank and quite exhausted from our long day, we returned to Otjiwarongo. Marica cooked a meal – and wow, that woman can really cook! – and after the meal, armed with a delicious box of leftovers for *padkos* (which means 'road food'), I said my goodnights.

In the morning I decided to do a quick shop before continuing north. At the traffic lights in the town I noticed a familiar-looking overlanding vehicle – familiar inasmuch as I'd seen pictures of it. I followed it around the corner and as we parked next to each other I recognised Neil and Julie,[127] who I knew had been on the road behind me. Although we had communicated we had not met. They sold overlanding stickers and these were the ones that I had been putting on my window throughout my journey. They kindly

---

127 www.instagram.com/overlandbirds

sought out some spares to replace the Cameroon and Nigeria stickers which had both been stolen in Cameroon, so it was a pleasure to finally meet them in person over a cup of tea before heading off in opposite directions.

ETOSHA

I decided to spend a quiet day or two catching up with myself at a nice campsite[128] before exploring Etosha National Park. It was a good decision. The camping spots, separated from each other by bushes, were on elevated ground looking over the pretty countryside, and the parking was empty but for me. Each spot had a tap and a luxurious patch of green grass, and while the ablutions were quite a walk away there were basins for me to wash some essentials as well as a good clean shower with hot water from a donkey boiler. It was now late July, making the nights and early winter mornings very cold.

At the camp's reception I could access WiFi and get cold drinks, and on my second afternoon I decided to sit and work on my laptop and then settle my bill before leaving the next morning. As I was sitting and working on the veranda Meisie, the receptionist, came over to chat with me and like others asked where I was from and where I was heading. I told her all about buying BlueBelle in the UK, building her interior in Barcelona, and then my drive through Africa to return to Zimbabwe. The conversation was memorable and ended something like this:-

Meisie: (*speaking to the groundsman who was watering the garden a couple of metres from the veranda*) You see what women can do? We can do whatever men do!

A laugh ensued from the groundsman.

Meisie: (*addressing me*) I am very proud to hear what you have done! Ha!

Me: Thank you.

Meisie: (*earnestly*) Although you will never get married you know. Never, *never*!

---

128 www.mondjilasafaricamp.com

Me:	Well, I'm not looking to get married, so that's OK!
Meisie:	Yes, but there is no chance now. If you can drive as well or better than him, and you have done such a journey, done your own DIY... A man who is with you will feel like... feel like...

She pondered, looking for the right phrase to express her opinion, and the groundsman finished her sentence:

"A lady!"

"Yes!" Meisie exclaimed with appreciation as she turned to me with a look of sympathy.

"You have no chance!"

I exploded with laughter. I had to appreciate what she said! I am now reminded of it every time I am 'mansplained' to and it has become one of my favourite anecdotes. At least now I know why I'm single – and likely to remain so!

I had read that Etosha National Park would open at 6.00am, which was well-timed as dawn is usually the best time to see wildlife. I was still an hour away from the park, so it meant an early start and driving in the dark as sunrise wasn't until around 7.45. I also hoped it would mean I could avoid the crowds.

The road was good, making my drive an easy one, and I was the second vehicle in the queue when I arrived just before 6.00... only to find out that in winter the opening times had changed to an hour later. No point getting stressed though: I was there, so I would just relax and wait. As vehicles arrived behind me, I noticed that people were going to the guard at the gate and collecting papers, which they were then filling out. I approached to find out what was going on, and with a piece of paper shoved at me I was informed that I would need to complete a form with my details before I could enter.

With my form completed and duly stamped, I followed the road and came to what looked like a camp with an office and shops. I paid my entrance fee at the office. Within the few minutes that I was there the room had filled with people and there were now queues at each of the open counters. The system of paying and accessing tickets seemed much more complicated than it needed to be, and I wondered how impressed the other visitors were. I had frankly expected better from a country that values tourism so much.

I eventually drove into the park and it was just glorious. I was in time to see the sun rising like a bright orange orb on my right and the sky burnished with fiery colours that rapidly faded into the bright blue of day. I breathed the air deeply, excited to be in a nature reserve and wondering what I would see first. The land was bone dry and dusty white, with few shrubs or bushes and very little grass. I had read the park was considering selling several thousand animals in order to sustain the remaining numbers with grass and water. Sad, but I could see why it would be necessary.

I stopped at my first waterhole and spotted a hyena running off on the opposite side. A small group of oryx were coming down to drink and a large vulture was sitting in the fork of a dead tree on the edge of the waterhole, some ten metres away from where I had stopped. *This* was what I loved to see: the crown jewels of Africa, wild and free!

I drove slowly in the direction of the next waterhole, looking out into the landscape to see any animals that might be camouflaged by it. When I was a child, it was a game to see how many I could spot before anyone else and I loved reliving that feeling! Joining the main rut-filled and dusty road, I found it wasn't long before glitzy 4x4 trucks were speeding past me like they were on a highway, followed by tourist-filled cars with people and cameras hurtling from one waterhole to the next and missing the animals that were standing quietly in the bush in between. I would spot them racing up behind, then overtaking me and kicking up great clouds of dust. I had to close my window so that I didn't choke, while of course the dust disturbed them not at all in their fully sealed, air-conditioned cabs.

I spotted a few of those awkward, incredibly powerful and positively prehistoric beasts, the beautiful but rare rhino, quietly grazing a few metres from the road; and then a small troupe of elegant giraffe. Everyone else had zoomed past them. Only the people who came after me were lucky enough to catch them, having seen me stop to look into the bush. This was far from the peaceful and respectful game drives I remembered from my earlier years. With all the rushing hordes I felt more like I was at an amusement park on a bank holiday weekend. Disturbingly, the wildlife seemed to have become accustomed to the presence of so many tin cans careering through their habitat.

A little while later I passed about fifteen vehicles. They were scattered around a triangular patch between three tracks and had unwittingly trapped a family of cheetah. Wildlife should be given their due respect and space: *never* corner them or hem them in. I was most perturbed at the safari operators, who were crowding in as close as they could to give their visitors a photograph, regardless of the consequences. I stopped briefly a safe distance away, and through my binoculars I observed the three lean, majestic animals pacing nervously. I wondered how many of their onlookers were truly appreciating the rarity of seeing cheetah in the wild, because for me this felt like the most *un*natural way to view them – more like a zoo than a wildlife reserve.

Despite that worrying incident, I had a superb morning viewing Africa's finest natural resources: giraffe, rhino, waterbuck, kudu, vulture, cheetah, hyena, jackal, elephant, wildebeest, weasel, sable, impala, oryx, warthog and zebra. Around lunchtime I was hot, hungry and certainly dusty, so I chose to find the camp within the reserve. I had been warned to book in advance, but all I needed was to find a parking space. I had a toilet of course and enough water and provisions to be self-sufficient and non-polluting.

The road to the camp was particularly rutted and quite a distance through the park from the main road – or perhaps the conditions just made it feel that way. On arriving in a neat little 'village' with offices, chalets and shops, I sought out the reception where the woman on duty did little to make me feel welcome. There was no accommodation, no parking, no recommendations, and really nothing African about the experience. I decided that I'd had enough of the dust and the inhospitable people. I'd had a good taste of wildlife here but I would definitely prefer exploring further in my native Hwange National Park, where I knew the experience would be much more pleasant.

CAPRIVI STRIP

I headed to Rundu, on the edge of the Caprivi Strip, and on the way I made an overnight stop in an expensive campsite in Tsumeb.

The Caprivi Strip is what is known as a *salient* of Namibia: a thin belt of land which protrudes from the north-east corner of the country for about four hundred and fifty kilometres inland, with its eastern tip on the Zambezi River about a hundred metres from Zimbabwe. This strip was negotiated by the German colonisers with the British in 1890 to give Namibia access to the Zambezi, which in turn gave them access to the east coast of Africa and their other colony at the time, Tanzania. A mere thirty-two kilometres wide at its narrowest point, Caprivi's landscape differs vastly from the rest of Namibia since it is situated on the fertile flood plains of four rivers that border or cross it: the Okavango, the Kwando, the Chobe and the great Zambezi.

It was marginally greener here and there were noticeably more trees, but the area was also beset by the drought which had been affecting the entire southern region. My camp in Rundu was a neat mix of cabins and camping areas, and just fifty metres from my spot I could see the Okavango River flood plain. The water levels were very, very low. I planned to stay only one night, but I found my bed ironically soaked through: while once again trying to fix my shower, I had left the head open and water had leaked through to the mattress. I had to sleep on the sofa and suffered a really bad night, straining my back and shoulder so that I awoke feeling miserable.

I decided to stay another night: my back problems and lack of sleep were not the recipe for a good day's driving. Then, in the early hours of the morning, it became evident that I had once again eaten something that did not agree with me. I couldn't pinpoint what it was, but I ended up with a slight fever too and was grateful again for my loo and bucket. I did fleetingly have a concern that it might be malaria, but I'd been out of the worst areas for some weeks and it would have appeared earlier. Fortunately by late afternoon I was feeling much better, and a couple of sips of colloidal silver and a good night's sleep saw me feeling almost normal again by the next morning.

I continued east and not far from Rundu I entered Bwabwata National Park. The road ran right through the park, and instead of the usual signs for different road conditions there were warning signs for elephants and a speed restriction (which was well within my limit). My first sighting of an elephant was a great matriarch standing at the side of the road, looking as though she was accustomed to the traffic and was waiting for me to pass. I stopped and watched as she crossed with two little ones, one a few years old and the other no more than a year. She lumbered swiftly across the road, keeping her youngsters close. I pondered how sad I was to see elephants that had been forced to adapt to human passage.

I had decided to keep my driving to a minimum. I wanted to ensure that I got a bit more rest before the final push to cross the last two borders to reach Zimbabwe, and my choice of Shamvura Camp[129] on the banks of the Okavango River was perfectly placed. I had been in contact with the owner, Charlie, on Facebook and she had invited me to visit her and her husband Mark some months before.

On arriving at Shamvura I was warmly met by the couple, who invited me into the camp lounge. On our way there I was greeted by several dogs and a goat. Inside the thatched building it was cool with a charming, eclectic and fun interior that I can best describe as a home away from home. Outside among the trees, where their foliage created an escape from the sun, there was a deck with a stunningly beautiful view overlooking the river and across into Angola; and accompanying this, the glorious surround sound of the great variety of birdlife which flitted around the greenery.

Charlie and Mark were great fun and we had a wonderful evening listening to each other's stories of Africa whilst observing the obligatory sundowner ritual. I spent a peaceful night in the yard of one of their secluded tented camps and gratefully used the donkey boiler-heated shower. I departed a little later than normal the next day after some more fun conversation with my hosts and must say I found it hard to say farewell to this lovely spot.

---

[129] www.facebook.com/groups/108179025871151

It was four hundred kilometres to my next stop, Katima Mulilo, located on the banks of my beloved Zambezi River. The town's name comes from the local Bantu language of siLozi and means 'quench the fire', referring to the nearby rapids. My camp for the night had the loveliest deck overlooking the water and the river felt so familiar, as though it was telling me I was almost home. The sun set over the wide waters as they drifted by and I imagined them flowing over the mighty Victoria Falls not too much further along the river. There were some clouds to add to the spectacle of another glorious technicolour African sunset, pink-tinged and gold-rimmed before the deep purples announced the falling of night and the mosquitoes emerged in force to drive me back to the safety of BlueBelle.

Chapter Eighteen – Botswana

7 August 2019

The Namibian border post was efficient and unmemorable, as was the crossing into Botswana, with the exception of being required to put all my shoes[130] into a chemical dip as well as BlueBelle's wheels. Botswana takes the spread of diseases such as foot-and-mouth, and others that might affect their livestock and wildlife, very seriously: the latter are a huge part of the country's tourism industry.

I had chosen to drive down through Botswana and enter Zimbabwe at Plumtree, which was closer to my final destination, my home town of Bulawayo. The alternative would have been to enter near the north-west of the country and drive down from there, but I was unable to determine the condition of the road on the other side and I wasn't in the mood for any surprises. A section of my drive that day was partly through Chobe National Park, Botswana's first national park and also its most ecologically diverse. The road was narrow but in good condition, and since I had heard reports of the strict traffic measures I stuck to my usual comfortable speed.

The landscape had changed from mixed grasslands and forests to swathes of grassland with only the occasional tree. It was early August and the grass was tall and yellow with bulging seed heads. I came across a herd of elephant standing on the side of the road, eagerly grabbing bunches of the grass with their trunks and stuffing their mouths greedily. From my observations the drought was having devastating effects in Botswana too, with many of the waterholes on which the wildlife relied drying up. This had caused great herds of animals to migrate into Zimbabwe, which in turn was exacerbating the water crisis in Hwange National Park. The rains, however, were at best still several months away.

I had been absent from this part of the world for almost thirty years and I was again surprised to see how much the wildlife had

---

[130] I confess I only admitted to two frequently used pairs!

become accustomed to the traffic, with both antelope and elephants waiting for cars to pass before crossing. I had to ponder on whether this was a good thing. At least there were fewer accidents, but accidents there still were, especially when vehicles insisted on driving at night and trucks particularly failed to issue due caution. I'm not convinced in the twenty-first century that man and nature really can coexist without nature suffering.

I passed a few more large family herds of elephant, and this was more familiar to me than the small groups I had seen in Ghana and Namibia. These gentle giants are such a wonder: so huge, so odd, with their large, round, flat-bottomed, padded feet and that extraordinary trunk. And yet they are the epitome of a caring society that has protected its kind for millennia, until the advent of the greedy hunter who wants to display them on his walls or use parts of their body to enhance his own puny body parts. Poaching and hunting are the theft of our crown jewels. There is one pay day, and when they are gone they will never return.

As I was driving along, by now out of the game reserve, I was struggling to stay awake on the good roads. I was also bored with listening to music so I decided to try a podcast. I had downloaded several on to my phone but never got around to listening to them. Since other overlanders had highly recommended them I decided it was time to give one a try. However, my brain was so intensely engaged by the topic being discussed that I got flagged down, and realised with a groan that I had not been paying sufficient attention to the road signs. Indeed there were the police, stopping me for failing to slow down when signed to do so… and this time I knew I was in the wrong.

I really detest paying fines. I'm always the one who pays parking fees and adheres to the speed limit, so I was really mad at myself. I was asked to get out of my van and witness the video.

I can't tell you what it was: perhaps that I was not safely in my van; or that I knew that I was in the wrong; or simply the fact that I was now so close to the end of this long, long journey home; but for the second time I burst into tears in front of the police. As much as I tried, all the emotion of the past eight and a half months came pouring out of me and I couldn't pull myself together. Trying to speak between sobs and gasps for air and biting my lower lip, I told the officer how I had driven all this way without getting a ticket and I was so stupid and I was so, *so* sorry. He probably thought he had broken me himself... But he kindly took pity on me and told me to go with just a warning to be careful. I couldn't believe what I was hearing, and when he repeated himself I thanked him, blessed him and walked shakily back to BlueBelle, thanking my angels and guardians for their help once again.

HOW DID I GET HERE?

There was one last stop before I crossed the final border. It was a perfectly nice lodge with indifferent staff, but the campsite was more expensive than I had expected and offered less value. They would not assist me to connect to the WiFi (which I hoped I could use to catch up on messages) and the drinks were horrifically overpriced. Eventually I gave up and parked BlueBelle for the night. The camp had good washing facilities but the parking was a shambles and had enough sand to make me very uncomfortable. Nonetheless I spent a peaceful last night of my journey.

The morning air was cold and there was no dew: there just wasn't any moisture in the air to spare. As the sun rose I took to the quiet road, expecting to be at the border by mid-morning.

Driving along peacefully it finally dawned on me that I was nearly home. How did I get here? For the past eight and a half months I had 'eaten the elephant', taking each road, each border, each obstacle and each pothole one bite at a time: staying the course, making adjustments; learning, laughing, getting irritated; sweating, freezing, delighting at every sunrise I woke up to and every sunset that ended another day and saw me safe. I had never doubted that the journey could be made, but at the same time I couldn't believe that I was almost there, almost done.

A voice in my head suddenly said, "What happens if we just carry on?" I considered what lay ahead with a tinge of trepidation. Would it be possible to return to a country I had left thirty-eight years before and not seen for more than thirty? I reflected on the countries, landscapes and borders I had crossed and smiled at the memories of the wonderful people I had met. It would be all right, I knew.

Letting go of my old world had opened up a surprising new world for me, one in which I knew that I could trust myself, trust the Universe and trust that my angels and guardians had my back – pretty much all the time if I allowed it. I had overcome what could feel like insurmountable obstacles and lived to tell the tale. The woman who left Europe was not the woman who came home. To be totally honest, the woman who left Europe didn't have a clue what it would take to make this journey: she wasn't fully kitted out, didn't know enough about what she would face; but the woman I found on the road was filled with determination, resourceful and able to think on her feet, and most importantly she learnt to laugh again. On my journey home, I had succeeded in finding myself through the journey within. I had found that I was capable, smart, adaptable, competent, brave, strong and worthy, and my heart was at peace. I had found my joy again. It was not the joy of my youth but a joy in the small things of each day: a beautiful sunrise, the kindness of a stranger, the waves and smiles of the African people, the stunning nature that surpassed all expectations, and the often annoying but constant red dust of Africa.

The woman who left Europe didn't care what happened to her. The sad truth was that when I started this journey I was depressed and had no interest in my life. But the woman who arrived home knew that there was work to be done. She had girls to educate so that fewer of them faced the future of the many thousands of girls she had seen carrying babies on their backs and water on their heads and living in the direst poverty. If she was able to travel twenty thousand kilometres through eighteen African countries over nearly nine months, she could confront that challenge too.

I had made it home to Africa and I was ready to face whatever I might find, knowing that while I still had no external riches, I now had a wealth of internal resources that I would never let go of again.

Chapter Nineteen – Zimbabwe

8 August 2019

As I crossed over the dry river bed to enter the country that I had left so many years before, but which had never left me, a feeling of incredulity overwhelmed me. Could it be possible that I had *actually* achieved what I had set out to do? Was I truly here or was it merely a mirage, a dream that the many months of heat had brought upon me? It was 8 August 2019: I had one more border post to complete and I would be done.

A host of new thoughts now pushed to the fore: would I be able to stay, would it have been worth it, would I be able to regain my nationality, would I find a way to make a living here… would… could… should…? I pushed these thoughts aside and did what I had done so many times before: I completed the task ahead… and crossed into Zimbabwe.

I parked my vehicle, picked up my folder of papers and walked steadily into the cool building. It all looked so very familiar and colonial; nothing here seemed to have changed over the long years that I had been away. The people were friendly and well-spoken and the queue moved along efficiently, not yet too long.

A part of me wanted to shout out to everyone that I had just driven twenty thousand kilometres, all by myself, just to get there. Another part of me felt that everyone should be looking at me with the awe I myself felt. Instead, I filled out the form, followed the queue, got the sticker in my passport that would allow me to stay for thirty days at a time (up to a maximum of ninety days) and my TIP (including insurance and carbon tax), again to be renewed every thirty days.

As I worked my way through the queue I started to smile and then to grin. I couldn't help it: I was still pinching myself that I was really and truly here! It had been two and a half years of preparation, sacrifice and great effort, along with the kindness of so many people, to bring me to this point… and yet here I was, against so many odds.

I left the building and at the customs check I told them that I had driven home. I got the feeling that they didn't really believe me, but they checked BlueBelle and were impressed that I had managed to build a home inside a van. They cleared me to go without further inspection and as I passed through the boom I wondered, for just a moment, whether I had done the right thing – but it was only a fleeting thought before I put my foot on the accelerator and introduced BlueBelle to her new country.

As I passed the town of Marula on pretty good tarmac, I turned to look to my right and my heart skipped a beat when I caught sight of the Matobo Hills. This UNESCO heritage landscape was the playground of my youth. I recalled the many weekends that had been spent climbing the balancing rocks and languishing with a picnic in the shade of the sparse trees by the side of a dam.

It was in that moment that I knew: I WAS HOME! – and I knew that I did not, *could not* regret a single moment of the journey that had brought me back here. Despite not having a 'home' to go to and only a vague future, my time on the road had prepared me for so many things that I knew I could conquer whatever lay ahead, as I had so many obstacles before.

I felt the sun beating down on me, delighted with the warmth that was not only outside but also growing inside me. I was prepared for a new adventure and started thinking ahead, wondering what the future might look like...

Epilogue

I have often been called crazy. I have no issue with being called crazy; in fact, I frequently used it to my advantage! But what I hope most is that I am seen as an ordinary woman, with hopes, fears, dreams and failings; and that if, at sixty, I could make this extraordinary journey using just my determination (and the support of the Universe), then I look forward to finding out what *you* can do when you allow yourself to pursue *your* dream – no matter what it looks like.

I will admit to the fact that when I left Europe I was very depressed. I had no idea whether I would be successful, and frankly the least of my worries was dying whilst attempting the journey; actually at the time that outcome would have been a relief. I mention this not to elicit any sympathy, but in the hope that those who face mental health challenges may be inspired to overcome them. I knew that I needed to make this journey to find my true self again, but it was only when I was on the road, both literally and figuratively, that I managed to change my mind about myself and so much more. I knew with certainty that what I had been doing for so many years had not changed anything. And while I'm not suggesting that everyone do something quite as radical as I did, I do recommend applying yourself to trying something different in order to attain a different result.

In writing this book I have looked back at all that I have done and seen the picture of an elephant that I have enjoyed every bite of – even the hard lessons that showed me the ultimate power of *me* when I worked with the Universe. I had too much incredible good fortune to even consider that I did it all alone. I remain grateful for all of it and admit, hand on heart, that I couldn't have done it without my many angels and guardians, including the human ones.

I'm loving being home and feeling at home. I have come full circle and, if I survive the production of this book, I may consider writing another one about what I have been up to since my return, which has certainly been both an eye-opener and quite eventful.[131]

I had the time of my life. It wasn't easy but it was surely worth it and I'm certain that this isn't the end of my adventures...

* * *

I took several hundred photographs along the way, some of them good enough to share, and a selection of these can be found alongside the story in the **online *Special Edition*** of this book. Since the cost of printing it is far too prohibitive at present, please visit www.goinghometoafrica.com for details.

---

[131] I will confess to just one negative side-effect from my journey: I merely have to feel a whisper of anything against my skin and I will tend to swat ferociously. I now suffer from mosquito stress trauma.

BLUEBELLE'S REPAIRS LIST

I cannot begin to recount the number of times men told me BlueBelle was an amazing, courageous and strong vehicle and deserved a medal. They got a gleam in their eyes as they inspected every part of her... and I agree she is a vehicle beyond excellent; however, I feel I didn't do too badly myself.

But for the men obsessed with the number of tyre changes I had to make, I will add that although I had two slow leaks repaired, not once during my entire journey did I need to make a change until I got to Namibia, when I replaced the front tyres that had come with the van.

Here is a full list of the repairs that were made:-

What	Where
Tyre puncture from a bolt, repair	Rabat, Morocco
Fuel tank emptied due to petrol, new fuel filter	Nouakchott, Mauritania
Rear-axle sump filled and resealed, new brake pads	Accra, Ghana
Oil and filter change	Lagos, Nigeria
Clutch change	Enugu, Nigeria
Fuel filter change, slow puncture fixed	Douala, Cameroon
Side doors welding	Pointe-Noire, ROC
Driver side suspension spring replaced, including wheel ball joints and steering 'thingies'	Pointe-Noire, ROC
Oil and filter change, fuel and air filter change, shock absorbers replaced, wheel ball joints, clutch adjustment	Windhoek, Namibia
Two new 'All Terrain' front tyres	Windhoek, Namibia

About the Author

Dot Bekker was born and raised in Bulawayo in the south-west of Zimbabwe. She has now lived in six countries across two continents: Zimbabwe, South Africa, the United Kingdom, Portugal, Luxembourg and Spain; but after thirty-eight years away from the country of her birth (twenty of those years in Europe), she decided to return. She has travelled extensively across much of the USA, including driving from Los Angeles to Edmonton in Canada, and she has seen much of Europe, some of Asia and about half of Africa. People often refer to her restless spirit, but she likes to think of it as "enjoying a change of scenery from time to time".

Having had more jobs than she can remember across a swathe of industries fulfilling a variety of roles, Dot found her passion in life. For the past eighteen years she has been a business and entrepreneur coach, supporting small business owners and solopreneurs to develop and grow their businesses both on- and offline.

She has also served on the boards of a variety of women's organisations in all the countries she has lived in, bringing to these her passion for human equality and equal opportunity rights for girls and women. Currently she is focused on providing scholarships for girls' secondary education in Zimbabwe – where two-thirds of girls are *not* in high school – and supporting entrepreneurship in her home town.

She has also decided to encourage more women to visit Africa and will be running small women-only group tours from 2022 in Zimbabwe, Namibia and South Africa. Watch her Facebook page for details of *Going Home to Africa Tours*.

At the time of writing Dot still lives in and travels with BlueBelle whenever possible and can be seen out and about meeting people and making things happen in her beloved Zimbabwe.

She is also already working on the sequel to this book, *Being Home in Africa*.

To find out about Dot's journey as it continues, look at @goinghometoafrica on Facebook and Instagram or on the website www.goinghometoafrica.com for blogs and updates.

To find out about the girls' education fund, look at @kusasa.africa on Facebook and Instagram or on the website www.kusasa.africa.

Printed in Great Britain
by Amazon

31861227R00269